Ethical Economy. Studies in Economic Ethics and Philosophy

More information about this series at
http://www.springer.com/series/2881

Experts and Consensus in Social Science

Carlo Martini • Marcel Boumans
Editors

Experts and Consensus in Social Science

 Springer

Editors
Carlo Martini
Department of Political and
   Economic Studies
University of Helsinki
Helsinki, Finland

Marcel Boumans
Department of Economics
University of Amsterdam
Amsterdam, The Netherlands

ISSN 2211-2707   ISSN 2211-2723 (electronic)
ISBN 978-3-319-08550-0   ISBN 978-3-319-08551-7 (eBook)
DOI 10.1007/978-3-319-08551-7
Springer Cham Heidelberg New York Dordrecht London

Library of Congress Control Number: 2014947216

Printed on acid-free paper

Springer is part of Springer Science+Business Media (www.springer.com)

Preface

The majority of contributions to this volume derive from papers presented at the 2012 workshop "Experts and Consensus in Economics and the Social Sciences" held at the University of Bayreuth, and organized by Carlo Martini, Marcel Boumans and Niels Gottschalk-Mazouz. The contributors to the workshop were Boumans, Maria Jimenez Buedo, Filip Buekens (with Fred Truyen), Frank den Butter (with Sjoerd ten Wolde), Robert Evans, Laszlo Kosolosky (with Jeroen Van Bouwel), Amir Konigsberg, Merel Lefevere (with Eric Schliesser), Martini, J.D. Trout, Aviezer Tucker, and Rafał Wierzchosławski. The 2-day workshop was a major success: the dialogue that ensued from the participants' presentations was so valuable that the authors felt the need to document that occasion in an edited volume, and to increase the number of participants in the on-paper discussion by inviting Roger Cooke and Julian Reiss to contribute. The result of these efforts is the present volume.

Helsinki, Finland   Carlo Martini
Amsterdam, The Netherlands   Marcel Boumans

Acknowledgments

The editors wish to thank the series editor Alexander Brink and the Springer editors Neil Olivier, Floor Oosting and Chris Wilby for their support and encouragement, the participants of the workshop for their valuable contributions, the Deutsche Forschungsgemeinschaft for a generous workshop grant, the Center for Philosophy and Economics of the University of Bayreuth for its hospitality and help in organizing the workshop, and Lauren N. Jung for her help in proofreading the manuscript. Carlo Martini would like to thank the Academy of Finland Centre of Excellence in the Philosophy of the Social Science for the financial support during the preparation of this volume. The editors would like to thank especially John B. Davis for his constructive suggestions and comments on the manuscript.

Contents

List of Figures

List of Tables

Chapter 1
Introduction: Experts and Consensus in Social Science

Marcel Boumans and Carlo Martini

Abstract The ideals of science as objectivity and consensus are – unsurprisingly – not so easy to attain in scientific practice. Science is ultimately a product of individual scientists with their own personal backgrounds and experiences, and there is no unique methodology to de-personalize and objectify knowledge. Social scientists, in particular, use a variety of tools for their investigations: They gather evidence from different sources, under different conditions and with different instruments. They are both the locus where different sources of evidence aggregate and also a direct source of evidence that comes in as intuitions and background knowledge. Acknowledging this wide variety of sources of evidence and methods in social science, different kinds of methodologies for reaching consensus have been developed. What kind of consensus is indicative of good science? What are the rules for consensus formation? And, is there a normative aspect to the formation of scientific and policy making consensus? The contributions of this book focus on experts: those institutional figures that act as a liaison between science and policy makers, politicians, governments, and other public domains.

1.1 Subjective Judgment in the Social Sciences

According to the Received View of science, the two main ideals of scientific knowledge are that it is "objective" and "unified". Although the specific meaning of each term can vary across different scientific contexts, they share the following connotations: "Objective" denotes knowledge that is impersonal, intersubjective,

M. Boumans (✉)
Department of Economics, University of Amsterdam, Valckenierstraat 65, 1018 XE, Amsterdam, The Netherlands
e-mail: m.j.boumans@uva.nl

C. Martini
Department of Political and Economic Studies, University of Helsinki, Unioninkatu 40A, office A509, Helsinki, Finland
e-mail: carlo.martini@helsinki.fi

© Springer International Publishing Switzerland 2014
C. Martini, M. Boumans (eds.), *Experts and Consensus in Social Science*,
Ethical Economy 50, DOI 10.1007/978-3-319-08551-7_1

unbiased and disinterested, and "unified" implies a consensus and sharing of language, laws, method and facts.

Perhaps the concept that comes closest to these ideals is Thomas Kuhn's use of "paradigm" to characterize "normal science". In the Preface of his *Structure of Scientific Revolutions*, Kuhn clarifies how he arrived at his particular usage of the concept of "paradigm". He had spent the year 1958–1959 at the Center for Advanced Studies in the Behavioral Sciences and observed the widespread disagreement that according to him distinguished the social from the natural sciences:

> [S]pending the year in a community composed predominantly of social scientists confronted me with unanticipated problems about the differences between such communities and those of the natural scientists among whom I had been trained. Particularly, I was struck by the number and extent of the overt disagreements between social scientists about the nature of legitimate scientific problems and methods. Both history and acquaintance made me doubt that practitioners of the natural sciences possess firmer or more permanent answers to such questions than their colleagues in social science. Yet, somehow, the practice of astronomy, physics, chemistry, or biology normally fails to evoke the controversies over fundamentals that today often seem endemic among, say, psychologists or sociologists. Attempting to discover the source of that difference led me recognize the role in scientific research of what I have since called 'paradigms'. These I take to be universally recognized scientific achievements that for a time provide model problems and solutions to community of practitioners. (Kuhn 1970, pp. vii–viii)

Kuhn saw the existence of extensive disagreement within one discipline as a clear indication that the specific discipline was not yet a science. Kuhn's observation was so influential that the argument from consensus to the recognition of scientific status of a certain discipline has been used again and again after the publication of his book (cf. Rosenberg 1994).

But ideals of science as objectivity and consensus are – unsurprisingly – not so easy to attain in scientific practice. Consensus is the end-state of a process for which hardly any methodology exists. Science is ultimately a product of individual scientists with their own personal backgrounds, and there is – again – no unique methodology to de-personalize and objectify knowledge. Even at the core of what the folk notion of science considers to be objective, say, in measurement, or statistical analysis, subjectivity is hard, or even impossible, to eliminate, nor, as some of the authors will argue in this book, do we need to.

Let us illustrate this with a distinction that Hempel (1952) made between two kinds of "imaginary experiments": the "intuitive" and the "theoretical". An imaginary experiment has the goal of anticipating the outcome of an experimental procedure that is not actually performed but just conjured up in the mind of the experimenter. Anticipation is guided by past experience concerning particular phenomena and their regularities, and occasionally by belief in certain general principles, which are accepted as if they were a priori truths. An imaginary experiment is called intuitive when

> the assumptions and data underlying the prediction are not made explicit and indeed may not even enter into the conscious process of anticipation at all: past experience and the – possibly unconscious – belief in certain general principles function here as suggestive

guides for imaginative anticipation rather than as a theoretical basis for systematic prediction. (Hempel 1952, p. 76)

In contrast to the intuitive experiment, a theoretical imaginary experiment

presupposes a set of explicitly stated general principles – such as laws of nature – and it anticipates the outcome of the experiment by strict deduction from those principles in combination with suitable boundary conditions representing the relevant aspects of the experimental situation. (Ibid.)

A theoretical imaginary experiment is an objective experiment: it is based on explicit and shared knowledge, and the outcome of this experiment does not require human reasoning but could also be run on a computer.

The intuitive imaginary experiment is clearly more personal than the theoretical one, and, differently from the latter, it could not be run on a computer, because it is based on intuitions, background information, and beliefs which may not even be conscious. But Hempel does not say to whose intuitions he is referring.

Other authors, among them Olaf Helmer, Norman Dalkey and Nicholas Rescher, have tried to make explicit whose intuitions are needed, namely those of experts. Helmer and Rescher (1958), in their paper titled 'On the Epistemology of the Inexact Sciences', written while working for the RAND Corporation, discuss what kind of knowledge requires subjective judgment. The paper opens with a quotation of Alfred Marshall ([1890] 1920, p. 32), where he compares the laws of economics with those of the tides, which are to be considered as "inexact":

The laws of economics are to be compared with the laws of the tides, rather than with the simple and exact law of gravitation. For the actions of men are so various and uncertain, that the best statement of tendencies, which we can make in a science of human conduct, must needs be inexact and faulty. (Marshall 1920, p. 32)

The key to Marshall's view lies in his claim that economic mechanisms work out their influences against a messy background of complicated factors, so that the most we can expect of economic analysis is that it capture the "tendencies" induced by changes in this or that factor. Helmer and Rescher saw these inexact laws, which they called "quasi-laws", as generalizations, less-than-universal principles, that are neither fully, nor even explicitly articulated, or even articulable. They require a different epistemology and methodology, namely, the systematic employment of expert judgment in structured decision making processes:

a knowledge about past instances or about statistical samples – while indeed providing valuable information – is not the sole and sometimes not even the main form of evidence [. . .]. In fact the evidential use of such prima facie evidence must be tempered by reference to background information, which frequently may be intuitive in character and have the form of a vague recognition of underlying regularities, such as analogies, correlations, or other conformities [. . .]. (Helmer and Rescher 1958, p. 30)

Helmer was a pioneer in futurology, the science that takes an interest in calculating the probability of future often large scale social and technological scenarios, and always advocated the involvement of experts in forecasting and prediction:

> The key to progress in this field has been the recognition that in dealing with the future, especially in 'soft' areas such as social, political, and economic developments, we have no firm laws providing the kind of predictive power associated with the laws of physics but must rely largely on intuitive understanding and perceptiveness of experts in relevant areas. (Helmer 1983, p. 20)

Social scientists use a variety of tools for their investigations. In fact, probably no scientist has exactly the same toolset as another scientist. They gather evidence from different sources, under different conditions and possibly with different instrumentation. They share at times different beliefs on the efficacy of a particular method or validity of a theory, even when they share a general paradigm. Particularly in the social sciences, scientists are both the locus where different sources of evidence aggregate, in no pre-determined way, as we will see in the next section, and also a direct source of evidence that comes in as intuitions, background knowledge, knowledge of initial conditions, and so on.

1.2   From Science to Policy Making

It is fair to say that in social science the sources of evidence, as well as the methods used, are more varied than in natural science. To exemplify, let us consider how recent experiments have been used to test model-based predictions in economics, how historical arguments and statistics support one another in sociology, or how, in psychology, mental models explain experiments and are in turn validated by them. In each of those fields the range of methods grow with technological improvements – increased computational power and new programming languages, use of crowdsourcing for experimental purposes, new networks of interdisciplinary collaboration, etc. We can only expect the trend to be sustained in the future by the engine of human inventiveness.

Acknowledging a wide variety of sources of evidence and methods in social science, different kinds of "triangulation" have been developed to reach convergence. The strategy of triangulation requires that more than one method, or more than one source of evidence, should be used to validate an observation. The rationale for this practice is that we can have more confidence in a certain result when different methods or sources of evidence are found to be congruent and yield comparable data (Jick 1979). The strategy of triangulation is similar to the strategy of "reproducibility". Reproducibility concerns closeness of agreement between results obtained by experiments on the some object or process carried out under changed conditions. Changed conditions may include: principle, method, observer, instrument, reference, location, conditions of use, and time. If an experiment cannot be reproduced, the result is not accepted as scientific evidence.

But a large variety in methods and sources of evidence carries along with it more coordination problems. For scientific evidence to support a policy stance, it has to be summarized and carefully packaged in a consensus. Disagreement is often taken to be the main drive of scientific discoveries and innovation, but consensus is the bedrock of decision making. Consensus is seen by the bystanders of democratic policy making as the sign that policies are being based on solid scientific and objective grounds. As Kuhn had observed, rightfully or wrongly, consensus is the hallmark of a mature science, and we would not like to base our policies on immature sciences. Jan Tinbergen ([1982] 2003) well illustrated this view when he called for a "synthesis" of the divergent economic views that dealt with the economic recession of the 1980s: "If we, economists, continue to oppose each other, we fail in our duty as scientists." Of course we may rightfully contend that there is so far little evidence that consensus goes hand-in-hand with justification, truth and good science, so one of the fundamental questions that future research will have to answer is what kind of consensus is indicative of good science.

But even before that, a more severe problem challenges us: how to gain consensus from increasingly diverse methods and sources of evidence. Unfortunately, facts and evidence do not have a way to impose themselves on the minds and hearts of researchers and policy-makers, and, despite statements to the contrary, they cannot always force irrelevant or biased theory out (cf. Blanchard 2009). Their evidential weight is gaged by the way they are collected, processed, and presented. To collect, process, and present evidence is the role of those working at the interface between science and politics, the so-called "experts". Experts are different from politicians, insofar as their concern is, at least to a greater extent, with the truth of the matter, but also from the pure scientists in that they focus on concrete problems and tasks. What the experts focus on may sometimes be assigned to them by others, rather than freely chosen. Experts are commonly employed as advisors to governments, national and private institutions like bureaus of economic analysis and lobbying organizations, political parties, and several other bodies that influence or determine social policies. Experts can also be directly involved in policy making, as it is the case for the monetary policies of most central banks.

1.3 Consensus or Disagreement

"Let a thousand flowers bloom!" So goes the motto that has at times been used to promote pluralism and diversity in science and society. But even if we agree that diversity and pluralism are the engines of inventiveness and progress – in good company of Feyerabend (1975), Hull (1988), Solomon (1994), Page (2007) – we believe that this metaphor should be extended to capture the whole picture: an engine without steering wheel (or with many uncoordinated ones) is highly inefficient and indeed destined for doom. Creativeness and plurality should not be under attack, but one must notice that they bring benefits only in the right place and at the right time. When it comes to decision making and policy making, the need to smooth out our differences and direct resources to the options we deem more worthy is just as pressing as the one of promoting creativity.

Even if we disagree with Kuhn on the consensual nature of mature sciences, there are at least three reasons for wanting consensus among experts, when they are in the role of advisors or policy makers. The first reason is logical: Reason-based policy making requires the reasons given to be at least non-contradictory. It is hard to motivate a stance when reasons support both it and its contradictory. The second reason is economic: Like all other human endeavors, also science has to satisfy unlimited wants (knowledge, problem resolution, etc.) with limited resources. Deciding where and how to employ scientific capital is part of the endeavor of maximizing resources, whereas renouncing any level of consensus in science would be tantamount to renouncing the view that scientists should not pursue the truth only for its own sake but for the sake of public utility as well (cf. Buekens and Truyen, Chap. 11, this volume). The third reason is epistemic, and even though it may seem an odd one, it is worth taking a look at it. If we consider decision making or advising groups as collective agents, as some literature has recently suggested that it is methodologically advantageous to do, then one of the fundamental requirements is that these agents possess coherent sets of beliefs (see List and Pettit 2011 and Tuomela 2013). The "coherentization" of beliefs within a group then requires some process of consensus formation.

But are there "rules" for consensus formation? And, moreover, is there a normative aspect to the formation of scientific and policy making consensus? Feyerabend (1975) has written that we should not look for a method in science because there are no exception-less or even useful rules in science. Even conceding the point, what about the need for applying science to problem solving and other social tasks? Sometimes we do not have the time or the window of opportunity for trying out all possible methods. Sometimes one choice of action precludes others, whether in synchrony or in the future. How do we decide which selection of facts, numbers, laws, observations to use and which to neglect? Thomas Edison is said to have proclaimed "Hell, there are no rules here – we're trying to accomplish something!" But in the age of Big Science the role of the maverick scientist is limited by the scale of resources she or he can employ. The tradition of amateur scientists who paved the way of science with their milestone experiments or theories—think of John Dalton or Gregor Mendel – is harder to maintain with the growth of large scale research, where testing a theory may require the collective efforts of hundreds or even thousands of scientists working on a single project (see Galison 1992). Big Science is not only natural science, we can expect (and hope) social science to require the same level of mobilization in the future (see Trout 2009).

But the efforts of Big Science require much coordination, and the view defended in this book is that such process of coordination and consensus formation should be a "well-ordered" one, to use the language of Kitcher (2001). What makes the contributions of this book unique is that here we focus on experts: those institutional figures that act as a liaison between science and policy makers, politicians, governments, and other public domains.

1.4   Seeking Expert-Based Consensus

The idea of expert-based consensus can be illustrated in analogy with the idea of model-based consensus (see Boumans, Chap. 3, this volume). The estimates of different models can be compared and synthesized analytically, and the resulting consensus – "colligation" – is taken as the evidence needed for formulating practical recommendations (den Butter and Morgan 1998). *Mutatis mutandis*, expert-based consensus analogously involves combining the judgments and reflections of experts into a "consensus summary". Clearly there are differences; perhaps the most salient ones being that models typically produce numbers, while experts produce anything from vague propositions to numerical estimates, and as a consequence, the elicitation and combination of expert judgments will be rather different from working with models.

The practice of seeking expert-based consensus has been investigated in several scientific fields at least since the work of the RAND Corporation in the 1950s and 1960s (Dalkey 1969; Dalkey et al. 1972). More recently, the field of engineering has seen much interest in relying on subjective judgment for eliciting, for instance, risk estimates in a number of practical applications: from nuclear risk assessment (Cooke 1991), to volcano eruptions (Aspinall 2010). Relatively little attention, however has so far been given to the field of the social sciences, despite the fact that there are several areas where the work of experts is constantly utilized. Examples of the latter practices are economic policy committees and evaluation of social policies. While some work has already been done (Collins and Evans 2007; Downward and Mearman 2008; Reiss 2008; Boumans 2008; Martini 2014a, b), in order to investigate, for instance, how economic committees work, and in order to draw some conclusions for a methodology of expert judgment in the social sciences, it is our belief that there is little communication among the various disciplines that study expert-based consensus.

1.5   The Contributions in This Volume

The contributions in this volume are written by philosophers, economists, sociologists and historians, each concerned with a specific aspect of the problems we highlighted in this introduction. It would be vain to attempt to unify under a common denominator the multiple facets of this book; to mention a few, the multiple ways consensus can arise on a given scientific or practical problem, the epistemological and sociological frameworks that justify different ways of consensus formation, and the implications that all of this has for democratic institutions. We hope that the reader will rather find value in this book in the attempt to make different disciplines talk to one another on shared problems and concerns, which was the goal of the workshop from which most of the contributions originate (see Preface).

Additionally, this volume is an effort to frame a special form of interdisciplinarity, namely "interventionist interdisciplinarity", that is, the practice of providing a platform for disciplines to interact. In a climate of calls for democratic participation in scientific efforts (see Kitcher 2001; Longino 1990), we should uphold at least two desiderata for the process through which consensus arises to be a fruitful one. The first one is that this process be reflective, if not rational. We know that consensus arises in societies for many different reasons (information cascades, leader's charisma, overreaction to information, herding, etc.), and that not all forms of consensus are equally desirable – take for example bank runs and witch hunts. If there needs to be consensus on topics like climate change, economic regulations, etc. we would prefer consensus to be a product of as little emotional and irrational factors as possible. So the first reason for studying the different facets, both descriptive and normative, of consensus formation is to understand both normatively and descriptively the interaction between science and society in modern science-based democracies. Here, understanding seems the key to preventing scientifically unjustified consensual stances, like those on phrenology or eugenics. The second desideratum for the process leading to "rational" consensus is that we wish to gain an understanding of what it means to be a scientific expert. Expertise is too much at risk of becoming just a label without a substance, and understanding what constitutes expertise is just as important as analyzing consensus.

What follows is a roadmap for the reader of this collection. We decided to organize this collection of articles in thematic sections, rather than disciplinary ones, and the choice reflects the interdisciplinarity of this volume: Rather than creating a set of compartmentalized disciplinary sections, we have let shared problems be treated together when different disciplines can contribute to their understanding. The choice reflects our belief that there are problems in the social sciences that should be dealt with by focusing on the contents of a contribution, rather than its perspective, in special case when the contributions are meant to look at the practice of science, rather than the theory. Indeed, the first Part is titled **Consensus in Practice**.

In some cases, consensus is required for policy making. *The Institutional Economics of Stakeholder Consultation* (Frank den Butter and Sjoerd ten Wolde) goes right to the heart of the matter from an economic perspective, with the concept of "matching zone" as a tool for "consultation and compromise finding between representatives of stakeholders". Economists and policy makers in general employ a number of tools and models at their disposal, and answer to different interests and institutional requirements. Agreement ought to be sought by defining and creating the necessary common grounds (matching zones) among stakeholders, as this will reduce transaction costs. A matching zone can be a complex tool to use; on the basis of a number of case studies, the authors lay out three sets of principles for (i) when to use a matching zone (strategic level); (ii) how to design a matching zone (tactical level); and (iii) how to manage a matching zone (operational level).

In other cases, experts are called upon to provide estimates of forecasts. Particularly in the so-called "inexact sciences", subjective expert judgment is a particularly precious source of evidence, but having a methodology for its use is paramount for avoiding biases and the possibility of manipulation. *Model-Based Consensus* (Marcel Boumans), advocates an adaptation of the Cooke Method to make it applicable to social science. The Cooke Method is a set of operational principles and a method for elicitation and aggregation of expert-based estimates, which has been employed in engineering, geology, and other technical fields (see also Roger Cooke, Chap. 10, this volume). Use of the Cooke Method implies the need of "seed variables", variables whose values are known beforehand, against which experts can be calibrated, and their judgments successively weighted. But in the social sciences good seed variables are hard to come by, and Boumans suggests, instead, to use experts in model-based consensus: We can find at least some level of consensus over the empirical validity of economic models, and we can use the experts to adjust the parameters and initial conditions of the models, rather than directly as estimators.

The distinction between seeking policy-making consensus and scientific agreement is not uncontroversial. Solomon (2007) considers the consensus conferences of the National Health Institute (NHI) and claims that they succeed in performing the former task, but not the latter; in other words, NHI consensus conferences only function when there already is an underlying scientific consensus. *Explicating Ways of Consensus-Making in Science and Society* (Laszlo Kosolosky and Jeroen Van Bouwel) analyzes the process of seeking consensus in science in two moments: peer-to-peer consensus, called "academic consensus" (acceptance of a certain stance within the scientific community) and peer-to-laypeople consensus, called "interface consensus" (the transmission of a certain scientific stance outside the boundaries of the scientific community, e.g. to policy makers). The authors reject Solomon's thesis that a consensus conference works better by voting rather than deliberation and list a number of epistemic benefits of deliberation.

The first part of this volume centered around the problem of what it means to seek for consensus in science from a practical (in the sense of arising from practice) viewpoint. But what is the kind of epistemology that underlies consensus seeking? In Part II we collect contributions that expose different philosophical **Frameworks of Consensus**. *Judgments About the Relevance of Evidence in the Context of Peer Disagreements and Practical Rationality* (Amir Konigsberg), deals with peer disagreement. Much of the disagreement that occurs in science is among peers (see also Kosolosky and Van Bouwel, Chap. 4, this volume), so what is a rational strategy to deal with this kind of disagreement, that is, what should we believe, when we find ourselves disagreeing with someone who is just as intelligent and well-informed as us? There are different sources of evidence for the statements (e.g. scientific ones) we defend: first-order evidence (the results of a scientist's model, her experimental evidence, etc.), and second-order evidence (the evidence coming from the peers of a scientist's, including the disagreeing ones). How to balance first- with second-order evidence, which one should bear more heavily on our stance on a given situation, is a matter of individual judgment and personal sensitivity to the given case.

So what is the drive to consensus in science (and in social science in particular)? *Seeking Consensus in the Social Sciences* (Carlo Martini) takes a step back and analyzes two old problems related to consensus and expertise: the disputes on "consensus versus disagreement" and "expert judgment versus mechanical rules". Is lack of consensus in social science to be cherished or deplored? Is relying on personal judgment and "soft knowledge" wise, or should we strive to axiomatize the scientia (not yet "science") of human behavior. This chapter defends two interrelated theses: The first one is that a meaningful question about consensus in science is not whether we should seek it or not, but rather what kind of consensus we should seek and what kind we should give up. A corollary of the first thesis is that, in the pursuit of scientific consensus, subjective expert judgment is not dispensable. Together, the previous observations motivate the defense of the second thesis: The meaningful question about the role of subjective expert judgment in science is not whether experts should play a role in the justification of scientific theories, methods, observations etc. but rather what role they should play, and how that role should be fulfilled.

Struggling Over the Soul of Economics: Objectivity Versus Expertise (Julian Reiss) tackles another "old problem" in debates on expertise: the clash between objectivity and expertise. Reiss considers the classical ideal of economic science as *objective* science from a number of perspectives: theory formation in economics, methodology of economics, and normative economics. He asks the question "why objectivity?" and analyzes the quest for objectivity in science in connection with the pursuits of truth and empirical adequacy. Finding flaws in these accounts, he proposes to consider objectivity as an instrumental concept, that is objectivity as a practice to promote trust in science. This turns the problem of expertise to a problem about *trust* – "which experts should we trust?" – and that is probably one of the most salient questions to be asked about expertise.

So, a recurrent key question is "Who are the experts? How do we identify them?". This is the problem of attributing expertise, the one that Part III, **Attributing Standards of Expertise**, deals with.

Epistemology as a Social Science (Aviezer Tucker) presents a take on the problem of how to identify experts that is based on the Neyman-Rubin causal model. Statistical correlation between certain beliefs and certain kinds of social groups can be, under certain circumstances, caused by expertise, in the sense of possessing "special knowledge". The analysis proposed by Tucker allows for a statistical understanding of the communities of experts, and some beliefs that are typically associated with those communities.

The Expert Economist in Times of Uncertainty (Maria Jimenez-Buedo) claims that there are two alternative conceptions of who is an expert and who is not. According to the realist conception, an expert is whoever possesses knowledge of her field of research; this is a very demanding requisite for expertise. We can often only say *a posteriori* whether an expert was right or wrong in her assessment (hence whether she really knew), and it is often hard to extrapolate future likely competence from past competence (see Roger Cooke, Chap. 10, this volume), yet the alternative is no less problematic. The alternative social conception of expertise says that someone is an expert if she is recognized by others as such, so expertise is considered to be a relational notion. While the latter conception is more flexible, its danger is that anyone could be an expert as long as she is recognized as such, and independently of any factual indication of expertise. The author defends the thesis that the two notions, however, are not incompatible, and that a mixture of both is necessary for attributing expertise.

Validating Expert Judgment with the Classical Model (Roger Cooke) tackles the aforementioned problem of extrapolating likely expertise from past performance. Cooke's method of elicitation and aggregation of subjective judgment (the Classic Model, see Cooke 1991) has been tested repeatedly over the past two decades, and that has given rise to an expert judgment database, kept at the Technical University of Delft and containing an extensive set of studies on expert calibration and performance. Cooke's "Classical Model" is a performance-based weighted average of expert assessments. The weights are derived from experts' calibration scores, as measured on "seed variables". Seed variables serve a threefold purpose:

1. to quantify experts' performance as subjective probability assessors,
2. to enable performance-optimized combinations of expert distributions,
3. to evaluate the combination of expert judgment.

The name "Classical Model" derives from an analogy between calibration measurement and classical statistical hypothesis testing. Calibration measures the correspondence between a set of experimental results ("seed variables") with the expert's assessments. Cooke and Goossens (2008) compare this performance weighted combination with combinations where the expert assessments are equally weighted.

In his contribution to this volume, Cooke investigates whether experts were more successful with performance weights or equal weights. In other words, should we give all experts' opinions the same weight, or should we weight their opinions based on their performance? Cooke reviews a method for answering that question developed in Clemen (2008), and finds it wanting. He then suggests an alternative method, and how it could be used for answering that question with the TU Delft database.

The Truth About Accuracy (Filip Buekens and Fred Truyen) distinguishes the quest for truth, in scientific investigation, from the quest for accuracy. While truth is a rather ideal, and mostly semantic, notion, in science we tend to rely on the instead normative notion of accuracy. This distinction bears on how we define expertise: In his program of "veristic social epistemology" Goldman (1999) had made the concept of expertise dependent on the notion of truth – roughly, experts are those who possess the most truths on a subject matter. But the authors find Goldman's characterization of expertise inadequate. What is needed is not the concept of truth, but rather that of accuracy, when individuating experts. How to define accuracy is yet another problem to be solved, but what one must notice is that there is a normative dimension (not only a semantic one) to the definition of expertise.

The last Part of this collection, **The Democratic Dimension**, deals with the political and democratic dimension of expertise. *Expert Advisers* (Robert Evans) asks the question whether consensus of experts is desirable or not in society. Consensus of experts is "easy" because they often share methods, values, forma-tion, etc. but it does not necessarily guarantee that all available perspectives of a problem have been considered. For a long time, this has been a problem for social studies of science – including the project carried forward in the past decades by Harry Collins and Robert Evans – and it has led to the call for a "democratization" of the process of consensus formation. But Evans warns against the extremes: science is not a democratic institution, and it is not meant to stand by the same rules. There needs to be a separation of the political from the technical phase of science, and, while this may in part be an ideal, because the political phase trumps the technical one under most circumstances, the distinction is still useful against the possible abuses of policy makers: on the one hand, the abuse of portraying a lack of evidence and agreement in science, when the science has actually settled a given issue. On the other hand, the abuse of creating a false impression of agreement on a certain issue, when the scientists are still in the process of settling the issue.

Related to the problem of democratization of expertise is also the next chapter in line *The Role of Experts in the Condominium Model* (Rafał Wierzchosławski). Experts tend to hold a privileged epistemic position against that of laics, but how does that fare in the context of the Spanish republican ideal of freedom and government? Wierzchosławski considers the republican model proposed by Philip Pettit in relation to the problem of expertise. The often-times conflicting opinions of experts versus laymen is one that needs careful consideration, and the chapter offers some strategies for resolution.

Private Epistemic Virtues, Public Vices (Merel Lefevere and Eric Schliesser) deals with the problem of responsibility in science. Should social scientists be responsible for the consequences of their policy recommendations, or even the unintended consequences that their theories imply for policy making? They start with Douglas's (2009) account of "collective negligence", by which it is hard to attribute guilt on a specific member of a scientific community because it seems that it was the whole community to be responsible for negligence. The authors reject this way of attributing, or rather, responsibility, and argue that the community of scientists should be held responsible even for unintended consequences of their theories or policy recommendations. At the same time, a way to avoid such unintended consequences is to promote pluralism.

References

Aspinall, W. 2010. A route to more tractable expert advice. *Nature* 463(21): 294–295.

Blanchard, Olivier. 2009. The state of macro. *Annual Review of Economics* 1: 209–228.

Boumans, Marcel. 2008. Battle in the planning office: Field experts versus normative statisticians. *Social Epistemology* 22(4): 389–404.

Clemen, R.T. 2008. Comment on Cooke's classical method. *Reliability Engineering and System Safety* 93(5): 760–765.

Collins, Harry, and Robert Evans. 2007. *Rethinking expertise*. Chicago: The University of Chicago Press.

Cooke, Roger M. 1991. *Experts in uncertainty: Opinions and subjective probability in science*. New York/Oxford: Oxford University Press.

Cooke, Roger M., and Luis L.H.J. Goossens. 2008. TU Delft expert judgment data base. *Reliability Engineering and System Safety* 93: 657–674.

Dalkey, Norman C. 1969. An experimental study of group opinion: The Delphi method. *Futures* 1 (5): 408–426.

Dalkey, N.C., D.L. Rourke, R. Lewis, and D. Snyder (eds.). 1972. *Studies in the quality of life: Delphi and decision-making*. Lexington: Lexington Books.

den Butter, Frank A.G., and Mary S. Morgan. 1998. What makes the models-policy interaction successful? *Economic Modelling* 15: 443–475.

Douglas, Heather E. 2009. *Science, policy and the value-free ideal*. Pittsburgh: University of Pittsburgh Press.

Downward, Paul M., and Andrew Mearman. 2008. Decision-making at the Bank of England: A critical appraisal. *Oxford Economic Papers* 60: 385–409.

Feyerabend, Paul. 1975. *Against method*. London: Verso.

Galison, Peter L. 1992. *Big science: The growth of large-scale research*. Stanford: Stanford University Press.

Goldman, A. 1999. *Knowledge in a social world*. New York: Oxford University Press.

Helmer, Olaf. 1983. *Looking forward. A guide to futures research*. Beverly Hills: Sage.

Helmer, Olaf and Nicholas Rescher. 1958. *On the epistemology of the inexact sciences*, RAND paper N. p 1513. The RAND Corporation.

Hempel, Carl G. 1952. Symposium: Problems of concept and theory formation in the social sciences. In *Science, language, and human rights*, eds. Roderick Firth and Max Black. 65–86. Philadelphia: University of Pennsylvania Press.

Hull, David. 1988. *Science as process*. Chicago: The University of Chicago Press.

Jick, Todd D. 1979. Mixing qualitative and quantitative methods: Triangulation in action. *Administrative Science Quarterly* 24: 602–611.

Kitcher, Philip. 2001. *Science, truth, and democracy*. Oxford: Oxford University Press.

Kuhn, Thomas S. 1970. *The structure of scientific revolutions*, 2nd enlarged edition. International encyclopedia of unified science, vol. 2, no. 2. Chicago/London: The University of Chicago Press.

List, Christian, and Philip Pettit. 2011. *Group agency: The possibility, design, and status of corporate agents*. Oxford: Oxford University Press.

Longino, Helen E. 1990. *Science as social knowledge: Values and objectivity in scientific inquiry*. Princeton: Princeton University Press.

Marshall, Alfred. [1890] 1920. *Principles of economics*, 8th ed. London: Macmillan.

Martini, Carlo. 2014a. The role of experts in the methodology of economics. *The Journal of Economic Methodology* 21(1): 77–91.

Martini, Carlo. 2014b. Experts in science: A view from the trenches. *Synthese* 191: 3–15.

Page, Scott E. 2007. *The difference: How the power of diversity creates better groups, firms, schools, and societies*. Princeton: Princeton University Press.

Reiss, Julian. 2008. *Error in economics: Towards a more evidence-based methodology*. London: Routledge.

Rosenberg, Alexander. 1994. If economics isn't science, what is it? In *The philosophy of economics: An anthology*, ed. Daniel Hausman, 376–394. Cambridge: Cambridge University Press.

Solomon, Miriam. 1994. *Social empiricism*. Cambridge, MA: MIT Press.

Solomon, M. 2007. The social epistemology of NIH consensus conferences. In *Establishing medical reality: Methodological and metaphysical issues in philosophy of medicine*, ed. H. Kincaid and J. McKitrick. Dordrecht: Springer.

Tinbergen, Jan. [1982] 2003. The need of a synthesis. In *Jan Tinbergen. The centennial volume*, ed. J. Kolpp, 303–306. Rotterdam University. Translation of De noodzaak van een synthese. *Economisch Statistische Berichten* 1-12-1982, 1284–1285.

Trout, J.D. 2009. *The empathy gap*. New York: Viking/Penguin.

Tuomela, Raimo. 2013. *Social ontology: Collective intentionality and group agents*. Oxford: Oxford University Press.

Part I
Consensus in Practice

Chapter 2
The Institutional Economics of Stakeholder Consultation; How Experts Can Contribute to Reduce the Costs of Reaching Compromise Agreements

Frank A.G. den Butter and Sjoerd A. ten Wolde

Abstract Complicated projects, policy plans and government regulation usually involve a number of stakeholders with diverging interests. A good infrastructure for the consultation of, and for the discussion between these stakeholders is needed in order to avoid high implementation costs. Following the theory of new institutional economics these implementation costs can be seen as transaction costs. This is especially relevant in Government-to-Business (G2B) and Government-to-Consumers (G2C) relationships where the projects and policy measures bring about (re)distribution problems. This chapter discusses various ways to organize these consultations with the help of experts as intermediaries, so that a compromise agreement is reached on the solution of the (re)distribution problem. These institutionalized structures of consultation are referred to as "matching zones". Practical experiences, mainly from the Netherlands, provide guidelines for the effective institutional setup of such "matching zones". Specifically, the design of a "matching zone" should try to adhere to the following principles: *(i)* there should be a common interest and ample incentives for reaching an agreement; *(ii)* there should be the prospect of long, repeated interaction; *(iii)* there should be a balance between representation and efficiency; *(iv)* the constraints should be clear from the onset of the matching zone; *(v)* fairness should be strived for; *(vi)* IC technology should be utilized optimally; and *(viii)* informal contacts and an amicable atmosphere should be promoted. Most importantly, however, independent experts appear to fulfil an important role in order to reach compromise agreements at sufficiently low implementation costs.

Ten Wolde's part of the research project was financed by the "Transactieland.nl foundation".

F.A.G. den Butter (✉) • S.A. ten Wolde
Department of Economics and RITM, VU University Amsterdam, De Boelelaan 1105,
1081HV Amsterdam, The Netherlands
e-mail: fbutter@feweb.vu.nl

17

2.1   Introduction

In modern economies, with full use of information and communication technology, the execution of projects and implementation of policy plans are becoming more and more complicated. Various stakeholders are involved. They want their interests to be safeguarded. So, clashes between the government, private parties (business or citizens) in these Government-to-Business (G2B) and Government-to-Citizen (G2C) relationships are ever more likely. For instance, infrastructural and building projects are increasingly prone to "NIMBY"[1] objections, thus increasing the need for *ex ante* discussion. In the meanwhile, regulatory pressure and government inefficacy continue to be major impediments to efficient business and the functioning of government services. It may lead to long and costly delays in the preparatory stage of large projects, and in high implementation costs of policy plans, and legal regulatory measures. In the Netherlands – a tightly-packed country with high levels of business activity and a strong regulatory government – this potential for large costs, which in a general sense can all be regarded as transaction costs, is even greater than usual. As such, there is ample opportunity for an improvement of the way in which interaction between the government and society is designed.

That is why, in the Netherlands, some practical experience has been obtained in the setup of an infrastructure for the strategic and policy discussions between relevant stakeholders in these projects, plans and regulatory measures. Part of it goes back to the (in)famous "polder model" where great efforts have always been made to reach consensus, or at least compromise agreements between stakeholders with different interests in matters of (re)distribution of welfare. Out of these experiences an institutional innovation has risen in the Netherlands, which has been labelled "matching zone". In a matching zone, the government organizes an institutionalized forum for decision-making between the government and society – the latter consisting of businesses and/or citizens. This forum is often mediated by experts with a broad overview of the policy situation, who can depoliticize the debate, and point out creative and effective solutions. The objective of this institutional innovation is to lower the transaction costs while optimizing policy outcomes.

Matching zones have proven their worth in both theory and practice. In practice, several matching-zone-type institutions have shown to demonstrate better outcomes than the *status quo ante* – often a setting in which the government decides on policy and subsequently runs into trouble implementing it because of societal obstruction. Regulatory pressure can be relieved, while the government itself may also avoid duplicating work. Moreover, transaction costs in establishing rules and/or regulatory measures and implementation are lowered. This has come about through carefully crafted organizational mechanisms, but also through institutional experimentation. Theoretically, matching zones also provide for the resolution of collective action problems between, for example, firms and citizens, or firms and

---

[1] Not In My Back Yard.

firms. Through repeated interaction, mutual trust and an incentive to cooperate are cultivated, so that parties spend more time on achieving efficient outcomes and less time on factional bickering and "trench warfare". Employing neutral experts in such situations of potential conflict is often essential for participants to put their trust in such institutions.

This chapter seeks to link the practical experiences of matching zones with the theory of new institutional economics (see e.g. Ménard and Shirley 2005). Although it is not yet possible to make a systematic evaluation of the transaction cost reduction that matching zones bring about, some broad lessons can be drawn from both practical and theoretical insights. Through a proper design and management of matching zones a fall in transaction costs and an improvement in policy outcomes can be obtained. In that case the design and management of the matching zone should adhere to a number of principles, as discussed in Sect. 2.5 of this chapter. Although the experiences described in this chapter mainly stem from the Netherlands, these principles have a general validity, and can be applied to a broad range consultation and compromise finding activities involving different representatives of stakeholders.

In line with the theme of this book, the chapter pays ample attention to the role of experts as intermediaries in the negotiations between stakeholders. It is essential for these experts to be independent and have no specific stakes in order to facilitate reaching compromise agreements at sufficiently low implementation costs. In that sense the chapter is not so much on reaching consensus but rather on reaching compromise with the help of experts. However, in order to come to a compromise agreement at lowest implementation costs, it is a prerequisite that there be consensus amongst the stakeholders that the compromise is the best possible one. In some of the cases discussed in this chapter it is therefore required that in the negotiation process unanimity on the compromise agreement is to be reached.

The contents of the remainder of this chapter are as follows. Section 2.2 discusses the meaning and significance of matching zones, it elaborates which different types of matching zones can be distinguished and explains the demand for matching zones. Section 2.3 then describes four cases in which matching-zone-type institutions were employed. Three cases stem from the Netherlands and one from Brazil. Given these practical examples, Sect. 2.4 investigates how the setup of consultation in matching zones can be embedded in, and be based upon modern theories of new institutional and transaction cost economics. Section 2.5 distils lessons at the strategic, tactical, and operational level for future matching zones from the preceding discussion. Section 2.6 concludes.

2.2 Matching Zones

2.2.1 Definition and Types

The term "matching zone" as a label for the institutional setup of consultation and compromise finding between representatives of stakeholders asks for a precise definition and a comparison with other similar concepts. Moreover, it is useful to make a number of analytical distinctions between different types of matching zones.

The aim of a matching zone is to provide an institutionalized infrastructure for the interplay between either representatives of businesses and the government or citizens and the government in order to reduce the implementation or transaction costs of projects and government intervention. A matching zone can therefore be defined as an institutionalized structure of consultation, in which the government interacts on a policy legislation development level with sectorial representatives of businesses. It is important that the matching zone brings together the relevant political and economic agents, in order to provide for an "arena" in which discussions and negotiations between different interests can be conducted in a cooperative way. A first prerequisite for a matching zone to be effective is that *only* relevant, but also *all* relevant stakeholders take part in the discussions.

There are a number of adjacent concepts. One of these is the notion of the "orchestration of chains" (Den Butter 2012; Van Veenstra and Janssen 2009). This orchestration involves the streamlining of the interaction between governments and firms (but not citizens). It entails coordinating government services and demands towards business, by intelligently establishing institutional structures that coax the different government parties into working together. The firm is regarded more as a "customer" than as a cash cow or an obstruction. This new framework is believed to relieve both governmental organizations and firms of an excessive regulatory burden. The term "chain restructuring" is largely a synonym for this orchestration as well (Taskforce Ketenherinrichting 2007).

Also related is the idea of "public-private partnerships" (Van Woelderen et al. 2006; Koppenjan 2005; Martimort and Pouyet 2008; Schaeffer and Loveridge 2002). In such partnerships, the costs of projects – often infrastructural – are borne partially by those benefiting most from the project, mostly firms. If these public-private partnerships are carried out well, lower costs may be achieved, while projects that otherwise would perhaps not even have been feasible can be tailor-made to fit the needs of important actors. Also, "white elephant" projects that do not live up to their grandiose ambitions are more easily avoided.

Yet, the matching zone is a more flexible concept. As stated before, matching zones may include firms, citizens, or both. Moreover, their objectives need not always be the same; rather, it is the central notion of government-guided discussion and negotiation between different interests that characterizes the matching zone.

A very broad distinction can be made between those matching zones that are instituted on a project base, and those that encapsulate a more wide-ranging array of responsibilities. *Project-based matching zones* may be invoked to facilitate decision-making on a specific issue, such as the construction of a new airport or a new tax policy. This matching zone may be either for a predefined time period, or for an indefinite period – though "one-shot-interactions" are not seen as matching zones here, as they cannot be regarded as institutionalized framing. *Broad-based matching zones*, on the other hand, are organized more comprehensively around a number of related issues or a fixed number of agents that are involved in a collection of issues. For instance, the Socio-Economic Council (SER) of the Netherlands is a corporatist advisory organ organized around the juxtaposition between trade unions and employers' organizations, with independent members providing mediation and advice on most issues of concerns to employers and employees (see e.g. Visser and Hemerijck 1998, p. 93). This case quite clearly illustrates the role of experts who facilitate reaching compromise agreements.

A second dichotomy is based on whether the matching zone is organized for a known and specified amount of time or for an undefined period – or even permanently. While project-based matching zones may be both finite and permanent, broad-based matching zones are unlikely to be finite. The duration of a matching zone is quintessential to its functioning, given that participants will take into account the benefits and costs of future cooperation and conflict. Generally, a longer duration can be expected to generate more cooperative outcomes. It implies, as will be elaborated later, that the discussions and compromise formation become part of a repeated game. However, matching zones of a limited duration may also be valuable when the project does not lend itself well for long-term evaluation, for instance.

A last distinction that can be made is whether the matching zone is geared more towards distributing costs and benefits, or towards regulation. When a matching zone is focused on costs and benefits, the form and shape of policies or projects are not part of the debate; rather, financing and (re)distributing gains are at the heart of the discussion. The many public-private partnerships that come into existence to finance infrastructural projects like highways provide an example of this. Often, bargaining about who pays for the highway and where the exit ramps will be located is more important than regulating the maximum speed and the like. On the other hand, regulation may also be an important topic for decision-making. If the government plans to impose new norms for pollution, both firms and households may want to discuss not only the costs and benefits, but also the exact content of regulation. Again in such discussions the trusted opinion of experts may facilitate coming to a compromise agreement with the consent of all relevant stakeholders so that implementation costs of regulation are minimized. Figure 2.1 summarizes these various types of matching zones.

	Undetermined/permanent	Finite
Project-based	Design + execution + maintenance/execution phase	Design phase Design + Execution phase
Broad-based	Corporatism, institutionalized input	Not likely

Fig. 2.1 A typology of matching zones

2.2.2 Project-Based Matching Zones

Often, matching zones are created around new, government-instigated projects. For instance, the building of a new airport usually involves a great number of stakeholders, some of which may be disadvantaged by the airport, while others profit from it. Since the issues arising from such projects are unlikely to be tackled in a single meeting, there may be a need for sustained discussion between interest groups. Characteristic of such a project-based matching zone is that it involves only a relatively limited number of issues, all strictly arising from the project itself. It would, for example, not be acceptable for firms to complain about high municipal taxes when the matching zone is focused on the building of an airport.

Every project of this kind has three phases: (1) the design phase, (2) the execution phase, and (3) maintenance and revision (Bovens et al. 2001). One of the prime questions facing policy-makers when setting up a matching zone is which of these phases to include. In general, the design phase will almost invariably be included, since it is often the most fundamental phase of a project. An exception is when the project has already been carried out; e.g., if a highway has already been built. It is, however, a well-known fact in the administrative sciences that plans may still be prone to substantial change, sabotage or even hold-up during their execution (Bovens et al. 2001). Hence, both firms and citizens may insist that the execution phase also be included, as a check on the actual implementation of plans. In the last phase, when the project has been executed, the issues for discussion are maintenance and minor changes. Agents may then be interested in such issues as the division of costs and benefits, and regulation. If these issues are important to the actors involved, a matching zone may be created for an undefined time period, rather than until the end of a given phase. However, the project may also be subject to major ex post revision; for example, an airport may want to build another runway. In this case, the project goes back to the drawing board, and the cycle starts again at the design phase. If major revisions are frequent, extending the matching zone to an undefined stretch of time may also be attractive to policy-makers. As such, project-based matching zones may vary from relatively short but institutionalized meetings between those affected, to infinitely running platforms to discuss design, execution and revision of projects. Here the role of independent experts is to design an appropriate institutional setup of the matching zone, where during the project the discussions with the stakeholders take place so that there is a broad support for the way the project is executed. Moreover, their role can also be to moderate discussions in an efficient and cooperative fashion.

Project-based matching zones may discuss a wide range of issues. In general, these issues can be subdivided into the following broad categories: (1) design, (2) regulation, and (3) finance. Design corresponds to the physical attributes of the project: For instance, when building a new business park, the matching zone may discuss such issues as the total area of the park, the number of parking lots, or the exact location. Such design issues are often the hardest to change after execution, hence giving the participants an incentive to bargain aggressively about them. Regulation refers to the rules governing the project. Hence, when building a new airport, a matching zone could decide on a noise pollution cap, or on a limited number of aircraft slots. Not only are regulations easier to change afterwards, they are also subject to changing trends, as demonstrated by changing safety rules for nuclear reactors, for instance. Issues of finance, lastly, are comprised by arguments over the division of direct costs and benefits: who pays for what, and who gets part of the incomes or profits generated? This is where expert knowledge comes in handy: independent experts will know which issues to address and how to discuss them. Moreover, they may have specific knowledge on matters of finance which the stakeholders in the discussion do not have.

2.2.3   Broad-Based Matching Zones

While consultation of civil society and business is often confined to specific projects, the realm of politics is also permeated by policy areas where (potential) conflict is more widespread and consultation must be based on a broader foundation. One way to handle such latent or manifest conflicts is through institutionalizing dialogue and negotiation between the opposed parties, and the government. One infamous example of this is the concept of "corporatism", pioneered in Mussolini's Italy and later employed by a wide range of regimes. Corporatism involves the creation of economic and social policy in conjunction with representative groups in society, such as trade unions and employers' organizations. Although the bad reputation of fascism has stuck to it, more transparent and democratic variants have been utilized successfully in advanced economies such as the Netherlands. Such corporatist bodies can also be regarded as matching zones.

There are several reasons why countries have come to institutionalize societal juxtapositions. One reason can be to dampen conflict and to optimize socio-economic outcomes. Through repeated interaction, the encapsulation in the system, and the supervision of the government, social agents may tone down their stance, and focus on cooperation not conflict. Another reason is that governments may want the continued input of societal partners in the policy process, but are not able to do so effectively through non-institutionalized channels. Broad-based matching zones may then provide a government with the means to adjust its policy to the wishes of important groups.

When matching zones are broad-based, they are unlikely to be of a temporary character. Given the wide range of issues, there is no obvious time limit. Moreover, if the matching zone is functioning well, there is no incentive to terminate it after a given period, since it is exactly the repeated interaction that breeds cooperation and trust. It is precisely this cooperation and trust which is needed to bring down the transaction costs of executing projects and implementing policy plans. So a major aim of the matching zone is to enhance the societal support for the project, policy plan or government regulation.

2.2.4 Explaining the Demand for Matching Zones

The coming into being of matching zones in the Netherlands, and similar structures in other parts of the world, corresponds to a need and demand for such apparatuses. There is a wide gamut of circumstances under which ordinary, ad hoc decision-making could be improved upon by such institutions. There are three main reasons to institute a matching zone: *(i)* excessive regulatory pressure, *(ii)* inefficient public services and excessive bureaucratic specialization, and *(iii)* the need to decide on new policy or regulate some specific domain.

2.2.4.1 Excessive Regulatory Pressure

With the expansion of governmental responsibilities since the Second World War, regulatory pressure has increased likewise in many Western societies (cf. Raad van Economische Adviseurs 2005). Both national and regional governments have an increased capacity to regulate society and business, and more and more expertise on regulation. This process has, nevertheless, also led to an explosion of the costs and time that citizens and firms incur in complying with these new rules. From an economic perspective, it is optimal to equate the "marginal returns" of regulation with the "marginal costs" of higher regulatory pressure. This exacts that only "necessary" regulation be implemented. In this case "necessary" regulation can be seen as that level of regulation which repairs market failure or complies with political preferences on redistribution in the most efficient way. However, in the Netherlands, and in many other countries, the feeling is that regulation exceeds this optimal level, leading to excessively high costs of regulation.

There are three theoretical mechanisms to explain this. One of these is that the benefits of regulation often accrue to the regulators themselves, while the costs of regulation are not borne by these politicians and civil servants. This is an argument from public choice theory which leads to a problem of "externalities" in crafting regulation. Matching zones may cause these externalities to be internalized, by passing on part of the costs of regulation to policy-makers.

A second explanation is the exponential effect of rules on regulatory pressures: research shows that new rules breed even more rules (Raad van Economische

Adviseurs 2005). As such, the proliferation of rules may be an explosive exponential process: because new rules lead to new and sometimes undesirable behavior, this new behavior is often again corrected by the creation of rules, hence creating a vicious cycle.

A third theoretical mechanism is that rules are often (ab)used by insiders with vested interests. Because of this, the removal of objectively redundant rules is often strongly delayed by those benefiting from them, while the spread of new rules is not slowed as strongly (Raad van Economische Adviseurs 2005). This status quo bias is widely spread and hard to combat by means of incremental policy-making.

The consequences of this increase in regulatory pressure are plenty and varied. The most important effect for business and the economy is an increase in transaction costs: doing business is rendered comparatively more expensive. Financial funds are allocated to unproductive activities, such as filling in forms, rather than physical production. Moreover, rigidities become more widespread, such that the welfare enhancing market forces are less able to do their work.

A second effect is an increase in monitoring costs as part of transaction costs at the side of the government: with every new rule, the government needs more capacity to enforce compliance with these rules. Moreover, new rules can cause popular support for regulation to wither if these rules are perceived as unjust or redundant. In this case, new rules can elicit unproductive behavior, if citizens also live up less to necessary and just rules.

A third negative aspect of regulatory pressure is that overly strict regulation may also slow down innovation. Even though unwanted behavior may be prevented by new rules, the desirable behavior may also be affected. Thus, firms and individuals will be restricted in their behavior and will not be able to innovate as much as they would otherwise.

2.2.4.2 Inefficient Public Services and Excessive Bureaucratic Specialization

One of the propelling forces behind productivity growth, and hence economic growth, is the intensification of labor specialization. As Adam Smith already contended, labor specialization lets tasks be performed more efficiently. However, there is also a downside: increasing specialization asks for more coordination and communication, because congruence between the different modules of a production chain is quintessential for the efficiency gains that come with it. If this congruence is insufficient, specialization may lead to inefficiency and mounting transaction costs, rather than economic progress. This is a well-known phenomenon within many bureaucratic apparatuses: citizens and firms get sent from one department to another, often getting stuck in a Catch 22-type situation. Along the way, economic actors incur high costs, and waste time and effort.

These transaction costs are caused by the fact that specialization has taken place without being accompanied by a fitting organizational structure. Due to this, each employee and department is often working on its own island (Van Veenstra and

Janssen 2009, p. 19). Moreover, as an organization's departments get older, they are often prone to a phenomenon called scope creep, in which the internal objectives stray away from the originally specified goals (ibid.). Several causes can be identified. First of all, governments often employ management techniques that rely on very limited measures of performance. Governmental tasks, however, are often very complex. Thus, incentives arise to focus on the measures, rather than the real goal at hand. This encourages isolation and excessive specialization. Secondly, different parts of a government organization may have their own clientele (Bovens et al. 2001, p. 218). This is often due to intensive contacts between parts of government and their "clients". Because of this, companies often have no problems in dealing with one part of a bureaucracy, while other parts work against them. For instance, firms are the core clientele of Chambers of Commerce in the Netherlands, while civil servants dealing with spatial planning often give more heed to other concerns than business's worries.

Hence, specialization within the civil service (and often also within companies and other organizations) may lead to inefficient policy-making and implementation. Rules are frequently unclear, and firms are told different things by different departments. Starting entrepreneurs and citizens themselves also run into these kinds of problems. This brings about higher transaction costs in the economy. Thus, streamlining bureaucratic processes more often than not is essential. Matching zones can be very helpful in enabling such streamlining, often by forcing the bureaucracy to arrange all contacts with the relevant part of society through one channel. In this setting experts with a broad knowledge of the various government departments, and with knowledge of the stakes and hobbyhorses of the departments, may very well contribute to reaching agreements.

2.2.4.3 New Policies and Projects

New projects and policies often run into "NIMBY"-type problems. Moreover, the original plans are often not geared perfectly towards those that would benefit from it. This may lead to unnecessary delays, inefficient implementation, or a project or policy that simply does not match society's needs. Any project or policy invariably has a number of beneficiaries and a number of disadvantaged groups. Bringing together these two parties before implementation starts is quintessential for optimizing outcomes and minimizing transaction costs. With increasingly vocal citizens and firms, ignoring society is simply not an option anymore. Matching zones can therefore be employed, bringing together the government, firms, and citizens, in order to forestall costs from running high.

2.3   Cases

This section gives four examples of the institutional setup of consultation and stakeholder participation, which can be regarded as successful matching zones. These cases are used in the following sections to illustrate the theoretical argumentation for the design of matching zones in various situations, and to derive practical recommendations for their design.

2.3.1   The Alders Table

Schiphol, one of Europe's busiest airports, is a major driver of the Dutch economy. Many companies are heavily dependent – either directly or indirectly – on the airport. At the same time, however, the endless air traffic elicits much frustration and consternation in the densely populated metropolitan area of Amsterdam. Contributing to this clash of interests are the continuing pressures to expand the airport. In its long-term strategic document of 2007, the Schiphol Group argued that a sixth runway would be paramount to the future economic development of the Netherlands (Schiphol Group 2007). While debate about any expansion of Schiphol had long been contentious, the looming inevitability of some form of extension triggered a more constructive response from many affected parties – negotiating on reasonable terms became more attractive than thwarting any new developments.

From this situation emerged a new forum for discussion and negotiation between the various stakeholders, in which the national and municipal governments, the inhabitants of the affected area, and the parties involved in aviation were drawn together to discuss mutually advantageous solutions.[2] This can be regarded as a matching zone. Rather than summoning all parties for a one-off negotiation about the future of the airport, the Ministry of Infrastructure and the Environment, and the (former) Ministry of Spatial Planning decided to institute a semi-permanent council, which would provide policy-makers of these two ministries with consensual advice.[3] This would all occur under the presidency of former Minister of Spatial Planning and Labour MP Hans Alders – accordingly, the matching zone was dubbed the "Alders Table" (Tafel van Alders). Here Alders, as chairman, obviously fulfilled the role of independent expert who facilitates that agreements between the various stakeholders were to be reached. His experience as a minister and a parliamentarian, with ample experience in resolving planning and environmental issues, endowed him with the necessary knowledge and stature.

In this case the parameters set by the initiating ministries are of special interest. Firstly, the task given to the matching zone was explicitly bound by the need for full

---

[2] http://www.alderstafel.nl/schiphol/start/

[3] http://www.alderstafel.nl/schiphol/opdracht/

agreement.[4] This included giving heed to the four prime interests of the different participants – further development of the aviation sector, limiting noise nuisance for inhabitants, improving the quality of living for the direct surroundings of Schiphol, and the efficient use of ground space. This specific task had the effect that factions within the matching zone could not span together and ignore other groups. Rather, all participants needed to work together on relatively equal footing, and all had to compromise. Although this could have led to small groups hijacking the debate by threatening with a veto, this seems not to have occurred – quite possibly because of the necessity to cooperate in the future.

Secondly, a specific deadline was given to complete the first assignment: The Alders Table was asked to provide an advice for the medium term before May 2008.[5] This created the necessary pressure to coax the participants into compromise and to avoid the usual procrastination and bickering. Of course, it is also possible that this deadline negatively affected the quality of the advice, although this would be hard to establish empirically.

Thirdly, the set of possible outcomes was limited from the onset by the ministries. Six different policy alternatives were given, leaving it up to the matching zone's actors to favor one over the other – although hybrid forms were allowed.[6] This selection of a limited set of alternatives effectively reduced the number of issues on which the participants could disagree. Also, endless quarrels about procedures and the order of discussion were avoided. Moreover, debate was tightly focused on the issue at hand, so that vaguely related issues were avoided. Also, the discussion was confined within the set of policy options that were deemed feasible and desirable by the two cooperating ministries. The flipside of this is, of course, that more creative solutions were avoided and that productive "horse trading" was quite hard.

Fourthly, the number of actors in the matching zone was heavily restricted. As such, the companies operating at and around Schiphol were not invited. Also, citizens suffering welfare losses were only invited to join through two interest groups, the Commission for Regional Discussion on Schiphol Airport (CROS) and the Society for Common Platforms (VGP). Moreover, municipalities that were only affected mildly by the expansion of Schiphol were not included, as well as NGOs focused on environmental preservation.[7] This facilitated efficient discussion and decision-making, and made it less arduous to keep all participants in check. However, it also provoked a backlash: entrepreneurs in the vicinity of Schiphol have complained extensively about their exclusion, and eventually came up with an alternative Alders Table – the so-called Economic Table for Schiphol (ETS) – in

---

[4] http://www.alderstafel.nl/schiphol/opdracht/

[5] http://www.alderstafel.nl/schiphol/opdracht/

[6] http://www.alderstafel.nl/schiphol/opdracht/

[7] http://www.trouw.nl/tr/nl/4324/Nieuws/article/detail/1201545/2008/12/04/Aan-de-Tafel-van-Alders-zijn-te-weinig-plaatsen.dhtml

November 2010. Thus, although efficacious discussion was facilitated by excluding actors, legitimacy also suffered.

Up until now, the Alders Table seems to have performed quite satisfactorily. The advice of 2008 was taken up by the government, and subsequently implemented.[8] Even the business alternative, the ETS, admits that the Alders Table works well.[9] Moreover, the Alders Table has resulted in the establishment of two additional matching zones with a similar task. These perform the same role, but with respect to Eindhoven Airport and Lelystad Airport, both deemed to be important future alternatives to the expansion of Schiphol. The Alders Table has also, however, been criticized for its lack of representativeness and lack of openness.[10] Although this critique by left-out, disgruntled stakeholders may very well be fair, it seems not to significantly have undermined the effectiveness of the matching zone.

2.3.2 The Social Economic Council (SER)

The post-bellum period in the Netherlands saw a strong determination to build up the country, rather than getting bogged down in class struggle between various interest groups in the socio-economic debate on policy matters. This led the government of Prime Minister Willem Drees to institute a "social economic council" in 1950 – dubbed the Sociaal-Economische Raad (SER) in Dutch.[11] In fact it is part of what can be called the industrial organization of policy preparation in the Netherlands (see Den Butter 2011). This council was set up to bring together trade unions, employers' organizations and so-called independent "crown members" in a tripartite, permanent institution. Although this institution preceded the concept of what this chapter labels "matching zone" it can be regarded as a prototypical one: it provides a well institutionalized framing of consultation in order to prevent societal clashes of interest and to come to compromise agreements. The principal task with which the SER has been entrusted is advising the government; although the government is not obliged to follow this advice, it is legally expected to consider it and provide a formal reply. Yet in most cases the government will indeed follow the advice as policy measures approved in the advices of the council will meet broad support when implemented.

There are a number of features that set the SER apart as a public institution. Firstly, the inclusion of independent crown members – members appointed by government decree – provides for a conciliatory and objective factor. Whenever the unions and employers dig their heels in the sand, they can facilitate a

---

[8] http://www.depers.nl/binnenland/181734/Nieuwe-vertrekroutes-Schiphol.html

[9] http://www.vlieghinder.nl/reacties.php?id=P5813_0_1_0

[10] http://www.trouw.nl/tr/nl/4324/Nieuws/article/detail/1201545/2008/12/04/Aan-de-Tafel-van-Alders-zijn-te-weinig-plaatsen.dhtml

[11] http://www.ser.nl/nl/Raad/Tijdbalk.aspx

breakthrough. Moreover, since many crown members are renowned scientists (including the president of the Dutch Central Bank and the director of the Central Planning Bureau), the SER benefits from recent scientific breakthroughs. In fact these crown members act as experts which are instrumental to reach agreement on the advices amongst the social partners. A major advantage of such experts joining the discussions in the SER is that they urge the participants from the social partners to base their arguments on solid scientific insights. It brings discipline to the discussions. For instance, the model based policy analysis of the Central Planning Bureau plays a major role in the macro-economic policy debate in The Netherlands (see Den Butter 2011). In their interventions in the SER all stakeholders are forced to frame their contributions in terms of this policy analysis. This may help to formulate optimal policies. Expert civil servants from the policy departments of the Ministries also attend the discussions in the SER but have no say. Formally this is correct as the government asks the SER for advice and it would be improper as representatives of the government would interfere in the discussions. However, through informal channels, and in consultation with the independent members, expertise at the Ministries may have its influence on the final compromise.

Secondly, by its permanent nature, the SER is likely to maintain its existence and prominence for many years to come. This brings a strong "repeated game" element into the relationship between its members. Both unionists and employers are perfectly aware that they will be dependent on each other in the future. This often breeds cooperation and concession politics (see Den Butter and Mosch 2003 for a further discussion).

Thirdly, the selection of participants is narrow. Three trade unions and three employers' organizations form part of the SER, hence giving them favored access over other, alternative organizations. On the one hand, this may lead to rigidity, especially in a country where union membership is quite low and where labour and capital are not always the central juxtaposition in the economy anymore (Visser and Hemerijck 1998, p. 100). The SER has thus been criticized for not responding to a changing society, while the trade unions specifically are often scolded for being unrepresentative. On the other hand, however, the efficiency of the policy process is greatly helped by not bringing in too many actors and by keeping interests clear. Moreover, it has been argued that the system encourages the trade unions and employers' organizations to look beyond their narrow constituency, and take into account the broader needs of society from the macroeconomic perspective.

Fourthly, casual contacts between the SER members are very common. Since the SER is interwoven with a number of other institutions and organizations, its members often see each other frequently on both a formal and an informal basis. It has been argued that this has led to a high degree of mutual trust among SER members, thus facilitating cooperation. There is, of course, also the critique that this has rendered the SER into an "inbred clique" that does not represent society's interests sufficiently and is slow to make decisions. Yet, as the independent members of the SER are also part of these formal and informal networks, their influence on consensus and compromise formation is also exerted through these channels.

Fifthly, there are a number of incentives that encourage reaching compromise agreements on the advices. One relatively recent development is the scrapping of the government's obligation to ask for the SER's advice on every single social or economic measure it takes. While beforehand this was widely expected to reduce the SER's influence, its actual effect was the opposite: because the Council now often had to give "unwanted" advice in order to influence government policy, the need for a coherent and consensual position was even greater. This led the SER to become less divided and more efficacious in its formulation of policy advice. Another important device that induces compromise agreements is the fact that both the trade unions and the employers' organizations have a number of sticks and carrots to employ. Trade unions have an official (conditional) right to strike, but also to sign collective agreements in name of all employees. Employers' organizations can decide to hire and fire workers, but are also able to represent the whole gamut of employers in collective bargaining. This enables both parties to issue credible threats *and* credible rewards, thus making cooperation more enticing.

Of course, the SER is no panacea for all economic ailments. Specifically, during the 1970s the Council was rife with division and disputes. During this time, the SER was often one of the many arenas in which unions and employers were slinging mud at one another. However, in the 1980s a new consensual mode was found, partly in response to the economic problems afflicting the Netherlands. In the two following decades, the so-called "polder model" became commonplace, in which societal groups aimed at mutually beneficial outcomes and not at conflict. This is reasoned to have produced significant economic gains, and above all a high degree of mutual trust within political and economic institutions, amongst which the SER was prime. Hence, the SER played a key role in promoting a political economy in which transaction costs in socio-economic collective bargaining were low, while outcomes were relatively optimal. In this sense, the Council's function as a "matching zone" is often evaluated quite positively, albeit that long delays in reaching compromise agreements are sometimes also regarded as hindrance to the process of policy making. Moreover, in recent years internal disputes within the trade unions have weakened the role of the Council.

2.3.3   Participatory Budgeting in Brazil

A somewhat more exotic variant on the matching zone can be found in contemporary Brazil: the so-called *orçamento participativo*, or "participatory budgeting". Responding to pressure for more local democracy in the end of the 1980s, the socialist PT party in the southern city of Porto Alegre implemented a radical new way of setting the municipal budget (Kunrath Silva 2003, p. 165). The idea was to involve citizens in the budgeting process, thus enhancing spending efficiency and popular representation, and reducing graft and waste. While political power has swapped hands ever since, the *orçamento participativo* has continued to play a key role in Porto Alegre's politics, and has even been copied in a great number of other

Brazilian cities. It is an interesting case to study because the prefecture of Porto Alegre has managed to effectively bring together citizens and the government, while keeping transaction costs down.

The *orçamento participativo* in Porto Alegre has evolved throughout the past two decades, but the underlying principle has remained the same. Each of the 16 subsections of the city has its own plenary meeting, and there are five thematic plenaries: Transport; Education, Culture and Leisure; Health and Social Assistance; Economic Development and Taxation; and City Planning and Urban Development (Fedozzi 1998, p. 259). In each of these institutional structures, there are three phases, with the budgetary choices and number of participants being narrowed down in each subsequent phase. There is an annual cycle. The most important axis of negotiation is between the government and different groups of citizens. Hence, the *orçamento participativo* can safely be regarded as an example of a matching zone, in which the government attempts to align its own objectives and interests with those of a wide gamut of societal actors.

Some institutional features set the *orçamento participativo* apart from other matching zones. First among these is the "funnel-shaped" structure of meetings, consisting of the aforementioned three phases (see Fig. 2.2). In the first phase, *all* citizens of the age of 16 and above residing in the area are allowed to join the meetings. In this phase, participants are presented with the outlay of the part of the budget that is designated to be decided upon by the *orçamento participativo*. (Since the prefecture also faces fixed costs, it cannot allot the whole budget to the assembly.) They jointly decide on the criteria and emphases that should apply to the eventual allocation of the budget. Most importantly, they decide on the division of popular delegates per neighborhood, who will then further their interests during the rest of the budget process.[12] In the second phase, things get more detailed, as the assembly decides on the policies and projects that will be enacted during the coming fiscal year. At this stage, all participants are still welcome, but a higher level of knowledge about the budget is expected and necessary to follow the discussions. During this phase, the popular delegates are actually elected, and will start consulting their constituents about policy. In the third phase, finally, only the delegates and government officials are allowed to join the discussion – the so-called Budgetary Council (Fedozzi 1998, p. 255). In this phase, debate gets quite technical, and the delegates are expected to be knowledgeable about the issues on the table. Effectively, this is where the experts get into the game, as representatives are often weathered in the specifics of their decision-making areas.

In practice this funnel model tries to achieve a balance between popular legitimacy and efficiency. While the initial phase leaves plenty of room for "agenda-setting" on the part of ordinary people, the election of representatives in the later phases prevents the process from becoming slow and murky. Moreover, the yearly election of these delegates makes sure that there is competition and that the assembly does not become detached from its social environment. In practice, this

---

[12] http://www.partizipation.at/fileadmin/media_data/Downloads/themen/A_guide_to_PB.pdf

Fig. 2.2 The funnel model

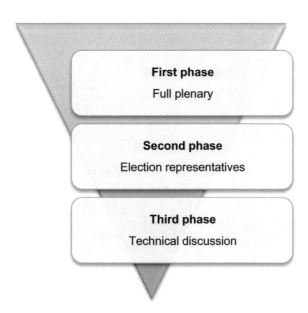

First phase
Full plenary

Second phase
Election representatives

Third phase
Technical discussion

has worked out well: the *orçamento participativo* has been widely hailed as an example of efficient but fair policy-making. In short, transaction costs have been kept low.

A second characteristic of participatory budgeting in Porto Alegre is that there are also constraints on the delegates (Kunrath Silva 2003, p. 172). Beforehand, the prefecture compiles a concise list of criteria to which the eventual budget should adhere. Since government officials also have a vote in the meetings, they are keen on monitoring adherence to these criteria. Moreover, there is the requirement that expenditures and incomes add up to zero, eventually. Hence, delegates cannot spend at will, but have to take into account financial constraints. Moreover, there is a strong incentive to produce consensus, as any failure to come to a conclusion will make the representatives come off as irresponsible and not worthy of re-election. In general, debate is cooperative and past assemblies have always managed to come to a consensual budget decision.

A third element is that, even while delegates take over during the third phase, the whole budget process is transparent and accessible. This has strongly diminished the opportunities for misapprehension of funds, collusion among delegates, or "blackmailing" from the side of the government. Moreover, it has increased the popular legitimacy of the process. Although it also means that every delegate is subject to scrutiny, and that there is thus an incentive to get as big a piece of the cake as possible, this seems not to have produced any problems in general, and is viewed as an essential element of these matching zones.

The result of this way of organizing the budget process is that, rather than making decision-making tedious and opaque, the inclusion of citizens may actually render the formulation of policy more efficient and just. Social and economic indicators in Porto Alegre seem to support the efficacy of the *orçamento participativo*, as the city strides forward where other Brazilian cities – such as Rio de Janeiro – struggle (Baiocchi 2006, p. 2). The key is to create a strong institutional foundation, with clear rules and a thought-out way to balance representation and efficiency. In this case the role of experts to come to compromise agreements differs somewhat from the other cases. Here, in a way, the "experts" are delegates which are sufficiently knowledgeable to follow the technical discussions in the third stage of the funnel model.

2.3.4 Imports of Animal Nutriments

The import of foodstuffs of animal origin, such as meat and fish, is often a cumbersome process, due to a plethora of (phyto)sanitary, logistical and legal regulations. Importing such foodstuffs through the port of Rotterdam involves a great many organizations, ranging from ship-owners to container-movers, from governmental sanitary institutions to the port of Rotterdam itself, and of course the customs authorities[13] In this production and logistic chain, many things can – and do – go wrong, slowing down trade.

To deal with this, the Dutch customs authorities initiated a matching zone – here the label of matching zone ("koppelzone" in Dutch) was in fact used (Boerma and Troquay 2010). It was set up in cooperation with a number of business organizations and governmental institutions, among which the prime Dutch government organization for sanitary and phytosanitary inspection, the Food and Consumer Product Safety Authority (VWA).[14] This was done under the aegis of the government organization specialized in matching-zone-type institutions, "Slim Geregeld, Goed Verbonden" (SGGV). The aim of the matching zone was to reduce transaction costs for Dutch importers of animal foodstuffs.

This matching zone has three striking characteristics. First, the project gravitates around the introduction of a specially developed piece of software, *Supd@x,* which centralizes all the necessary requests for importing animal products (IVW 2010, pp. 8–9). Thus, the project reaps the full benefits from IC technology. Cumbersome paperwork is avoided and there is one central database in which all the parties involved can find what they need. Also, the set of information that needs to be provided was broadened (Van Veenstra and Janssen 2009, p. 40). Paradoxically, this seems to have reduced transaction costs, because "follow-ups" for more information are now less frequently needed.

Second, from the government's point of view, responsibility is centralized and vested in the customs authorities. These authorities manage the matching zone and can thus be seen as both the mouthpiece and the director of the institution. This has

---

[13] http://sggv.nl/casussen/sggv-in-een-wereldhaven/omschrijving

[14] http://sggv.nl/casussen/sggv-in-een-wereldhaven/omschrijving

two advantages: (i) firms only have to deal with one organization, and (ii) there are clear and hierarchical lines of responsibility, thereby preventing "bureaucratic isolationism". Apparently here government officials chair the negotiations in the matching zone, although they may rely in technical matters, and also in matters of institutionalizing the discussions, on help by independent management consultants as experts. That is how in this case the input of experts is organized in order to come to compromise agreements.

Third, the rules for importing have been made more flexible. Because the production and logistic chain is more integrated and coherent, there is less need for burdensome rules, and more space for the careful interpretation of regulations. As such, both importers and government authorities were relieved from the burden of checking minute details.

Although only installed relatively recently (starting in 2009), this program seems to function well. The partners in the chain have decided to extend the Supd@x program to other forms and modalities of import, such as Schiphol Airport (ICTU 2011). Total reductions of costs have been estimated to be around €6 to €8 million per year.[15] A striking feature of this matching zone is that particular attention has been paid to the management of information streams (Van Veenstra and Janssen 2009, p. 43). This corresponds with the idea that one of the prime objectives of instituting a matching zone is to facilitate the easy flow of information.

2.4 Theoretical Framework: The Added Value of Matching Zones

Matching zones offer a number of advantages over the usual *status quo*. The theoretical basis for these advantages is broad, ranging from simple economic mechanisms to issues of justice. This section seeks explanations from the theoretical perspective why the previous examples of matching zones worked well.

2.4.1 Externalities

Externalities, both positive and negative, play a major role in a modern densely populated society with much social and economic interaction and entanglement. The more players with different objectives and incentives there are, the larger these externalities will be. Hence, interactions with such diverse actors as governments, firms and citizens will tend to be replete with inefficiencies due to externalities causing welfare losses. An example of a negative externality discussed before is the incentive for civil servants to increase regulatory measures, while not having to

---

[15] http://www.inspectieloket.nl/domeinen/zeehavens/projecten/supdx2010615232822.aspx

incur the costs of these. Externalities between citizens and firms also abound: pollution, use of infrastructure, but also monopoly pricing are examples of these kinds of market failures.

The issue with externalities is that economic agents' rational, self-interested behavior is not aligned with the "social optimum". Hence, if agents were to align their behavior with the public interest, they could attain a higher overall welfare. This alignment, however, is subject to what is often called "collective action problems", because every agent will still have an incentive to free-ride on others. The key feature of *matching zones* is that they enable participants to overcome these collective action problems and hence internalize externalities. The role of experts in the different settings of the matching zones is that they may enhance the awareness of the various stakeholders in the matching zone of these externalities. Thus, achieving higher welfare will often be possible through coordinating actions. There are four different types of such economic improvements, which are discussed below.

2.4.2 Economic Welfare Improvements

From the perspective of compromise agreements in discussions on welfare gains from projects and policy plans where different stakeholders are involved, there are two main axes on which the analysis of efficiency improvements should be based:

1. Do all parties involved gain instantaneously from the improvement in efficiency?
2. Is there any redistribution of economic means after the improvement?

Please note that "dynamic efficiency" is not considered here; merely "static efficiency gains". If one combines these two axes, the typology of economic welfare improvements is obtained as depicted in Fig. 2.3.

The implications of these different types of economic improvement can differ vastly. The following list gives a definition of each of them and some examples.

- *Clash of interests.* When an improvement leads to a loss for at least one party, while overall welfare and efficiency increase, then one can speak of a "clash of interests". This will often spark conflict and discontent on the side of the disadvantaged parties. A classic example is that of the "enclosure movement" in England in the late eighteenth century: Rich landowners (forcefully) appropriated land from poor peasants, who were not compensated for this and thus ended up worse than in their initial situation, even though enclosure is often praised for bringing about higher efficiency in agriculture.
- *Pareto improvement.* If an improvement can be made with all parties better off in an absolute sense, then we have a Pareto improvement. Since all economic agents gain, they are assumed to agree with such a solution. There are, however, two caveats. First, issues of fairness can and do play an important role in

Do all parties gain?		Ex post redistribution?	
		Yes	No
	Yes	"Fair" Pareto improvement	Pareto improvement
	No	Kaldor-Hicks improvement	Clash of interests

Fig. 2.3 A typology of economic welfare improvements

bargaining, even if economic theory does not predict so. We will further discuss this under the "fair" Pareto improvement. Second, Pareto improvements are not as common as one would like them to be. Specifically, it is often posited that countries in an advanced stage of development have "picked the low-hanging fruit" – i.e. obvious Pareto improvements.[16] An oft-cited example of a Pareto improvement is the introduction of the intermodal ISO container for freight ships (although even this advance may have disadvantaged some parties).

- *Kaldor-Hicks improvement.* Because of the relative rareness of Pareto improvements, in practice the (re) distribution of the welfare gain will more often be subject to the "Kaldor-Hicks criterion". If some economic agents lose out initially, but can be compensated *ex post*, then a situation may move towards Pareto efficiency without any agent objecting. This is, however, subject to critique: for instance, Stringham (2001) remarks that a government would need to be impossibly knowledgeable if it is to apply this criterion in general equilibrium. Nonetheless, there are plenty of instances in real life where this principle appears to have worked: providing inhabitants of seedy neighborhoods with new housing, so that the neighborhood can be rejuvenated, is a fine example.
- *"Fair" Pareto improvements.* Even if all parties gain from a Pareto improvement, some may gain far more than others. Different from what orthodox economic theory suggests, people often do place a strong weight on the fairness of a process and its outcome, even up to the point of opposing measures that would have made them better off in absolute terms (Husted and Folger 2004). This is why "fair" Pareto improvements are also a possibility (please note that the notion of "fair" is open to considerable debate and that this chapter will not try to provide a definition for it). In this case the discussions in the matching zone are confined to come to a "fair" distribution of the welfare gains from the project or policy measure.

---

[16] http://www.economist.com/node/18276872?story_id=18276872

Repeated interaction?	Hierarchic ?		
		Yes	*No*
	Yes	Matching zones	Repeated games
	No	Government consultations	One-shot transactions

Fig. 2.4 Different types of economic interaction

2.4.3 Types of Economic Interaction

The above typology suggests that there are different types of outcomes in achieving efficiency. At least as important, however, are the *means* through which such outcomes are reached. Figure 2.4 illustrates the two main questions that are to be answered in this case.

Thus, matching zones are asked for if there is a need for both repeated interaction/institutionalization and for enforcement of the agreements. Through this potent combination, it is possible to internalize externalities and come to agreements that are perceived as fair and mutually beneficial.

2.4.4 Transmission Mechanisms

Matching zones thus have two major advantages in public policy. Firstly, they reduce transaction costs when trying to achieve economic welfare improvements through projects and policy plans. Secondly, they lower the chance of hold-up problems and reneging on agreements *ex post*.

There are at least three transmission mechanisms through which these improvements are achieved, and which give matching zones an edge over the other forms of coordination in a great number of situations:

1. Enforcement of agreements
2. Repeated interaction
3. Actor participation and fairness

2.4.4.1 Enforcement of Agreements

Agreements between parties are often prone to cheating, lying and outright reneging. If a firm has an agreement with a group of citizens that it will cut its noise pollution in return for citizens' backing of an expansion of the firm's premises, it may be tempted to simply ignore the citizens after they have given their consent. Similar situations are common in one-off interactions between firms or between citizens. This is especially the case if the agreement has not been put in writing, or if the legal system is not well-suited for enforcing the specific agreement. The involvement of the state may thus make compliance more likely, since it is the only body able to truly enforce agreements, by virtue of its sovereignty.

An issue here is the trustworthiness of government itself. While higher layers of government will usually stick to their promises, given their high visibility, lower layers (e.g. municipal or provincial governments) are much more able to fly under the radar, tempting them to renege on agreements. An essential feature is thus citizens' ability to enforce agreements made with the state through the courts. While this feature of constitutional law is usually enshrined quite well in many advanced democracies, it is an essential feature of matching zones.

In order to show how to model the enforcement aspect of matching zones, the example of an agreement between a firm and a group can be used. The firm and citizens can either strike an agreement or fail to produce consensus (see Fig. 2.5). If the two parties cannot make a deal, the status quo ensues, leaving each party with a payoff of 0. If they do strike a deal, the citizens are assumed to make the first move – e.g. consenting with an expansion of the firm.[17] Subsequently, the firm has to decide whether it lives up to its promises, or does not comply. If it does comply, a mutually satisfactory outcome (A, A) results. It is also possible, however, to ignore the citizens and achieve the higher payoff C. Since this was not the citizens' intention, they obtain a lower payoff B. Hence, we have the payoff profile (B, C), and the following ranking:

$$B < A < C$$

It is obvious then, by backward induction, that the group of citizens will not even strike an agreement if $B < 0$. Since the citizens make a concession, while the firm sticks with the status quo, this must be the case by definition. Hence, the mutually advantageous cooperation will be impossible to achieve.

The question now is about the role of the government in this game. The government can drastically change the payoff profile of the firm through either financial or non-monetary punishment of reneging on agreements. Let this punishment be denoted by F. Then, the total payment for the firm if it does not comply will be $(C-F)$ instead of C. Hence, for the punishment to be effective, the following condition must hold:

$$(C - F) < A \quad \text{or, equivalently,} \quad F > (C - A)$$

Hence, if the government is sufficiently successful in convincing parties that non-compliance leads to severe punishments, then it may be able to induce

---

[17] Please note that the below argument works symmetrically; i.e. it could also be the firm that makes the first move, and the citizens that decide whether to comply or not.

Fig. 2.5 A cooperation game

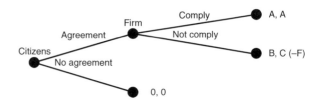

cooperation. Specifically, the institution of a matching zone is well-suited for guaranteeing this kind of government oversight.

2.4.4.2 Repeated Interaction

It is common knowledge that it is often easier to cooperate with people one thoroughly knows than with complete strangers. Part of this is due to human nature: we tend to feel more at ease when we are used to somebody's ways and rarities, and when we know what to expect. Perhaps equally important, however, is the notion that repeated interaction breeds cooperation through the incentives that future cooperation brings. Since matching zones are institutionalized as long-run mechanisms for convening, all participants know that they will have to negotiate about more than just the issue on the table. A necessary condition for a cooperative outcome, however, is a sufficiently patient attitude of the participants.

A way to formalize this is to model the interaction as a repeated game. Like the previous game, we call the cooperative gains A, the gains for the firm from reneging C, and the payoff for the citizens if they are being cheated is B. The difference is that, this time, the game is played an infinite (or, equivalently, unknown) number of times. If one of the agents does not keep its promise, the other one is not willing to cooperate anymore for the rest of the time. We then have the following payoff per actor, assuming the discount factor δ:

$$\pi_{Cooperate}^{Firm} = A + \delta A + \delta^2 A + \delta^3 A + \cdots + \delta^\infty A = \frac{A}{1-\delta}$$

$$\pi_{Cheat}^{Firm} = C + 0 = C$$

So for the firm, we have the following condition:

$$\delta \geq 1 - \frac{A}{C}$$

In words: the larger the gains from cooperation, the more likely cooperation, and the larger the gains from cheating, the less likely.

2.4.4.3 Fairness and Transaction Costs

In transaction cost economics, the "fairness" of transactions is often not an issue. Only absolute gains matter, not relative distributions. In reality, however, most people react strongly to matters of fairness and justice. If governance does not take this factor into account, transactions costs may quickly run high (Husted and Folger 2004, p. 719). Economic actors will not be willing to make economic exchanges, or may be slow in ascertaining the implications, and will thus falter in deciding.

One can identify two forms of fairness: procedural fairness and outcome fairness. Procedural fairness refers to the notion that people want a *say* in the outcome; even if the eventual result isn't to their liking, they will still have the feeling of being heard (ibid., p. 725). This includes such factors as respect, telling the truth, trust, etc. When such procedural fairness is not present, participants are more likely to hinder the functioning of the governance mechanism (ibid., p. 726).

Outcome fairness, on the other hand, is an assessment of the situation *ex post*. Having a voice in the outcome is not essential; rather, what is important is that participants get their "fair share" of the pie. This is up to every participant's individual, subjective judgment. However, there are often general principles guiding the perceived fairness, such as proportionality, need, merit, and the like. If a governance system does not generate such outcomes, it is more likely to have high transaction costs or even to fail (ibid.).

Matching zones may provide for both of these types of fairness. Procedural fairness is achieved if actors get a say in the decision-making process. This relates to the "funnel model" discussed in the context of Porto Alegre's *orçamento participativo*. Outcome fairness is also more likely, because parties often have a veto or strong bargaining power in the matching zone. Hence, it is harder to exclude important economic agents. Therefore, making fairness part of the considerations in the matching zone negotiation should lead to lower transaction costs.

The considerations to include the concept of fairness in the discussions and negotiations between stakeholders in the matching zone are much related to the lessons from a positive economic theory of fairness. This theory and its practical examples illustrate how the perception of fairness between the various stakeholders can be framed in such a way that there is a divergence between individual non-cooperative rationality and group wealth maximization (Isaac et al. 1991). In other words, the (re)distribution of welfare gains from a project or policy plan must meet the test of fairness shared by all participants in the discussions and negotiations. That will enhance the societal support for the project or plan and reduce the transaction costs considerably.

2.5 Learned Lessons

The empirical cases we have seen above and the theoretical considerations of matching zones bring to light a number of lessons that can be drawn for the real-world application of matching zones. While every problem needs its own bespoke matching zone, a number of broad principles can be identified that will work almost invariably. These principles can be organized into three categories: those at the strategic level, at the tactical level, and at the operational level. Together, these lessons are essential to a well-functioning matching zone.

They are not, however, sufficient conditions. As always, the devil is in the details, and matching zones will have to be adjusted to the specific subject, political playing field, and local culture. As yet, the notion of the matching zone shows that much can be achieved through institutional innovation. It is therefore highly recommendable to experiment with different forms of matching zones, in order to find out what works best in a particular setting.

2.5.1 The Strategic Level: When to Use a Matching Zone

The most important decision to make when it comes to matching zones is whether to institute a matching zone at all. In this decision, the government needs to take into account its own capabilities and wishes, and those of societal actors. A prerequisite is that the matching zone must *add value*: it should provide for an improvement over the status quo or any alternative institutional set-up.

Broadly spoken, a matching zone is only a desirable option when one or more of the following three conditions are fulfilled:

1. The government has trouble fulfilling its obligations towards society satisfactorily, due to a lack of coordination with societal actors
2. Societal actors have trouble fulfilling their obligations towards the government satisfactorily, due to a lack of coordination with the government, and/or due to a lack of coordination between governmental departments
3. Representation of important affected parties is indispensable, due to popular demand and/or likely obstruction of implementation by these parties

If the government is unable to perform its services towards its citizens and firms in a decent way, it may be opportune to institute a matching zone. This depends on whether such a dysfunctional performance is due to a lack of consultation of the government's clientele and affected actors. For instance, if a local government is responsible for handing out subsidies to small enterprises, but these subsidies do not find their way to these kinds of businesses, it may be wise to set up an institutional consultation of such businesses to improve the government service.

In the same fashion, if firms or citizens have trouble complying with the government's requirements, such as paying taxes or administrative duties, a matching zone may help. If communication between the government and society, or within the government internally (and thus ultimately with society), is lacking, institutionalized consultation may help to improve the flow of information and reduce the burden of government rules and requirements.

Representation is almost inevitable in modern democratic societies. This may be due to the public's opinions on representation (i.e. a call for legitimacy) or because the concerned actors may frustrate the implementation/execution of policy. If such is the case, a matching-zone-type construction is desirable for both practical and ethical reasons. For instance, now that Lelystad airport is to be expanded, it would be highly reasonable to have an institutionalized consultation mechanism including the affected people and businesses.

If at least one of the three conditions stated above is fulfilled, and if there is no better, cheaper or more efficient way to solve the problem, then setting up a matching zone is strategically desirable. Although this cost-benefit analysis is hard to quantify in practice, it is essential that policy-makers give sufficient thought to these requirements.

Developing and highly divided societies bring along added difficulties in instituting matching zones. Where trust in government institutions is low, the division between labor and capital is strong, or short-term thinking trumps long-term cooperation, matching zones are more likely to fall apart. For example, many Latin American countries have institutions where the government, trade unions and employers' organizations are brought together, yet these councils are rarely more than another arena for scolding each other. Nonetheless, these sorts of situations also offer the largest improvement over the status quo, since the initial situation is often one of virtually no dialogue. In that respect, the example of Porto Alegre's *orçamento participativo* shows that employing matching-zone-style institutions is far from impossible in these countries.

2.5.2 The Tactical Level: How to Design a Matching Zone

If the government decides to institute a matching zone, the ensuing question is: how to design it? The preceding cases and theoretical analysis have revealed six guidelines for matching-zone design:

1. Create an incentive for reaching an agreement
2. Create the expectation of repeated interaction
3. Strike a balance between representativeness and efficiency
4. Institute impartial arbitration (e.g. by participation of experts)
5. Make clear what the constraints are
6. Properly use IC technology

First of all, there must be a strong incentive for reaching an agreement. This can be achieved through a formal need for unanimity on the agreement – i.e. every participant has a veto –, or by making clear that any decision based on a small majority will be discarded by the government. This principle prevents factionary politicking and implementation problems afterwards. There is, however, a trade-off between unanimity and efficiency, since a veto implies excessive bargaining power. Hence, if full unanimity is unattainable, the matching zone should aim for as large a majority as possible, so as to prevent politicization of the issue at hand.

Second, there has to be an element of a repeated game in the matching zone. Hence, the participants must have the expectation that they will have to deal more often with the other actors, in order to induce a cooperative attitude. With some broad-ranging issues, this may be achieved through making the matching zone (semi-) permanent, such as the SER. With project-based matching zones, including the implementation and revision phase in the matching zone can yield a similar effect, since participants can frustrate the execution of the project afterwards if they are not content with the outcome.

Third, one has to strike a subtle balance between the representativeness and efficiency of the matching zone. While including all affected actors individually will lead to a very cumbersome decision-making process, excluding too many parties will on the other hand bring about discontent and a lack of legitimacy. An instrument for striking such a balance is through the use of the "funnel model", as employed in the *orçamento participativo* in Porto Alegre. By narrowing down the number of actors as the participation process progresses, one ensures that agenda-setting is not overly limited, while the discussion of contentious issues and technical details is left up to those who have the time, resources and knowledge.

Fourth, one needs impartial arbitration. This may be done through installing an independent president; a trusted figure who is seen as being "above the parties" and who is gifted with a talent for bringing people together. Another, complementary, way to achieve such arbitration is through the use of "independent experts", such as the independent members in the SER. These may provide the matching zone with the necessary scientific and technical expertise, while often being a highly conciliatory factor in discussions. It is absolutely essential that these arbitrators have no stakes in the issue at hand.

Fifth, there must be clear constraints from the outset of the matching zone. When starting the discussion, the participants should be aware of the allotted funds, the deadlines that need to be met, the criteria to which any solution must adhere, and any other lateral constraints. This will prevent participants from making outlandish demands, while also imposing some structure and discipline on the matching zone. Moreover, it may be beneficial to restrict the number of possible policy options from which participants can choose, as has been done in the Alders Table. This can focus debate and preclude any options that are unfeasible beforehand.

Sixth, reaping the benefits from IC technology is highly conducive to an efficient exchange of information. Although ICT should not distract from the importance of face-to-face contact, the possibilities for information centralization and sharing are very large, lowering substantially the costs of sharing and retrieving such information (cf. Janssen and Gortmaker 2005).

If the design of a matching zone adheres to these principles, and moreover is suited to the specificities of the policy area, the chances of the matching zone becoming a success are strongly enhanced.

2.5.3   The Operational Level: How to Manage
a Matching Zone

Having the right design is not a guarantee for success: efficient management of the matching zone is essential to its functioning, and is a process that never stops. The gist of the analysis of this chapter is that a cooperative attitude is the most important trait to cultivate in order to keep transaction costs down and optimize outcomes. Three guidelines on management can be distinguished to achieve this:

1. Maintain procedural and outcome fairness
2. Breed an atmosphere of mutual trust and informal contact
3. Hold on to constraints and earlier agreements

First, at all times a sense of fairness should be maintained. Since the execution phase of any project or policy also requires at least some degree of public support, it is paramount that people directly involved be satisfied with both the process and the outcome. Giving all participants some voice in the outcome and preventing excessive social pressure is hence key to achieving *ex post* satisfaction.

Second, fostering an atmosphere of mutual trust and informal contact between the members of the matching zone can help to smoothen bargaining and propagate a cooperative attitude. This effect works both on a psychological level and through the repeated-game argument seen above. If participants are at ease and are better aware of each other's intentions and reasoning, they are more likely to cooperate. Independent experts can be helpful, for instance in their role of chairperson or moderator, to create such atmosphere of ease. Also, if participants are likely to see each other in more venues than just the matching zone, it pays off to behave collaboratively. There is, however, a risk in this: if participants get too close and friendly, there is a chance they become overly cooperative and lose sight of their constituents. This, in turn, puts into jeopardy the legitimacy and long-term functioning of the matching zone. Hence, it is also up to the managers of the matching zone to maintain a professional atmosphere in which participants are expected to be reliable representatives of their constituency.

Third, it is important that the participants are made to honor any *ex ante* constraints placed upon them, as well as any collective agreements they have made earlier. If agreements are not respected, the matching zone may descend into chaos, with trust breaking down easily. Hence, it is up to the (impartial) chairperson to hold participants up to their agreements.

2.6 Conclusion

The modern-day interaction between government and society is rife with unnecessary transaction costs and suboptimal decision-making. This chapter has explored the potential of institutionalizing the setup of consultation and compromise finding with stakeholders to render this interaction more efficient, by lowering transaction costs and optimizing decisions. In these so called matching zones, the government organizes a forum for decision-making between the government and citizens and/or firms. Through a number of cases the chapter demonstrates that matching zones come in many shapes and sizes, but that they all have in common that important political and economic actors are brought together to rationally and cooperatively discuss their different interests. Another common feature of these matching zones is that independent experts, albeit as chairpersons or as moderators, may be helpful in the process of reaching compromise agreements. It is showcased that, in practice, such matching-zone-type institutions may indeed improve upon the *status quo ante*. This has come about through carefully crafted organizational mechanisms, but also through institutional experimentation. Subsequently, the chapter explores a number of theoretical considerations that give backing to the matching zone's potential for efficiency improvement. The main conditions here seem to be hierarchical enforcement of agreements, repeated interaction between parties, and improved transaction fairness.

Although there are no systematic empirical evaluations of matching zones, some broad lessons can be drawn from both practical and theoretical insights. Specifically, the design of a matching zone should try to adhere to a set of strategic, tactical, and operational principles At the *strategic level*, instituting a matching zone is only worth the effort if it adheres to at least one of the following three conditions: *(i)* the government has trouble performing its services toward society satisfactorily, due to a lack of information about societal actors; *(ii)* societal actors have trouble fulfilling their obligations towards the government satisfactorily, due to bad communication with the government, and/or due to a lack of coordination between governmental departments; and *(iii)* representation of important affected parties is inevitable, due to popular demand and/or likely obstruction of implementation by these parties. Moreover, the matching zone should be the most efficient way of alleviating one of these problems.

At the *tactical level*, the design of a matching zone should adhere to the following six principles: *(i)* there should be ample incentives for consensus, or at least for the will to reach compromise agreements; *(ii)* there should be the prospect of long, repeated interaction; *(iii)* the design should strike a balance between representation and efficiency; *(iv)* there must be an impartial arbiter of some sort (the independent expert); *(v)* the constraints should be clear from the onset of the matching zone; and *(vi)* IC technology should be utilized optimally.

At the *operational level*, there are three management principles the chair of the matching zone should adhere to: *(i)* procedural and outcome fairness should be strived for; *(ii)* an atmosphere of frequent, informal contact and trust should be fostered; and *(iii)* ex ante constraints and agreements made should be respected.

There is still much scope for additional research on the optimal setup of matching zones. Although the four cases discussed in this chapter show how experts may, in different settings, contribute to reach compromise agreements, their role should be studied more closely in order to come to some archetypical function of experts in the matching function. A further road to follow is to combine the experiences with framing in communication and negotiation theory with the lessons from new institutional economics in the design of matching zones (see e.g. Putnam and Holmer 1999; Brummans et al. 2008). Yet, this is exactly what makes the concept of the matching zone so exciting: it allows for institutional innovation, bringing a breath of fresh air to the oft-traditional domain of politics. Although there are likely to be many pitfalls along the way, the key lesson remains that creativity and institutional experimentation can yield surprising new forms of governance. In a world that asks for dynamism, adaptation, and creative competitiveness, such innovations will be ever more borne out of necessity, rather than luxury.

References

Baiocchi, G. 2006. The citizens of Porto Alegre. In which Marco borrows bus fare and enters politics. *Boston Review,* March/April. http://bostonreview.net/BR31.2/baiocchi.php.

Boerma, N., and T. Troquay. 2010. *Samenwerken in Ketens: Koppelzones in Actie.* Den Haag: Transaction Management Centre.

Bovens, M.A.P., P. 't Hart, M.J.W. van Twist, and U. Rosenthal. 2001. *Openbaar Bestuur. Beleid, Organisatie en Politiek.* Alphen aan den Rijn: Kluwer.

Brummans, B.H.J.M., L.L. Putnam, B. Gray, R. Hanke, R.J. Lewicki, and C. Wiethoff. 2008. Making sense of intractable multiparty conflict: A study of framing in four environmental disputes. *Communication Monographs* 75: 25–51.

den Butter, F.A.G. 2011. The industrial organisation of economic policy preparation in the Netherlands. In *The politics of scientific advice; Institutional design for quality assurance,* ed. J. Lentsch and P. Weingart, 177–214. Cambridge: Cambridge University Press.

den Butter, F.A.G. 2012. *Managing transaction costs in the era of globalization.* Cheltenham: Edward Elgar.

den Butter, F.A.G., and R.H.J. Mosch. 2003. The Dutch miracle: Institutions, networks and trust. *Journal of Institutional and Theoretical Economics* 159: 362–391.

Fedozzi, L. 1998. Esfera pública e cidadania: A experiência do orçamento participativo de Porto Alegre. *Ensaios FEE, Porto Alegre* 19(2): 236–271.

Husted, B.W., and R. Folger. 2004. Fairness and transaction costs: The contribution of organizational justice theory to an integrative model of economic organization. *Organization Science* 15(6): 719–729.

ICTU. 2011. *Van 2010 naar 2011. Mijlpalen en Perspectieven.* Den Haag: Stichting ICTU.

Inspectie Verkeer en Waterstaat. 2010. *Toezichtplan Vervoer over Water 2010.* Den Haag: IVW.

Isaac, R.M., D. Mathieu, and E.E. Zajac. 1991. Institutional framing and perceptions of fairness. *Constitutional Political Economy* 2: 329–370.

Janssen, M., and J. Gortmaker. 2005. Orchestreren van ketenprocessen. *Webservice Orchestratie in E-government* 46(5): 18–22.

Koppenjan, J.F.M. 2005. The formation of public-private partnerships: Lessons from nine transport infrastructure projects in the Netherlands. *Public Administration* 83(1): 135–157.
Kunrath Silva, M. 2003. A expansão do orçamento participativo na região Metropolitana de
Porto Alegre: Condicionantes e resultados. In *A Inovação Institucional no Brasil: o Orçamento
Participativo*, ed. L. Avritzer and Z. Navarro. São Paulo: Cortez. http://www.democraciaejustica.
org/cienciapolitica3/sites/default/files/a_expansao_do_orcamento_participativo_na_regiao_metropolitana_
de_porto_alegre_marcelosilva.pdf.
Martimort, D., and J. Pouyet. 2008. To build or not to build: Normative and positive theories of
public-private partnerships. *International Journal of Industrial Organization* 26: 393–411.
Ménard, C., and M.M. Shirley. 2005. *Handbook of new institutional economics*. New York:
Springer.
Putnam, L.L., and M. Holmer. 1999. Framing, reframing and issue development. In *Communica-
tion and negotiation*, Sage Annual Reviews of Communication Research 20, ed. L.L. Putnam
and M.E. Roloff, 128–155. Newbury Park: Sage.
Raad van Economische Adviseurs. 2005. *De Wetten en Regels die Droom en Daad Verstoren;
Bureaucratisering en Overregulering*. Den Haag: Tweede Kamer der Staten-Generaal.
Schaeffer, P.V., and S. Loveridge. 2002. Towards an understanding of types of public-private
cooperation. *Public Performance & Management Review* 26(2): 169–189.
Stringham, E. 2001. Kaldor-Hicks efficiency and the problem of central planning. *The Quarterly
Journal of Austrian Economics* 4(2): 41–50.
Schiphol Group. 2007. *Een Wereldwijd Netwerk voor een Concurrerende Randstad*. Schiphol:
Schiphol Group.
Taskforce Ketenherinrichting. 2007. *De Groei Ontketend: Overheid en Ondernemers On-line.
Meer Ruimte voor Ondernemen, Betere Dienstverlening en Lagere Lasten voor Ondernemers*.
Den Haag: Taskforce Ketenherinrichting.
van Veenstra, A.F., and M. Janssen. 2009. *Orchestratie van Ketens. Techniek, Bestuur en
Organisatie*. Den Haag: Alliantie Vitaal Bestuur.
van Woelderen, S., T. van Liebergen and J. van Helvoirt. 2006. *Publiek-private Samenwerking.
Sectorstudie Decentrale Overheden II*. ING Economisch Bureau/Nyenrode Business
University.
Visser, J., and A. Hemerijck. 1998. *Een Nederlands Mirakel. Beleidsleren in de Verzorgingsstaat*.
Amsterdam: Amsterdam University Press.

Chapter 3
Model-Based Consensus

Marcel Boumans

> *Science aims at rational consensus, and methodology of science must serve to further this aim.*
>
> Roger Cooke, *Experts in Uncertainty.*

Abstract The aim of the rational-consensus method is to produce "rational consensus", that is, "mathematical aggregation", by weighing the performance of each expert on the basis of his or her knowledge and ability to judge relevant uncertainties. The measurement of the performance of the experts is based on the expert's assessment of "seed variables". These performances are used to determine the weights of the expert's judgments in the aggregation of them. The disadvantage of the rational-consensus method in social science is the lack of agreed upon seed variables, and that it does not instead use the shared knowledge captured by models. Moreover, there seems to be sufficient evidence that combining models with expert judgments leads to better judgments. This is even more evident with respect to forecasts.

3.1 Introduction

In science, there seems to be a broadly shared consensus about which epistemic genre can be considered as most scientific, namely the experimental method, and more precisely, the "laboratory ideal" of experimentation, that is "designing manipulated, well-controlled, isolated experimental systems" (Schwarz and Krohn 2011). Since the nineteenth century, however, scientists and philosophers are aware that there are many natural and social phenomena that cannot be studied in a laboratory. For these phenomena the most prominent alternative method since the 1950s became the method of statistical modeling. Instead of experimenting on the real phenomena, one could experiment on the objects existing in the world of the model (Morgan 2012). Both illustrative as well as representative for this general understanding are the comments by Olaf Helmer in a 1953 internal Rand

M. Boumans (✉)
Department of Economics, University of Amsterdam, Valckenierstraat 65, 1018 XE, Amsterdam, The Netherlands
e-mail: m.j.boumans@uva.nl

© Springer International Publishing Switzerland 2014
C. Martini, M. Boumans (eds.), *Experts and Consensus in Social Science*,
Ethical Economy 50, DOI 10.1007/978-3-319-08551-7_3

Corporation memorandum 'Experimentation in the non-experimental sciences'[1]:
"in economics and political science it is our unwillingness and, often, inability to
interfere with social institutions as well as the seeming impossibility of achieving
the prerequisites of all experimentation, the reproducibility of like circumstances"
(Helmer 1983, pp. 23–24). Instead, he suggested, "the real world is first replaced by
an analogue (usually mathematical, sometimes physical), the experiment with real
objects is replaced by one with fictitious objects" (p. 24).

One of the major problems for a social science is that the social world is too
complex, too idiosyncratic, and too irregular to be captured sufficiently in our
models or theories (Bogen and Woodward 1988). As a result, social science is
inexact. This discussion "that there is, or may be, a science" of social phenomena,
started with John Stuart Mill's *A System of Logic* ([1843] 1911).[2] Mill did not
regard a social science such as economics to be an "exact science" (p. 553). The
basic premises of any social science state accurately how specific causal factors
operate, but, according to Mill, they are statements of tendencies and are inexact
rather than universal generalizations. Social scientists know the major causes of
social phenomena, but there are many "inferences" or "disturbing causes"
(Hausman 1992, p. 124).

In an exact science, explanation is complete: "the greater causes, those on which
the principal part of the phenomenon depends", Mill writes, "are within the reach of
observation and measurement; so that if no other causes intervened, a complete
explanation could be given not only of the phenomenon in general, but of all the
variations and modifications which it admits of" (Mill [1843] 1911, p. 552). A
science is exact when "its phenomena have been brought under laws
comprehending the whole of the causes by which the phenomena are influenced,
whether in a great or only in a trifling degree, whether in all or only in some cases,
and assigning to each of those causes the share of effect which really belongs to it"
(p. 553).

In opposition to this, in an inexact science

> the only laws as yet accurately ascertained are those of the causes which affects the
> phenomenon in all cases, and in considerable degree; while others which affect it in
> some cases only, or, if in all, only in a slight degree, have not been sufficiently ascertained
> and studied to enable us to lay down their laws, still less to deduced the completed laws of
> the phenomenon, by compounding the effects of the greater with those of the minor causes.
> (Mill [1843] 1911, p. 553)

Mill refers to the science of tides as an example of an inexact science. Scientists
know the laws of the great causes, the gravitational attraction of the sun and the
moon, but they are ignorant of "circumstances of a local or casual nature, such as
the configuration of the bottom of the ocean, the degree of confinement from shores,
the direction of the wind, &c" (p. 553).

---

[1] Parts of this memorandum have been reproduced in Helmer (1983).

[2] See Hausman (1992), in particular, his Chapter 8, for a detailed discussion of inexactness in
economic theory, which is based on his interpretation of Mill's account of inexactness.

Since social scientists, in Mill's view, know only the laws of the "greater causes" of the phenomena, they are unable to infer invariably and precisely what actually occurs. A social theory considers only some of the "great causes" of social phenomena. Any social science is in this way an inexact science. This inability is a consequence of inexactness within the theory, not merely of faulty data or mathematical limitations.

About 40 years later, Alfred Marshall made the same comparison with the science of tides, to discuss economics as an inexact science (see also Chap. 1, this volume). Marshall devoted chapter 3 (of Book I) of the *Principles* to a discussion of the nature of "economic generalizations or laws". Why, he asked, should the "laws of economics" be less predictable and precise in their workings than the law of gravitation? The key to Marshall's view, according to John Sutton (2000, p. 4), lies in his claim that economic mechanisms work out their influences against a messy background of complicated factors, so that the most we can expect of economic analysis is that it captures the "tendencies" induced by changes in this or that factor.

> [N]o one knows enough about the weather to be able to say beforehand how it will act. A heavy downpour of rain in the upper Thames valley, or a strong north-east wind in the German Ocean, may make the tides at London Bridge differ a great deal from what had been expected. (Marshall 1920, p. 32)

This chapter will discuss methodologies where completeness is attained by adding expert judgment, which encapsulates knowledge about idiosyncratic and messy conditions. Experts are the carriers of expert knowledge. But expert knowledge is personal, and experts tend to disagree. Since expert judgments are unavoidably "personal", "subjective", or "biased", any methodology based on expert judgments has to include a strategy to ensure objectivity. Strategies that have been developed for this purpose share the idea that individual expert judgments have to be combined such to reduce subjectivity and disagreement. This chapter will focus on cases of expert consensus, where the combination of experts is instantiated by a model.

To clarify this specific kind of expert consensus, Sect. 3.2 first will describe the historical background from which this model-based approach of expert consensus arose. Particularly, its first ideas were developed in the 1950s when the difference between natural and social science were discussed among economists and philosophers connected to the RAND Corporation. The search for a methodology of an inexact science resulted in the Delphi method. The main critique on this method was that it was not clear whether the consensus reached by this method would indeed be more accurate than expert judgments taken individually. Section 3.3 will discuss a method of expert consensus developed in the 1990s by Roger Cooke with the aim of arriving at a more accurate result. The core idea is that expert judgments should be aggregated as a weighted average where the weights are determined by the performance of the individual expert's assessment of "seed variables". The problem with the Cooke method is that it is developed for applications in natural science and engineering where there is sufficient consensus on the values of appropriate seed variables. In social science, however, this is not the case. Instead of using seed variables, Sect. 3.4 will suggest the use of "seed models" instead. In economics, there is much more consensus on the empirical adequacy of certain models than on the accuracy of the values of specific economic facts. Particularly, with respect to forecasting, recent studies by Philip Hans Franses show that the combination of model forecasts adjusted by experts improves the accuracy of the forecasts. However, for these cases the "expert" is not an individual scientist but a team of experts employed by a scientific institution that is also the proprietor of the relevant model. The idea of model-based consensus is not new, particularly in the context of Dutch economic consensus policy, which is based on Jan Tinbergen's view of the role models should have in relation to settling policy issues. Section 3.5 will show that this Tinbergian kind of model-based consensus is conditioned on the assumption that economics eventually can be an exact science. The methodology developed here is based on the presupposition that economics is fundamentally an inexact science.

3.2   A Methodology for an Inexact Science

In 1952, an 8-week seminar, 'The Design of Experiments in Decision Processes', was held at Santa Monica accommodating the game theorists and the experimenters associated with the RAND Corporation (Thrall et al. 1954), to discuss the "symmetrical roles" of experiment and mathematical model in economics and psychology. The economist Oskar Morgenstern presented a paper 'Experiment and computation in economics'[3] in which he made an useful distinction between two kinds of experiments to discuss the similarity between experiment and model:

> (1) Experiments of the *first kind* are those where new general properties of a system are to be discovered by its manipulation on the basis of a theory of the system;
> (2) experiments of the *second kind* do not primarily rely on a theory but aim at the discovery of new, individual facts. (Morgenstern 1954, p. 499)

Using these definitions, Morgenstern's main "thesis" was: "Every computation is equivalent to an experiment of the first kind and vice versa" (p. 499). This equivalence was, according to Morgenstern, already emphasized by Ernst Mach by his notion of thought-experiment.

> Its methods involve imagining conditions that differ from the known conditions and then attempting to identify the proper factor to which the imagined variations could be ascribed. This procedure consists in the drawing of implications and like other experiments may lead to the discovery of new facts. (Morgenstern 1954, p. 486)

---

[3] This paper was not published in the seminar proceedings (Thrall et al. 1954), but with a slightly extended title in a volume Morgenstern edited in *Economics Activity Analysis* (1954).

Thought-experiments were, according to Oskar Morgenstern, "vitally affected" by the new possibilities created by computers.

This distinction that Morgenstern made between first kind and second kind of experiments is closely related to a distinction the philosopher Carl Hempel made in the same period. In a paper on the differences between methods in the natural and social sciences, Hempel (1952) distinguishes between two kinds of "imaginary experiments": the "intuitive" and the "theoretical" (see also Chap. 1, this volume). An imaginary experiment is aimed at anticipating the outcome of an experimental procedure which is just imagined. Anticipation is guided by past experience concerning particular phenomena and their regularities, and occasionally by belief in certain general principles or laws as if they were *a priori* truths. An imaginary experiment is called *intuitive* when

> the assumptions and data underlying the prediction are not made explicit and indeed may not even enter into the conscious process of anticipation at all: past experience and the – possibly unconscious – belief in certain general principles function here as suggestive guides for imaginative anticipation rather than as a theoretical basis for systematic prediction. (Hempel 1952, p. 76)

In contrast to the intuitive experiment, a "theoretical kind of imaginary experiment"

> presupposes a set of explicitly stated general principles – such as laws of nature – and it anticipates the outcome of the experiment by strict deduction from those principles in combination with suitable boundary conditions representing the relevant aspects of the experimental situation. (Hempel 1952, p. 76)

This distinction between "theoretical" and "intuitive" is subsequently used to distinguish between idealizations in economics and those in the natural sciences. According to Hempel the idealizations in economics are intuitive:

> the corresponding 'postulates' are not deduced, as special cases, from a broader theory which covers also the nonrational and noneconomic factors affecting human conduct. No suitable more general theory is available at present, and thus there is no theoretical basis for an appraisal of the idealization involved in applying the economic constructs to concrete situations. (Hempel 1952, p. 82)

It should be noted that Hempel did not explicitly account for who should run the intuitive imaginary experiment, who should have the appropriate intuitions. Morgenstern, however, did, for economics: it should be an economist, well-informed by economic theory. But economic theory is not exact, therefore it should be to "a very high extend in addition related to non-constructively obtained material, such as personal experience" (Morgenstern 1963, p. 88).

In the 1950s, imaginary experiments were considered as an appropriate alternative for real experiments, a shared view that was strengthened by the contemporaneous development of the computer. But an experiment run on a computer – today called a simulation – requires "explicitly stated general principles", for example laws of nature. In economics, there are not so many of these principles, if there are any. Economics is an "inexact science", which makes deductions such as predictions unreliable, also noted by Morgenstern (1928):

> Economic processes, and therefore the data in which their action is registered, are not
> characterized by a degree of regularity sufficient to make their future course amenable to
> forecast, such 'laws' as are discoverable being by nature "inexact" and loose, and therefore
> unreliable. (Marget 1929, pp. 313–314)[4]

Olaf Helmer, like Hempel a student of Hans Reichenbach,[5] had developed rather similar ideas about the usage of statistical models as experiments but also about the incompleteness of models and theories in the social sciences, see above. In a paper 'On the Epistemology of the Inexact Sciences', which first appeared as a RAND working paper (Helmer and Rescher 1958), and was published the year after in *Management Science* (Helmer and Rescher 1959), he, together with Nicholas Rescher, discussed what kind of knowledge was needed to complete a statistical model. The RAND paper opens with a long quotation of Alfred Marshall ([1890] 1920, p. 32) stating that the "laws of economics" are not like the "simple and exact law of gravitation" but instead are "inexact and faulty" (see also Chap. 1, this volume). Helmer saw these inexact laws, which he called "quasi-laws", as generalizations, less-than-universal principles, that are neither fully, nor even explicitly articulated or even articulable. They require a different epistemology and methodology, namely, the systematic employment of expert judgment: "background information, which frequently may be intuitive in character and have the form of a vague recognition of underlying regularities, such as analogies, correlations, or other conformities" (Helmer and Rescher 1958, p. 30). For "quasi-laws", we need "knowledge of regularities in the behavior of people or in the character of institutions, such as traditions and customary practices, fashions and mores, national attitudes and climates of opinion, institutional rules and regulations, group aspirations, and so on" (Helmer and Rescher 1958, p. 30).

The source for this kind of non-explicit background knowledge is the expert. The expert has

> at his ready disposal a large store of (mostly inarticulated) background knowledge and a
> refined sensitivity to its relevance, through the intuitive application of which he is often
> able to produce trustworthy personal probabilities regarding hypotheses in his area of
> expertness. (Helmer and Rescher 1958, p. 31)

To develop a methodology for an inexact science that relies on expert judgments, Helmer designed at the RAND corporation the "Delphi method", "undoubtedly the best-known method of eliciting and synthesizing expert opinion" (Cooke 1991, p. 12). The Delphi method is based on structural surveys and makes use of "the intuitive available information of the participants, who are mainly experts" (Cuhls 2005, p. 96). There is not one Delphi methodology, instead there is a general agreement that it is an expert survey in two or more rounds in which in the second

---

[4] Morgenstern 1928 has never been translated into English, but Arthur Marget's extensive review article of this book summarizes it adequately.

[5] According to Rescher (2006), Hempel and Helmer constitute the "middle generation" of the Berlin School of Logical Empiricism because both were students of Reichenbach. For more biographical details and the interrelationships between Hempel and Helmer, see Rescher 2006.

and later rounds of the survey the results of the previous round are given as feedback. Thus, the experts answer from the second round on under the influence of the other experts' opinions.

In the middle 1960s and early 1970s the Delphi method found a variety of applications. Most applications are concerned with technology forecasting, but the method has also been applied to many types of policy analysis. We shall only be concerned here with the forecasting type of the Delphi method.

In forecasting, the team conducting the Delphi method seeks experts who are most knowledgeable on the issues in question, and seeks to achieve a high degree of consensus regarding predicted developments.[6] Its basic approach can be described as follows (see Cooke 1991, pp. 13–14): A monitoring team defines a set of issues and selects a set of respondents who are experts on the issues in question. A respondent generally does not know who the other respondents are, and the responses are anonymous. A preliminary questionnaire is sent to the respondents for comments, which are then used to establish a definitive questionnaire. This questionnaire is the sent to the respondents and their answers are analyzed by the monitoring team. The set of responses is then sent back to the respondents, together with the median answer and the interquartile range, the range containing all but the lower 25 % and the upper 25 % of the responses. The respondents are asked if they wish to revise the initial predictions. Those whose answers remain outside the interquartile range for a given item are asked to give arguments for their prediction on this item. The revised predictions are then processed in the same way as the first responses, and arguments for outliers are summarized. This information is then sent back to the respondents, and the whole process is iterated. A Delphi exercise typically involves three or four rounds. The responses on the final round generally show a smaller spread than the responses on the first round, and this is taken to indicate that the experts have reached a degree of consensus. The median values on the final round are taken as the best predictions.

Cooke (1991, p. 15) notes that one of the most important later variations of the Delphi method was the involvement of letting the experts indicate their own expertise for each question. Only the judgments of the experts claiming the most expertise for a given item are used to determine the distribution of judgments for that item. It was claimed to improve accuracy. This claim however was challenged by a study showing that self-ratings of participants did not coincide with "objective expertise" as measured by relative deviation for the true value on fact-finding and forecasting tasks.

---

[6] See Cooke's (1991) *Experts in Uncertainty* for a more detailed discussion of the Delphi method. The brief exposition of this method is based on Cooke's (1991) account.

3.3 The Cooke Method

According to Roger M. Cooke (1991), the kind of consensus reached by the Delphi method is not "rational": Delphi consensus does not imply convergence or accuracy, or more generally is not "scientific". Therefore, he proposed five "principles" to formulate "guidelines for using expert opinion in science" (p. 81):

– Reproducibility

> It must be possible for scientific peers to review and if necessary reproduce all calculations. This entails that the calculational models must be fully specified and the ingredient data must be made available (p. 81).

– Accountability

> The source of expert subjective probabilities must be identified (p. 81).

– Empirical control

> Expert probability assessments must in principle be susceptible to empirical control (p. 82).

– Neutrality

> The method for combining/evaluating expert opinion should encourage experts to state their true opinions (p. 83).

– Fairness

> All experts are treated equally, prior to processing the results of observations (p. 83).

Cooke (1991, p. 84) concluded this discussion of the "rational" principles for expert consensus with the remark that "There is no method at present which satisfies all of the above principles. There is every reason at present to develop these methods". And so he did. Over the last 20 years, at Delft University of Technology, Cooke has developed procedures to support the formal application of expert judgment to acquire "rational consensus". These procedures are set out in a 'Procedures guide for structured expert judgment' (Cooke and Goossens 1999), which was developed for a uncertainty study of accident consequence codes for nuclear power plants using structured expert judgment, commissioned by the European Commission and the United States Nuclear Regulatory Commission.

In this Guide the "principles for rational consensus" (p. 15) were slightly revised, into:

– Scrutability/accountability: all data, including experts' names and assessments, and all processing tools are open to peer review and results must be reproducible by competent reviewers.
– Fairness: experts are not pre-judged.
– Neutrality: methods of elicitation and processing must not bias results.
– Empirical control: quantitative assessments are subjected to empirical quality controls.

This revision implies a shift emphasis in the principles of fairness and neutrality: from aiming at unbiased judgments of the individual experts to aiming at a method of combining the individual expert judgments such that the "consensus" is unbiased.

Unlike the Delphi method the consensus is not based on an agreement of the experts. "If rational consensus requires expert agreement, then rational consensus is simply not possible in the face of uncertainty", even "be quarantined [...] the experts would disagree" (p. 15). The proposed rational consensus is a weighted average of the individual expert judgments. So, the main problem is the determination of these weights.

In a survey article discussing 15 years of research in expert judgment at Delft, other considerations are given for preferring a rational consensus, that is, a "mathematical aggregation" above an "agreement among experts":

> a group of experts tends to perform better than the average solitary expert, but the best individual in the group often outperforms the group as whole [...]. This motivates the elicitation of the assessments of individual experts without any interaction, followed by mathematical aggregation in order to obtain a single assessment per variable, thereby weighting the individual experts' assessments based on their quality [...]. (Goossens et al. 2008, pp. 234–235)

So, over the years, the term "rational consensus" received a more specific meaning, namely "mathematical aggregation", that is, a weighted aggregation, where the judgment of each expert is weighted on the basis of his or her knowledge and ability to judge relevant uncertainties. So, an essential element of the method of rational consensus is the weighting of the experts. This element will be discussed below.

The method, also called the "Cooke method", has found successful applications for cases where one cannot build up historical data to quantify risk models and has proven to be "most effective when data are sparse, unreliable or unobtainable" (Aspinall 2010, p. 294). For these cases,

> Expert judgment is used to obtain results from experiments and/or measurements, which are physically possible, but not performable in practice. Such experiments are 'out of scale' financially, morally, or physically in terms of time, energy, distance, etc. they may be compared to thought experiments in physics. Since these experiments cannot in fact be performed, experts are uncertain about the outcomes, and this uncertainty is quantified in a formal expert judgment exercise, so as to obtain the information that we require. (Cooke and Goossens 1999, p. 24).

In a video interview made at Resources for the Future,[7] Cooke expressed this as follows:

> so we never built up historical data to quantify our risk models by the nature of the case. So in building a risk model and quantifying this model we must have recourse to expert judgment, and this has been a theme throughout my work and a lot of risk analysis is

---

[7] Since September 2005 Cooke is appointed to the Chauncey Starr Chair in Risk Analysis of Resources for the Future.

directed to this. We really want to look at expert judgment as a new form of scientific data which we can use in a methodological proper way to quantify our models and make this whole process transparent. (Cooke 2009, transcription by the author)

Instead of performing a physical experiment, experts are asked to do a "hypothetical experiment":

First you have to be very clear what you want to ask, and this is a very difficult part of an expert judgment exercise to formulate a protocol of the questions you exactly ... exactly what you want to know. I like to think of it as follows: that expert judgment is just a different way of doing experiments. And you should have questions that you could in principle ask the nature, but for various reasons practically you cannot do so. So you ask these questions to experts who are familiar with the whole field and who can tell you what they think what will probably happen, and what their uncertainty is on what is going to happen if you could do such experiment. (Cooke 2009, transcription by the author)

If a parameter is uncertain, and if the uncertainty cannot be quantified with historical and/or measurement data, then the analyst must ask the expert how the values *would* be determined if suitable measurements could be performed. Although these experiments are hypothetical, i.e. they cannot be performed in practice, they must be physically possible. The values are known to depend on a large number of physical parameters which cannot all be measured or controlled on any given experiment. Moreover, the functional form of the dependence is not known. Hence, if a controlled experiment is repeated many times, different values will be found reflecting different values of uncontrolled and unknown physical parameters. If a measurement set-up is described to an expert, s/he can express his/her uncertainty via a subjective distribution over possible outcomes of the measurement. In such cases the experts are questioned directly about uncertainty with respect to model parameters.

So, the Cooke method is an approach where purposely experts are being used to run imaginary experiments, that is, the Cooke method is a combination of the approaches of Helmer (expert elicitations) and Hempel (imaginary experiments).

A formal expert judgment exercise is called an "elicitation". And because this exercise is to reveal and quantify the expert's uncertainties, Cooke considers the preparation for elicitation as "really nothing more than carefully designing these hypothetical experiments, so as to obtain the information that we require" (Cooke and Goossens 1999, p. 24).

And then we look at experts really as statistical hypotheses. When an expert says he has a certain uncertainty distribution over the range of outcomes of some possible experiments: that is a statistical hypothesis. And that is how we look at it. (Cooke 2009, transcription by the author)

In describing this hypothetical experiment to the expert, the physical factors which may influence the outcome of the experiment are first identified by the "analyst". Each relevant physical factor will fall into one of the two classes: (1) The case structure assumptions; and (2) the uncertainty set. Some relevant factors will have their values stipulated by the assumptions of the study, as reflected in the case structure. Other factors may influence the outcome of the hypothetical

Fig. 3.1 Format for eliciting continuous variables (Source: Figure 5, Cooke and Goossens 1999, p. 27)

Conditional on

< values of factors in the case structure assumptions >

Please give the 5%, 50% and 95% quantiles of your uncertainty in

< Hypothetical experiment >

taking into account that values of

< uncertainty set >

are unknown

experiment, but their values are not stipulated by the case structure. These factors belong to the uncertainty set. The expert is made aware that these factors are uncertain, and should fold this uncertainty into their distributions on the outcome of the hypothetical experiment. The general format for elicitation is given in Fig. 3.1.

An important phase of the procedure is the "identification" of the expert. An "expert for a given subject" is defined as a "person whose present or past field contains the subject in question, and who is regarded by others as being one of the more knowledgeable about the subject" (pp. 29–30). These experts are designated as "domain" or "substantive" experts. The following general selection criteria are recommended (p. 30):

- Reputation in the field of interest
- Experimental experience in the field of interest
- Number and quality of publications in the field of interest
- Diversity in background
- Awards received
- Balance of views
- Interest in and availability for the project.

These selection criteria are probably chosen to meet the rational consensus principle of scrutability/accountability.

Once the experts are selected, they are requested to provide their assessments on the query variables. The next crucial phase is the determination of the weight of these assessments. It is for this determination that the last "principle for rational consensus", "empirical control", comes into play.

> Empirical control is built in the elicitation procedure by asking experts to assess 'calibration or seed variables'. 'Seed variables' are variables whose values are or will be known to the analyst within the frame of the exercise but not to the expert. Seed variables are important for assessing the performance of the combined experts' assessments. Seed variables also form an important part of the feedback to experts, helping them to gauge their subjective sense of uncertainty against quantitative measure of performance. (Cooke and Goossens 1999, p. 28).

Although it is explicitly noted that expert assessments should not be treated "as if they were physical measurements in the normal sense, which they are not" (p. 10), experts are assessed as if they are measuring instruments, namely by calibration. Calibration and gauging are typical techniques for increasing the reliability of a measuring instrument, but here they are applied to experts: "expert judgment is recognized as just another type of scientific data, and methods are developed for treating it as such" (p. 10).[8]

Empirical control of the expert's performances is used to determine the weights of the expert's judgments in the aggregation of them. This performance is measured by the expert's assessment of "performance variables", "calibration variables" or "seed variables". As Cooke and Goossens (1999, p. 12) explain, seed variables may sometimes have the same physical dimensions as the variables of interest. This arises when the variables of interest are not practically measurable for reasons of scale, e.g. great distances, long times, high temperatures; whereas measurements can be performed at other scales. In this case, unpublished measurements or experiments can be used as seed variables. When such seed variables are not available, variables can be chosen which "draw on the relevant expertise" yet do not have the same dimensions as the variables of interest. As a loose criterion, a seed variable should be a variable for which the expert may be expected to make an educated guess, even if it does not fall directly within the field of the study at hand.

The identification of appropriate seed variables is a difficult task of the "uncertainty analyst":

> It is impossible to give an effective procedure for generating meaningful seed variables. If the analyst undertakes to generate his own seed variables, he must exercise a certain amount of creativity, perhaps supported [by] the experts themselves. (Cooke and Goossens 1999, p. 28)

Seed variables falling squarely within the experts' field of expertise are called "domain variables". In addition to domain variables, it is permissible to use variables from fields which are adjacent to the experts' proper field. These are called "adjacent variables". Adjacent variables are those about which the expert should be able to give an educated guess. Seed variables may also be distinguished according to whether they concern predictions or retrodictions. For predictions the true value does not exist at the time the question is answered, whereas for retrodictions, the true value exists at the time the question is answered, but is not known to the expert. Cooke and Goossens (1999) come with the following evaluation of these four different kinds of seed variables:

> In general, domain predictions are the most meaningful, in terms of proximity to the items of interest, and are also the hardest to generate. Adjacent retrodictions are easier to generate, but are less closely related to the items of interest. (Cooke and Goossens 1999, p. 29)

---

[8] Though experts are not considered to be measuring instruments, their judgments are considered as measurements.

Combining these notions they arrived at a table "with a crude evaluation" of the different types of seed variables, see Table 3.1.

3.4   Model-Based Forecasting

Both the Delphi method and the Cooke method are developed by mathematicians and engineers specifically for applications in relation to engineering problems. This impedes the application of the Cooke method to the typical problems in social science. The identification of appropriate seed variables concerning retrodictions is more difficult in social science than in natural science because the use of seed variables for calibration purposes presumes scientific consensus on their true values. In social science it will be very hard to find variables for which there is scientific consensus and at the same time are unknown to the expert.

This does not yield for seed variables concerning predictions. By their nature they are unknown to the expert when s/he is solicited about them. Moreover, in Cooke and Goossens's "crude evaluation", domain predictions appear as strongest seed variables, see Table 3.1. Therefore, for the discussion of the involvement of expert judgments in social science we now focus on "judgmental forecasting".

In the Cooke method, expert consensus presupposes consensus on the values of the seed variables. This consensus is crucial to the method because these values are used to calibrate the expert judgment, that is, to give the expert judgment a "weight". In a science like economics, values of variables do not and will never have this decisive role, because their supposed values will have too much uncertainty. In economics, for example, it is therefore not customary to talk in terms of "true values", but instead of "estimates" or "approximations".

In economics, instead of consensus on values of variables, one will find consensus on the validity of specific empirical models, in particular when they are developed at recognized economic institutions, like a central bank. Therefore, to enable the application of the Cooke method to social science, I suggest a shift from consensus on specific facts to consensus of specific empirical models. The rational-consensus method does not optimally use this systematic and shared knowledge captured by models. According to the rational-consensus procedures, models are considered to be more personal. The individual expert can bring "their written rationales", these include "consult of sources, do some modeling, do some calculations, run some codes", but these "rationales" are personal and not necessarily shared intersubjective knowledge (Cooke and Goossens 1999, p. 33). This may be true for engineering, but in economics there is much more consensus on the validity of the models used at e.g. central banks.

The weighting of experts should therefore not be based on calibration using seed variables, but instead should be based on calibration with seed models.

In a recent article in the *International Journal of Forecasting*, Philip Hans Franses (2008, p. 31) called for "more interaction between researchers in model-based forecasting and those who are engaged in judgmental forecasting research".

Table 3.1 Classification of seed variables, crude evaluation

	Predictions	Retrodictions
Domain	+++	++
Adjacent	++	+

Source: Cooke and Goossens (1999, p. 29)

His call is built on some positive evidence on the successful interaction between models and experts. According to Franses, there seems to be sufficient evidence that combining models with expert judgments leads to better judgments. This seems even more evident with respect to forecasts. "Indeed, a model's forecast, when subsequently adjusted by an expert, is often better in terms of forecasting than either a model alone or an expert alone" (Franses 2008, pp. 32–33). The reason is that "a model will miss out on something, and that the expert will know what it is" (p. 32).

In the context of the use of economic models for forecasting purposes, the reason of having the involvement of expert judgments is similar to the reason for using the Delphi or the Cooke method mentioned above, to correct for obvious known shortcomings in the economic model or to mimic the effects of economic events occurring outside the model.

> Shortcomings can occur when actual time series do not fit well with the estimated behavioural equation, for example because of revisions of the national accounts. Outside economic effects can involve specific knowledge for the near future about contracts or plans or the creation of temporally higher or lower effects of economic behaviour of households or firms because of sudden shocks in confidence or announced changes of tax rates. (Franses et al. 2007, p. 7)

In model-based forecasting, expert judgments can be used in two different ways, namely by interfering with the specification of the model structure or by adjusting "add factors". An add factor is an additional factor in the equations of the model concerning the behavior of households and firms. The add factor can be used by the forecaster to adjust the outcome of the equation.

Published forecasts are rarely based on the model outcome only; adjustments are often made to the model-based predictions in arriving at a final forecast. Thus published forecasts reflect in varying degree the properties of the model and the skills of the model's proprietors. This is illustrated by two figures (Fig. 3.2 and Fig. 3.3).

The first figure, Fig. 3.2, is presented in a discussion by Michael Lawrence, Paul Goodwin, Marcus O'Connor and Dilek Önkal (2006) on 25 years of "judgmental forecasting" and pictures the steps in forecasting. The figure is explained in terms of a case on the sales of a product:

> We propose viewing the total set of data useful for forecasting as made up of two classes; the history data and the domain or contextual data. The history data are the history of the sales of the product. The domain data are in effect all the other data which may be called on to help understand the past and to project the future. This includes past and future promotional plans, competitor data, manufacturing data and macroeconomic forecast data. The data usually input to a forecasting decision support system are the history data and occasionally promotion data. The adjustment review process is informed by both the history data and all the non-history data. (Lawrence et al. 2006, p. 494)

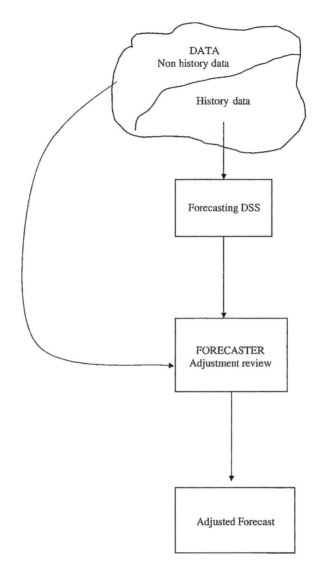

Fig. 3.2 Forecasting steps (Source: Lawrence et al. 2006, p. 494)

The second figure, here Fig. 3.3, was developed to clarify macroeconomic forecasting of the CPB Netherlands Bureau for Economic Policy Analysis (CPB). In January 2011, the CPB organized two meetings to inform journalists and policy makers about the models being used at the CPB and how forecasts are made, under the title 'Models and Forecasting: a look in the engine room of the CPB'. One key message was that the CPB does not blindly trust on computer calculations. The results are always assessed by experts on subfields (Verbruggen 2011).

Although it is already a long practice in forecasting to have expert judgments involved, there is however still a lack of studies concerning the "weighting" of the individual experts, concerning the "empirical control" of the expert judgments to

Schema production process

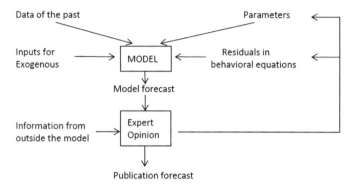

Fig. 3.3 Scheme of the production of a published forecast (Translated from Verbruggen 2011, slide 6)

enhance "rationality". Lawrence et al. (2006, pp. 506–510), however, discuss strategies for improving judgmental forecasts, of which two can be considered as a possible strategy for empirical control of expert judgments in social science.

The first improvement strategy they discuss is provision of outcome feedback. This strategy, however, suffers the same problem as seed variables concerning retrodiction, "most recent outcome contains noise and hence it is difficult for the forecaster to distinguish the error arising from a systematic deficiency in their judgment from the error caused by random factors" (p. 507).

A second strategy that may be used for weighting the expert judgments is the use of statistical forecasting methods to forecast the error in judgmental forecasts. The predicted error can then be used to correct the judgmental forecast. This correction method is appropriate when the biases associated with judgmental forecasts are systematic and sustained, e.g. a tendency of forecasters to overweight recently released information (p. 509). Because this method presumes a longer record of judgmental forecast it is not so much applicable to an individual expert, but more to correct the aggregated judgmental forecasts. The disadvantage of this method is that it leads back to the earlier problem of how to aggregate expert judgments rationally.

This latter problem, however, can be evaded by taking the "expert" not to be an individual scientist but a specific scientific institution, where a team of experts is employed. In the Delphi method and the Cooke method, the individual experts have a dominant role, but this became to be so because of the nature of the cases where these methods are applied. For these cases, there is generally no strong consensus about which model would be the most appropriate. Moreover, although expert judgments are needed to make an explanation complete, this requirement does not say who or what the carrier of this expert knowledge should be. My suggestion is that to deal with issues that have to be treated in social science, the carrier of expert knowledge is a scientific institution. To be scientific, an institution has to meet the same criteria as an individual expert, like the ones listed by Cooke and Goossens (1999), see Sect. 3.3. An institution has a longer record of forecast, and if such an institution houses both a model and a team of experts, like the CPB, judgmental forecast can be evaluated and eventually compared with other institutions' forecasts.

If we look at judgmental forecast made by institutions and not individual experts, we can use the above mentioned second strategy of weighing expert judgments as an appropriate empirical control of scientific institutions. A good example of such a calibration is a study by Franses et al. (2011), in which they evaluated macroeconomic forecasts of the CPB for the period 1997–2008.

As mentioned above, the published forecasts of the CPB are never simply the model forecasts. Before being published, all forecasts are scrutinized by various experts who assess the accuracy and adequacy of the model forecast and suggest judgmental adjustments. It is these adjusted forecasts which are made publicly available. Fortunately, and "in complete contrast to other forecasting areas" (Franses et al. 2011, p. 483), the CPB has kept track, at least since 1997, of the nature and size of these judgmental adjustments. Franses, Kranendonk and Lanser could therefore use this database to compare the accuracy of the model forecasts with that of the judgmentally adjusted forecasts, to know how effective and useful these adjustments are.

Their main findings are that the CPB model forecasts are not accurate, "biased", for a range of variables, but at the same time the associated expert forecasts, that is, the outcomes of the model filtered by experts, are more often accurate; and that expert forecasts are far more accurate than the model forecasts, in particular when the forecast horizon is short. In summary, "the final CPB forecasts de-bias the model forecasts and increase the accuracy relative to the initial model forecasts" (p. 494).

3.5 Model-Based Consensus

The idea of a model-based consensus is not new. It is originally conceived by the inventor of macro-econometric models, the Dutch economist Jan Tinbergen. He built the first two macro-econometric models, the first of the Dutch economy (Tinbergen 1936a) and the second of the US economy (Tinbergen 1939). His method of econometric modeling was new and controversial at that time (see Morgan 1990 for an extensive history of these models and the debates to which they led). Therefore, while working on his second model for the *League of Nations*, Tinbergen wrote a memorandum to explain and justify this new method. The "method" he had developed was aiming to understand the causation of business-cycle phenomena, and "essentially starts with a priori considerations about what explanatory variables are to be included. This choice must be based on economic theory or common sense" (Tinbergen 1939, p. 10). He was quite aware of the fact that economists did not agree upon what the most important causes of the business-cycle phenomenon were.

> It is rather rare that of two opinions only one is correct, the other wrong. In most cases both form part of the truth [. . .] The two opinions, as a rule, do not exclude each other. Then the question arises in what 'degree each is correct'; or, how these two opinions have to be 'combined' to have the best picture of reality. [We can] combine these different views, viz. by assuming that the movements [. . .] can be explained by some mathematical function of all the variables mentioned. We then have not a combination in the physical sense – an addition of two quantities or of two amounts – but a combination of influences. In many cases the mathematical function just mentioned may be approximated by a linear expression. (Tinbergen 1936b, pp. 1–3)

In a later recollection on this period, Tinbergen (1979) explained that he had learned this method from his mentor and Ph.D. thesis supervisor, the physicist Paul Ehrenfest. Ehrenfest had taught him that

> to formulate differences of opinion in a 'nobler' way than merely as conflicts. His favourite formulation was cast in the general form: if $a > b$, scholar A is right, but if $a < b$, then scholar B is right. The statement applied to a well-defined problem, and both a and b would generally be sets of values of elements relevant to the problem treated, with possibly a number of components of qualitative nature. (Tinbergen 1979, p. 331)

This view on models and on how to use them in dealing with differences of opinions would never leave him. In a 1982 article 'The Need of a Synthesis', Tinbergen repeated his lifelong credo:

> In quantitative terms one can also say that in certain regression equations some of the coefficients indicate what the weights are of the explanatory variables, as these are put forward in the competing theories, in the explanation of the independent variable. In the search for a synthesis what matters is that, as has been stated by Klein: 'It is less important that the effort be labeled Keynesian, monetarist, neoclassical or anything else, than that we get good approximation to explanation of this complete system . . .'. Indeed, the criterion by which we test the various competing views, has to be in the best possible explanation of the developments observed [. . .]. The point with which I want to end this argument is that the synthesis is only completed when such partial studies – the usefulness of which I accept fully – are made part of a complete model. The reason for that I gave earlier already: consistency with the other 'blocs' of a complete model. That is why, we cannot do without our largest model factory, the Central Planning Bureau, in establishing the synthesis intended. (Tinbergen [1982] 2003, pp. 303, 305–306)

According to him, models are "an order of thinking. They make it possible to localize differences of opinion: to indicate the equation about one disagrees, the term of that equation, or the term that is lacking, or the variable that is lacking" (Tinbergen 1987, p. 106; translated by the author).

Tinbergen was the first director of the CPB, founded in 1945, and became as such one of the most important designer of Dutch consensus-based policy, also called the "Polder model". Today, economic policy analysis at the CPB is still very much in the tradition of its first director:

> Many policy measures in the macroeconomic sphere can only be understood and discussed properly with the help of a model which sets out the key relationships between

macroeconomic variables. Such a model is an important instrument in considering relevant relationships. (Don and Verbruggen 2006, p. 146)

In a panel discussion to explore policy makers' perspectives on their experiences of the modeling-policy interaction, Henk Don, director of CPB from 1994 to 2006, explained the unique role models have in Dutch policymaking, when compared to other countries:

> Perhaps the most important one is to use models as an information processing device: to monitor the economy, to monitor the budget outlook in particular, and to provide information about different scenarios that the near future might bring. In Dutch policy-making there is still another use of economic models, which is to use it as a tool in consensus building. [. . .] Using the model may help to locate exactly where the political differences are and whether these are differences of preferences in what people would like the economy to produce or whether these are difference in analysis of what the economic trade-offs really are. The model helps very much in assessing all these difference and in getting as much common ground as you can get. (Don, quoted in Morgan 2000, pp. 264–265)

In this Tinbergenian kind of model-based consensus, however, the role of the expert is different from the one discussed above: The economist is only invited to identify the set of potential influences, which magnitudes then will be measured by the statistician to see whether they are significant in the causal explanation of, for example, the business cycle. According to Tinbergen's account, the "additional information" of the expert can be measured statistically, that is, estimated. The problem remains that we also need experts to add non-measurable information, that is, information for which we do not have statistics. For this kind of information, the role of the expert judgment is to provide a "measurement" when no statistical measurement is possible. The evaluation of this latter kind of expert judgment cannot be conducted by measurement as Tinbergen proposed.

3.6   Conclusions

Any methodology for an inexact social science needs to account for the involvement of expert judgments. Because experts judgments are subjective, this methodology needs also to include an account of reaching consensus to increase objectivity. This chapter has proposed to use Cooke's rational consensus method as a framework to develop such an account for reaching consensus in social science. Therefore Cooke's method requires the following modulations.

Firstly, the evaluations (weighting) of experts should not be limited to point predictions, but should include a broader range of predictions about behavior patterns, like frequencies, trends, phases, lags and amplitudes. An expert on volcanoes, a volcanologist, is not expected to predict timing of a volcanic eruption, but instead to be able making an adequate analysis of the observed changes in certain conditions and based on this analysis to make an adequate prediction about a probable eruption with a probable magnitude within a probable period.[9] Experts who in the past regularly made good "predictions" of trends and turning points gain a higher "weight" in the aggregated judgment.

Secondly, not individual experts should be evaluated but institutions that function as "centers of expertise". Institutions like the CPB or a central bank do not work with sole experts but with teams of experts who are in a sense anonymous. It is not the individual expert that is weighted but the institution as a whole. A forecast by such an institution is a model-based judgment. A model-based judgment is a combination of a model outcome corrected by expert knowledge, where this expert knowledge is the combined expertise of the institute's researchers.

References

Aspinall, W. 2010. A route to more tractable expert advice. *Nature* 463, 21 January, 294–295.
Bogen, J., and J. Woodward. 1988. Saving the phenomena. *Philosophical Review* 97(3): 303–352.
Cooke, R.M. 1991. *Experts in uncertainty: Opinions and subjective probability in science.* New York/Oxford: Oxford University Press.
Cooke, R.M. 2009. *Resources for the future.* Researcher Spotlight Roger Cooke. http://www.rff. org/Researchers/Pages/ResearcherSpotlightCooke.aspx.
Cooke, R.M., and L.H.J. Goossens. 1999. *Procedures guide for structured expert judgment*, Report EUR 18820. Luxembourg/Brussels: European Commission.
Cuhls, K. 2005. Delphi method. In *Delphi surveys, teaching material for UNIDO foresight seminars*, ed. K. Cuhls, 93–112. Vienna: United Nations Industrial Development Organization.
de Jong, J., M. Roscam Abbing, and J. Verbruggen. 2010. *Voorspellen in Crisistijd. De CPB-Ramingen tijdens de Grote Recessie* [Forecasting in Time of Crisis. The CPB-Forecasts during the Great Recession], CPB Document No. 207. The Hague: CPB.
Don, F.J.H., and J.P. Verbruggen. 2006. Models and methods for economic policy: 60 years of evolution at CPB. *Statistica Neerlandica* 60(2): 145–170.
Franses, P.H. 2008. Merging models and experts. *International Journal of Forecasting* 24: 31–33.
Franses, P.H., H.C. Kranendonk, and D. Lanser. 2007. *On the optimality of expert-adjusted forecasts*, CPB Discussion Paper No. 92. The Hague: CPB.
Franses, P.H., H.C. Kranendonk, and D. Lanser. 2011. One model and various experts: Evaluating Dutch macroeconomic forecasts. *International Journal of Forecasting* 27: 482–495.
Goossens, L.H.J., R.M. Cooke, A.H. Hale, and Lj. Rodic-Wiersma. 2008. Fifteen years of expert judgment at TU Delft. *Safety Science* 46: 234–244.
Hausman, D.H. 1992. *The inexact and separate science of economics.* Cambridge: Cambridge University Press.
Helmer, O. 1983. *Looking forward. A guide to futures research.* Beverly Hills: Sage.
Helmer, O., and N. Rescher. 1958. *On the epistemology of the inexact sciences*, 1513, October 13. RAND.

---

[9] This analogy with volcanology is made in a CPB report (de Jong et al. 2010, p. 61) to underline the reports main conclusion: "due to the character of macro-economic short-term forecast, it is most unlikely that CPB and other forecasting institutes will be able to forecast the next financial crisis adequately" (p. 3). The report was written to answer the question why CPB "did not see the credit crisis coming, nor did it predict that the Dutch economy would shrink in 2009" (p. 3). The presentation 'Models and Forecasting' by Verbruggen, discussed in Sect. 3.5, see also Fig. 3.3, was based on this report. So, the report also discusses explicitly the necessary role of experts.

Helmer, O., and N. Rescher. 1959. On the epistemology of the inexact sciences. *Management Science* 6(1): 25–52.

Hempel, C.G. 1952. Symposium: Problems of concept and theory formation in the social sciences. In *Science, language, and human rights*, 65–86. Philadelphia: University of Pennsylvania Press.

Lawrence, M., P. Goodwin, M. O'Connor, and D. Önkal. 2006. Judgmental forecasting: A review of progress over the last 25 years. *International Journal of Forecasting* 22: 493–518.

Marget, A.W. 1929. Morgenstern on the methodology of economic forecasting. *Journal of Political Economy* 37(3): 312–339.

Marshall, A. [1890] 1920. *Principles of economics*, 8th ed. London: Macmillan.

Mill, J.S. [1843] 1911. *A system of logic. Ratiocinative and inductive*, 8th ed. London: Longmans, Green and Co.

Morgan, M.S. 1990. *The history of econometrics ideas*. Cambridge: Cambridge University Press.

Morgan, M.S. 2000. The relevance of economic modelling for policy-making: A panel discussion. In *Empirical models and policy-making: Interaction and institutions*, ed. F.A.G. den Butter and M.S. Morgan, 259–278. London/New York: Routledge.

Morgan, M.S. 2012. *The world in the model. How economists work and think*. Cambridge: Cambridge University Press.

Morgenstern, O. 1928. *Wirtschaftsprognose. Eine Untersuchung ihrer Voraussetzungen und Möglichkeiten*. Vienna: Springer.

Morgenstern, O. 1954. Experiment and large scale computation in economics. In *Economic activity analysis*, ed. O. Morgenstern, 484–549. New York/London: Wiley/Chapman & Hall.

Morgenstern, O. 1963. *On the accuracy of economic observations*, 2nd ed. Princeton: Princeton University Press.

Rescher, N. 2006. The Berlin school of logical empiricism and its legacy. *Erkenntnis* 64: 281–304.

Schwarz, A., and W. Krohn. 2011. Experimenting with the concept of experiment: Probing the epochal break. In *Science transformed? Debating claims of an epochal break*, ed. A. Nordmann, H. Radder, and G. Schiemann, 119–134. Pittsburgh: University of Pittsburgh Press.

Sutton, J. 2000. *Marshall's tendencies. What can economists know?* Leuven/Cambridge, MA: Leuven University Press/The MIT Press.

Thrall, R.M., C.H. Coombs, and R.L. Davis (eds.). 1954. *Decision processes*. New York: Wiley.

Tinbergen, J. 1936a. Kan hier te lande, al dan niet na overheidsingrijpen, een verbetering van de binnenlandse conjunctuur intreden, ook zonder verbetering van onze exportpositie? [Could here in this country, whether or not after government intervention, set in an improvement in the domestic economy, even without improving our export position?] In *Prae-adviezen voor de Vereeniging voor de Staathuishoudkunde en de Statistiek* [Pre-advices for the Society of Economics and Statistics]. The Hague: Nijhoff.

Tinbergen, J. 1936b. *Memorandum on the continuation of the League's business cycle research in a statistical direction*, Unpublished memorandum. Archive of the League of Nations, Geneva.

Tinbergen, J. 1939. *Business cycles in the United States of America 1919–1932. Statistical testing of business-cycle theories II*. Geneva: League of Nations.

Tinbergen, J. 1979. Recollections of professional experiences. *Banca Nazionale del Lavoro Quarterly Review* 32(131): 331–360.

Tinbergen, J. 1987. Over modellen [On models]. In *Lessen uit het Verleden. 125 jaar Vereniging voor de Staathuishoudkunde*, ed. A. Knoester [Lessons from the Past. 125 year Society of Economics], 99–112. Leiden/Antwerpen: Stenfert Kroese.

Tinbergen, J. [1982] (2003). The need of a synthesis. In *Jan Tinbergen. The centennial volume*, ed. J. Kol, 303–306. Rotterdam University. Translation of De noodzaak van een synthese. *Economisch Statistische Berichten* 1-12-1982, 1284–1285.

Verbruggen, J. 2011. De 4 'ellen' van het voorspellen: SAFFIER II. CPB presentation. http://www.cpb.nl/publicatie/presentatie-de-4-ellen-van-het-voorspellen-saffier-ii.

Chapter 4
Explicating Ways of Consensus-Making in Science and Society: Distinguishing the Academic, the Interface and the Meta-Consensus

Laszlo Kosolosky and Jeroen Van Bouwel

Abstract In this chapter, we shed new light on the epistemic struggle between establishing consensus and acknowledging plurality, by explicating different ways of consensus-making in science and society and examining the impact hereof on their field of intersection, i.e. consensus conferences (in particular those organized by the National Institute of Health). We draw a distinction between, what we call, academic and interface consensus, to capture the wide appeal to consensus in existing literature. We investigate such accounts – i.e. from Miriam Solomon, John Beatty and Alfred Moore, and Boaz Miller – as to put forth a new understanding of consensus-making, focusing on the meta-consensus. We further defend how (NIH) consensus conferences enable epistemic work, through demands of epistemic adequacy and contestability, contrary to the claim that consensus conferences miss a window for epistemic opportunity (Solomon M, The social epistemology of NIH consensus conferences. In: Kincaid H, McKitrick J (ed) Establishing medical reality: methodological and metaphysical issues in philosophy of medicine. Springer, Dordrecht, 2007). Paying attention to the dynamics surrounding consensus, moreover, allows us to illustrate how the public understanding of science and the public use of the ideal of consensus could be well modified.

4.1 Introduction

In our society, there are these moments in which establishing a *scientific consensus* seems imperative to solve urgent problems, for instance, as concerns climate change; achieving consensus on the causes and extent of global warming would

---

The authors are listed in alphabetical order and have contributed equally to the chapter.

L. Kosolosky (✉) • J. Van Bouwel
Centre for Logic and Philosophy of Science, Ghent University, Blandijnberg 2, 9000 Gent, Belgium
e-mail: Laszlo.Kosolosky@UGent.be

© Springer International Publishing Switzerland 2014
C. Martini, M. Boumans (eds.), *Experts and Consensus in Social Science*,
Ethical Economy 50, DOI 10.1007/978-3-319-08551-7_4

facilitate policymaking and, moreover, send a convincing signal that doing nothing will have dire consequences. On the other hand, philosophers studying plurality and heterodoxy in science have raised questions concerning the ideal of the scientific consensus and the pernicious effects the consecration of scientific consensus might have.

Several philosophers of science have developed interesting accounts on how to deal with this tension between plurality and consensus; how scientific plurality, dissent, and consensus-making can go hand in hand. And, in relation hereto, how consensus conferences manage to deal with the tension between plurality and consensus. In what follows, we want to analyze some of these accounts about how science goes or should go from scientific plurality to scientific consensus, introducing an important distinction between consensus-making among scientists – establishing an *academic consensus* – on the one hand and consensus-making at the interface between science and society – establishing an *interface consensus* – on the other hand.

This analytical distinction will help us (a) compare the differences among philosophers in understanding consensus-making, (b) develop our social-procedural account of scientific consensus (analogous with social accounts of objectivity) paying attention to *meta-consensus*, and (c) spell out how to modify the public understanding of science and the public use of the ideal of consensus.

4.2   Aspects of *Scientific Consensus*: The Intra-scientific Consensus and the Science-Society Interface

If we aim to elaborate on the tension between consensus and plurality mentioned above, we first need to establish what aspects of scientific consensus we would like to address here. We draw a distinction between a "technical, academic consensus" and an "interface consensus".[1] The former points at a consensus being established among scientists or experts in a certain field related to a certain topic. The latter relates to a consensus being established at the border between science and society, typically including a wider range of actors apart from scientists (i.e. laypeople, interactional experts, government representatives, etc.). The most intuitive way to grapple this distinction is by distinguishing two problems or two moments of decision-making that should be analytically separated, i.e. the actual move from plurality to consensus among scientists or experts on the one hand and the moment of dissemination and justification towards or within society on the other hand.

---

[1] We grant at once that talking about consensus can at the same time apply to academic as well as interface consensus. The distinction is meant to be non-exclusive. What we seek to elaborate are ideal types of consensus that can be used to classify or evaluate the plethora of non-ideal or mixed cases that dominate the research practice. These moments might de facto coincide, but might be distinguishable, e.g., as concerns the way in which uncertainties are weighted.

Another way to comprehend the distinction is by describing it in terms of the relation between its actors and/or the conditions that need to be fulfilled beforehand. The relationship at play within academic consensus is one between experts. In the academic world, every scientist/academic is regarded to be an (equal) peer and everyone serves as an authority within his or her field. These people are generally regarded to be on the cutting edge of research and are expected to be among the first to notice changes occurring within their field of expertise. The relationship at play within the interface consensus is one between expert and layman, grasping the interface between science and society. This type entails a relation between expert and layman grounded on authority, trust, and mutual respect, where the actors are not regarded to be on equal (epistemic) footing. The difference in interaction is important to bear in mind when we want to have a look at what's at stake in each of them. This brings us to our second point, namely the conditions that need to be fulfilled beforehand. As for academic consensus, we could argue that the community should enable critical interaction among academic experts and have significant evidence available on the basis of which a conclusion can be formulated. As for interface consensus, some form of academic consensus or a first attempt to establish consensus is required to start up the interface process.

A helpful example to illustrate how this distinction might be used are consensus conferences. To demonstrate this, we briefly sketch the workings and goals of the National Institutes of Health (NIH) Consensus Conferences: The NIH consensus development program constructs major conferences that aim to produce evidence-based consensus statements addressing controversial issues in medicine important to health care providers, patients, and the general public. The conferences aspire to provide an independent look at the issues through an unbiased panel. These conferences are run on a type of "court model", in which the panel members serve as a jury. They are supposed to have no financial or career interests related to the topic and they are highly regarded in their own fields, but are in no way closely aligned with the subject under scrutiny.

Due to the stress on providing an evidence-based consensus, the NIH itself differentiates between Consensus Development Conferences and State-of-the-Science Conferences. Consensus Development Conferences are typically undertaken when there is a solid body of high-quality evidence, such as randomized trials and well-designed observational studies. State-of-the-Science Conferences are generally utilized in cases where the evidence base is weaker. In both cases the statement is a report evaluating scientific information on a given biomedical or public health intervention with the purpose of resolving a particular controversial issue in clinical practice. Each report handles a series of five to six questions concerning efficacy, risk, clinical applications, and directions for future research. As sketched out in the NIH guidelines, these conferences have set two goals for themselves: On the one hand, they aspire to bring about rational consensus on controversial health topics, and, on the other hand, they intend to spread the medical information across to the broader public. We could say that the NIH conferences carry the task of contributing both to "academic consensus" as to "interface consensus", to the former by establishing a consensus within the scientific community and to the latter by providing and transmitting this established scientific consensus to the larger community (NIH, website).

Obviously, as thinking the example through shows, there might be an overlap between both moments and there might be causal influences in both directions. In the following sections, we will show how our analytical distinction helps in explicating different understandings of the structure and functions of consensus-making in the philosophical literature. First, in Sect. 4.3, it will be made clear how the example of the NIH consensus conferences already captures differences among philosophers in understanding consensus making.

4.3 Consensus-Making Conferences: Miriam Solomon on the Two Moments of Consensus-Making

Miriam Solomon (2007) argues that the National Institutes of Health consensus development conferences do not bring about rational consensus on controversial health topics. Solomon insists that a consensus usually exists beforehand, at least among the researchers, as opposed to what the NIH claims to be the case. According to her, these conferences can only serve a (subsidiary) goal of spreading the information across to a more general public.

Put bluntly, although Solomon will agree that a consensus conference can contribute to *interface consensus*, she will not agree that consensus conferences contribute to *academic consensus*, because the latter consensus already existed before the conference started. According to her, consensus conferences miss the intended window of epistemic opportunity: they typically take place after the experts have reached consensus.[2]

In her understanding of the role of consensus conferences, Solomon (implicitly) distinguishes between the two moments identified above. She claims that the actual (NIH) consensus conferences should be seen as a moment of disseminating knowledge, justifying a clinical practice, ... not as a place for doing science and establishing an intra-scientific consensus, that already happened beforehand. The consensus conference is then a ritual, a choreographic epistemic performance, creating authoritative knowledge; it is the moment of the *interface consensus* addressing the public intended. In her own words, consensus conferences can be merely a "[...] rhetorically efficacious way to get the word out, to interested intermediaries such as professional groups, pharmaceutical companies and health insurance companies who will then adapt the statements for their own particular purposes" (Solomon 2007, p. 175).

Her account, however, is left with a couple of open problems. First, the way in which Solomon argues for such a quite substantial claim raises questions. If one

---

[2] In previous work, we analyzed her claim and found it to be wanting, mainly because the examples she gives in favor of her account do not suffice (cf. Kosolosky 2012).

gazes upon the history of NIH consensus conferences one can see that the NIH already organized over 157 conferences. Solomon discusses two of them in further detail, which are supposed to serve as central examples to clarify what NIH consensus conferences actually entail. However, when push comes to shove, she omits to say why these two are typical examples. So the question remains whether they really are as typical as she supposes them to be and on what grounds she (can) make(s) this assumption. Moreover she does not address how exactly the establishment of the intra-scientific, academic consensus came to be; Does establishing an academic consensus go further than published studies pointing in the same direction? And if the consensus conference is merely a ritual, if the only epistemic surplus/value is that it authorizes knowledge, then why was there a different outcome in NIH consensus conference 1977 and the Danish consensus conference 1983 (both on breast cancer screening)?[3] Do we have the same academic consensus (preceding consensus conferences) in both cases and a different interface consensus (as a result of the consensus conferences) because of the difference in publics intended?

We will return to this matter below. In this section, we presented the role scientific consensus plays in consensus conferences and the way in which consensus is established, whereby two moments of consensus-making can be distinguished. According to Solomon, consensus conferences serve to the second one, i.e. the elaboration of an interface consensus, while the first one, the making of the academic consensus, happens beforehand (cf. Solomon 2007, p. 173), "the rational basis for that consensus is made clear by AHRQ formal assessment of that evidence" (AHRQ is the *Agency for Healthcare Research and Quality*).

4.4 Consensus-Making and the Meta-Consensus I: Deliberative Choreographies, Aggregation and Contestability

Besides distinguishing the academic from the interface consensus, we would also like to introduce the notion of the meta-consensus. Instead of focusing on the simple level, that is, on the result of alternative theories/models tested against one another eventually – thought to be – leading to some consensus *outcome*, we could learn a lot by shifting to the analysis of the meta-consensus that stipulates the *procedure* to

---

[3] The first Danish medical consensus conference was held in 1983, on the topic of early detection of breast cancer. It did not recommend general mammographic screening, even for women over 50 years of age, thus coming to a different conclusion from the first NIH Consensus conference held in 1977 (see Jorgensen et al. 2009). "The role that consensus conferences can play in making policy explains why different countries hold consensus conferences on the same topics. For example, recommendations for mammograms to screen for breast cancer may be different in countries with different resources or different values. For instance, in the UK, mammograms are not routinely offered to elderly women because they are not cost effective at that age; in the USA cost effectiveness is not valued so highly." (Solomon 2011, p. 248)

be followed. In Sect. 4.6, we will explore the idea of meta-consensus a bit further in theoretical terms, but let us first continue to scrutinize Solomon's analysis of consensus conferences and now focus on the procedures at play. Solomon scrutinizes NIH Consensus Development Conferences, as it is a good example of a social, deliberative epistemic procedure.

Advocates of rational deliberation as a most desirable social epistemology have been claiming that it reveals bias and presuppositions, corrects errors, generates additional evidence, and that more can be accomplished through rational deliberation among two or more individuals than by individuals working alone. For some, for instance, Helen Longino (1990), this rational deliberation and critical interaction are constitutive of scientific objectivity, provided that the interaction respects some norms.[4] The NIH consensus program also works hard to be perceived as objective (cf. Solomon 2007, p. 174), although it may not actually achieve objectivity *qua* freedom from all bias:

> The consensus program 'science court' is not designed to be free of biases such as, for example, group dynamics, ordering of speakers, rhetorical force of speakers, peer pressure, chair style, general medical practice biases (e.g. intervention is generally favored over non-intervention), unsystematic evaluation of evidence, the effects of sleep deprivation and conservativeness or radicalism of panel members. The only biases it is designed to eliminate (and it may or may not succeed in doing so) are those of governmental pressures, commercial pressures and biases from one's own prior research in the area. (Solomon 2007, p. 169)

Here, Solomon emphasizes via her discussion of consensus conferences that rational deliberation does not deliver what it promises as it is subject to groupthink, suppression of dissent and other biases typical of deliberating groups (also see her 2006). Instead of the procedure of deliberation, Solomon wants to defend the procedure of aggregated judgment, in which members of a group typically do not deliberate with each other, but instead cast their votes or give their views independently. This might even make the NIH consensus conferences obsolete: "A more recent epistemic concern about the idea of consensus development is, wouldn't it be quicker, more timely, and at least as good to do a meta-analysis of the available evidence? Such a formal analysis would have a similar claim to be free from bias." (Solomon 2007, p. 169)[5,6] Should the conferences play an epistemic role at all, that

---

[4] We do want to add, though, that for Longino objectivity comes in degrees and she does not consider the "closure" of controversy or critical interaction as the outcome to be obtained – plurality and dissent have their value. This is contrary to most consensus conferences where the "closure" of intellectual controversy and the establishment of a consensus is imperative.

[5] A bit further in her paper Solomon correctly describes that meta-analysis of evidence is nowadays part of the NIH Consensus Conferences preparations. She thus asks whether there is still room for consensus conferences when meta-analyses have already been performed. What Solomon refers to here as meta-analysis is the systematic literature review prepared by the Agency for Healthcare Research and Quality (AHRQ), which is a literature review that tries to identify, appraise, select, and synthesize all high quality research evidence relevant to a particular research question (Kosolosky 2012).

[6] See also Sunstein (2006) for a development of this line of criticism, we will not engage with that here.

is: "Consensus conferences seem to miss the intended window of epistemic opportunity: they typically take place *after* the experts reach consensus." (Solomon 2007, p. 170)

But, is the epistemic work done, if one limits the procedure to aggregation? Are we not losing **epistemic adequacy** and **contestability** (linked to *epistemic responsibility*) out of sight? Returning to the analytical distinction between an academic and an interface consensus, Solomon seems to presuppose that an aggregative procedure establishing academic consensus does all the epistemic work (and establishing an interface consensus could possibly be understood as doing merely policy work). However, the NIH conferences could perform epistemic functions that the aggregation neglects.

(a) *epistemic adequacy*

In her analysis of NIH conferences, Solomon notices that: "The NIH consensus program has never been assessed for the accuracy of outcomes. No-one has ever investigated, for example, whether the outcomes are better – more 'true' or whatever – than those achieved by other methods such as non-neutral panels or formal meta-analysis of evidence." (Solomon 2007, p. 174) When she scrutinizes social deliberative epistemic procedures wondering whether they yield the desired kinds of products, she focuses on the accuracy of outcomes, not on their adequacy. Adequacy seems to be an afterthought.

Let us briefly illustrate the difference between accuracy and adequacy that we have in mind here. Speaking about (a) *accuracy*, we think of the relation with reality, preciseness of the answer given, while (b) *adequacy* points at what the explainee expects of an answer or how it fits with the explainee's epistemic interests. To clarify these criteria and the idea that there often is a trade-off to be made between them, let us compare the answers given to the questions of a consensus conference with maps. A subway map like the one of the Paris Metro is *adequate* for its users because it *accurately* represents specific types of features (e.g. direct train connections between stations, number of stations between two given stations, . . .) while other features are consciously *less accurately* represented (the exact distances between the stations, the relative geographical orientation of the stations, . . .). If the latter would be represented more accurately, the map could become less *adequate* for its intended users and a perfectly accurate representation mirroring every detail would be utterly useless. Other maps (e.g. Paris' shopping or tourist attractions maps) require other kinds of information (relating to, e.g., distances, details about street names, house numbers, etc.) in order to be useful – the best trade-off between accuracy and adequacy differs depending on the interests or desiderata at play. Thus, on the one hand, because of different interests or desiderata, it is impossible to make a map that is ideal in all possible situations. On the other hand, not all maps are equally good, as one can make claims of superiority that are bound to specific situations. The same can be said about the answers that are formulated in a consensus conference.

In Solomon's understanding of what NIH conferences actually do, the *accuracy* of outcomes should not be a worry, given she claims that there is already an academic consensus before the conferences take place which seems to make the consensus conference itself obsolete from an epistemic point of view. She sees NIH conferences as the (interface) moment in which the wording or the articulation of this consensus is done in an *adequate way* ("user-friendly"): "Second, formal meta-analysis of research, classified into grades of quality of research, is hardly user-friendly. The NIH consensus statement is written so as to be intelligible not only to primary health care practitioners but to health care administrations and the general public. NIH conferences are not only rhetorical forces; they make the research more widely accessible." (Solomon 2007, p. 175) However, this understanding of the relation between accuracy and adequacy, between the academic moment and the interface moment, is too unidirectional, as if adequacy concerns do not touch upon accuracy concerns, as if there would be no trade-off. According to our understanding, the adequacy concerns can be articulated in the interface moment, which then should be fed back into the academic moment in order to trade-off accuracy and adequacy concerns. In that sense the interface moment is not merely a moment of user-friendly dissemination, but also one of critique and contestability of the academic moment (highlighting epistemic interests that have not been addressed).

Solomon defends her claim in relation to the NIH conferences, by drawing on two examples, i.e. the 'Helicobacter Pylori in Peptic Ulcer Disease conference' (1994) and the 'Management of Hepatitis C Consensus Development Conference' (2002). By analyzing both in detail, we can show how the interface moment does highlight epistemic interests that have not been addressed at the academic moment and thus point at the epistemic role of the interface moment in terms of adequacy.[7]

First, according to Solomon, "the 2002 Consensus Development Conference 'Management of Hepatitis C' repeats recommendations that were already stated by the FDA in the previous year" (Solomon 2007, p. 170). The two 2001 studies dealing with hepatitis C issued by the Food and Drug Administration are: 'Ribavirin and chronic hepatitis C infection' (FDA 2001) and 'From the FDA' (Schwetz 2001). What both studies acknowledge is the fact that the FDA has issued two approvals involving the use of Rebetol capsules (ribavirin) to treat patients with chronic hepatitis C. Now if we look at the outline of the final NIH report, we notice that the report deals with the following five questions: (1) What is the natural

---

[7] As is stated on the NIH website, the consensus conference examples serve merely an historical and epistemological purpose to defend claims on consensus formation. The actual statements referred to from within any of the reports should thus not be judged for their truth today: "This Archive of Older Conference Statements is provided solely for historical purposes. Due to the cumulative nature of medical research, new knowledge has inevitably accumulated in these subject areas in the time since these statements were prepared. Thus some of the material is likely to be out of date, and at worst simply wrong. The statements may, however, continue to be useful to the research community as a reference for understanding what was known about a topic at a particular point in time, including whether gaps in research identified at the time of each conference have since been filled. It is for this purpose that the conference statements will remain available in this format indefinitely. For reliable, current information on these and other health topics, we recommend consulting the National Institutes of Health's MedlinePlus http://www.nlm. nih.gov/medlineplus/ (NIH, website on the consensus development conference program)".

history of hepatitis C?, (2) What is the most effective appropriate approach to diagnose and monitor patients?, (3) What is the most effective therapy for hepatitis C?, (4) Which patients with hepatitis C should be treated?, and (5) What recommendations can be made to patients to prevent transmission of hepatitis C? (NIH 2002, p. 7). In response to the question that comes closest to the one being answered by the FDA report, i.e. 'What is the most effective therapy for hepatitis C?', the NIH report says that "combination therapy results in better treatment responses than monotherapy, but the highest response rates have been achieved with pegylated interferon in combination with ribavirin. [...] Currently the best indicator of effective treatment is an SVR, [...]" (NIH 2002, p. 17). A crucial nuance is at stake here: whereas the FDA reports talk about an appropriate method of dealing with hepatitis C, namely taking ribavirin, the NIH report addresses the question what the best (or most effective) therapy for hepatitis C is. An FDA report does not address the question of most effective therapy, it merely "[...] requires drugs to be tested only relative to placebos. This means that an FDA approval is, at best, a signal that the approved drug is better than taking a sugar pill, not that it's better than an existing treatment" (Reiss 2010, p. 9). Moreover, the other types of questions the NIH report dealt with were not addressed in any of the FDA reports. Taken all together, the NIH report displays something more substantial than merely repeating FDA recommendations, it takes these recommendations to another level and incorporates them in a larger framework. Addressing the adequacy in this case, means answering the above five questions, a task the NIH consensus conferences set out to do. The multitude of questions were not yet addressed in academic literature, nor the question what the best therapy might be.[8] Clearly an example of how epistemic interests modify the academic moment.

Second, according to Solomon, the 'Helicobacter Pylori in Peptic Ulcer Disease conference' (1994) "took place after the important clinical trials [...] and after research scientists, and many prominent clinicians, had reached consensus on the use of antibiotics for peptic ulcers" (Solomon 2007, p. 170). The NIH report reflects all the scientific studies that established a disturbing epidemiologic relationship between H. pylori and gastric malignancies, concluding that "such studies have given rise to the hypothesis that H. pylori is a major etiologic factor in peptic ulcer disease and that diagnosis and eradication of the organism are necessary for optimal therapy of the disorder" (NIH 1994, pp. 3–4). However, this is not the only matter this report investigated. Similar to the 2002 report mentioned above, this report brought together specialists in gastroenterology, surgery, infectious diseases, epidemiology, and pathology, as well as the public, to address multiple questions: (1) What is the causal relationship of H. pylori to upper gastrointestinal disease? (2) How does one diagnose and eradicate H. pylori infection? (3) Does eradication of H. pylori infection benefit the patient with peptic ulcer disease? (4) What is the

---

[8] This is a critique that transcends this particular report, as most (if not all) NIH consensus reports address a multitude of questions targeted at the needs and interests of the people (see also the NIH website on the consensus development program).

relationship between H. pylori infection and gastric malignancy? (5) Which H. pylori-infected patients should be treated? (6) What are the most important questions that must be addressed by future research in H. pylori infections? After presentations by experts and discussion by the audience, the consensus panel weighed the evidence and prepared their consensus statement. Among their findings, the panel concluded that: (1) ulcer patients with H. pylori infection require treatment with antimicrobial agents in addition to anti-secretory drugs whether on first presentation with the illness or on recurrence; (2) the value of treating non-ulcer dyspepsia patients with H. pylori infection remains to be determined; and (3) the interesting relationship between H. pylori infection and gastric cancers requires further exploration (NIH 1994, pp. 3–4). Solomon's claim that there was a pre-established consensus on the use of antibiotics for peptic ulcers seems a bit too straightforward, as the answer to the fifth question warrants further research to be conducted, at least for some of the patients intended:

> There are ample data to support the antimicrobial eradication of H. pylori infection in patients with peptic ulcer disease. All patients with gastric or duodenal ulcers who are infected with H. pylori should be treated with anti-microbials regardless of whether they are suffering from the initial presentation of the disease or from a recurrence. H. pylori-infected peptic ulcer patients who are receiving maintenance treatment with antisecretory agents or who have a history of complicated or refractory disease should also be treated for the infection. The presence of NSAID's, including aspirin, as a contributing factor should not alter the antimicrobial regimen, but whenever possible, these drugs should be discontinued. *However, in asymptomatic H. pylori-infected patients without ulcers, the data are not sufficient to support prophylactic antimicrobial therapy to prevent ulcer disease in the future to reduce the likelihood of developing gastric neoplasia. Also, no convincing data exists to support routine treatment of patients with nonulcer dyspepsia who are infected with H. pylori. Thus, at the present time there is no reason to consider routine detection or treatment of H. pylori infection in the absence of ulcers. Carefully controlled prospective studies are needed to assess the benefits of treating nonulcer dyspepsia patients with H. pylori infection. It is self-evident that no patient should be treated for H. pylori unless one of the sensitive and specific tests previously discussed demonstrates infection.* (NIH 1994, p. 14, our italics).

This answer suggests how for some cases definitive answers need to be postponed as long as prospective studies remain absent. Another example here is how the question whether eradication of H. pylori infection prevents gastric cancer can only directly be answered by use of a long and costly study, which was not present. The NIH report therefore suggests an alternative approach to conduct studies looking at the intermediate endpoints that are thought to predict the evolution of malignancy and their response to H. pylori eradication. Also, the report recommends that more epidemiological studies would be needed to define more precisely the subset of H. pylori-infected individuals who will develop gastric cancer (NIH 1994, p. 17). Moreover, a causal relationship between H. pylori and peptic ulcer disease is more difficult to establish (as opposed to a causal relationship between H. pylori and chronic superficial gastritis) from the available data in part because of the lack of an animal model and because only a small proportion of individuals harboring the organism develop ulceration (NIH 1994, p. 5). All of these are thus obstacles H. pylori research is confronted with in ascribing the correct use of antibiotics. Adequacy concerns, as mentioned above, can thus be articulated in the interface moment, in which participants can advance epistemic interests that have not been addressed, which then should be fed back into the academic moment in order to trade-off accuracy and adequacy concerns. In this case, a requirement for prospective studies, intermediate endpoint studies, epidemiological studies and animal models serve as a feedback loop, where the interface moment, by addressing the question of appropriate medication, gives advice on what research still needs to be conducted to be able to serve the needs of those infected.[9] In that sense the interface moment is not merely a moment of user-friendly dissemination, but also one of critique and contestability of the academic moment.

Perhaps the easiest way to grasp the opportunity the NIH consensus conferences leave for adequacy concerns is in how they consider the patient's well-being as most central in their discourse. For instance, in the 2000 consensus conference on osteoporosis, it says that: "until there is good evidence to support the cost-effectiveness of routine screening, or the efficacy of early initiation of preventive drugs, an individualized approach is recommended" (NIH 2000, p. 19). Taking into account adequacy during consensus conferences will thus influence the content of the academic consensus – which makes the conference more than merely dissemination and choreography.

(b) *contestability* *(and epistemic responsibility)*

Different epistemic interests to be addressed, and the related trade-offs between accuracy and adequacy, might result in a variety of outcomes in which the idea of articulating *the* scientific consensus becomes more nuanced. Adequacy concerns explicated during the interface moment put the plurality of epistemic interests up front. Interface assures contestability and raises questions about the degree of

---

[9] In other cases, such as the NIH consensus conference on management of hepatitis B (2008), similar demands for further research as to be able to answer the question for treatment appropriately reemerge. The conclusion of this report goes as follows: "Hepatitis B is a major cause of liver disease worldwide, ranking as a substantial cause of cirrhosis and hepatocellular carcinoma. The development and use of a vaccine for hepatitis B virus (HBV) has resulted in a substantial decline in the number of new cases of acute hepatitis B among children, adolescents, and adults in the United States. However, this success has not yet been duplicated worldwide, and both acute and chronic HBV infection continue to represent important global health problems. Seven treatments are currently approved for adult patients with chronic HBV infection in the United States: interferon-a, pegylated interferon-a, lamivudine, adefovir dipivoxil, entecavir, telbivudine, and tenofovir disoproxil fumarate. Interferon-a and lamivudine have been approved for children with HBV infection. *Although available randomized, controlled trials (RCTs) show encouraging short-term results – demonstrating the favorable effect of these agents on such intermediate markers of disease as HBV DNA level, liver enzyme tests, and liver histology – limited rigorous evidence exists demonstrating the effect of these therapies on important long-term clinical outcomes, such as the development of hepatocellular carcinoma or a reduction in deaths. Questions therefore remain about which groups of patients benefit from therapy and at which point in the course of disease this therapy should be initiated*" (NIH 2008, p. 4, our italics). The NIH report here tries to meet these questions on patient treatment, that purely on the basis of scientific evidence (academic consensus in Solomon's account), are left unaddressed.

answerability/responsibility of the experts/scientists. Contestability – providing participants the possibility to challenge homogenization, marginalization of epistemic interests, etc. and diminish these tendencies – can be found both on the simple level of finding consensus as well as on the meta-level, i.e. the consensual setting in which the interaction takes place (and on which there is some form of meta-consensus).

An aggregative procedure misses contestability, in the sense that, as Alison Wylie puts it: "well functioning aggregation [...] preserves systematic bias as faithfully as it preserves the information and empirically probative insights held by members of a group" (Wylie 2006, p. 46).[10] Moreover, in many occasions, we lack the knowledge, means and time to assess whether the conclusions being put forth are the right ones. When we take one's testimony for granted, we do this often purely based on trust. For this we must have good reasons to trust the other person, in other words, he or she must be deemed trustworthy (Hardwig 1991, pp. 697–700).[11] The question that springs to mind is whether we can expect of people to trust a judgment that was taken through aggregation, where the possibility exists that the group decision does not correspond with any individual opinion defended in the group. When, for instance, a group is polarized on an issue and the decision is but an average not defended by any of the people involved. A dubious policy that no one actually endorses, would thus be the result of a strongly divided group. Aggregative procedures are but quasi-transparent processes: when there is no opportunity for debate and no arguments are given in favor or against a certain take on things, it remains difficult for the general audience to acquire on which grounds a decision was taken (Baartmans and Kosolosky in print).

Thus aggregative procedures obscure the opportunity for contestability, as part of the process remains in the dark for most of the people involved. An interface moment could allow for contestability as it offers opportunity both to (1) question bias, as well as, (2) acquire insight into how certain positions and decisions came to be. The NIH general procedure allows for both moments of contestability: Because they want to provide an independent look on the topic, they opt for a type of "court model", instating an unbiased panel. The review-process itself is structured as follows: First, there is an in-depth presentation of evidence to the panel. This includes a systematic literature review prepared by the Agency for Healthcare Research and Quality (AHRQ). In addition, recognized experts on the topic give presentations to the panel and the audience. Finally, formal periods of public discussion are held. The conference program contains approximately 21 speakers: 3 of them present the information found in the systematic review of the literature;

---

[10] As an example Wylie investigates research concerning gender prejudices. She mentions there being research in which professors were to judge a fictive candidate for a job on the basis of a resume. When the candidate was named Mark Miller, he was hired by two thirds of the professors. However, when the identical resume made mention of Karen Miller, the candidate was but hired by less than half of the professors (Wylie 2006, p. 46).

[11] For a detailed insight into how trust, and its counterparts of distrust and mistrust play an important role in everyday and scientific communication, see (Primiero and Kosolosky 2013).

the other 18 are experts on the topic at hand, have likely published on the matter, and may have strong opinions or beliefs on the topic. Crucial here is that where multiple viewpoints on a topic exist, every effort is made to include speakers who address all sides of the issue (NIH, website). It is only but through the procedure that moments of contestability become possible.

Examples of contestability concerning meta-consensus, i.e. the procedure, can be found, for instance, in relation to the NIH Consensus program, as we learn from Solomon's analysis (2011, p. 244):

> So we see particular concerns about 'objectivity' of panel members, fairness of chairs, time pressure and late night sessions, balanced assessment of the evidence, and so forth. The NIH CDC Program has been evaluated on a number of occasions: internal review in 1980, a University of Michigan Study in 1982, a Rand Corporation review in 1989, an IOM study in 1990, and most recently by a NIH working group in 1999 [Perry and Kalberer 1980; Wortman et al. 1982; Kanouse et al. 1989; IOM 1990; Leshner et al. 1999]. Concerns have regularly been expressed about panel selection to ensure 'balance and objectivity,' speaker selection that represents the range of work on the topic, representation of patient perspectives and more careful and systematic assessment of the quality and quantity of scientific evidence. Concerns have also been expressed about the time pressure to produce a statement in less than three days, and especially the lack of time for reflection or gathering of further information. Such concerns have in fact been behind some changes over time in the NIH CDC Program, and also behind the creation of different procedures at other kinds of consensus conferences, in both the national and the international scene.

Rolin (2009) stipulates the epistemic role outsiders to particular scientific communities can play. She argues that an epistemically responsible scientist has a duty to respond to outside criticism in certain circumstances insofar as it includes an appropriate challenge to her views. A meta-consensus taking contestability into account differs from both aggregated judgment – in supporting dynamical, diachronic interaction – and rational deliberation – avoiding groupthink via contestation. Obviously, contestability comes in degrees and is present to a greater or lesser extent in the existing formats for consensus-making.

Having pointed at the epistemic importance of considerations of adequacy and contestability, we can conclude that the role of the consensus conference is not merely choreographic or "just" a matter of policy. We highlighted clear epistemic roles, both in explicating adequacy and in assuring contestability – it is an epistemic role which Solomon misses in her critique;

> If the topic is not a scientific topic but is, instead, a matter of policy, the use of a consensus conference can be appropriate. The scientific community can tolerate—even celebrate— research disagreements. Policy decisions usually require the *joint action* of individuals, groups and nations. A well-negotiated consensus is widely thought of as the ideal foundation for joint action. So those European Consensus Conferences which consider questions of policy are more appropriately designed to attain their goals than, for example, the NIH CDC Program. (Solomon 2011, pp. 247–248)

4.5   Experts and Consensus-Making: John Beatty on the Two Moments of Consensus-Making

Whereas Solomon's work teaches us a lot on the "interface moment", John Beatty's focus is in the first place on the scientific experts establishing a consensus among themselves, the *academic consensus*. Obviously, the possible societal impact and consequences are taken into account – leading to some kind of self-censorship (cf. Beatty 2006) – but there is no consideration of an explicit *public* moment, during which an *interface consensus* would be established.

In his earlier work on experts (2006), Beatty already captures part of the tension between consensus making on the one hand and the intrinsic value of plurality on the other hand. Through a case study of the maximal admissible dose of radiation for humans, he concludes that craving consensus might widen the gap between expert and novice in two distinctive ways. First, what he calls simplification, entails that scientists instead of simply telling us what they know, they might tell us simply. In this manner, a lot of crucial information gets lost along the way. Second, what he identifies as the intentional withholding of information, means that scientists often agree amongst one another as to retain information from the public or silence discussions, which results in a distorted view of consensus amongst the public and nourishes the ill-conceived expectations they might have. Both pitfalls find their reasoning on either paternalistic or protective grounds, as Beatty elaborates. The former meaning that experts state that it might actually be in the public's advantage if they speak with one voice rather than with many, whereas the latter hints at the fact that experts, in this manner, could in fact guarantee that their status remains intact and can prohibit others from gaining the authority and trust to do their work.

Building on these striking insights on how scientific consensus is actually achieved, Beatty (together with Alfred Moore) works out an account of consensus formation that is partly procedural and partly substantive,[12] i.e. a notion of *deliberative acceptance*. In their paper 'Should we aim for consensus?' (2010), they start from an account of consensus-making set forth by Margaret Gilbert (1987). Gilbert captures a notion of what she calls joint acceptance: "A group jointly accepts *p* if and only if the individual members have openly agreed to let *p* stand as the position of the group" (Gilbert 1987, p. 194). Beatty and Moore emphasize two characteristics of this account of consensus. First, consensus understood in this sense tackles the notion on a rather different level: there is no talk of consensus on a certain proposition *p*, but consensus to let *p* stand as the position of the group. On *p* itself there could be considerable disagreement. Let us clarify this with a simple example. Suppose your faculty board wants to hire a new full-time professor in ethics, and after discussion and voting they opt to go with candidate A. You, however, preferred candidate B, based on the previous experiences she acquired and the

---

[12] In Sect. 4.6 we clarify in detail what they mean by both parts of the definition.

impression she gave during the interviews. Candidate A however is put forth as the department's choice. Now, in the same manner you can disagree as an expert on p, but yet again acknowledge the consensus recommending p (Beatty and Moore 2010, p. 206). Moreover, in Gilbert's terms, one is thought not to publicly disagree with the group opinion, of course one is not expected to lie, but any dissenting views should be rather carefully expressed (Beatty and Moore 2010, p. 207). Second, according to Beatty and Moore, defining consensus as such renders the notion meaningless. One can endorse a rather weakly defined notion as the consensus opinion, on which everyone agrees, but in such a case it is nothing more than an empty shell (Beatty and Moore 2010, p. 208).[13]

Beatty and Moore, develop their own notion, partly inspired by Gilbert, of consensus formation, i.e. *deliberative acceptance*: "A group deliberatively accepts p if and only if the individual members, based on the quality of their deliberation, have openly agreed to let p stand as the position of the group" (Beatty and Moore 2010, p. 209). As opposed to joint acceptance, this view allows for an explicit moment where dissenting opinions could be heard and noticed through deliberation (expanded with a system of voting when necessary). Beatty and Moore are convinced that their approach surpasses the difficulties set forth for Gilbert's account:

> Deemphasizing consensus on substantive issues (though not entirely), and stressing consensus on deliberative quality would not only take away the temptation to hide a persistent minority position, but would instead provide a good use for it. What better way to inspire confidence in a deliberative outcome than to show that (1) the position in question had been tested against a worthy alternative; (2) the minority felt that they had been heard, that they had been treated as deliberative equals; and (3) having been heard, even the minority agreed to let the position in question stand as the group's. (Beatty and Moore 2010, p. 209).

---

[13] An historical example arguing in favor of this remark is the consensus report (and table) published by Peter Mitchell to support his chemiosmosis hypothesis over the dominant chemical or direct-interaction coupling theory, to explain how and why ions move from an area of high concentration to an area of low concentration. Mitchell, however, presented a distorted view of consensus in the scientific discipline in 3 respects: (1) He does not identify all the expert members dealing with this topic, as this better fits his view of consensus on his hypothesis growing steadily over the years. (2) He ascribed some of the experts a wrong position. For example, the table mentioned experts being already halfly convinced that his route was the way to go, whereas it turned out they were actually convinced of his approach being half right. (3) He omits to specify the full extent of the cognitive content of consensus and forgets to show how it coincides with the views of the scientists. The consensus view he put forward seemed to be fairly evident, whereas upon careful examination it turned out that every scientist fills in the definition of chemiosmosis rather different. The consensus approach was thus based on a basic version of chemiosmosis, however, "the scientific content of this basic version was minimal; so much so that it could be and frequently was endorsed by those who described themselves and were described by others as strongly opposed to chemiosmosis as well as by those who claimed to be fervent supporters of the theory" (Gilbert and Mulkay 1984, p. 130). With Gilbert's understanding of consensus as joint acceptance, you might obtain situations like the Abilene paradox, where no one wants to "rock the boat", and, eventually, the consensus position that is accepted is counter to the position of every individual.

However, we think their account faces a couple of open problems. First, "let the position stand" is too passive to be able to capture the interaction between opinions and dissenting views. This phrasing omits the fact that in scientific and interface discussions there are not only persistent minority positions (sometimes there even might not be any position that convinces more than half of the participants), but in most occasions continually present minorities who are not that eager to just give in. This relates to our second objection, i.e. the position of the minority. Deliberative acceptance in a sense is aiming too high. According to this view, there will be a time when the minority has to admit that they were heard and that some kind of epistemic justice has occurred, that they were found to be unconvincing, and that they should correspondingly endorse the consensus position of the group. Although Beatty and Moore spell out this objection themselves, they find it unconvincing to aim lower (Beatty and Moore 2010, p. 209). Finally, moving from an academic consensus to an interface consensus, opens up the question what the responsibilities of the scientific expert are and what the responsibilities of society or policy-makers are, i.e. those that set-up expert committees and decide upon their functioning. As sketched out above, Beatty and Moore's account rather functions on the level of academic consensus. Interesting to see, however, would be how their account would tackle the issues raised above, e.g. how the minority-majority dynamics in the deliberation among experts could be affected in an interface moment – bringing up adequacy concerns and contestability.

Summarizing, Beatty and Moore focus on the formation of the academic consensus, keeping an eye on how the consensus could be sold to the public by the experts, and taking into account the expectations of the public (cf. Sect. 4.7), but there is no consideration of an explicit *public* moment, during which an *interface consensus* would be established. Neither is the epistemic contribution of interactions between the academic and the interface moment explored (an interaction in which minority positions might play an important role).

4.6 Consensus-Making and the Meta-Consensus II: A Social-Procedural Account of Scientific Consensus

In developing their account of consensus, Beatty and Moore rely on democratic theory, just like we have done before (see Van Bouwel 2009). We think this points at an important characteristic of consensus-making, in solving the tension between plurality and consensus, which is not always made explicit in accounts of consensus as knowledge-based: in both moments, there is a meta-consensus or a meta-agreement in play. As stipulated above, instead of focusing on consensus on the simple level, that is, as the result of alternative theories/models tested against one another leading to some consensus *outcome*, we could learn a lot focusing on the meta-consensus that stipulates the *procedure* to be followed. Understandings of consensus-making differ in how much weight they place on procedures relative to substantive considerations about the quality or characteristics of the outcomes of these processes. Let us elaborate this distinction further:

(a) Focusing on *outcome*, the substantive approach to consensus-making: Researchers agree on what they agree (in its ideal form mostly understood as a unanimity in which every participant comes to hold the same position for the same reasons) and the outcome satisfies certain conditions to assure that the consensus is right/correct and/or knowledge-based. Thus, there is a defined desirable outcome or decision (the outcome has to be right, living up to procedure-independent qualities), and in that sense, an implicit presumption of what a collective process or procedure has to generate qua collective decision; the existence of a consensus is presupposed. In this account, complete unanimity is not required, but only that if dissent exists, it is marginalized and suppressed (Miller 2013).

(b) Focusing on the *procedure*, the procedural approach to consensus: Researchers might agree on the procedure through which to aim for a collective decision/consensus. Call it a form of meta-agreement or meta-consensus, without specifying requirements on the substance, on the outcome, that this procedure eventually should produce. Here, there are no procedure-independent criteria to assess the quality of the correct outcome; it is the procedure itself that matters and that has to satisfy certain normative criteria. An outcome is legitimate if the collective decision-making procedure itself satisfies certain conditions and these conditions (the appropriateness of the procedures) might be satisfied in degrees (cf. infra) (Longino 2002, chapter 6).

(c) Focusing partly on *procedure* and partly on *outcome*: Both the procedures and the outcome should be correct. Beatty and Moore's account presented in Sect. 4.4 is a nice example: There is reference to substance in the act of accepting or letting the outcome stand. This acceptance might then be "based on the quality of your deliberation", which seems to bring it very close to a procedural view, but nevertheless omits to go all the way. According to this view, you might associate the idea of a substantive consensus with the idea of normative unanimity, that is, everybody coming to hold the same position for the same reasons. In much deliberative theory (Mansbridge et al. 2010, pp. 66, 68), it is thought that if a deliberative group cannot reach consensus in this sense, then the proper role of deliberation is simply to clarify and structure the disagreement, which sets the scene for a decision by some other (non-deliberative) method, usually a vote. Now what Beatty and Moore outline in the paper with the idea of joint acceptance and deliberative acceptance is a kind of consensus that is less than normative unanimity (in which scientists can speak as one without having to say that they were in full agreement), but more than simply the preferences of the participants combined under some decision rule, which need have no reference at all to substance.[14]

---

[14] We thank Alfred Moore for clarifying this.

Thus, the solution for the tension between plurality and consensus could be sought in some form of meta-consensus or meta-agreement. The resulting account of consensus will be a social one – not stipulating the characteristics the outcome should have, but stipulating the social procedure that has to be followed. Obviously, it is self-evident that an account of consensus is social. Consensus is always a product of sociality. However, we want to emphasize the parallel of our thinking in terms of a meta-consensus with *social accounts of objectivity*.[15] Another intuitive way to grapple the difference is to imagine when one calls a certain decision democratic in contemporary political theory: this is not because the decision or outcome of the procedure has certain intrinsic characteristics that make it democratic, but because itself is the result of going through a democratic procedure. Shifting the focus from the product to the epistemic processes resulting in an outcome, also implies that consensus comes in degrees, depending on the extent to which the procedure has been followed, repeated, etc.

The debate about *scientific consensus* then moves to consensus on epistemic procedures, i.e. finding a form of meta-consensus. Thus, the tension between scientific plurality and consensus is not tackled on the simple level, but on the meta-level. This is analogous to how democratic societies deal with value pluralism; the focus is not on getting rid of value pluralism, but on establishing a framework – a meta-consensus – within which pluralism can be dealt with satisfactorily. The meta-consensus can be one that prescribes rational deliberation (in line with models of deliberative democracy), or aggregation (stipulating a procedure for adding up the available views), or agonistic pluralism (developing a procedure or constellation – conflictual consensus – that wants to optimize the *epistemic fecundity* via agonism, cf. Van Bouwel 2009), etc.

4.7 Modifying the Public Understanding of Scientific Consensus

Establishing scientific consensus is highly valued by philosophers,[16] scientists and the public. The emergence of a scientific consensus replacing competing accounts is often interpreted as a proof of scientific progress and a marker of truth; ideally all scientific inquiry and debate would result in a consensus. Finding scientific

---

[15] The most well-known example here is Helen Longino's social account of objectivity (cf. Longino 1990, 2002). See also Douglas (2004) for a good analysis.

[16] There are also other philosophers that have dealt with the value of pluralism and consensus. A similar example as to the way we dealt with both terms in this chapter, is the recent work by Martin Carrier (2012). Carrier, in his analysis, clearly focuses on academic consensus and omits to consider the interface consensus. He zooms in on the epistemic attitude, an attitude that differentiates the scientific community from the broader society, as science allows to eventually reach consensus on any given topic. However, as we have mentioned above, persistent disagreement is also a characteristic of science.

consensus is then understood as a proof for the validity of a theory and – indirectly – of the public policy based on the consensus theory.

The back side of the coin is that the lack of scientific consensus often is used to undermine or criticize science and the public policy based on it (e.g., former US President Bush on climate change). When scientists agree, their results are taken more seriously than when they disagree, even though such an agreement or consensus might hinder scientific progress because of critical, heterodox theories not being taken seriously (e.g., the theory of continental drift was accepted by geologists only after 50 years of rejection, and the theory of helicobacter pylori as the cause of stomach ulcers, was at first widely rejected by the medical community).

These observations might question scientific consensus as an ideal or as the goal of inquiry and marker of truth; enforcing "consensus" might be dangerous or not desirable, hence the importance of scrutinizing carefully what is actually going on in establishing scientific consensus; i.e. which moments one can distinguish, the epistemic and non-epistemic value of those moments as well as the different procedural set-ups – just like we have been doing above in distinguishing the academic, interface and meta-consensus. Communicating this variety of formats to the public, helps qualifying the actual span of scientific consensus-making and the oracle like features it might sometimes have. Our reasoning is in line with Inmaculada de Melo-Martin and Kristen Intemann's recent paper, where they show, by analyzing conflicts on GMO's and climate change, that "focusing on dissent as a problematic activity sends the message to policy-makers and the public that any dissent undermines scientific knowledge" (de Melo-Martin and Intemann 2013, pp. 232–233). Encouraging and providing mechanisms of dissent can also be important to reassuring the public that the consensus view has undergone rigorous scrutiny. Events such as "climate-gate" reinforce the public perception that climate scientists are resistant to criticism and have a "bunker mentality" (Grundmann 2012).

Pointing at some of the undesirable effects too high expectations about consensus-making might have, we refer to Churchill's famous dictum: "Democracy is the worst form of government, except for all those other forms that have been tried from time to time." (from a House of Commons speech on November 11, 1947). Similarly, science and consensus-making mechanisms create fallible knowledge.

These insights taken together do not foreclose scientific consensus-making, but stress the need for a mentality change in society about what scientific research consists of and what it can entail for policy making. As such, "in a scientific community, different individuals can weigh evidence in different manners through the use of different standards. In the best case,[17] science puts forward a robust

---

[17] A sentiment shared by other researchers: "The idea of consensus in science does not imply the fact that all the scientists have internalized and agreed upon the truth of the statements that make up a certain consensus. In this sense, what is called a 'scientific consensus' in the literature can be the product of compromise, negotiation, and only under special circumstances a truly consensual resolution" (Martini 2011, p. 152).

consensus based on a research process that allows continued scrutiny, re-examination, and revision" (Oreskes 2004, pp. 369–370).[18]

4.8 Conclusions

Through our analysis we have argued in favor of the following claims:

(a) Consensus-making as discussed by philosophers of science, should be aware of the difference in aiming for an *academic consensus* or an *interface consensus* in science and society. A broader understanding of the different structures and functions of consensus-making helps us to see more nuances.

(b) The difficulties of achieving consensus understood as an unanimous outcome – a seldom-attained ideal stipulated by a range of criteria – should make us shift to a procedural approach in which the emphasis is not so much on establishing the consensus, but dealing with plurality in a consensual way, i.e., framed within a meta-consensus that agrees on how to disagree.

(c) Taking into account epistemic adequacy and contestability as important characteristics of sound epistemic processes, we questioned Solomon's account of consensus conferences as just being moments of deliberative choreographies, repeating work that has already been done by the aggregation of expert opinions.

(d) Solomon's idea of (what is the valuable) scientific consensus as, basically, an idea of *academic consensus* as we described it, holds on to an ideal which we also encounter among the public in general. According to us, it is too high an ideal, that eventually can be used against science; it is therefore more recommendable to think in terms of degrees of consensus and adequacy for the public addressed while keeping an eye on the variety of consensus-making formats.

Acknowledgements Research for this chapter was supported by subventions from the Research Foundation (FWO) – Flanders through research project G.0122.10. The authors would in particular like to thank Alfred Moore, Boaz Miller, Carlo Martini, Jan de Winter, Anna Leuschner, the anonymous reviewers and the audiences at TiLPS EPS seminar, EPSA13, VISU2013, SPSP2013, LOBSTER and the Bayreuth2012 workshop for their comments on previous versions of this chapter.

---

[18] This quote can be read, as Miller would probably do, saying that this is not always the case, still thinking that only consensus that has certain properties should be trusted. (based on personal communication with Boaz Miller) However, we read "in the best case" as pointing out the fact that in many cases no robust consensus will be found, but nevertheless consensus-seeking might be optimized to (1) acquire the best result possible, (2) prevent forced consensus being established, and (3) allow trust to be generated.

References

Baartmans, T., and L. Kosolosky. in print. *Tijdschrift voor Filosofie*. Groepsbeslissingen: kwaliteit, autoriteit en vertrouwen.

Beatty, J. 2006. Masking disagreement among scientific experts. *Episteme* 3(1-2): 52–67.

Beatty, J., and A. Moore. 2010. Should we aim for consensus? *Episteme* 7(3): 198–214.

Carrier, M. 2012. Values and objectivity in science: Value-ladenness, pluralism and the epistemic attitude. *Science and Education* 22(10): 2547–2568.

Churchill, W. 1947. House of Commons speech on Nov. 11, 1947.

De Melo-Martin, I., and K. Intemann. 2013. Scientific dissent and public policy: Is targeting dissent a reasonable way to protect sound policy decisions? *European Molecular Biology Organization Reports* 14(3): 231–235.

Douglas, H. 2004. The irreducible complexity of objectivity. *Synthese* 138(3): 453–473.

FDA. 2001. Ribavirin and chronic hepatitis C infection. *Consumer* 35(5): 3.

Gilbert, M. 1987. Modeling collective belief. *Synthese* 73(1): 185–204.

Gilbert, G.N., and M. Mulkay. 1984. *Opening Pandora's box: A sociological analysis of scientists' discourse*. Cambridge: Cambridge University Press.

Grundmann, R. 2012. The legacy of climategate: Revitalizing or undermining climate science and policy? *Wiley Interdisciplinary Reviews: Climate Change* 3(3): 281–288.

Hardwig, J. 1991. The role of trust in knowledge. *Journal of Philosophy* 88(12): 693–708.

Institute of Medicine (IOM). 1990. *Consensus development at NIH: Improving the program. Report of a study by a committee of the Institute of Medicine Council on Health Care Technology*. Washington, DC: National Academy Press.

Jorgensen, K.J., P.H. Zahl, and P.C. Gotzche. 2009. Overdiagnosis in organised mammography screening in Denmark. A comparative study. *BMC Women's Health* 9(1): 36.

Kanouse, D.E., R.H. Brook, and J.D. Winkler. 1989. *Changing medical practice through technology assessment: An evaluation of the National Institutes of Health Consensus Development Program*. Santa Monica: Rand Corporation.

Kosolosky, L. 2012. The intended window of epistemic opportunity: A comment on Miriam Solomon. In *Logic, philosophy and history of science in Belgium II*, ed. Bart Van Kerkhove, Thierry Libert, Geert Vanpaemel, and Pierre Marage. Brussel: Koninklijke Vlaamse Academie van België.

Leshner, A., et al. 1999. Report of the working group of the advisory committee to the director to review the office of medical applications of research. At http://www.nih.gov/about/director/060399a.htm. Accessed 8 June 2008.

Longino, H. 1990. *Science as social knowledge*. Princeton: Princeton University Press.

Longino, H. 2002. *The fate of knowledge*. Princeton: Princeton University Press.

Mansbridge, J., et al. 2010. The place of self-interest and the role of power in deliberative democracy. *The Journal of Political Philosophy* 18(1): 64–100.

Martini, C. 2011. *Consensus and disagreement in small committees*. Phd-thesis. ISBN: 978-94-6191-092-9.

Miller, B. 2013. When is consensus knowledge based? *Synthese* 190(7): 1293–1316.

National Institutes of Health. 1994. Helicobacter pylori in peptic ulcer disease. *NIH consensus statement*. February 7–9, 12(1):1–23. Available online: http://consensus.nih.gov/1994/1994HelicobacterPyloriUlcer094PDF.pdf. Accessed on July 7, 2014.

National Institutes of Health. 2000. Osteoporosis prevention, diagnosis, and therapy. *NIH consensus statement* 17 (1):1–45. Available online: http://consensus.nih.gov/2000/2000Osteoporosis111PDF.pdf. Accessed on July 7, 2014.

National Institutes of Health. 2002. Management of hepatitis C. *NIH consensus statement* 19(3): 1–46. Available online: http://consensus.nih.gov/2002/2002HepatitisC2002116PDF.pdf.

National Institutes of Health. 2008. *NIH consensus development conference statement on management of hepatitis B* 25(2):1–29. Available online: http://consensus.nih.gov/2008/hepbstatement.pdf. Accessed on July 7, 2014.

National Institutes of Health. Website on the Consensus Development Conference Program. Available online: http://www.consensus.nih.gov. Accessed on July 7, 2014.

National Institutes of Health: Official Site, Web Site: Available online: http://www.nih.gov/. Accessed on July 7, 2014.

Oreskes, N. 2004. Science and public policy: What's proof got to do with it? *Environmental Science and Policy* 7: 369–383.

Perry, S., and J.T. Kalberer. 1980. The NIH consensus-development program and the assessment of health-care technologies: The first two years. *The New England Journal of Medicine* 303(3): 169–172.

Primiero, G., and L. Kosolosky. 2013. The semantics of untrustworthiness. *Topoi.* doi:10.1007/s11245-013-9227-2.

Reiss, J. 2010. In favour of a Millian proposal to reform biomedical research. *Synthese* 177: 427–447.

Rolin, K. 2009. Scientific knowledge: A stakeholder theory. In *The social sciences and democracy*, ed. J. Van Bouwel, 95–119. Basingstoke: Palgrave Macmillan.

Schwetz, B.A. 2001. From the food and drug administration. *The Journal of the American Medical Association* 286(10): 1166.

Solomon, M. 2006. Groupthink vs. the wisdom of the crowds: The social epistemology of deliberation and dissent. *The Southern Journal of Philosophy* 44(S1): 28–42.

Solomon, M. 2007. The social epistemology of NIH consensus conferences. In *Establishing medical reality: Methodological and metaphysical issues in philosophy of medicine*, ed. H. Kincaid and J. McKitrick. Dordrecht: Springer.

Solomon, M. 2011. Group judgment and the medical consensus conference. In *Handbook of the philosophy of science: Philosophy of medicine*, ed. D. Gabbay and J. Woods, 239–254. San Diego: North Holland.

Sunstein, C.R. 2006. Deliberating groups versus prediction markets (or Hayek's challenge to Habermas). *Episteme: A Journal of Social Epistemology* 3(1): 192–213.

Van Bouwel, J. 2009. The problem with(out) consensus. The scientific consensus, deliberative democracy and agonistic pluralism. In *The social sciences and democracy*, ed. J. Van Bouwel, 121–142. Basingstoke: Palgrave Macmillan.

Wortman, P.M., A. Vinokur, and L. Schrest. 1982. *Evaluation of NIH consensus development process*. Ann Arbor: University of Michigan. NIH-80-301.

Wylie, A. 2006. Socially naturalized norms of epistemic rationality: Aggregation and deliberation. *The Southern Journal of Philosophy* 44(S1): 43–48.

Part II
Frameworks of Consensus

Chapter 5
Judgments About the Relevance of Evidence in the Context of Peer Disagreements and Practical Rationality

Amir Konigsberg

Abstract This chapter addresses a core topic in the recent debates about disagreement between peers, namely whether and how you ought to revise your beliefs if you discover that you are disagreeing with a peer – a colleague, fellow expert, or simply someone that you have reason to believe is just as competent as you are on the matter at hand. The topic of disagreement and more specifically the problem of how to respond to disagreement, is relevant in many areas in life where the same information is available to different people that come to hold different beliefs in regard to what that information *means*. The topic also bears on questions relating to epistemic warrant, namely to what extent one's beliefs can be justified by evidence, to first-person conviction, epistemic humility, normative epistemology, and self-servicing beliefs.

In this chapter I approach this topic differently to how it has been approached in the recent literature. I believe that there is a difference between addressing the disagreement problem hypothetically, or in theory, as an abstraction of *a case of disagreement*, and regarding this same problem when it is considered from a *practical* point of view, in consideration of features that characterize *actual* cases of disagreement. I believe that the core difference between these two cases relates to judgments relating to the relevance of second-order evidence (roughly, evidence about the viability of inferences made from what we regularly treat as evidence). In actual cases of disagreement, as opposed to hypothetical abstractions of such cases, what is or isn't relevant depends on how uncertain the situation is seen to be by the person in question. And this depends on the level of confidence as perceived by that person's subjective first-person judgment. In what follows I show that subjective confidence about first-order judgments can swamp second-order evidence – against a plausible view that it shouldn't. And I believe that this is a significant problem in practical rationality that is brought into focus by disagreement problems. I focus on the problem of *relevancy judgments* and how they relate to the calibration of

A. Konigsberg (✉)
The Center for the Study of Rationality and Interactive Decision Theory, The Hebrew University of Jerusalem, Jerusalem, Israel
e-mail: amirkonigsberg@gmail.com

© Springer International Publishing Switzerland 2014
C. Martini, M. Boumans (eds.), *Experts and Consensus in Social Science*,
Ethical Economy 50, DOI 10.1007/978-3-319-08551-7_5

first-person judgments with statistical data, and I demonstrate how this impinges on disagreements when these are considered from the first-person perspective.

5.1 Introduction

Recent debates dealing with the epistemic significance of peer disagreement have sought to provide responses to cases in which peers disagree about the epistemic import of a shared body of evidence.[1] Various responses have been suggested in the literature.[2] The problem, as typically addressed in the literature, takes the following general form:

If persons A and B are epistemic peers – meaning roughly that it is equally probable that A and B will be correct on matters relating to the domain in which they are peers – and on a particular unexpected occasion they happen to find out that they disagree about whether a particular proposition P (pertaining to that domain) is true given the evidence that is equally available to them both, and assuming that neither party has any independent reason to discount the dissenting party's conclusion, they ought to respond to this discovery ... *in such and such a way.*

The responses to this problem in the literature vary, and can roughly be divided into three types of response: (1) the *bootstrap* response; (2) the *conciliatory* response, and (3) the *egalitarian* response. I think that some of these responses have considerable appeal. But I also think that some make sense theoretically, but do not make sense from a practical point of view, and that others are simply unreasonable. All the same, I do not believe that the goal of establishing *which* of these responses is better, as a good deal of the recent debate has been focused on doing, actually address the important but understated problem of practical rationality that underlies the disagreement problem stated above.

Customarily, the problem of disagreement asks about the appropriate response (typically the response of a peer) upon encountering a disagreement between peers. The literature offers different solutions to the problem, each of which has more or less normative appeal. Yet none of these solutions seems to engage with what seems to be the *real* problem of disagreement. It is my aim in this chapter to highlight what the real problem of disagreement is. It is, roughly, the problem of deciding *whether* a revisionary tactic is appropriate following the discovery of disagreement, as well as deciding *which* revisionary tactic is appropriate. This non-standard approach to the disagreement problem exposes a slippery and inevitable difficulty that any discussion of disagreement ought to deal with. Once recognized, the real problem

---

[1] Another subject matter in the literature on disagreement is whether responses to peer disagreement ought to be the same (i.e., should entail the same revisionary response) in all domains. This question is discussed in Konigsberg 2013a.

[2] Such as the Equal Weight View (Elga 2007), the Total Evidence View (Kelly 2009), the Common Sense View (Enoch 2010) as well as a number of other closely related approaches (Feldman 2006, 2007; Christensen 2007; Matheson 2009; Moss 2011).

of disagreement reflects on the standard question addressed in the literature about *which* revisionary tactic is appropriate for dealing rationally with disagreement. The problem also generalizes to broader problems in practical rationality.

The above-mentioned approaches (1–3 above) are characterized by the different tactics that they propose for dealing with disagreement. But these tactics only appear to be relevant after the truly hard work of deciding *whether* they are relevant in each actual case of disagreement has been done. And this, I believe, is a huge problem that has not been adequately recognized in the literature or has even largely been missed until now. It is, in a word, *the problem of judgments about relevancy*.

The epistemic significance of this problem extends beyond debates surrounding disagreement, since relevancy judgments involve the subjective appreciation of evidence made about the reliability of inferences made from evidence. It is my aim here to draw attention to this general problem which, I believe, also lies at the heart of debates surrounding disagreement. It is my contention that *actual* cases of disagreement, as opposed to *possible* cases of disagreement, must deal with this inevitable situation.

The chapter will proceed in two stages. In the next section I outline what I take to be the real problem of disagreement, setting forth my core argument. But I will start with some preliminaries. After that I will present three approaches that I take to characterize the solutions that have been proposed in the literature. In the course of doing so I will show why most of these do not address the real problem of disagreement. But I will also suggest which of the approaches in the literature is most plausible in view of its partial recognition of the underlying difficulty brought about by the inescapability of relevancy judgments. My foremost aim in this chapter is to highlight a fundamental difficulty relating to first-person judgments about the relevance of second-order information – roughly, information which is applicable to specific cases by virtue of their location in a broader statistical framework. I aim to demonstrate how this difficulty impinges on actual situations where revisionary responses to disagreement are called for.

5.2   The Real Problem of Disagreement – *Setting the Stage*

The crux of the matter lies in a practical paradox of sorts, which is inevitable. This paradox relates to judgments about evidence made from subjective standpoints. Before I present this practical paradox I will start by clarifying what I mean by disagreement.

5.2.1   *Disagreements Between Ordinary People*

Disagreements as I shall refer to them here are situations in which *people* disagree. More specifically, these types of disagreements involve cases where one person finds out that another person, typically someone whose relevant epistemic capabilities are similar, holds a different opinion, view, or belief on the same matter.[3] The fact that I will be referring to ordinary people in this context is important, and I make note of it here because it imparts that I wish to relate to the normative question of how *human* reasoners ought to respond to disagreements in situations that are characterized by uncertainty about who or what is correct. This approach contrasts to another, prevalent in the economic as well as the philosophical literature, in which rational agents rather than human reasoners are the focus.[4] The rational behavior of rational agents is typically different to that of human reasoners, and so as to set the stage for addressing the problem, the distinction must be made.

5.2.2   A Brief Note on Disagreements in the Economic Literature

In the economic literature there has been an ongoing debate since the mid-1970s surrounding the question of disagreement.[5] The core of this debate focuses on the possibility of rational disagreement between rational agents. The question posed is whether it is possible that agents who are expected to conditionalize on information in the same way, can agree to disagree (Aumann 1976). The debate considers whether it is possible for rational agents to disagree *rationally*.

In the cases of disagreement referred to in the economic literature the types of agents referred to are *not* human agents. And the rationality that is attributed to these agents is perhaps *not* human rationality. Human rationality, in the context of disagreement, relates to human reasoners that encounter evidence to which they know that they may respond imperfectly. The problem of disagreement is thus located in the wider context of human fallibility and regards disagreements as opportunities for corrective measures aimed at mitigating erroneous consequences of imperfect reasoning.

---

[3] While opinions, views, and beliefs may suggest different meanings, each suited more than the other for a particular context; I use them here interchangeably as referring to what a person regards as true.

[4] By rational agents I have in mind something similar to what Thaler and Sunstein have recently referred to as *Econs*. See (Thaler and Sunstein 2008).

[5] See for instance (Aumann 1976) and (Geanakoplos and Polemarchakis 1982; Cave 1983; Moses and Nachum 1990; Rubinstein and Wolinsky 1990; Hanson 2003; Dégremont and Roy 2009; Hansen and Cowen 2004; Milgrom and Stokey 1982).

5.2.3   Human Imperfection and Its Implications for Practical Reasoning Problems

There are two critical senses in which human imperfection impinges on disagreements. The first relates to the gathering of information, the second to inferring conclusions from it. People's capacities in both these areas are limited, and they commonly make mistakes. In the course of my discussion I will assume that people are typically aware that they make mistakes – that we know that we are not normally capable of taking all or perhaps unlimited information into account when we deliberate in uncertain conditions. Moreover, we are normally also aware of the fact that when we do possess information that is relevant to our beliefs, our responses – characteristically the inferences that we make from this information – are often imperfect. And by 'imperfect' I have in mind, approximately, three things.

5.2.4   Imperfection and Reasoning

Firstly, when people infer conclusions from evidence, however limited or encompassing this evidence may be, they are not always correct in what they infer. And people commonly recognize this about themselves. What this actually means is that they recognize that their reasoning is error prone, and thus imperfect.

Secondly, while people generally know that their reasoning is error prone, they do not always recognize the occasions in which it is so. Because of this, people often think they are right when they are wrong, and therefore incorrect reasoning sometimes goes unrecognized.

Thirdly, because they know that they may sometimes be wrong about what they believe, and because they also know that they do not always recognize the occasions when this is so, people should not always be certain that what they believe is correct. Indeed, it appears that in general we ought to have some reservations about the viability of our responses, particularly when they encounter dissent from an esteemed counterpart or a fellow expert.

5.2.5   When Subjective Credence Plays Against Facts of the Matter

In many situations of uncertainty, evidence may be more or less convincing, and this seems to play subjective credences against perhaps unknown facts of the matter. All the human reasoner has to go by is his subjective credence, which is assumed to mirror the strength of the evidence that he has. In cases such as this, an individual's subjective flaws as an evidence evaluator prescribe some type of risk mitigating strategy so that inferences whose impact on credence is partly subjective, can be weighed against some type of objective standard that is not based on the same error prone reasoning.

5.2.6   First-Order and Second-Order Evidence

A helpful distinction has been made in the literature between two kinds of evidence.[6] The distinction provides a convenient taxonomy for considering corrective standards for mitigating erroneous tendencies in reasoning. The distinction is between first-order evidence and second-order evidence and it can be understood as making a point about two kinds of epistemically relevant considerations, or evidence.

First-order evidence refers to the kind of evidence the presence of which can increase or decrease subjective credence in a particular proposition. And by increase, I mean that it can make one more confident about the proposition than before – either by moving one's belief towards that expressed by the proposition, or by strengthening one's belief. In the same way, first-order evidence can decrease one's confidence too. Moreover, if first-order evidence is epistemically insignificant, it may neither increase nor decrease credence.

The notion of second-order evidence refers to evidence that bears on whether one's beliefs, or the credences that one has assigned, are likely to be correct.[7] For our purposes what is entailed by first-order evidence is partly subjective because credences that are based on first-order evidence are estimates of a proposition's truth value, based on subjective assessments of first-order evidence. Credences might appear precise because they are usually expressed in numerical form, but let's remember that credences are people's estimates of truth values, expressed as probabilities. As opposed to first-order evidence, which usually relates to a person's present judgment, second-order evidence is typically evidence that is based on past epistemic performance, or experience, and as such does not depend on corroboration by present judgment.

Here is an example illustrating this distinction. The first-order evidence (FOE) that I encounter may be the Candlestick in the Hall, which supports my belief that Colonel Mustard did it (P): $<FOE \vdash P>$, or else it increases credence in the belief that he did it. The second-order evidence (SOE) that I possess may be prior knowledge that in the past, when I inferred *who* was guilty on the basis of weapon and location alone (FOE), I was wrong 70 % of the time. In this case second-order evidence is the knowledge that I have about my past performance in inferring conclusions in similar conditions (using the same variables).[8] It tells me how likely it is that my inference – e.g., $<FOE \vdash P>$, is correct.

In the context of disagreements between peers, first-order evidence will be the evidence that each peer encounters and which consequently leads each to believe as

---

[6] Kelly (2009), Christensen (2007), and Feldman (2006) also refer to this distinction.

[7] Compare Kelly's discussion of Downward Epistemic Push (Kelly 2009, sec. 5.3).

[8] Second-order evidence, conceived as I am presently suggesting, provides information about the likelihood of some event, outcome or possibility in some general population of events, outcomes, or possibilities. It may take many different forms and prior experience or performance is only one such form.

he does in the first-place. Therefore if the disagreement is, for instance, between weather forecasters, and concerns the weather forecast for tomorrow, first-order evidence is the evidence on which each person bases his belief about tomorrow's weather. More generally, we might think of this as the type of evidence that is normally needed for a weather forecaster to make up his mind about tomorrow's weather, prior, that is, to finding out what his peer believes about it. Thus first-order evidence in this context may perhaps be temperature maps (TM), atmospheric factors (AF), and other metrological features (MF) on which weather forecasters typically base their predictions. Let E denote a particular piece of evidence. In this case a prediction based on FOE will look like this: $<ETM; EAF; EMF \vdash P>$.

Second-order evidence will typically be evidence that relates to the belief-forming circumstances in which conclusions are inferred from first-order evidence. This may for instance include considerations about how likely it is that the inferences made from first-order evidence are correct. In disagreement problems, second-order evidence will characteristically relate to prior knowledge about a person's competence in inferring conclusions from first-order evidence (typically stated in probabilities based on prior performance), or perhaps knowledge about the person's susceptibility to error.

The widely consensual position in the literature is that in reasoning problems that involve first and second-order evidence, subjective credences that are based on first-order evidence ought to be balanced by probabilities derived from second-order evidence based on past performance (in the same way circumstantial indicators in Bayesian reasoning problems are weighed against base-rate information). The general contention is that not to take into account second-order evidence, usually prior probabilities, where these are informative and thus epistemically relevant to the assessment of the viability of present evidence, is a failure of reasoning. To be more specific, it is a failure to consider objective – i.e., second-order as well as subjective – i.e., first-order – factors, both of which are of epistemic value. Otherwise put, to only consider first-order evidence and not to consider second-order evidence is a failure to consider *all* the relevant evidence.

This insight has been expressed in the literature. Kelly, for instance, articulates it as follows: "what it is reasonable to believe about the world on the basis of one's evidence is constrained by what it is reasonable to believe *about* one's evidence" (Kelly 2009, sec. 5.3). So too, Christensen notes that "the rationality of first-order beliefs cannot in general be divorced from the rationality of certain second-order beliefs that bear on the epistemic status of those first-order beliefs" (Christensen 2007, 18). To apply this insight to our previous example, this would mean that if, after encountering the Candlestick in the Hall I infer that Colonel Mustard did it, without considering that second-order evidence suggests that my inference that Colonel Mustard did it is 70 % likely to be wrong, I would be neglecting relevant and thus epistemically valuable evidence.

5.2.7   Theoretical and Practical Prescriptions

The prescription to consider second-order evidence in conjunction with first-order evidence appears to be unproblematic in theory. In situations of uncertainty, second-order evidence – usually prior probabilities – should be weighed against subjective likelihoods derived from first-order evidence, typically in accordance with Bayes' rule.[9] But while in theory this appears unproblematic and straightforward, there seems to be a difficulty in realizing this prescription in practice.

Because the normative prescription is that second-order evidence ought to be incorporated in judgment in situations of uncertainty, it is subjective judgment that is responsible for determining a situation *as* uncertain, and consequently for determining *whether* second-order evidence is relevant as a risk-mitigating measure for addressing this uncertainty. But because determining whether a situation is uncertain depends, at least in part, on how confident the person is about first-order evidence, it can make the subjective judgment about *whether* second-order evidence is relevant dependent on the very unlawful outcome it is there to mitigate. And this is what paves the way to the real problem that a person that encounters first-order evidence appears to face.

The reason this is a practical rather than a theoretical problem is because in theory there is no apparent difficulty of incorporating second-order evidence in judgments about first-order evidence; in these kinds of theoretical cases, any judgment based on first-order evidence will be weighed against the second-order evidence that applies to that judgment. Why? Well because this is the normative thing to do; second-order evidence *is* the means by which an individual judgment is put in the context of passed judgments and thus undergoes statistical corroboration. It is what is needed so that the viability of an individual judgment can be properly assessed. But in practice, whether or not second-order evidence applies to an individual judgment depends on how uncertain the person is or how compelling first-order evidence appears to be. If first-order evidence is compelling, second-order evidence may be taken to be irrelevant or inapplicable to that judgment because statistical corroboration appears unnecessary or inappropriate. Hence second-order evidence can be regarded as more or less applicable depending on the diagnostic value of individual judgment, which it was initially aimed to corroborate.

The normative problem that I am trying to outline is a problem of disagreement between peers considered from a practical point of view. And it is importantly different to theoretical abstractions of such disagreements. In theory, if you and I are peers and we disagree (even though each of us is confident about what we

---

[9] Bayes's rule, or theorem, is a rule for operating on numerically expressed probabilities to revise a prior probability (in other words, the base-rate) into a posterior probability after new data have been observed. According to the theorem, the posterior probability for event H1 *after* data D is observed and accounted for is: $p(\mathrm{H1}|\mathrm{D}) = p(\mathrm{H1})\,p(\mathrm{D}|\mathrm{H1})/p(\mathrm{D})$, where $p(\mathrm{H1})$ is the prior probability assigned to H1 *before* D is observed.

believe), second-order evidence about our peerhood is the means by which we locate ourselves in a statistical framework. The fact that we may find first-order evidence compelling seems to be neither here nor there; because disagreement exists between the two of us, and we are equally competent reasoners, second-order evidence must be used, since second-order evidence will have to be judged relevant to the case at hand in some sense and to some degree. In this case the question that remains is how to deal with first-order and second-order evidence in relation to each other. And this is what has traditionally been debated in the literature. But in practice, if you regard first-order evidence as sufficiently compelling, you will probably not regard the evidential situation as uncertain. And as such, the corroboration of your belief with second-order evidence may seem irrelevant or even damaging to your subjective evaluation. In such a case, the fact that your peer disagrees may be evidence in favor of their being wrong. But it is important to see that even if, in such a case, you do not regard your situation as uncertain this does not mean that you are denying that there is a case of peer disagreement. You're not. Peer disagreement can still be a problem even if you yourself are confident about the first-order evidence. I mention this here because one might object that if you find that there is no uncertainty, then this is in fact a denial that there is a case of peer disagreement. But this only seems to be the case if one assumes that an agent's uncertainty about first-order evidence alone merits his using second-order evidence to corroborate his belief.

5.2.8 Practical Problems with Theoretical Prescriptions in Disagreement Problems

The practical difficulty with implementing the normative prescription to weigh first-order evidence against second-order evidence in situations of uncertainty is that from the first-person standpoint second-order evidence often has ambiguous implications. To see this, consider a hypothetical situation. Assume that I know that based on past performance I am 70 % likely to be correct in my predictions. On first thought, I can take this to mean that there is a 70 % chance that my next prediction will be correct and a 30 % chance that it won't. Now, having made my next prediction there appears to be no way for me to ascertain, independent of relying on my present judgment and the various considerations that support it, whether my prediction falls in the positive or negative percentiles of chance. That is to say, I have no way of knowing whether my present belief is an instance affirming the 70 % chance that I am correct or the 30 % that I am not. My probability of being correct, based on past performance, is second-order evidence the inclusion of which appears to depend on my present level of confidence about first-order evidence. And if I my confidence is high, I may regard my present judgment as being an affirming instance of the positive likelihood of my being correct (in line with how second-order evidence can be understood), rather than an uncertainty in need of corroboration. And because, on this interpretation, *I am* correct, there is no need to weigh my present level of confidence against second-order evidence.[10] Note that I am not suggesting that I would necessarily be justified in neglecting the 70:30 base-rate. Rather, what I am suggesting is that the significance of the 70:30 base rate can mean different things in terms of epistemic justification.

This suggests that aside from the normative prescription to weigh first-order evidence against second-order evidence I appear to also have a normative obligation to treat first-order evidence in accordance with the level of epistemic warrant that it provides. It does after all seem to be uncontroversial that different evidential situations warrant varying levels of confidence. And it seems that proper incorporation of new information about these situations depends on the epistemic warrant that is provided by first-order evidence. A person in a first-person standpoint may consequently be faced with two, possibly conflicting, normative prescriptions, from which the suspected practical paradox arises:

(1) Respond to first-order evidence in accordance with how convincing it appears to be.
(2) Mitigate the risk of being wrong by weighing first-order evidence against second-order evidence.

As noted, the practical problem here is that there is no independent way to ascertain which prescription – (1) or (2) – applies, and there is no immediately obvious or straightforward way of combining them. And this situation, in which we are asked about an individual's appropriate response once conflict with a peer is discovered, appears to be reflective of a class of epistemically ambiguous situations in which the crux seems to lie in an individual's ability to determine the appropriate revisionary response to the situation. And because doing so is largely a matter of how confident the individual is about the first-order evidence, the inclusion of second-order evidence seems to depend, at least in part, on the selfsame risk-prone reasoning it is there to mitigate. And this, it seems, is inevitable. As long as subjective judgment is responsible for deciding *whether* second-order evidence is relevant, it doesn't appear to matter that second-order evidence is independent of current judgment, the risk of fallible subjective judgments remains.

5.2.9   The Real Problem of Disagreement – A Practical Paradox

If the normative prescription is that an individual in a decision circumstance ought to decide whether or not second-order evidence is relevant to that circumstance, he

---

[10] Kelly states of cases such as these that "one's first-order evidence not only confirms the belief in question; it also confirms a proposition to the effect that it is reasonable for one to hold that belief" (Kelly 2009, sec. 5.3).

must have the ability to distinguish when it is and when it isn't relevant. We assume that this is a function of how ambiguous the evidence is, perhaps how weak the evidence is (Enoch 2010; Kelly 2005), or how uncertain he is about what he has inferred from the evidence. In each case it is on the basis of such considerations that the individual deems second-order evidence relevant or irrelevant. And this seems to lead to a situation where the judgment of relevance has no independent evidence to go by. Hence theoretically, Bayes rule may well offer a precise way to weigh beliefs, and philosophers writing about disagreement may well make suggestions about which responses are appropriate for peers that encounter conflicting beliefs. But tactics such as these only seem to be relevant *after* the hard work of deciding relevancy has been done, and this, as I have tried to show, is theoretically an underdescribed problem that I believe has largely been missed until now.[11]

5.3 Responses in the Literature

I believe that responses to peer disagreement in the recent philosophical literature can be divided into three kinds. In the next section I will address each of the approaches in the literature in relation to the problem highlighted in Sect. 5.2. Before doing so I will sketch a pseudo-particularized example of disagreement on the basis of which the plausibility of each of the approaches can be assessed.

5.3.1 A Case of Peer Disagreement

Jill and Jack are two equally ranked chess masters. As it happens, Jill and Jack have other things in common aside from sharing the same title and rank at chess. They have both been playing chess for the same number of years and they have won the same number of games, at equally ranked tournaments, against equally classed players, using similar game strategies. Additionally, Jill and Jack also know all of this about each other.

On a particular occasion, Jill and Jack are each independently asked by an examiner which color has the advantage in a particular chessboard arrangement. Jill tells the examiner that she thinks that White has the advantage; Jack tells the examiner that he thinks that Black has the advantage. Then each of them is told by the examiner about what the other thinks. What should Jill and Jack do in regard to their beliefs after being given this information, assuming that is, that neither one of

---

[11] Elsewhere I discuss the epistemic significance of relevancy judgments. In this context see also Maya Bar-Hillel's seminal "The base rate fallacy in probability judgments" (Bar-Hillel 1980), which focuses on relevancy judgments in establishing whether or not base rates ought to be incorporated in probability judgments. See also: (Bar-Hillel and Fischhoff 1981; Bar-Hillel 1982; Welsh and Navarro 2012; Barbey and Sloman 2007; Ajzen 1977).

them has any non-question-begging reason to think that the other happens to be reasoning in sub-standard conditions – that, for instance, the other isn't drunk, dazed, tired, or anything of the sort? More specifically, should the discovery that they believe differently make either of them lose confidence in their own beliefs?

5.3.2   The Bootstrap Approach[12]

The bootstrap approach with regards to disagreement makes use of a person's own reasoning about the issue at hand to support his revised reasoning about the issue at hand. It suggests that because P is true it doesn't matter that a peer disagrees about this, *because* P *is* true, and one's peer is therefore wrong. This is blatantly question-begging reasoning. And it is reasoning that fails to appreciate the epistemic significance of disagreement.[13] Moreover, for disagreement to have no epistemic impact is in fact a failure to appreciate it as relevant evidence.[14]

The bootstrap response ignores second-order evidence concerning peerhood and contends that the appropriate response to the discovery of disagreement is to act in accordance with what first-order evidence suggests.[15] This would mean that Jill would take her belief that White has the advantage to support the belief that Jack is wrong *because* White has the advantage.[16] She would thus *not* adjust her credence in White having the advantage because from her standpoint she has no reason to. Her disagreement with Jack appears to be at once both epistemically

---

[12] Elga (2007) also discusses the problem of bootstrapping, as do Kelly (2009) and Enoch (2010). I do not discuss either of these views regarding bootstrapping here.

[13] This is why David Enoch has fittingly called it the "*I don't care view*" (Enoch 2010, p. 15); the view is attributed to Thomas Kelly (2005). Neither Enoch nor Kelly contend that this is a plausible response to disagreement, largely because it completely ignores the epistemic significance and corrective role that other people's opinions can have on our own judgment.

[14] Matheson presents a novel argument for why evidence of disagreement is, after all, *relevant* evidence. According to Matheson, if, to continue our chess example, Jill were to ask Jack which color he thinks has the advantage on the present chess-board position, she would be justified in believing Jack on this matter, since she relies on Jack (in fact she relies on Jack on these matters as much as she relies on herself). If this is so then Jack's belief *does* provide Jill with evidence that Black has the advantage. And it is therefore evidence for Jill regardless of what she believes (Matheson 2009).

[15] In doing so it violates what Christensen has recently called "independence": "In evaluating the epistemic credentials of another's expressed belief about P, in order to determine how (or whether) to modify my own belief about P, I should do so in a way that doesn't rely on the reasoning behind my initial belief about P" (Christensen 2011).

[16] This is someone reminiscent of Kelly's view according to which a disagreement is already an indication that asymmetry exists between peers; the fact that there is disagreement (and assuming epistemic permissiveness is not permitted) already indicates that someone is right and someone is wrong. And supposedly, the one who got it right should *not* revise his beliefs (Kelly 2005). See also Enoch for a critical evaluation of Kelly's early view (Enoch 2010).

insignificant, *because he is wrong* and thus what he thinks is irrelevant, and misguiding, because he is *wrong.*[17]

The bootstrap approach is normally referred to as a limit case expressing the tempting appeal of the kind of unwarranted reasoning that unregulated internal standards for justification can sometimes give rise to.[18] All the same, what characterizes the bootstrap approach is that it only lets subjective credence in relation to first-order evidence influence its judgment. Second-order evidence has no effect. The bootstrap approach is especially dangerous because the person using the bootstrap approach may well argue that his tactic *is* to use the outputs of first-order evidence *and* second-order evidence but that occasionally the output of first-order evidence overrides the output of second-order evidence and thus makes it *irrelevant.*

What seems to be the core problem with bootstrapping is that second-order evidence is relevant after all, even in those cases where it is supposedly swamped by the epistemic force of first-order evidence. What makes it relevant is that the viability of any single judgment that belongs to a statistical data set of similar judgments ought to be established in reference to that data set, or, more specifically, it ought to be weighed against second-order evidence pertaining to it. Nonetheless, what is intuitively appealing about bootstrapping, is that whether a single judgment belongs to a particular data set will depend on the level of certainty with regards to the case at hand. If there is uncertainty, then corroboration is in order. If there isn't uncertainty, or if the degree of uncertainty is small, then this may merit exclusion from the data set to which such an instance would otherwise belong.

5.3.3 The Conciliatory Approach

The conciliatory approach is probably the most intuitively reasonable approach because it appreciates the epistemic significance of disagreement and respects the corrective role that other people's beliefs can have on individual reasoning that is often wrong. This approach recognizes both the normative requirement to respect the epistemic force of first-order evidence and the normative requirement to

---

[17] This line of thought is somewhat reminiscent of Kripke's dogmatism paradox. Gilbert Harman transmitted Kripke's Dogmatism Paradox (Harman 1973), which is also presented in revised form in (Kripke 2011). See also Kelly's treatment of the paradox in relation to disagreement and higher-order evidence (Kelly 2008).

[18] It is, in this context, sometimes referred to as the Extra Weight View. See Elga 2007; Kelly 2009; Enoch 2010. In a wider context, the bootstrap approach disregards the awareness that people normally have of their own fallibility and the corrective role that they attribute to other people's opinions as a means for arriving at better conclusions. It grants first-person conviction about first-order evidence a justificatory role that is normally attributed to independent standards. In so doing it uses circular reasoning to bootstrap the justification of a belief to conviction about it. In itself, this doesn't necessarily pose a problem, yet once relevant second-order evidence is available, dismissing it altogether is wrong.

consider second-order evidence when things are uncertain. Accordingly, that Jack believes differently to Jill about what color has the advantage in the present alignment of the pieces on the board *is* epistemically significant evidence and should be incorporated into Jill's response once she finds out what Jack believes. In fact, recognizing that Jack believes differently ought to make Jill doxastically shift in the direction of Jack's belief (Matheson 2009).

The conciliatory approach contends that Jill's confidence in White being advantageously positioned should be revised following her discovery of Jack's belief. But it does not state *how* it should be revised, or more specifically, to what degree.[19] The answer to this question seems to depend on how *relevant* Jill believes Jack's belief is for her revised response. It depends on the measure of epistemic significance that she grants it.

We shall return to the conciliatory approach momentarily, after examining the egalitarian approach. In the meantime let us note that the merit of the conciliatory approach appears to be that it recognizes that what an equally competent person believes *is* relevant evidence. Moreover, it prevents bootstrapped dismissals of what other people think. All the same it leaves open the question regarding the weight that ought to be granted to prior knowledge concerning peerhood. And on this matter the egalitarian approach, which is a particular kind of conciliation, provides an answer concerning the appropriate weight that ought to be granted to second-order evidence so as to reach rational epistemic compromise.[20]

5.3.4   The Egalitarian Approach

The egalitarian approach to disagreement says the following. If two people are equally likely to be correct and they unexpectedly discover that they hold different beliefs about what *is* correct then they ought to recede their confidence in their own belief being correct to the conditional probability that would be granted to their being correct in considering, prior to the actual disagreement, the appropriate response were such a situation to occur.[21] And because they are equally likely to be correct, the appropriate conditional probability that they ought to grant their own beliefs would be 0.5. Why 0.5? Because from the theoretical vantage point, the probability that they would be correct if such a situation would occur is equal. If there were more than two peers involved in such a scenario that the probability that

---

[19] Matheson (2009) clarifies and defends weak and strong conciliatory responses, from very little movements to strong movements, entailing, for instance, the suspension of judgment.

[20] See also Konigsberg 2013b.

[21] This is largely based on Elga's formulation for the Equal Weight View (Elga 2007): "Upon finding out that an advisor disagrees, your probability that you are right should equal your prior conditional probability that you would be right. Prior to what? Prior to your thinking through the disputed issue, and finding out what the advisor thinks of it. Conditional on what? On whatever you have learned about the circumstances of the disagreement" (Elga 2007).

any one of them is correct conditional on a disagreement occurring would be $1/n$. Otherwise put, if two peers disagree and neither has any reason aside from the other's opinion to think that the other is wrong, such as their possession of more or better evidence or perhaps superior conditions for inferring from the evidence in the present circumstance, then the epistemic weight of first-order evidence ought to be ignored, and the revised credence ought to be based on second-order evidence alone.

The egalitarian approach suggests what Sarah Moss has called a "perfect com-promise[22]" (Moss 2011). If A assigns credence C_1 to P, and B assigns credence C_2 to P, then a "perfect compromise" would be for A and B to assign $(C_1 + C_2)/2$ credence to P (Moss 2011). It is important to see that according to Moss' position, the credence value of C_1 and that of C_2 are given equal weight – e.g., each of them is given 0.5, as above.

The egalitarian approach amasses its conclusions from theoretical thinking about a *possible* disagreement occurring. It contends that if two people know that based on their prior performance and capabilities they share an equal probability of being correct on some hypothetical occasion, and they also consider (from this same hypothetical perspective) the probability of their each being correct on the occasion of such a hypothetical disagreement occurring, then their *actual* response ought to be equal to their hypothetical response, that is, treating each belief as equally probable.

Aside from the fact that the egalitarian response suggests to completely swamp first-order evidence with second-order evidence, it doesn't take into account that in an *actual* case of disagreement each of the parties involved has reasons for believing as they do and possibly also epistemic grounds for dismissing the purely hypothetical revisionary suggestion. The actual disagreement as opposed to the hypothetical disagreement appears to possess an epistemic factor that the theoret-ical consideration neglects to consider. In the actual disagreement one person may have reason to think that they are correct in light of the epistemic force of first-order evidence, and as a consequence to think that the other person is incorrect.[23] From the theoretical vantage point this kind of playing of subjective credence against second-order evidence is unwarranted. But from the actual perspective of a person in the midst of disagreement the justificatory weight of subjective credence is not only plausible but also appears to be a normative requirement – a requirement to

---

[22] Adam Elga's (Elga 2007) and David Christensen's (2007) views are two examples of what I take to be the egalitarian approach to peer disagreement. On both of these accounts, if disagreement is apparent, each peer ought to revise their confidence in alignment with what second-order evidence dictates.

[23] And in the actual disagreement this might be explained in a number of ways. The dissenting person, in view of his divergence of opinion, may be thought to have slipped in performance – made a mistake that is, a performance-error, perhaps misapplying the proper rules of inference. Alternatively, the divergence itself may be regarded as a reason, or perhaps even a proof, that that person ought to be demoted from the level of peer.

respond to the evidence in a manner that is sanctioned by *that* evidence (prescription #1 above).[24]

The merit of egalitarian suggestions for belief revision is that they obey prior probabilities in the absence of any non-question-begging circumstantial indicators. Their limitation is that they eradicate the epistemic weight of the first-order considerations such as those on the basis of which Jill came to believe as she did in the first place. Egalitarianism contends that if there is to be compromise the only compromise there can be is perfect compromise, while actual disagreements suggest that it isn't at all clear that this is so.

There is a danger in the egalitarian approach. It is the danger of rigid reasoning. If a person does not honor the prior probabilities entailed by second-order evidence but instead defers to them completely, his beliefs and behavior will be more rigid; new experiences will be classified on the basis of previously established probabilities and information will be absorbed less for its intrinsic value and more according to whether it meets the terms of a bet. Hence the question becomes how the diagnostic value afforded by first-order evidence can be respected while the dictates of second-order evidence are honored too.

5.3.5   Back to the Conciliatory Approach

Once we recognize that actual disagreements involve reasoning on the basis of everything that is epistemically available to us, including subjective contentions regarding the conclusiveness of first-order evidence, the dangers of bootstrapping seem to be inevitable. All the same, to completely overrule first-order evidence on the basis of second-order evidence, as the egalitarian approach suggests, seems wrong. In this sense the dangers of bootstrapping are dangers that we will perhaps have to live with (Enoch 2010). But without preserving an individual's normative obligation to deal with these dangers we would seem to have to give up too much of what good reasoning amounts to and what plausible revisionary approaches to disagreement ought to offer. Indeed, to eradicate the possibility of error altogether by dismissing any possibility of inaccuracy would seem to compromise our ability to encounter and conditionalize on new evidence.

The conciliatory approach seems to provide the most plausible tactic for responding to disagreement. But because it doesn't specify a specific rule for how to balance first-order evidence with second-order evidence, it appears to leave much of the hard work to the individual's sense of judgment. In doing so it is perhaps less explicit in its rules for revision but it is, nonetheless, more attuned to the complexity involved.

---

[24] To dismiss first-order evidence altogether, as egalitarian positions seek to do, leads to a sort of real-world skepticism (Feldman 2006, p. 415), according to which the level of credence attributed to many of our commonly held beliefs ought to be reduced, which is implausible.

5.4   Kelly's Total Evidence View

The Total Evidence View proposed by Thomas Kelly (2009) appears to recognize some of the concerns that I have raised here. Kelly rightly contends that upon encountering disagreement with a peer, the interaction between first-order and second-order evidence can be a complicated affair. And that in such cases what it is right to believe "depends on both the original evidence as well as on the higher-order evidence that is afforded by the fact that one's peers believe as they do" (Kelly, in: Whitcomb 2011, p. 201). The merit of Kelly's Total Evidence View appears to be that it acknowledges that there is a difference between theoretical problems of disagreement and actual problems of disagreement, a difference that I have focused on here. But unfortunately Kelly doesn't peruse the normative significance of these observations further.[25] There are lines of similarity between what I am proposing here to be the real problem of disagreement and Kelly's Total Evidence View. I do not mean for my view and Kelly's to exclude each other in any way. As noted, I think that Kelly recognizes the difficulty posed by egalitarian solutions and he also notes the importance of psychological considerations relating to first-order evidence.[26] All the same, what I have proposed here takes Kelly's observations one step further.

Given the importance of incorporating first-order evidence as well as second-order evidence, and recognizing that psychological persuasion about first-order evidence can sometimes swamp the weight of second-order evidence, whether or not it *will* swamp second-order evidence appears to depend on the subjective point of view. In effect this means that whether or not second-order evidence will be weighed or downgraded, and to what extent, will depend on what is deemed appropriate, on grounds of relevancy, by subjective appraisal. And therefore, as I have tried to argue, the real problem of disagreement is that one must respect the epistemic force afforded by first-order evidence while honoring the dictates of second-order evidence. And this inevitably leads to a situation where the epistemic force of first-order evidence determines whether or not second-order evidence is relevant. Revising beliefs without attending to first-order evidence seems implausible. But letting conviction about first-order evidence determine whether or not

---

[25] Kelly has recently pursued this direction further in his, "Disagreement and the Burdens of Judgment," unpublished but available online at: http://www.princeton.edu/~tkelly/datbj.pdf

[26] Kelly also observes that a person's psychological persuasion about first-order evidence may determine the way in which they consider second-order evidence: "In some cases, the first order evidence might be extremely substantial compared to the higher-order evidence; in such cases, the former tends to swamp the latter. In other cases, the first order evidence might be quite insubstantial compared to the higher order evidence; in such cases, the latter tends to swamp the former" (Kelly, in: Whitcomb 2011, p. 202). This appears to be an important observation about human reasoning and in particular it emphasizes the force that psychological conviction can have on the assessment and evaluation of evidence.

second-order evidence is relevant paves the way to the error prone reasoning that revisionary tactics are there to mitigate.

And in recognizing this core problem, perhaps Kelly's Total Evidence View is not a revisionary tactic for dealing with disagreement at all, but rather an acknowledgment of I) the need to weigh first-order as well as second-order evidence, and II) an appreciation of the role that psychology has in determining whether or not second-order evidence should be taken into account in practical situations of belief revision in the context of disagreements. My account of the real problem of disagreement and the emphasis on practical difficulties with the subjective appreciation of second-order evidence takes disagreement to point to a more general phenomenon of practical reasoning, in which relevancy judgments – such as determining whether second-order evidence is appropriate and should be applied – form a central part.

5.5 So What, After All, Can We Do?

As we saw, subjective judgments relating to second-order evidence can be dangerous because they may be based on circular reasoning. All the same, to avoid these dangers by dismissing the dictates of subjective judgment altogether upon encountering disagreement is implausible because it will entail that many beliefs about which we are perfectly confident will have to be dismissed. And it will also undermine the ability to attain new information whenever disagreement is encountered. The appropriate response to disagreement ought to honor both the normative requirement to consider second-order evidence and to respect first-order evidence in proportion to the epistemic force that it provides. How these two requirements should be considered in an actual case of belief revision – how much weight ought to be granted to each – is something that must inescapably be left to the judgment of the subject that is aware of these two requirements. And this, as I said at the outset, is inevitable.

What I have tried to do here is to highlight a neglected problem distinct from the problem of disagreement as it is usually discussed. This problem stems from an intrinsic property of second-order evidence that can make otherwise clear data, typically prior probabilities, practically ambiguous. In actual situations of disagreement the problem of determining how relevant second-order evidence is appears to be more fundamental than establishing the rational way of combing first and second-order evidence. And incorporating second-order evidence often depends on determining whether it is epistemically appropriate, and this, as I have tried to show, will often be a function of the subjective appreciation of the epistemic force of first-order evidence.

As a concluding remark, and so as to make sure that the problem I have raised here is not mistaken as being merely another position in the existing debate, let me point to why the present observation is novel. The problem of relevancy judgments and the ambiguous practical implications of second-order evidence suggests that even if a particular revisionary response is considered rational in theory – suggesting for instance such-and-such a combination of first and second-order evidence – in practice it may be deemed inapplicable on grounds of the epistemic force, or diagnostic value, of subjective judgments about first-order evidence.

References

Ajzen, Icek. 1977. Intuitive theories of events and the effects of base-rate information on prediction. *Journal of Personality and Social Psychology* 35(5): 303–314.

Aumann, Robert J. 1976. Agreeing to disagree. *The Annals of Statistics* 4(6): 1236–1239.

Barbey, Aron K., and Steven A. Sloman. 2007. Base-rate respect: From ecological rationality to dual processes. *The Behavioral and Brain Sciences* 30(3): 241–254. discussion 255–297.

Bar-Hillel, M. 1980. The base-rate fallacy in probability judgments. *Acta Psychologica* 44(3): 211–233.

Bar-Hillel, Maya. 1982. Ideal evidence, relevance and second-order probabilities. *Erkenntnis* 17 (3): 273–290.

Bar-Hillel, Maya, and Baruch Fischhoff. 1981. When do base rates affect predictions? *Journal of Personality and Social Psychology* 41(4): 671–680.

Cave, Jonathan A.K. 1983. Learning to agree. *Economics Letters* 12(2): 147–152.

Christensen, David. 2007. Epistemology of disagreement: The good news. *Philosophical Review* 116(2): 187–217.

Christensen, D. 2011. Disagreement, question-begging, and epistemic self-criticism. *Philosophers' Imprint* 11(6): 1–22.

Dégremont, Cédric, and Olivier Roy. 2009. Agreement theorems in dynamic-epistemic logic. In *Logic, rationality, and interaction*, ed. Xiangdong He, John Horty, and Eric Pacuit, 105–118. Berlin/Heidelberg: Springer.

Elga, Adam. 2007. Reflection and disagreement. *Noûs* 41(3): 478–502.

Enoch, David. 2010. Not just a truthometer: Taking oneself seriously (but not too seriously) in cases of peer disagreement. *Mind* 119(476): 953–997.

Feldman, Richard. 2006. Epistemological puzzles about disagreement. In *Epistemology futures*, ed. Stephen Hetherington, 216–326. Oxford: Oxford University Press.

Feldman, R. 2007. Reasonable religious disagreements. In *Philosophers without gods: Meditations on atheism and the secular*, ed. Louise Antony, 194–214. Oxford: Oxford University Press.

Geanakoplos, John, and Heracles M. Polemarchakis. 1982. We can't disagree forever. *Journal of Economic Theory* 28(1): 192–200.

Hansen, Robin, and Tyler Cowen. 2004. *Are disagreements honest?* Unpublished manuscript. Accessible at http://hanson.gmu.edu/deceive.pdf. Last accessed 20 May 2014.

Hanson, Robin. 2003. For Bayesian wannabes, are disagreements not about information? *Theory and Decision* 54(2): 105–123.

Harman, Gilbert. 1973. *Thought*. Princeton: Princeton University Press.

Kelly, T. 2005. The epistemic significance of disagreement. In *Oxford studies in epistemology*, vol. 1, ed. John Hawthorne and Tamar Szabo Gendler, 167–196. Oxford: Oxford University Press.

Kelly, Thomas. 2008. Disagreement, dogmatism, and belief polarization. *The Journal of Philosophy* 105(10): 611–633.

Kelly, T. 2009. Peer disagreement and higher order evidence. In *Disagreement*, ed. Ted Warfield and Richard Feldman. Oxford: Oxford University Press.

Konigsberg, Amir. 2013a. On uniform solutions to peer disagreement. *Theoria* 79(2): 96–126.

Konigsberg, A. 2013b. Epistemic value and epistemic compromise: A reply to moss. *Episteme* 10 (1): 87–97.

Kripke, Saul A. 2011. Two paradoxes of knowledge. In *Philosophical troubles, Collected papers*, vol. I, ed. Saul A. Kripke. Oxford: Oxford University Press.

Matheson, Jonathan. 2009. Conciliatory views of disagreement and higher-order evidence. *Episteme* 6: 269–279.

Milgrom, Paul, and Nancy Stokey. 1982. Information, trade and common knowledge. *Journal of Economic Theory* 26(1): 17–27.

Moses, Yoram, and Gal Nachum. 1990. Agreeing to disagree after all. In *Proceedings of the 3rd Conference on Theoretical Aspects of Reasoning About Knowledge*, 151–168. TARK'90. San Francisco: Morgan Kaufmann Publishers Inc.

Moss, Sarah. 2011. Scoring rules and epistemic compromise. *Mind* 120(480): 1053–1069.

Rubinstein, Ariel, and Asher Wolinsky. 1990. On the logic of 'agreeing to disagree' type results. *Journal of Economic Theory* 51(1): 184–193.

Thaler, Richard H., and Cass R. Sunstein. 2008. *Nudge: Improving decisions about health, wealth, and happiness*. New Haven: Yale University Press.

Welsh, Matthew B., and Daniel J. Navarro. 2012. Seeing is believing: Priors, trust, and base rate neglect. *Organizational Behavior and Human Decision Processes* 119(1): 1–14.

Whitcomb, Dennis. 2011. *Social epistemology: Essential readings*. Oxford: Oxford University Press.

Chapter 6
Seeking Consensus in the Social Sciences

Carlo Martini

Abstract In this chapter I clarify some of the terminology used in debates over the value of scientific consensus. I distinguish between an investigative phase of science and a disseminating one and defend the first main thesis in this chapter: The meaningful question about consensus in science is not whether we should seek it or not, but rather what kind of consensus we should seek and what kind we should give up. The second issue I pursue in this chapter is how we should seek consensus in science. I will defend the second main thesis of this chapter: consensus should not be sought "in the science", but rather "among the scientists". In other words, subjective expertise is not a dispensable source of evidence in the social sciences, and one of the goals of methodologists should be to find the right place for expertise in the pursuit of scientific inquiry. The point of the second thesis is that there is no real contraposition between the value of subjective expertise, and the value of other (objective) methods, but both can and should contribute to the formation of scientific consensus.

6.1   Debates on Consensus and Expertise

The term "consensus" is an easily abused one in scholarly discourse. Consensus among scientists helps build public trust in science, a precondition for the existence of science as a large-scale public enterprise (so-called "Big Science"). Lack of consensus among scientists leaves room for interest groups to enter the policy making debate with parochial agendas and little or carefully hand-picked

C. Martini (✉)
Department of Political and Economic Studies, University of Helsinki, Unioninkatu 40A, office A509, Helsinki, Finland
e-mail: carlo.martini@helsinki.fi

© Springer International Publishing Switzerland 2014   115
C. Martini, M. Boumans (eds.), *Experts and Consensus in Social Science*,
Ethical Economy 50, DOI 10.1007/978-3-319-08551-7_6

evidence.[1] If so, consensus should be greatly valued as a means of creating a relation of trust with society at large. But consensus can also harm scientific goals: it tends to eliminate fringe theories that are potentially groundbreaking, and that can thus significantly impact the course of science; it tends to make scientists conservative, seeking peer validation more than the pursuit of knowledge. Therefore, disagreeing scientific positions should be cherished, because suppression of dissent easily slips into the suppression of knowledge, and because scientific endeavor is fallible, which implies that scientific knowledge is also knowledge of errors (Mill 1859). Instead of seeking consensus, we should "let a thousand theories bloom" (Hull 1988, p. 472), cherish diversity and pluralism. But then let us take one step forward towards policy advising: what should we do with a thousand theories? Too many stances, each pulling in a different direction, make clear and unambiguous advice hard to come by, let alone policy making. An eternally disagreeing scientific community might just have to renounce its public role, thereby renouncing the very resources that make large-scale scientific endeavors possible. And now we have come full circle, back to the stance this paragraph started with: consensus is a valuable goal for science.

The (hypothetical) repartee portrayed above could go on indeterminately. Both sides of the quibble—supporters of the value of dissent and defenders of consensus—have a wealth of reasons on their sides, but much of their disagreement is merely verbal. In this chapter I will argue that the circle in which the debate seems to be stuck is grounded on ambiguity, and the goal of the next sections will be to break that circle. In Sect. 6.2, I plan to clarify some of the terminology used in debates over the value of scientific consensus, and take a stance on the issue that starts from the distinction between an *investigative* phase of science and a *disseminating* one (see also Kosolosky and Van Bouwel, Chap. 4, in this volume[2]). Of course the two phases are interdependent and may partly overlap, but that does not imply that the investigative phase of science should be made identical to the disseminating one. Understanding what is involved in the process of consensus making in science will help understand what kind of consensus is desirable in science, and motivate the first thesis defended in this chapter:

Thesis 1 The meaningful question about consensus in science is not whether we should seek it or not, but rather *what kind of* consensus we should seek and *what kind* we should give up.

---

[1] Defenders of intelligent design like to highlight alleged disagreement on the evidential status of the theory of evolution, in order to push their creationist agenda into education programs (see Pennock 2011).

[2] Kosolosky and Van Bouwel (Chap. 4, this volume) distinguish between an academic and an interface consensus, the former focused on scientific outcomes—what scientists agree on—the latter on procedures—what procedures scientists employ to reach a collective decision or statement. Their account is structurally similar to the account presented in this chapter, but, while I use my account to motivate the two theses outlined below in this section, Kosolosky and Van Bouwel use theirs in order to discuss Solomon's stance on consensus in science.

Once we clarify the first problem—what kind of consensus is desirable for science—there is still another pressing problem to be dealt with: How should we pursue consensus in science? The focus and examples I will use are related to economics, although clearly the problem is a general one. The Received View tells us that consensus is the natural outcome in the pursuit of rational inquiry: As long as scientists abide by the accepted methods of science, previously diverging views will converge to a consensus. The stronger, realist, version of this view associates consensus with truth, while the weaker version with empirical success and rational inquiry. I take the former stance to be a rather controversial one, and investigating it would require a long digression into the metaphysics of science. But in Sect. 6.2 I will argue that even the weaker, and possibly more defensible, version is misguided, at least in the social sciences. I will refer primarily to examples from economics, where empirical success is often not driven by, nor the product of, existing methodological or theoretical consensus. Rather, the empirical success is typically produced by the coordination of subjective expertise, joint with the normative goal of reducing subjective differences in the pursuit of a common goal. Consensus, to put it in a slogan, is among the scientists, not in the science. That puts the focus on the intersubjective aspect of scientific research.

A long-running academic debate has seen objective methods of rational inquiry (modeling, actuarial rules, controlled experiments, etc.) in opposition to the idea that scientific inquiry is a product of subjective heuristics and methods of investigation (experience, hunches, tacit knowledge, etc.). Of course even the staunchest defenders of objectivity in science recognize that experts' intuitions and background knowledge play a role in the determination of what counts as a scientific claim and what does not; but, at the same time, they tend to hold the view that such a state of affairs is an imperfect one, and that the goal of rational inquiry is to limit the role of subjectivity, in favor of more transparent, shareable, and, in short, *objective* methods (Kydland and Prescott 1977; Trout 2009). There are good reasons for seeking objectivity; for at least fifty years research has provided much evidence for skepticism about the value of expert judgment:

- Experts consistently underperform mechanical rules in a number of tasks, especially in forecasting (Meehl 1954; Grove and Lloyd 2006).
- Experts are biased, on a number of counts: ethical, cognitive, professional, etc. (Faust 1984; Trout 2009).
- Experts do not always perform better than laypeople (Stael von Holstein 1972; Armstrong 1980; Yates and McDaniel 1991).

This chapter cannot provide a satisfactory answer to the problem of expertise vs. mechanical rules, but Sect. 6.4 will provide some rationale for the second thesis defended in this chapter:

Thesis 2 Subjective expertise is not a dispensable resource in the social sciences, and one of the goals of methodologists should be to find the right place for expertise in the pursuit of scientific inquiry.

The point of the second thesis is that there is no real contraposition between the value of subjective expertise, and the value of other (objective) methods, but both can and should contribute to sound decision making. Of course, one should not trivialize the matter, it's not that anything goes; rather, we should try to understand what is the role for subjective judgment—when it should be relied on and when not—and how it should be exercised. The last sections of this chapter will try to partly address those challenges (see also Martini 2014).

6.2   Consensus in Science

Even though the concept is not often mentioned explicitly, philosophers, historians, and methodologists of science have been talking about scientific consensus at least since the start of the twentieth century. The importance of logical positivism and empiricism was that they sought to establish on what grounds consensus can arise in science, and, with it, epistemic progress. Formal languages and empirical verification are often taken to be connected, in the mind of the positivists, with truth; but even more, they are connected with the possibility of consensus. A sentence should be verifiable because the scientific community can agree on its validity or otherwise reject it. Naturally, verifiability requires a certain level of formalization and systematization of knowledge; Porter (1996) has investigated how the necessity of formalization and systematization of social knowledge is intimately related to the desire for consensus and accountability, so I will not enter that debate here.

The close link between the positivist pursuit of truth and the desire for consensus in science is a problematic one, because it is hard to claim that the search for truth in science is intrinsically connected with the formation of consensus. Among the several arguments that Mill (1859) mentions, one is particularly relevant for us. Disagreement is necessary in science because the strength of a scientific truth is increased if it survives severe and repeated testing. This is a Popperian point: failed attempts to disconfirm a theory (to disagree with it) strengthen its validity— "corroboration" in Popper's terms; (see Popper 1959, Chapter 10). So cultivating dissenting views in science assures that there is always a testbed for corroborating theories.

But Thomas Kuhn ([1962]1970) moved perhaps the most important arguments against the ideals of verifiability and epistemic progress in science. His central idea of paradigm is tightly connected with the idea of a consensus among scientists on what methods to use and what problems to focus on. Without such a consensus there can be no normal science, and revolutions are the result of a breakdown of consensus. According to Kuhn, the hallmark of maturity in a science is the existence of paradigms, and his claim that paradigms are incommensurable implies that scientific progress is relative to the problems that that science itself has selected at a given time in its history: There is no scientific progress, Kuhn argues, in an absolute sense; rather, science *evolves* through paradigms as organisms do,[3] whose evolutionary advantage is relative to their environment. Yet Kuhn is clear in stating that the existence of paradigm in science is necessary for normal science, that is, for problem solving, inasmuch as paradigms *select the problem space* of a science at a given time (Kuhn 1970, pp. 34–37).

Does the existence of agreement (perhaps even paradigms) in the social science help problem solving? I think the answer is "no", although the matter will have to be postponed until the next section. For now, let us consider that, in Kuhn's mind, paradigms and the problem space they delimit are selected by the scientific community itself. But that is not a realistic assumption in social science,[4] for which the problems are not typically selected by the scientific community, but at least partly by society at large. This fact is explicitly recognized by Kuhn himself in *The Road Since Structure* (Kuhn 1970). There are plenty of examples in economics: the failures of mercantilism and successes of capitalism were perhaps the single most important motive for Adam Smith to attempt an explanation of how nations could increase their wealth; the Great Depression was to many economists a wake-up call on the flaws of general equilibrium theory, and for John Maynard Keynes the chance to write his *General Theory* (Keynes 1936); widespread racial segregation in the U.S. provided fertile ground in the 1960s and 1970s (and funds from the RAND corporation) for Schelling's models of segregation (Schelling 1971); and the list could continue.

I think the best strategy to defend consensus seeking in social science is not by linking consensus to either truth or empirical success, but, more pragmatically, to the legitimation of policy making and the normative dimension of social science. In support of that stance, it will be useful to distinguish an *investigation phase* in science from an *organizational phase*. The activities involved in scientific investigation may involve a number of processes that the philosophy of science literature has individuated—postulating hypotheses, corroborating, extending the applicability of a hypothesis, etc.[5]—and are subject mostly to theoretical desiderata, empirical adequacy, verifiability, replicability, etc. But these criteria are not sufficient in the phase of organization, where the results of empirical or theoretical investigation are transformed into policy relevant knowledge, and possibly, passed on in the form of advice or policy recommendations.

The organization of scientific knowledge involves a number of additional desiderata, for example relevance (to a given problem), or the inclusion of risk considerations, which are inherently normative requirements. Organizing scientific knowledge involves gathering the wealth of evidence and methods that a certain

---

[3] Although Kuhn is careful about pushing the analogy too far, his evolutionary understanding of progress in science is explicit (Kuhn 1970, pp. 172–173).

[4] There is ample evidence that the same holds for all sciences but generalizing this point is beyond the scope of this chapter, and here I will limit my claims to the social sciences.

[5] I'm not committed here to a precise, or even definite set, I take it that the debate is very much alive about what this phase involves and what it does not.

segment of scientific research has made available on a given problem, and "package" them in a way that is both relevant to a particular problem, and transmissible to a wider audience than the specialists only. Besides those that I already mentioned, and possibly many more, the pursuit of consensus is one of the desiderata for the organizational phase of science. Consensus is not a theoretical desideratum, it is not linked with truth or success in science (though the latter point will be justified in the next sections); it is a normative desideratum for scientific knowledge that aims at being relevant and transmissible.

We may (and probably should) accept that in a scientific community both a certain empirical or theoretical claim and its contradictory can coexist; that is, that disagreement may flourish. There may be different circumstances of how that happens: a certain claim—for example "a rate of inflation below $x\%$ causes a $y\%$ reduction in investment"—may be believed by a majority, and disbelieved by the remaining minority of a community. The existence of dissenting minorities will be good for testing the claim. In 2009 U.S. President Barack Obama declared that "there is no disagreement that we need action by our government, a recovery plan that will help to jumpstart the economy". The Cato Institute paid for full-page ads stating "With all due respect Mr. President—that is not true." Signatories of the ad were about 250 economists from several U.S. universities that opposed government intervention. No matter what the specific situation is, scientific disagreement is valuable and should be cultivated in scientific investigation. From the philosophical point of view, how the conflict of coexisting theories in science can be solved within an epistemology or metaphysics of science is a legitimate problem, but one that has limited relevance for the practice of science.

The most pressing problem, and a desideratum for the organizational phase of science, is how to deal with conflicting normative claims such as the following ones: "in order to achieve a 0.6 % GDP increase, the Federal Funds Rate should be decreased by 0.5 %"; and "in order to achieve a 0.6 % GDP increase, the Federal Funds Rate should be left unchanged". If science accepts the challenge of producing policy relevant knowledge, then a phase of consensual formulation of "public knowledge" should follow the messy and disagreement-ridden phase where all scientists are battling each other over the best hypotheses, models and methods. To conclude this part, consensus is one of the non-theoretical desiderata for social science in the organizational phase. The next problem to be addressed is how consensus ought to form among scientists. Is it a natural process that occurs when the science is ready, or is it a social one? Can we take evidence and facts alone to force themselves in the minds and hearts of scientists? This is what Blanchard thinks happens in economics:

> Facts have a way of eventually forcing irrelevant theory out (one wishes it happened faster), and good theory also has a way of eventually forcing bad theory out. The new tools developed by the new-classicals [economists] came to dominate. The facts emphasized by the new-Keynesians forced imperfections back in the benchmark model. A largely common vision has emerged [. . .]. (Blanchard 2009, p. 212)

   In the next sections, I will counter two claims: the first is that we can take Blanchard's claim to be an accurate descriptive statement. In other words, does the existence of a paradigm in economics (see Rosenberg 1994) hold scrutiny? Secondly, is it the case that the existence of a paradigm in economics helps problem solving, as it is the case when considering Kuhn's paradigmatic science? I will show that there are several cases of successful economics, which have been accomplished not just without the existence of an established paradigm, but probably thanks to lack of one; that is, thanks to the theoretical contributions from different paradigms and methods, even incompatible ones.

6.3 Consensus in Economics: Does Economics Have a Paradigm?

The first claim to be analyzed here is that economics is a paradigmatic (also, mature) science in Kuhn's sense of "possessing a paradigm". Besides Blanchard (2009), quoted in the preceding section, the claim can also be found in Rosenberg (1994, pp. 54–56). According to Rosenberg, economics is a science both because its textbooks are uniform in content and style, and because it has a common language, that is, mathematics. If we follow Kuhn's definition, then economics would fall into the category of mature sciences. However, the signs of presence of a paradigm in economics are only illusory, as I plan to motivate in this section.
   In the first place, the fact that economic textbooks are rather uniform should not be taken for granted. Textbooks are usually representative of a science as a whole, but this is hardly the case for economics. First of all, one could argue that in the light of new economic research textbooks will soon have to be rewritten in a rather different language from the one that is now in use. Both experimental economics and neuroeconomics have challenged economic theory in several ways, but they are also helping to establish new standards for a science that for a long time was thought of having no experimental dimension (Colander 2007, p. 15). Sooner or later, the empirical method will necessarily have to be considered more seriously in economics textbooks, but that is hardly a guarantee that homogeneity among textbooks will remain intact, as some may decide to focus on the empirical side of economics, while others may focus on the theoretical one.
   So the uniformity of economic textbooks seems only contingent on the current status of economics. Still, we could argue that there is perhaps more uniformity than, say, in sociology, or psychology. But even that degree of uniformity that does in fact exist among economics textbooks is misleading, because textbook economics leaves out important sources of evidence in the discipline. Subjects like history of economics, economic history, computer simulations, experimental economics,

and more, are typically not the subject of current economic textbook, and are possibly left for advanced training at the master's or doctorate levels.[6]

Why these are important sources of evidence in economics, despite being left out from textbooks, will become clearer in the following sections, where I will be discussing some of the "success stories" of economics. To anticipate briefly, one ought to note that the sources of evidence treated in economic textbooks are only a small part of the evidence that economic practitioners take into account when they deliberate in the "decision rooms". That provides a rationale for siding with Reiss on the acceptable sources of economic evidence:

> The position defended here [...] accepts that there is a plurality of methods for gathering evidence: indeed observation with the naked senses; instrument-enhanced Scientific observation, statistical methods (such as data-reduction and analysis techniques, index numbers, regression, ANOVA etc.); mathematical modelling; computer-based methods such as simulations; laboratory experiments, thought experiments and the analysis of natural experiments; testimony and expert judgment. (Reiss 2008, p. 3)

To sum up, the textbook argument seems a rather weak one for considering economics a paradigmatic science. Even according to Kuhn the existence of textbooks is mostly an incidental aspect of paradigmatic sciences,[7] but perhaps a different argument fares better; namely, the observation that economists speak a common language. The common language of economics is mathematics, and there is at least some evidence that modeling in economics has produced a certain degree of consensus over the epochs and perhaps even a number of paradigms: Ricardian (or Classical) economics, the Austrian School (though it rejected the imperialism of mathematical analysis), Neoclassical economics, etc.

But the common-language argument has a problem: The rationale of a paradigm in a science is that it allows scientists to delimit the space of possible problems that they can aim to solve. A paradigm adopts a set of methods that work better than others at resolving the problems the paradigm itself has isolated. While we could well argue that a number of paradigms have formed at different stages of economic thought, it is far from clear that they have been successful at dealing with a particular class of economic problems. In fact, most economic "paradigms" have, in the course of history, battled each other on the social planning field. They have even proclaimed themselves as overarching frameworks for all economic science,

---

[6] It would be nice to have some metrics on the core requirements of typical economic curricula, although I dare guess that such metric would not yield any surprising observations. As far as I know such metrics are not readily available. Colander (2007) does not contain one, and it may be hard to come up with a representative one given the ever-changing nature of academic curricula, new hires and retirements from departments, and other factors. That said, the standard economics curricula of most universities are nowadays available online, and a brief look at the major English-speaking Schools of Economics seems to confirm my observations in this section.

[7] In *The Structure of Scientific Revolutions* Kuhn talks repeatedly about textbooks (see esp. Chapter V: The Priority of Paradigms) but it is clear that he sees science textbooks as the byproduct of a paradigm, and only secondarily as indicators of their existence: "An increasing reliance on textbooks, or their equivalent, was an invariable *concomitant* of the emergence of a first paradigm in any field of science" (Kuhn 1970, p. 137; my italics).

and in recent decades have reached out to cover more and more aspects of human behavior (a phenomenon described as "economic imperialism"; see Mäki (2009), Mäki and Marchionni (2011)). Looking closely, it does not seem as if the predominant trends in the history of economic theory could really be considered paradigms in the relevant sense, that is in the sense of convergence over the methods and problem-space (the range of possible problems that the science has selected for itself) which enables the science to progress.

So far, I have argued that economics does not have a consensus or, speaking in Kuhnian terms, a paradigm, but *should* it have one? Would the existence of a paradigm make for better (more empirically successful) economics? In the next section I intend to show that success in economics does not come from the existence of a paradigm; quite the opposite, it comes from the concerted contribution of very diverse methods, and possibly the coexistence of different "paradigms".

6.4   Economic Experts

Most sciences rely on a handful of methods, those around which the scientists' views tend to converge. Of course there is, at times, formation of consensus in rational inquiry. In fact we hope that rational inquiry, by different methodologies, may produce plenty of consensus. Directing scientific resources towards the best tested paradigms would be good for the economics of scientific research. But the devil is in the details: sometimes rational inquiry produces consensus by overwhelming evidence, sometimes it produces consensus by somewhat arbitrarily eliminating contrary evidence because it is not good enough or it cannot easily be accounted for by the standard methods, language, etc. This phenomenon has a couple of official names in the scholarly literature: sampling bias and selection bias—the two are alike: we tend to discard evidence that doesn't fit well with our theoretical, linguistic, or model-based preconceptions (Hamill et al. 1980). Should we be hopeful that economics will achieve more durable states of consensus? Are there indications that a paradigm would help economics be more successful?

There are a number of examples that show exactly the opposite: these are episodes of economic success, and the take-home lesson from their analysis is that success came not from the application of a paradigm, but from the interaction of different methods and sources of evidence. In the rest of this section I will examine two cases. The first one is taken from Guala (2001) and Alexandrova and Northcott (2009). They describe the design of Spectrum Auctions—auctions used in the past decades by governments to sell the rights to operate over specific bands of the electromagnetic spectrum. The design of such auctions is considered one of the most successful application of economics to policy making. Reporting the views of John McMillan and Preston McAfee, Alexandrova and Northcott (2009, p. 316) write that the successes of those auctions were to be attributed to the development of game theoretical microeconomic models and of game theory in general. If that was the case, we could say that a particular paradigm (or a subset of, say, the game theoretical paradigm) was successful in solving an economic problem. In fact there was a lot more going on in the design of the Spectrum Auctions.

Alexandrova and Northcott (2009) write that what emerges from the analysis of the Federal Communication Commission 1994–1996 Spectrum Auctions are "two main competing accounts [. . .] roughly, those of theorists and those of experimentalists". In fact, even the theory used was not very conciliatory: some theory supported open auction, while other theory argued against (Alexandrova and Northcott 2009, p. 317). Guala (2001, p. 455) writes that the economists designing the auction used "theoretical models, experimental systems, simulations, public and private demonstrations of the properties of different economic machines." A lot of effort was needed to combine and put to work different theoretical assumptions. Experience, intuition, and personal judgment were paramount for the success of the auctions. Different accounts of the FCC spectrum auctions are uniform in attributing the success to the combination of a number of factors[8]: a solid game-theoretical foundation, the possibility of running simulations, the personal skills and experience with experimental methods of those involved in the project. There was not one single paradigm, not even one single methodology, at work in the FCC spectrum auctions, but a multiplicity of them. The same is true for the next example of this section: Central Banks and the practice of monetary policy by committee.

Most Central Banks' monetary policies are nowadays run by committees. From the Federal Reserve, to the Bank of England, the ECB and the Bank of India, interest rates and other monetary policy mechanisms are controlled by groups of experts who meet periodically to decide on the course of a bank's monetary operations. In *The Quiet Revolution*, Blinder (2004) describes how, starting in the 1990s, central banking across the world passed from the hands of one or a few individuals, their decisions cloaked in secrecy, to the works of more and more transparent committees, which started to regularly divulge their methods, data, and even, in some cases, records of their meetings. Despite recent criticism moved to the target of current monetary policy (inflation targeting), there is widespread agreement that monetary policy by committees has been overall successful at achieving price stability (Greenspan 2004; Bowen 2007). The material that is

---

[8] The success story of economics in its contribution to the Spectrum Auctions has not gone unchallenged. Mirowski and Nik-Khah (2007) and Nik-Khah (2008), have argued that the success rhetoric surrounding the FCC auctions is unjustified. Going over their arguments in the short space of this chapter would not do justice to their elaborate historical reconstruction. I just note here that, first, the authors focus on the success of game theory per se, whereas I take the success story to be representative of economics in general, in the employment of a diverse set of models and theories for a determinate goal. Secondly, from the analysis of the authors it transpires that the success of the FCC auctions was not a success for the regulators, but rather for the companies involved in buying the FCC licenses, who employed economists in order to understand the technicalities of the auctions involved and successfully lobby the regulators. If that was true, it would only show that there was a failure of the regulators in preventing lobbying, not that the economic agents (game theorists and experimentalists) employed in the design of the auction were unable to come up with meaningful and useful recommendations, as Guala (2001) argues, albeit the fact that they fell short of providing a unanimous recommendation for the type of auction that was to be employed.

available on monetary policy committees lets us investigate the background of this success story. As before, what I intend to show is that it was not the existence of a paradigm, but the ability to merge and discuss a range of very diverse sources of economic evidence, that allowed monetary policy committees to achieve their goals.

Here, I will only mention some of the main elements of monetary policy decisions in the Federal Open Market Committee (FOMC), the committee of the Federal Reserve, which is the one for which most material is publicly available, including full documentation and transcripts of the meetings. The FOMC relies on a wealth of evidence for taking policy decisions, mostly related to the adjustment of the Federal Funds Rate. Each month, the staff of the Board of Governors prepares a report called "Green Book", which summarizes the current economic and financial trends in the U.S. and abroad. The Green Book contains tables of past data, extensive textual analysis of past and projected economic performance, and, most recently, several *fan charts*[9] on various economic indicators (see Evans, Chap. 12, this volume, for a discussion of these charts).

The staff at the Board of Governors also produces the so called "Blue Book", officially called "monetary policy alternatives". The report contains a collection of textual analysis and model projections, which provide extra evidence on the possible impact of a number of monetary policy alternatives that the FOMC may consider. For instance, there are charts estimating the degree to which the market is able to predict changes in monetary policy, estimated from federal funds futures— they are indicators of the market's ability to predict the actions of the FOMC. The Blue Book contains long-term scenario analysis and short-term policy alternatives, given in table-format with associated rationale and risk assessment. Together with the Green Book and the Blue Book, the members of the FOMC receive, prior to each meeting, a so-called Beige Book, compiled by the Reserve Bank staff. The Beige Book hardly contains any charts or numbers; it is a detailed description of the current economic conditions for each of the districts of the Federal Reserve. It is compiled from direct interviews with the business sector, anecdotal information, historical data, etc.

The example of the FOMC highlights the same point that was made with respect to the design of the FCC auctions: Designing a monetary policy is a matter of selecting among various sources of evidence, by using the different theoretical backgrounds that characterize the members of the committee. The transcripts that the FOMC publishes highlight the same point. Historical arguments are used alongside model projections, anecdotical evidence can be used to adjust model-based forecasts, in a process of model-based consensus that is very similar to the one described by Boumans (Chap. 3, this volume).

In short, it is hard to see a single economic paradigm at work in monetary policy, or in designing spectrum auctions. Despite the lack of a paradigm, or of the kind of

---

[9] The famous fan charts, introduced by the Bank of England in 1997, are a convenient way to represent future projection together with confidence intervals.

uniformity among methodologies that Kuhn refers to as the hallmark of a paradig-matic science, economics has undoubtedly achieved a certain degree of success with respect to a number of economic issues. What seems to be at work in the cases of success described is not uniformity of method, but the concerted effort of experts in the pursuit of a common goal. This concerted effort, and the existence of an institutional design to make the effort feasible in the first place is, in the view I defend in this chapter, the condition for achieving consensus in economics. When economists are back in their narrow role of scientists, they pursue economic knowledge each with their own theoretical commitments. There are econometri-cians, microeconomists, macroeconomists, historians of economics, experimental-ists, and many more special disciplines within the umbrella term of "economic sciences". It would be both unrealistic to expect, and misguided to suggest, that economics could thrive better with less heterogeneity. But when those very same economists are concerned with problem solving (the kind of problems that the more general public entrusts them with), then a certain mechanism for assuring homog-enization of answers to a common problem will be fruitful, as it was illustrated in the examples mentioned in this section. Committees, working groups, and other similar institutional arrangements facilitate the formation of economic consensus over concrete problems.

Unfortunately, the process is far from perfect. Economics does not often achieve the level of success that the examples in this section have shown. But that is not because economics is lacking a paradigm, because its theories are weak, or for lack of evidential support, or due to other theoretical factors. The main lack of empirical success in economics should be sought in the lack of institutional settings where economists can share their expertise and pursue common goals. Among these mechanisms, we can think of the proposal by den Butter and ten Wolde (Chap. 2, this volume) as one of them: the setting up of "matching zones". The point here is that we don't need a different *kind* of economics, we need better tools for making the most out of the different methodologies that already exist in economics. This is not to say that new tools shouldn't be developed—the examples of experimental economics and simulations testify for the positive contributions that new methods can bring to economic science—but rather that, irrespective of the tools we use, success as a science can be achieved primarily by using the tools better.

To sum up this section, the variety of methods and sources of evidence in economics are an asset for the economic practitioner, and it is especially when a method is devised for bringing together these sources that economics succeeds at its best. Clearly there is a lot more that can be done, but it is not the attempt to establish a paradigm in economics. With respect to the problem of gaining a better method-ology of applied economics, I have suggested in other work (Martini 2014), specific directives for the employment of expertise to problem solving. In the next section I will address some of the issues related to the idea I have suggested here, which resembles an idea that has been in the philosophical literature for some time: well-ordered science.

6.5 Well-Ordered Science or Well-Organized Scientists

Polanyi (1945) thought that "science can continue to exist on the modern scale only so long as the authority that it claims is accepted by large groups of the public." But he also held on to the view, later shared by Kuhn, that the best organization of scientific research is the spontaneous coordination of individual efforts in the pursuit of internally-determined[10] scientific goals. Many instances in which that spontaneous coordination has failed to achieve the desired results have prompted scholars to dig deeper into the mechanisms by which science contributes to non-scientific (social) goals. The effort has given rise to the idea of *well-ordered science*.

Maxwell (1984), Kitcher (2001), and Cartwright (2006) have suggested ways in which science could be organized to work better than it does in its current state. I cannot do justice to those works in the limited space of this chapter, nor to several other similar attempts to expound the idea and principles of a well-ordered science. Instead, I will limit myself to suggesting an alternative (or probably a complement) to well-ordered science: a well-structured scientific community.

Kitcher's idea of well-ordered science seems to focus on importance of judging which kind of inquiries should or should not be pursued by means of a deliberative and reflective democratic process (Kitcher 2001, Chapters 8–10): well-ordered science, then, in Kitcher, targets the *goals* of scientific inquiry. Cartwright, instead, parts from Kitcher and focuses on evidence and warrant: well-ordered science should ask not only "'What warrants a theory,' but rather, 'What warrants the conclusions we draw on the basis of that science in putting it to use?'" (Cartwright 2006, p. 985). Both accounts seem to focus on standards for *science*, rather than for *scientists*.

But if my analysis in the previous sections of this chapter is correct—that the successes of social science[11] is dependent on the organization of expertise—then focusing on expertise will be at least one of the foci of well-ordered science. Many scientists (Polanyi was one of them) feel uneasy with the idea that we can intelligently select what kinds of evidence are legitimate in scientific inquiry, or what kinds of problems scientists should pursue, as it were, from without, rather than from within science itself. But we may well require science that in the process of organizing scientific knowledge (the organizational phase of science I introduced earlier) they abide by a number of good epistemic practices and principles. Some of these have been discussed extensively in the literature (see Colander 1992, 1994; Shanteau and Stewart 1992; Reiss 2008; Martini 2014; Cooke 1991; Cooke and Goossens 2000), but a lot more work needs to be done.

---

[10] For Kuhn, it is the scientific community that selects which problems it will try to solve, through a paradigm, and which standards of verification it is ready to accept.

[11] I presented a case for economics, but it is arguable that other similar successes stories could be found in for different social sciences.

What I am suggesting is not virtue epistemology, although it is probably quite compatible with it. It is the idea that we should go about using diverse and possibly interdisciplinary knowledge resources—sources of evidence, different investigative methods, different theoretical tools and assumptions—by smoothing disagreements in a coordinated and informed manner. If asked how a group of scientists who are tackling a concrete problem should join efforts to provide solutions, most people would probably answer that the scientists should sit around a table and "work together". Open panel discussion seems to be the most natural way to think about expert coordination, even though there is ample evidence that that is not always the case. How should a group of experts coordinate if the problem is forecasting when the next slump in the economic cycle will be? There is ample evidence that some form of aggregation will work much better than deliberation.

Of course the costs of organizing expertise should be commensurate with the stakes. Some failures in coordinating scientific efforts are more costly than others. Failing to achieve a working consensus on climate change, or on how to increase employment, might be extremely costly, whereas failing to reach a consensus on the status of quantum mechanics might not be as devastating. Of course, there should be organisms allowing the creation of consensus. Some have long been established—e.g. the NIH consensus development program (see Solomon 2007, 2011)—some have developed more recently and in the urgency of the situation, like the *The Consensus Project* on climate change (Cook et al. 2013). What is important is that the existence of a consensus project does not mean that the underlying research (the investigative phase) comes to a halt, although it may be affected to some extent. Disagreement can still exist, as it should, and we would want a mechanism for making sure that every consensus could be reevaluated in due time. The concept of "due time" is, again, a normative as well as empirical and pragmatic problem to be settled in concert with the policy makers, but it would guarantee that every scientific consensus is taken "with a pinch of salt", as any reasonable consensus should be taken, over a matter—science—which is by nature constantly correcting and perfecting itself.

To sum up, in this chapter I have argued that both consensus and experts are needed assets in science, despite the qualms many prominent scholars have expressed with the idea of consensus, and the wealth of evidence on the imperfect state of affairs concerning the employment of expertise in science. They are also, conceptually, a major focus of concern in the "well-ordered science movement": what I have called a well-structured scientific community, which focuses on rules for experts (the scientists) in the organizational phase of science, rather than rules that apply in the investigative phase of research.

References

Alexandrova, Anna, and Robert Northcott. 2009. Progress in economics: Lessons from the spectrum auctions. In *Oxford handbook of philosophy of economics*, ed. Harold Kincaid and Don Ross, 306–336. Oxford: Oxford University Press.

Armstrong, J. Scott. 1980. The seer-sucker theory: The value of experts in forecasting. *Technology Review* 82(7): 16–24.

Blanchard, Olivier. 2009. The state of macro. *Annual Review of Economics* 1: 209–28.

Blinder, Alan S. 2004. *The quiet revolution: Central banking goes modern*. New Haven/London: Yale University Press.

Bowen, Alex. 2007. The Monetary Policy Committee of the Bank of England: Ten years on. *Bank of England Quarterly Bulletin* Q1. Available at SSRN: http://ssrn.com/abstract=977475

Cartwright, Nancy. 2006. Well-ordered science: Evidence for use. *Philosophy of Science* 73(5): 981–990.

Colander, David. 1992. Retrospectives: The lost art of economics. *The Journal of Economic Perspectives* 6(3): 191–198.

Colander, D. 1994. The art of economics by the numbers. In *New directions in economic methodology*, ed. Roger E. Backhouse, 35–49. London: Taylor and Francis.

Colander, D. 2007. *The making of an economist, redux*. Princeton: Princeton University Press.

Cook, John, et al. 2013. Quantifying the consensus on anthropogenic global warming in the scientific literature. *Environmental Research Letters* 8(2): 024024.

Cooke, Roger M. 1991. *Experts in uncertainty*. New York/Oxford: Oxford University Press.

Cooke, R.M., and L.H.J. Goossens. 2000. Procedure guide for structured expert judgment in accident consequence modeling. *Radiation Protection Dosimetry* 90(3): 303–309.

Faust, David. 1984. *The limits of scientific reasoning*. Minneapolis: University of Minnesota Press.

Greenspan, Alan. 2004. Risk and uncertainty in monetary policy. *The American Economic Review* 94(2): 33–40.

Grove, William M., and Martin Lloyd. 2006. Meehl's contribution to clinical versus statistical prediction. *Journal of Abnormal Psychology* 115(2): 192–194.

Guala, Francesco. 2001. Building economic machines: The FCC auctions. *Studies in History and Philosophy of Science* 32(3): 453–477.

Hamill, Ruth, Timothy D. Wilson, and Richard E. Nisbett. 1980. Insensitivity to sample bias: Generalizing from atypical cases. *Journal of Personality and Social Psychology* 39(4): 578–589.

Hull, David L. 1988. *Science as a process: An evolutionary account of the social and conceptual development of science*. Chicago: University of Chicago Press.

Keynes, John Maynard. [1936] 2007. *The general theory of employment, interest and money*. London: Macmillan.

Kitcher, Philip. 2001. *Science, truth, and democracy*. Oxford: Oxford University Press.

Kuhn, Thomas S. [1962]1970. *The Structure of Scientific Revolutions. Second Edition Enlarged*. Chicago: The University of Chicago Press.

Kuhn, T.S. 1970. *The road since structure*. Chicago: The University of Chicago Press.

Kydland, Finn E., and Edward C. Prescott. 1977. Rules rather than discretion: The inconsistency of optimal plans. *The Journal of Political Economy* 473–491.

Mäki, Uskali. 2009. Economics imperialism concept and constraints. *Philosophy of the Social Sciences* 39(3): 351–380.

Mäki, U., and Caterina Marchionni. 2011. Is geographical economics imperializing economic geography? *Journal of Economic Geography* 11(4): 645–665.

Martini, Carlo. 2014. Experts in science: A view from the trenches. *Synthese* 191: 3–15.

Maxwell, Nicholas. 1984. *From knowledge to wisdom: A revolution in the aims and methods of science*. London: Blackwell Publishing.

Meehl, Paul E. 1954. *Clinical versus statistical prediction: A theoretical analysis and a review of the evidence*. Minneapolis: University of Minnesota Press.

Mill, John Stuart. [1859] 2002. *On liberty*. Mineola: Dover Publication.

Mirowski, Philip, and Edward Nik-Khah. 2007. Markets made flesh. In *Do economists make markets?: On the performativity of economics*, ed. Donald A. MacKenzie, Fabian Muniesa, and Lucia Siu. Princeton: Princeton University Press.

Nik-Khah, Edward. 2008. A tale of two auctions. *Journal of Institutional Economics* 4(1): 73–97.

Pennock, Robert T. 2011. Can't philosophers tell the difference between science and religion?: Demarcation revisited. *Synthese* 178(2): 177–206.

Polanyi, Michael. 1945. The autonomy of science. *Scientific Monthly* 60: 141–150.

Popper, Karl. [1959] 2002. *The logic of scientific discovery*. London: Routledge.

Porter, Theodore M. 1996. *Trust in numbers: The pursuit of objectivity in science and public life.* Princeton: Princeton University Press.

Reiss, Julian. 2008. *Error in economics: Towards a more evidence-based methodology.* London: Routledge.

Rosenberg, Alexander. 1994. If economics isn't science, what is it? In *The philosophy of economics: An anthology*, ed. Daniel M. Hausman. London: Routledge.

Schelling, Thomas C. 1971. Dynamic models of segregation. *Journal of Mathematical Sociology* 1 (2): 143–186.

Shanteau, James, and Thomas R. Stewart. 1992. Why study expert decision making? Some historical perspectives and comments. *Organizational Behavior and Human Decision Processes* 53: 95–106.

Solomon, Miriam 2007. The social epistemology of NIH consensus conferences. In *Establishing medical reality: Essays in the metaphysics and epistemology of biomedical science*, vol. 16, ed. Harold Kincaid and Jennifer McKitrick, 167–177. Dordrecht: Springer.

Solomon, M. 2011. Group judgment and the medical consensus conference. In *Philosophy of medicine*, Handbook of the philosophy of science, vol. 16, ed. Fred Gifford, Dov M. Gabbay, Paul Thagard, and John Woods, 239–254. Amsterdam: North Holland.

Staël von Holstein, Carl-Axel S. 1972. Probabilistic forecasting: An experiment related to the stock market. *Organizational Behavior and Human Performance* 8: 139–158.

Trout, J.D. 2009. *The empathy gap.* New York: Viking/Penguin.

Yates, Frank J., and Linda McDaniel. 1991. Probability forecasting of stock prices and earnings: The hazards of nascent expertise. *Organizational Behavior and Human Decision Processes* 49: 60–79.

Chapter 7
Struggling Over the Soul of Economics: Objectivity Versus Expertise

Julian Reiss

We now have a situation where social and psychological theories of human thought and action have taken the place of [the individual's] thought and action itself. . . . Not live human beings, but abstract models are consulted; not the target population decides, but the producers of the models. Intellectuals all over the world take it for granted that their models will be more intelligent, make better suggestions, have a better grasp of the reality of humans than these humans themselves.

(Feyerabend 1999)

When the crisis came, the serious limitations of existing economic and financial models immediately became apparent. Arbitrage broke down in many market segments, as markets froze and market participants were gripped by panic. Macro models failed to predict the crisis and seemed incapable of explaining what was happening to the economy in a convincing manner. As a policy-maker during the crisis, I found the available models of limited help. In fact, I would go further: in the face of the crisis, we felt abandoned by conventional tools.

In the absence of clear guidance from existing analytical frameworks, policy-makers had to place particular reliance on our experience. Judgment and experience inevitably played a key role.

(Trichet 2010)

Abstract The topics of this chapter are the notion of objectivity and the role for experts in economics. It will argue that core methodological debates are at heart debates about the notion of objectivity and about how objective a science economics can and should be. It will then introduce an alternative notion and show that for economics to be objective in the new sense, expert judgments are likely to play a much more prominent role than they currently do (or, more precisely, ought to do following the traditional ideal). It is quite obvious, however, that making expert judgments more prominent alone won't suffice. The right kind of expert judgment

J. Reiss (✉)
Department of Philosophy, Durham University, 50 Old Elvet, Durham DH1 3HN, UK
e-mail: julian.reiss@durham.ac.uk

© Springer International Publishing Switzerland 2014
C. Martini, M. Boumans (eds.), *Experts and Consensus in Social Science*,
Ethical Economy 50, DOI 10.1007/978-3-319-08551-7_7

is needed. The chapter will therefore end with some thoughts about what a better economic expertise might look like.

7.1   Introduction

This is the golden age for philosophers of economics. When I first entered the subject in the late 1990s, the economics profession seemed all fine and dandy. In macro, a "new synthesis" between new Keynesian and the new classical schools had just emerged, micro experienced an exciting revival fuelled by new findings in behavioral economics and micro econometrics, and economic policy subscribed to the Washington Consensus. Of course, outsiders such as heterogeneous economists and practitioners of history and philosophy of economics such as myself had our complaints but they were perceived as just that: economics dilettantes' grumbles.

This has changed over the years but most dramatically with the 2008 financial crisis. Suddenly we hear insiders to the profession make the same or similar complaints we had made, except couched in a more flamboyant language. We hear that "the economics profession went astray because economists . . . mistook beauty . . . for truth" (Krugman 2009), that economists "killed America's economy" because of unrealistic models (Stiglitz 2009), and that the crisis has made clear a "*systemic failure of the economics profession*" as it had systematically disregarded key factors responsible for outcomes such as the crisis (Colander et al. 2009; emphasis original) – all from highly prominent members of that very failing profession.

These are good times for making methodological remarks, then. The remarks in this chapter concern the notion of objectivity and the role for experts in economics. I will argue that core methodological debates are at heart debates about the notion of objectivity and about how objective a science economics can and should be. I will then introduce an alternative notion and show that for economics to be objective in the new sense, expert judgments are likely to play a much more prominent role than they currently do (or, more precisely, ought to do following the traditional ideal). It is quite obvious, however, that making expert judgments more visible alone won't suffice. The right *kind* of expert judgment is needed. I'll therefore finish with some thoughts about what a better economic expertise might look like. To start us off, I'll tell the tale of a fascinating case of failing economics, which highlights just the aspects of economic analysis I will focus on throughout this chapter.

7.2   A Fascinating (and, Embarrassing) Case

This short story begins with a 2010 paper in which two Harvard economists Carmen Reinhart and Kenneth Rogoff purported show that a country's level of debt and GDP growth are negatively correlated (Reinhart and Rogoff 2010). Their evidence seemed to indicate an important non-linearity: "the relationship between government debt and real GDP growth is weak for debt/GDP ratios below a threshold of 90 % of GDP. Above 90 %, median growth rates fall by one percent, and average growth falls considerably more" (ibid., p. 1). 90 % debt/GDP thus looked like a tipping point beyond which growth drops sharply.

In their paper, Reinhart and Rogoff were careful not to draw strong policy conclusions from their findings or even to read them causally. But other statements they made lent themselves to causal interpretation ("In a series of academic papers with Carmen Reinhart ... we find that very high debt levels of 90 % of GDP are a long-term secular *drag* on economic growth that often lasts for two decades or more", Rogoff 2012; my emphasis), and they certainly regard the 90 % threshold an important indicator for policy (e.g., "Our analysis, based on these cases and the 23 others we identify, suggests that the long term risks of high debt are real.", Reinhart and Rogoff, op. cit., p. 23).

The timing of this research could hardly have been better. Many governments ran huge budget deficits to finance fiscal stimulus packages in the aftermath of the recent financial crisis. As a consequence, public debt/GDP ratios soared all over the world between 2008 and 2012: from 64.8 to 101.6 in the US, 44.5–89.8 in the UK, 66.2–93.1 in the Eurozone, 64.9–81.6 in Germany, 105.4–161.6 in Greece. Alas, not all countries could handle the increased levels of debt equally well: the US steered dangerously close to a fiscal cliff, several European countries such as Greece and Cyprus had to be bailed out by IMF and the EFSF, and, probably, the best is yet to come. IMF and EFSF grant financial assistance only after a "country program" with the requesting government has been agreed on, and these programs invariably contain numerous austerity measures. The Reinhart-Rogoff findings appear to justify austerity. Until an Amherst grad student cooked their goose.

Thomas Herndon tried to replicate the Reinhart-Rogoff findings as an exercise for a term paper in an econometrics class. But no matter what he tried, his results kept deviating from those published by the prominent economists. So he asked them for their spreadsheet, received it and found the sources of discrepancy: a stupid coding error, mysterious data exclusions and dubious methodological choices Herndon et al. (2013). When corrected for the mistakes, growth remains slightly lower for countries with a debt/GDP ratio above 90 % but the difference is not at all dramatic. I haven't seen any evidence to the effect that Reinhart-Rogoff deliberately tweaked results. Thus far, they have admitted to the coding error but defended other aspects of their study (Cook 2013). It is pretty clear, however, that the original analysis did not quite receive as much attention as it should have, especially considering the likely policy consequences of research of this kind.

I do not want to pass any judgment on this case here. What it does in my view is to highlight challenges with respect to three aspects of economic analysis: theoretical, methodological, and ethical. One should note, first, that Reinhart and Rogoff established their result on the basis of an empirical study alone, with no theory supporting or explaining the result (I mean "theory" here in the broadest sense of either macro or micro economic abstract principles, historical and institutional background knowledge and so on). Second, Herndon et al. (2013) point out certain problems concerning selective data analysis, weighting and other methodological choices Reinhart and Rogoff made. But who is to say that the former are right and the latter wrong? On what methodological principles could we tell? Third, the case raises *ethical* challenges. One the one hand there are issues concerning scientific integrity. Even if no foul play was at work here, arguably, Reinhart and Rogoff did not take the appropriate care in making sure their evidence supports their claims. Or perhaps it is peer review that should have seen to that. Whoever made the mistake, something went wrong here. On the other hand, one might wonder whether research results that have a degree of politically effectiveness such as these should not come with warning labels. Once more, in the original paper Reinhart and Rogoff never talk about causation, just of association. However, it must have been clear to them that in policy and public arenas subtleties such as this will be ignored. A later reply by the authors shows that their actual views on the issue are a lot subtler than they were taken to be (Reinhart and Rogoff 2013). Perhaps they should have made that clear when they first published their results?

7.3 The Traditional Ideal of Objectivity in Economics: Abstract, Mechanical, Value-Free

There is a "received view" in economics about how good theory and good methodology ought to look like, and how economists ought to address ethical issues. This received view, I submit, stems from certain ideas regarding the notion of objectivity in science. Good science ought to be objective, and objectivity with respect to theory formation, methodology and ethics has a very specific meaning. In this section I will trace this three-pronged idea of objectivity in economics.

7.3.1 Objectivity in Theory Formation: Abstracting the Reality Behind the Phenomena

According to a widely held view concerning the aims of science, science ought to describe, and to some extent succeeds in describing, the objective reality behind the phenomena. Phenomena, that is, objects and events of scientific interest in the form in which they appear to us, are, or so this view goes, co-produced by reality *and* the idiosyncrasies of our particular points of view such as details of our perceptual apparatus, expectations formed by upbringing and culture, local and historical details of the conditions under which the observation was made and so on. As a consequence, phenomena in their full empirical concreteness are too complex for fruitful scientific theorizing. One reason is that science aims at establishing laws, that is, truths of high generality. As the precise details of an individual observation will never be exactly replicated, theorizing cannot be about the results of observations. Therefore, science has to abstract as much as possible from the details pertaining to a scientific observer's standpoint and examine reality behind the phenomena. It is in the nature of this reality that it cannot be observed. However, scientists can theorize about reality and test alternative theoretical conceptions against the observations they make.

While this "two-worlds view" (there is, first, a world of concrete ephemeral things with smells and warmth and colors and locations, and there is, second, a world of real things stripped off of most of these properties but which are more enduring and more frequently reappearing) has entered Western philosophy back in antiquity, it was probably Galileo whose science presents the first thoroughgoing and tremendously successful application of it. Galileo is responsible for the distinction between secondary and primary qualities, that is, qualities (characteristics) whose existence depends on us (such as odors and colors) and those that would continue to exist were all conscious beings wiped out from the universe (*The Assayer*, see Galilei 1623 [1960]). And Galileo is responsible for developing the method of analysis of synthesis, according to which phenomena are first broken into their simplest parts, the laws of these simple parts are established, and finally, the different laws of the various parts are combined to make a prediction about a new phenomenon (cf. Naylor 1990).

It took nearly 200 years for the two-worlds view to find its way into economics. Adam Smith's economics ([1776] 2008) was still deeply affected by his approach to moral philosophy, which required moral judgments about a phenomenon be made in consideration of all relevant detail (albeit from an impartial perspective, see Raphael 2007, Ch. 5). Only with David Ricardo (1817) did economics become an abstract science. Ricardo solved policy problems by building a simplified model of the situation within which the policy relevant question could be addressed unambiguously. The best-known application of this approach we find of course in Ricardo's theory of the comparative advantage, which he demonstrated using a two-countries/two-goods model and used to advocate the abolishment of the Corn Laws.

Ricardian economics, and not Smithian economics, has won the day. There were of course a few periods of uproar. Richard Jones, a nineteenth century political economist and close friend and ally of John Herschel, William Whewell and Charles Babbage (see Snyder 2011), developed a view of political economy in which phenomena in their concrete embedding in the cultural and moral contexts of their time were the subject of theorizing, in direct opposition to Ricardo's toy models (1817). But shortly after the publication of his book John Stuart Mill presented arguments to the effect that Jones' approach could not possibly be of use in political economy (Mill 1843, 1844), arguments that many methodologist would still regard as compelling today.

The most famous controversy arose towards the end of the nineteenth century when Carl Menger, founder of the Austrian School of economics, attacked members of the German Historical School and specifically Gustav Schmoller for their methodological aberrations. Schmoller contended that the starting point for all economic investigations be found in the concrete and comparative study of economies in all their gory detail through history and statistics, much like Richard Jones had. He had no patience for Ricardian economics:

> Once abstract economics had achieved a great system, its source of power dried up because it volatilised its results too much into abstract schemes, which no longer had any connection to reality. (Schmoller 1883, p. 978; quoted from Haller 2004, p. 8)

Menger, by contrast, regarded history and statistics as at best "auxiliary sciences" and saw the best way to study economics in finding the laws that apply to the simplest elements through the use of reason. Once more the objectivists prevailed: the Historical School essentially disappeared with Schmoller, except for its effect on American Institutionalism, which has, after World War II, itself all but disappeared from the face of the earth (Yonay 1998).

From Mill and Menger we learn that it is not only "abstract" and "simplified" that characterize this idea of objectivity. There is also the view that economics describes (or theorizes about) a privileged aspect of the social world. This privileged aspect, the "economic aspect", is given by the proper understanding of the nature of economics, which is captured in a definition. Mill's definition, for instance, reads:

> The science which traces the laws of such of the phenomena of society as arise from the combined operations of mankind for the production of wealth, in so far as those phenomena are not modified by the pursuit of any other object. (Mill 1844)

Menger does not define economics explicitly but it is clear from his writings that he regards (theoretical) economics as the science that traces the (strict) laws pertaining to the satisfaction of human needs. Theorizing, then, proceeds not only by abstracting and simplifying some aspect of the social world but by focusing on a specific aspect. There are slight differences in the precise understanding of what this is among different economists but all agree that there is such an "economic aspect".

A final battle I want to mention here is the "Measurement Without Theory" debate of the late 1940s. Again we find proponents of an approach to economics that begins with concrete phenomena and studies them comparatively through history and statistics – in this case the National Bureau of Economic Research economists Arthur Burns and Wesley Mitchell – who were attacked by Tjalling Koopmans for not grounding their studies in "economic theory" (1947). According to Koopmans, measurement and observation, causal inference and policy analysis all had to be guided by abstract economic theory in order to succeed. And again, most economists went with Koopmans.

The reason to present this potted history of methodological controversies here is twofold. On the one hand I want to show that certain criticisms that have been advanced against contemporary economics in the wake of the financial crisis are hardly new but rather have been made over and over again in the history of economics ever since economics left the embrace of philosophy after Adam Smith. On the other hand, the history of economics shows that the issue is at heart one about objectivity. Proponents on one side of the debates defend an ideal of objectivity that regards claims about an abstract, simple economic reality behind the phenomena as objective, whereas their opponents demand that the subject of economic investigations be these phenomena in their full complexity.

7.3.2   Objectivity in Methods: Creating Results by Mechanical Means

There is a second "traditional" sense of objectivity that doesn't pertain to the *products* of science (such as scientific claims about an abstract reality behind the phenomena) but rather to its *procedures*. To say that science is objective in this second sense is to say that its methods are free from personal elements, that in principle anyone (as long as they have the required technical skills) who employs these methods would come to the same conclusions. In other words, science is objective to the extent that it uses mechanical methods instead of human judgment.

In the history of economic thought there have been numerous controversies whether economics be a deductive or an inductive science. Richard Jones, for instance, developed his own inductive, Baconian approach against the deductive, Ricardian mainstream, Mill's methodology of economics has been termed "deductive *a priori*" (Hausman 1992), and Schmoller's inductivist (though for a critical view on that label, see Reiss 2000).

However, the categories "deductive" versus "inductive" are rather too coarse to get to the heart of the matter. For one thing, contestants on both sides (with the possible exception of Carl Menger) defended the view that an appropriate economic methodology makes use of a combination of inductive and deductive elements. Mill, for instance, only argued against the method of *specific experience*: since we will never find two situations (say, two economies) that are exactly alike except with respect to one factor, we cannot apply his method of difference to economic matters for causal inference (Mill 1844, Mill [1843] 1874). Nor do we need the method of difference. Since we already know the most basic principles of human behavior (people seek wealth and avoid labor) and technology (the law of diminishing returns) *inductively from generalized experience*, we can apply these fundamental principles to a specific situation to make a prediction. Schmoller, similarly, thought that induction and deduction are inextricably linked and equally needed for scientific reasoning like two legs are necessary for walking:

> What has been achieved is just as much the result of deductive as of inductive reasoning. Anyone who is thoroughly clear about the two procedures will never maintain that there are sciences explanatory of the real world which rest simply on one of them. (Schmoller 1900, vol. I, p. 110; translation in Hutchison 1994, p. 279)

The issues that divide the camps therefore concern not so much induction or deduction on its own but rather how much of each and at what stages of the investigation and how much and what kind of experience is needed for a good inductive argument.

So what is a good inductive argument? That is the subject of today's most hotly disputed methodological issue in economics and many other social sciences. This debate has most aptly been referred to as the "causal wars" and described as follows:

> The causal wars are about what is to count as scientifically impeccable evidence of a causal connection, usually in the context of the evaluation of interventions into human affairs. The most recent battles are between those arguing that only the use of RCTs should be accepted as providing acceptable evidence (sometimes, the exotic regression discontinuity (RD) design is also allowed). The RCT or *randomly controlled trial*, is an experimental design involving at least two groups of subjects, the control group and the experimental group (a.k.a. study group, or treatment group), between which the subjects are distributed by a strictly random process (i.e., one with no exceptions), and which are not further identified or distinguished by any common factor besides the application of the experimental treatment to the experimental group. (Scriven 2008, p. 11)

The RCT is essentially a probabilistic version of Mill's method of difference. Proponents maintain that a good argument in favor of some result R must contain the premise "R was tested in a randomized trial" – in apparent defiance of Mill's views of the applicability of the method of difference in economics.

But the defiance of Mill is only apparent. In fact, deduction from first principles, Mill's method of difference, the ideal RCT and a number of other methods (such as instrumental variables and related method defended by proponents of "Mostly Harmless Econometrics", Angrist and Pischke 2008) are all of a kind Nancy Cartwright calls "clinchers" (see Cartwright 2007). All clinchers have in common that their conclusion is certain, given the assumptions (these methods can be said to "clinch" their conclusions). The model is the deductive proof: if all the assumptions are true and no mistake was made in the derivation, the conclusion must be true.

What matters here is not so much that the conclusions are certain given the assumptions but rather that they are established "mechanically", with as little subjective judgment as possible. In consequence, results are established independently from the team of economists doing the experiment or derivation and in a way that is transparent to everyone who bothers checking them. Especially transparency is often used as a selling point for RCTs:

> If politicians can be convinced of the benefits of a particular policy or program for their constituents, they may be willing to adopt it, particularly if the results are presented as rigorous and transparent. (Cohen and Easterly 2009, p. 18)

Mechanical objectivity contrasts with a method of "considered judgment" (*cf.* Elgin 1996). A *considered* judgment about a scientific hypothesis involves taking into account all the evidence relevant to the assessment of the hypothesis, which requires judgments about relevance, about the quality of the evidence, about weighing difference pieces of evidence, about the amount of evidence needed to accept or act on the hypothesis, about whether or not additional evidence should be sought in the light of the cost of doing so, and so on. Many of these judgments do not follow strict rules and are therefore "subjective" in the eyes of some. This concerns especially certain value judgments that are required, for instance, to determine how much evidence is "enough", and to which we will now turn.

7.3.3   Objectivity in Ethics: The Social Scientists Qua Scientist Makes No Value Judgments

There is a third "traditional" sense of objectivity. The first two, which we may refer to as "product objectivity" and "process objectivity", respectively, can be found as much in natural as in social science. The third sense originates in social science and has to do with the fact that social science concerns human action, and human action cannot be understood without evaluations.

This sense goes back to Max Weber and his widely cited essay '"Objectivity" in Social Science and Social Policy'. In this essay Weber ([1904] 1949) argued that the idea of an a-perspectival social science was meaningless:

> There is no absolutely objective scientific analysis of ... 'social phenomena' independent of special and 'one-sided' viewpoints according to which – expressly or tacitly, consciously or unconsciously – they are selected, analyzed and organized for expository purposes. (Weber [1904] 1949, p. 72)

All knowledge of cultural reality, as may be seen, is always knowledge from particular points of view. (Weber [1904] 1949, p. 81)

The reason for this is twofold. First, reality is too complex to admit of full description and explanation. So we have to select. But, perhaps in contraposition to the natural sciences, we cannot just select those aspects of the phenomena that fall under laws and treat everything else as "unintegrated residues" (p. 73). This is because, second, in the social sciences we want to understand social phenomena in their individuality, that is, in their unique configurations that have significance for us.

Values thus solve a selection problem. They tell us what research questions we ought to address because they inform us about the cultural importance of social phenomena:

> Only a small portion of existing concrete reality is colored by our value-conditioned interest and it alone is significant to us. It is significant because it reveals relationships which are important to use due to their connection with our values. (Weber [1904] 1949, p. 76)

It is important to note that Weber did not think that social and natural science were different in kind. Social science too examines the causes of phenomena of interest, and natural science too often seeks to explain natural phenomena in their individual constellations. The role of causal laws is different in the two fields, however. Whereas establishing a causal law is often an end in itself in the natural sciences, in the social sciences laws play an attenuated and accompanying role as mere means to explain cultural phenomena in their uniqueness.

Nevertheless, for Weber social science remained objective in some way. By determining that a given phenomenon is "culturally significant" a researcher reflects on whether or not a practice is "meaningful" or "important", and not whether or not it is commendable: "Prostitution is a cultural phenomenon just as much as religion or money" (p. 81). An important implication of this view came to the fore in the so-called "*Werturteilsstreit*" (quarrel concerning value judgments) of the early 1900s. In this debate, Weber maintained against the "socialists of the lectern" around Gustav Schmoller the position that social scientists qua scientists should not be directly involved in policy debates because it was not the aim of science to examine the appropriateness of ends. Given a policy goal, a social scientist could make recommendations about effective strategies to reach the goal; but social science was to be value-free in the sense of not taking a stance on the desirability of the goals themselves.

Schmoller, of course, demurred. To him the issue was one of making economics more ethical and at the same time making ethical debates more scientific. It is important to note that he did not think that it would be a good idea to load economics with class or group or individual-specific interests. He believed, rather, that ethically sensitive social problems, especially those concerning economic justice, had demonstratively better and worse solutions and that economists were in a good position to help finding the better ones (Nau 2000). For him, there was therefore no conflict between acting as an economist *qua* economist and contributing substantively to political debates at the same time.

Many if not most contemporary economists stand firmly on Weber's side in this controversy. For a concise statement of the current mainstream view on the issue, consider Faruk Gul and Wolfgang Pesendorfer's widely cited paper:

> However, standard economics has no therapeutic ambition, i.e., it does not try to evaluate or improve the individual's objectives. Economics cannot distinguish between choices that maximize happiness, choices that reflect a sense of duty, or choices that are the response to some impulse. Moreover, standard economics takes no position on the question of which of those objectives the agent should pursue. (Gul and Pesendorfer 2008, p. 8)

7.4 Why Objectivity?

This is not the place to resolve these debates. Just to take a stance, I do think that compelling arguments have been made on the side of those who reject the respective ideal of objectivity in all three cases. First, even if there were an abstract economic reality behind the phenomena, we would never know it because economic factors tend not to combine additively but rather interactively. Therefore, the "law" that tells us what any given factor does in isolation from all others or when all others are held constant is not very informative about what that factor does when others are present or not constant. For policy purposes we should then study phenomena that are as close as possible to the policy situation we wish to change or bring about (Reiss 2008, Ch. 5). Second, there's a lot wrong with mechanical methods, and much has been said about this by people eminently more qualified than I am (Blalock 1991; Scriven 2008; Cartwright 2007; Deaton 2010). Some of the problems are: mechanical methods tend to be able to address only narrow sets of issues, a predicament which often results in changes in research question from one we want to answer to one we can address using the method; RCTs in particular are costly and may affect the populations studied; in social science, blinding – one of the major benefits of RCT methodology – is seldom an option; average results may mask dramatic differences in effect size among sub-populations; etc. Third, few learned men and women would any longer agree with Milton Friedman's dictum that differences about values are "differences about which men can ultimately only fight" (Friedman 1953), and rather turn to Amartya Sen who argues that rational argument concerning ethics is possible (Sen 1970). Moreover, economists are often in a privileged position to contribute to ethical debates (Atkinson 2001).

Rather than going through these arguments again what I want to do here is ask why we want a science that is objective in the first place. The first, and in my view most plausible, candidate is truth. For scientific realists, truth is an important (or the most important or the only) aim of science and there is a case to be made that only objective science – in the three-pronged sense of objective – can lead us to the truth.

The best argued and most coherent view of economics along these lines stems from Carl Menger. He argued that the aim of theoretical economics was to establish the laws pertaining to the "strict types" of the economic world, which could never be given in empirical circumstances because empirical types are always sullied by impurities:

> For even natural [as opposed to social] phenomena in their 'empirical reality' offer us neither strict types nor even strictly typical relationships. Real gold, real oxygen and hydrogen, real water – not to mention at all the complicated phenomena of the inorganic or even of the organic world – are in their full empirical reality neither of strictly typical nature, nor, given the above manner of looking at them, can exact laws even be observed concerning them. (Menger [1887] 1963)

In order to gather the truth, then, we have to depart from the phenomena and consider the strict types that are revealed to us by reasoning. These types and their strict laws, discovered ("mechanically") by deduction from first principles, describe the economic aspect of the phenomena of society. Ethics has no place in this vision of economics because it concerns the evaluation of states of affairs. But the economic laws are there whether or not we like them.

The problem with this vision, coherent as it might be, is twofold, epistemic and practical. The epistemic problem is that there is no way to arbitrate between different views on the matter of "economic truth". Menger starts his *Principles* with a definition of (economic) goods in terms of human needs, a thing's ability to satisfy a need, the needy person's knowledge of this ability and her command over it (Menger [1871] 1950). This is not an innocuous definition of economic good. Menger's objectivist conception of needs differed from the other neoclassical economists subjectivist conception of wants or preferences. Neoclassical economics ignored issues of information and knowledge until very recently. Nor is "having command over a thing" something about which most neoclassical economists would worry a great deal. But then, on a Mengerian conception of economics, how could we tell who is right?

The practical problem is that predictions concerning empirical phenomena depend on our knowledge of the strict laws of all aspects of the phenomena. So even if we knew the economic aspect for sure (but see above), we'd have to know every other aspect plus the (meta-)law for combining aspects. This is clearly a tall order but also one that may face in-principle obstacles, *viz.*, when aspects do not combine in a neat lawful way.

The next candidate for why we want objectivity is that it may guarantee us empirical adequacy. But this is not the case. As pointed out above, there is no guarantee that economic factors add linearly. To the contrary, there is much evidence to the effect that what a factor does depend on the constellation of all other factors. Therefore, the method of analysis and synthesis described above in Sect. 7.3.1 is unlikely to be successful. It certainly doesn't guarantee success. An RCT is, in a sense, a "holistic" method. If, say, we want to learn whether handing out bed nets for free, for a symbolic price or at cost is the most effective strategy to reduce malaria infections, we implement these strategies in affected population's otherwise unaltered habitat. We do not seek to establish what bed nets do to malaria infections in isolation from all other factors. But the RCT guarantees its result only under highly restrictive assumptions which, in most applications cannot be known to have been met. And there certainly have been many failures of policies established on the basis of RCTs.

Arthur Fine argues that we want objectivity, specifically procedural objectivity, in science because we want to trust scientists and their results: "Where the process of inquiry has certain built-in procedural features ('safeguards', we sometimes call them) we are inclined to trust it more than we would a procedure that fails to have those features" (Fine 1998, p. 17). It has been argued, for instance, that RCTs in medicine, while certainly no guarantor of the best outcomes, were adopted by the U.S. Food and Drugs Administration (FDA) to different degrees during the 1960s and 1970s in order to regain public trust in its decisions about treatments, which it had lost due to the thalidomide and other scandals (Reiss and Teira 2013; Teira 2010). To rid science of values can, similarly, be defended by appeals to attempts to ensure the trustworthiness of science. If social and moral values are personal, and this assumption is standardly made by economists (recall Lionel Robbins' "If we disagree about ends, it is a case of thy blood or mine – or live and let live ... But, if we disagree about means, then scientific analysis can often help us resolve our differences", Robbins 1932, p. 150), one will have a hard time trusting claims advanced by someone whose values one does not share. One might of course disagree on factual claims too but these disagreements, or so the story goes, can be settled on the basis of evidence.

But here comes the snag: the financial crisis has shown, if nothing else, that people do not trust economics. If even *The Economist*, a magazine not normally known for Marxist leanings or otherwise hostility to economics, blames the crisis on a failure of (macro and financial) economics (The Economist 2009, see below), we clearly have to worry about trust in the discipline.

What the crisis has shown is that objectivity in the three-pronged sense hasn't worked: economics has been criticized for being objective in all three senses in its wake. So what might be alternative strategies to win back trust in economics?

7.5 What's Wrong with Economics Experts?

Suppose for a moment we gave up objectivity in the three-pronged sense. In the resulting economics expert judgment would play a much more overt role than in traditional objectivist economics. If there is no privileged "economic aspect" of phenomena one can abstract from everything else and theorize about in isolation, someone has to make a selection of which features of the experienced phenomena that are worth theorizing about. If mechanical methods of inference fail, judgments about relevance and importance, quantity and quality of evidence that go into an inductive argument have to be made. If economics cannot be value free, someone has to decide which values to use in the process of scientific investigation. And who might this someone be? "The economics expert" is the answer that suggests itself.

But it would clearly be preposterous to assume that by giving a more prominent role to expertise alone the public would regain trust in economics. If *The Economist* laments "that macro and financial economists helped cause the crisis, that they failed to spot it, and that they have no idea how to fix it", the magazine does not refer to an impersonal behemoth called "economic science" that churned out the wrong kinds of predictions in the run-up to the crisis but rather economics experts who used the wrong theories or methods or assumptions, or used them in wrong ways.

The point is, we don't need just a more prominent role for expertise in economics, we need a better kind of expertise. Existing economics expertise is very heavily influenced by objectivist thinking. Let me give two apparently extreme but not untypical examples. The first is from an interview of Eugene Fama, Chicago economist and hero of financial economics (or so I was taught when I read finance), with *The New Yorker*'s John Cassidy. Fama not only says that the crisis left the efficient-market hypothesis unscathed, he also makes the following rather astonishing remarks:

Cassidy: Many people would argue that … there was a credit bubble that inflated and ultimately burst.

Fama: I don't even know what that means. People who get credit have to get it from somewhere. Does a credit bubble mean that people save too much during that period? I don't know what a credit bubble means. I don't even know what a bubble means. These words have become popular. I don't think they have any meaning.

Cassidy: I guess most people would define a bubble as an extended period during which asset prices depart quite significantly from economic fundamentals.

Fama: That's what I would think it is, but that means that somebody must have made a lot of money betting on that, if you could identify it. It's easy to say prices went down, it must have been a bubble, after the fact. I think most bubbles are twenty-twenty hindsight. Now after the fact you always find people who said before the fact that prices are too high. People are always saying that prices are too high. When they turn out to be right, we anoint them. When they turn out to be wrong, we ignore them. They are typically right and wrong about half the time.

Cassidy: Are you saying that bubbles can't exist?

Fama: They have to be predictable phenomena. I don't think any of this was particularly predictable. (Cassidy 2010)

Thus, there hasn't been a bubble in the real-estate market prior to the crisis. Perhaps this is an extreme case, but it's not uncommon that economists perceive phenomena through abstract theory – which, after all, describes the reality behind the phenomena. The second example concerns ethics. In his presidential address to the Eastern Economic Association, Harvard economist, one-time chairman of the Council of Economic Advisors and hero qua author of several undergraduate textbooks, Gregory Mankiw argues, quite amusingly, against a utilitarian foundation of optimal tax policies by deriving an apparent absurdity from it: an optimal tax system in which taller people pay higher taxes for the same income levels than shorter people (one reason is that height is an indicator of productivity). He calls his alternative moral foundation a "just deserts theory" and circumscribes it as follows:

> That is, each person's income reflects the value of what he contributed to society's production of goods and services. One might easily conclude that, under these idealized conditions, each person receives his just deserts. (Mankiw 2010, p. 295)

In equilibrium, and let's assume we are in equilibrium, every person receives his or her marginal product, this is just what he or she deserves, and under a just deserts theory this is a fair outcome. The problem is only that this "theory" ignores centuries of ethical argument. Let me give one instead of many. Individuals' incomes are usually determined by bargaining (whether at the individual level or that of groups such as workers in an industry). And, as Adam Smith, an ethically more sensitive economist, pointed out, the outcome of bargaining processes depends on a host of factors other than people's contributions such as the availability of outside options, the number and education of the individuals on each side of the bargain, their relative wealth, what they know and so on (Smith [1776] 2008, Book I, Ch. 8). Without an analysis of the conditions under which a bargain (or any exchange for that matter) is struck, one should not assume that people get what they deserve.

Paul Feyerabend didn't like scientific experts very much, for the reasons alluded to here (Feyerabend 1999). To him, an expert is primarily a specialist, one who tries to achieve excellence in an exceedingly narrow field at the expense of what he calls a "balanced development" – *some* knowledge of a variety of disciplines and fields such as history, philosophy, classics, the arts, pop culture and so on. Feyerabend describes living in a society in which experts (in this sense) have much influence on politics and society with his characteristic fervor:

Now, the peculiar situation in which we find ourselves today is that these inarticulate and slavish minds have convinced almost everyone that they have the knowledge and the insight not only to run their own playpens, but large parts of society as well, that they should be allowed to educate children, and that they should be given the power of doing so without any outside control and without supervision by interested laymen. [...] Should we allow a bunch of narrow-minded and conceited slaves to tell free men how to run their society? (Feyerabend 1999, p. 119)

I don't know about conceited, but one can hear that current economic experts tend to be too narrow-minded for the discipline's own good hither and yon. Our own Gregory Mankiw admits this much:

I should say at the outset that the issues I will discuss with you here involve not only economics but also some political philosophy. Because I am not a political philosopher by training, I hope you will forgive me if my occasional philosophical ruminations seem like those of an amateur. If I am right that the issue of redistributive justice will be at the heart of the coming policy debate, it will be hard to leave the topic to the philosophical experts. And in light of the inextricable linkages between philosophy and economics that characterize this topic, I hope it is possible that those experts might learn something from humble economists like me. (Mankiw 2010, pp. 285–6)

What Mankiw says about himself, other economist note about the profession: economists don't read enough history (Hoover 2012, p. 3), not enough humanities (McCloskey 2003, pp. 167 ff.), not enough ethics (Atkinson 2001). Far be it from me to suggest that economists are universally ignorant about these topics. But what one can say with some confidence is, I believe, that "reading widely" is not a value young economists are taught in graduate schools, certainly not in the leading ones. This is widely perceived to be a deficiency in the economics curriculum, for instance among employers of economists (Coyle 2012).

Let me give just one more piece of evidence. One way to read Mankiw's admission of ignorance of political philosophy is as displaying the virtue of modesty. An alternative is to read it as a display of the vice of arrogance. Here we have a world-class economist who, on the one hand, believes that there are "inextricable linkages between philosophy and economics" but, on the other hand, does not see the need to read up on what philosophers (and economists! – see e.g. Buchanan 1975) have said about the topic. At a recent conference I attended a very prominent economist (I cited one of his works here, but this is the only clue you will get) mocked my use of the word "ontology" – it being a word he does not understand. Lesson: many in economics regard ignorance, and not reading widely, as a virtue.

7.6 Economics Experts: Which Ones Should You Trust?

There is an alternative conception of objectivity, which contrasts sharply with the above. This conception is more pragmatist in character and thus starts from the end result and works its way back. Now, as we have seen, the purpose of doing science in an objective fashion is to gain trust. The alternative conception regards any trust-making feature of science as objective (Fine 1998, p. 18). That is, anything goes – as long as the practice promotes trust in science. In contraposition to the three-pronged traditional conception, we may call this conception "instrumentalism" about objectivity.

Instrumentalism makes the issue what features of the process of scientific investigation count as objective an empirical and contextual one. It is empirical in that anything that stands in the right kind of causal relation with public trust will count as an objective feature of science. There is no way to tell *a priori* what these features might be. It is contextual in that there is at least the possibility that these features vary with time, place, discipline and other contextual elements. It may well be, for instance, that the three-pronged traditional understanding once has promoted trust in economics, even if it no longer does so. It may also be that it is these features that promote trust in other sciences. And it may be that trust-making features vary with social and political circumstances – different features may be salient in different stages of development or between war and peace times and so on.

It is thus in the nature of the instrumentalist conception of objectivity that there is no answer to the question, "What is objectivity?" without an empirical study of the question "Which kinds of experts do you trust?". To end this chapter, I will nevertheless make a number of five, fairly mundane, recommendations of strategies that might be tried for success.

7.6.1 Strategy 1: Read More Widely

The great economist (and philosopher and legal scholar) Friedrich Hayek once said, "But nobody can be a great economist who is only an economist – and I am even tempted to add that the economist who is only an economist is likely to become a nuisance if not a positive danger" (Hayek 1956). To find out what else an economist needs to be in order not to become a nuisance, consider another great economist (and philosopher and statesman), John Maynard Keynes:

> The paradox finds its explanation, perhaps, in that the master-economist must possess a rare combination of gifts. He must reach a high standard in several different directions and must combine talents not often found together. He must be mathematician, historian, statesman and philosopher – in some degree. He must understand symbols and speak in words. (Keynes 1925, p. 12; quoted from Colander 2012, p. 11)

That an economist must also be a mathematician hardly needs defense these days. Still, two comments are in order. First, as David Colander argues, there are some reasons to believe that economists need more mathematics rather than less (ibid., p. 12). To model economies more adequately, an economist must understand how complex non-linear systems of heterogeneous agents work – which cannot be done using the simple linear dynamic models *en vogue* today. Second, and relatedly, economists need to use simulations models more than they currently do (Reiss 2011).

Simulations are a lot more flexible tool than analytically solvable mathematical models and can more readily capture the behavior of complex systems such as economies.

Through the study of economic history, the economist will gain some perspective, fill law schemata with empirical content and, in particular, understand that things could have been different. Richard Jones singlehandedly refuted a number of doctrines from Ricardo and Malthus that had become received wisdom at the time by simple appeal to the facts of history. For instance, he showed that Ricardo's universal definition of a rent relationship between a landowner and his tenant in fact only applied to England, Holland and parts of the United States at the time of his writing and that elsewhere and at other times other kinds of relationships prevailed. Similarly, he showed that Malthus's population principle wasn't even true of England's own history by comparing the contemporary state of population growth and food supply with that of pre-Elizabethan times (Snyder 2011, p. 124).

A statesman the economist has to be in at least two senses. She first has to know the institutional landscape at home and abroad. Even the most widely applicable economic principles hold only on account of an underlying institutional structure, and differences in institutional structure afford differences in causal relationships. Moreover, individuals act within institutional strictures. If a prediction of an economic outcome is to have any chance of success, it therefore must take into account these strictures.

Second, economics isn't (or shouldn't be) a science that discovers truths for the sake of truth, and even less one that promotes the interests of a small élite. The economist as statesman should know of the social problems of her time and aim to discover exactly those truths that help to resolve these problems.

Finally, the economist has to be part philosopher to understand that there is more to scientific method than deduction from first principles and RCTs as well as to follow the relevant ethical debates.

Rather than being a specialist in one thing, the economics expert who knows a little bit about everything will command public trust to the extent that the public realizes that there is no one talent that makes for a good economist and that knowledge of institutional and historical facts is as important as that of economic principles and the ability to make reasoned value judgments.

7.6.2 Strategy 2: Invite Non-economists to Economics Experts Committees

Not everyone can be expected to know everything and have all the required talents. Nor is this necessary. Many problems require interdisciplinary collaborations, so depending on the problem, one can import the expertise asked for. Unfortunately, economists tend not to like to talk to non-economists. But they should.

There are areas that are more obviously interdisciplinary. Economists, psychologists, philosophers and political scientists all engage in the study of well-being and its measurement for instance. But non-economists tend to be suspiciously absent from expert committees when it matters. The Advisory Commission to Study the Consumer Price Index or "Boskin Commission" after its chair Michael Boskin, for instance, had exclusively economists as members. But a price index measures the changes in the cost of living, and well-being experts other than economists surely have to say something about that (Reiss 2008, Ch. 2).

Similarly committees such as the Council of Economic Advisors would gain in credibility if its members had a broader range of expertise. Why not invite a financial historian? A philosopher? A legal scholar?

7.6.3   Strategy 3: Put Your Values on the Table

I used Mankiw's presidential address above as a example of economists' ignorance of discussions outside of economics and their taking pride in it. But Mankiw's discussion of optimal taxation policy is quite exemplary also in a different, a positive sense. Mankiw does not pretend that the topic can be studied in a way that is free of value judgments. To the contrary, he analyses the value framework of the standard approach, offers an alternative, and argues in favor of his alternative by pointing to some apparently untenable consequences of the standard view. His own view might, too, be untenable, but he does not hide it behind a tangled mass of apparently value-neutral mathematics.

Mankiw is quite unusual in this respect. Standard welfare economics is taught and usually presented as though it was a continuation of positive economics and did not involve substantive normative commitments at all (Gul and Pesendorfer 2008). At any rate, the normative commitments that are being made are seldom explicitly discussed (Atkinson 2001).

The situation is worse in positive economics. Perhaps this point is more controversial but strong arguments to the effect that value judgments are all over the place in positive economics are not difficult to make (Reiss 2008, 2013). And these do certainly get swept under the rug.

Hiding where one is coming from is not a good recipe if the goal is to inspire trust. The obvious alternative is, much like Mankiw, to make one's normative commitments explicit in order to allow critical scrutiny of these commitments by others, other experts and laypeople.

7.6.4   Strategy 4: Distinguish Value-Ladenness
          from Interest-Ladenness

Now, there are of course reasons why economists (and other scientists) prefer science to be value-free. One of the reasons is that science is different from partisan politics. Scientific results should serve as neutral arbiters between different positions and serve politicians of all colors, not just those who happen to agree with the scientist.

But science – economics – can play this role without being value free. To be value-laden does not necessarily mean to be laden with the interests of particular groups. There are various mechanisms that would help to make the difference clear. One might, for instance, derive a range of results under different sets of assumptions expressing different normative frameworks. Each of the derivations would be value-laden, but the economist would not necessarily present a result or policy that best agrees with her own convictions. Or one might subject the normative assumptions one must make for deriving results to public debate. Rather than using one's own views, the public would feed directly into the determination of the normative commitments.

7.6.5   Strategy 5: Admit that Rational Disagreement is Possible, in Matters of "Fact" as Much as Concerning "Values"

Among economists the view prevails that disagreements about values are, essentially, disagreements of taste and therefore cannot be rationally resolved whereas disagreements concerning facts can, at least in principle, be resolved by attending to empirical evidence. Let me quote Milton Friedman once more, as he makes the point so vividly:

> I venture the judgment, however, that currently in the Western world, and especially in the United States, differences about economic policy among disinterested citizens derive predominant from different predictions about the economic consequences of taking action – differences that in principle can be eliminated by the progress of positive economics – rather than from fundamental differences in basic values, differences about which men can ultimately only fight. An obvious and not unimportant example is minimum-wage legislation. Underneath the welter of arguments offered for and against such legislation there is an underlying consensus on the objective of achieving a 'living wage' for all, to use the ambiguous phrase so common in such discussions. The difference of opinion is largely grounded on an implicit or explicit difference in predictions about the efficacy of this particular means in furthering the agreed-on end. [. . .] Agreement about the economic consequences of the legislation might not produce complete agreement about its desirability, for differences might still remain about its political or social consequences but, given agreement on objectives, it would certainly go a long way toward producing consensus. (Friedman 1953)

It is quite ironic that today, 60 years on, there isn't an iota more consensus on the issue than at the time Friedman wrote, despite quantum leaps in both econometric technique and the availability of data. And the disagreements are not, or not only, about "fundamental differences in basic values".

There are at least two reasons to expect disagreements to persist. One is the entanglement of fact and value mentioned above. A disagreement about underlying values can therefore lead to a disagreement about the facts, even when data and observations are shared. The other is the complexity and evanescence of economic phenomena and the pace with which political agendas change. Even if we have much better econometric techniques than we had 60 years ago, they all work only against a backdrop of assumptions, many of which will seldom if ever be met. How different methods apply to non-ideal cases is always a matter of judgment and can seldom be resolved entirely unambiguously. Moreover, even relatively unambiguous cases will require a great deal of time for their resolution, and time is a scarce resource in the policy arena.

Economists should admit that rational disagreement is possible simply to show respect for other people. But it is also likely to promote trust in their science. If even enduring topics such as the costs and benefits of minimum wages cannot command consensus in economics, to deny rational difference of opinion amounts to admitting one's own irrationality. And who would trust a science whose practitioners think of themselves as foolish?

References

Angrist, J.D., and J.-S. Pischke. 2008. *Mostly harmless econometrics: An Empiricist's companion.* Princeton: Princeton University Press.

Atkinson, A. 2001. The strange disappearance of welfare economics. *Kyklos* 54(2–3): 193–206.

Blalock, H. 1991. Are there really any constructive alternatives to causal modeling? *Sociological Methodology* 21: 325–335.

Buchanan, J. 1975. Utopia, the minimal state, and entitlement. *Public Choice* 23: 121–126.

Cartwright, N. 2007. Are RCTs the gold standard? *BioSocieties* 2(1): 11–20.

Cassidy, J. 2010. Interview with Eugene Fama. *The New Yorker*, January 13, 2910.

Cohen, J., and W. Easterly. 2009. Introduction: Thinking big versus thinking small. In *Thinking Big and thinking small. What works in development*, ed. J. Cohen and W. Easterly, 1–23. Washington, DC: Brookings Institution.

Colander, D., M. Goldberg, A. Haas, K. Juselius, A. Kirman, T. Lux, and B. Sloth. 2009. The financial crisis and the systemic failure of the economics profession. *Critical Review* 21(2–3): 249–267.

Colander, D. 2012. What makes a good economist. In *What's the use of economics? Teaching the dismal science after the crisis*, ed. Diana Coyle. London: London Publishing Partnership.

Cook, C. 2013. *Reinhart-Rogoff recrunch the numbers.* FT Data http://blogs.ft.com/ftdata/2013/04/17/the-reinhart-rogoff-response-i/?

Coyle, D. (ed.). 2012. *What's the use of economics: Teaching the dismal science after the crisis.* London: London Publishing Partnership.

Deaton, A. 2010. Instruments, randomization, and learning about development. *Journal of Economic Literature* 48(2): 424–455.

Elgin, C. 1996. *Considered judgment.* Princeton: Princeton University Press.

Feyerabend, P. 1999. Experts in a free society. In *Knowledge, science and relativism*, ed. J. Preston, 112–126. Cambridge: Cambridge University Press.

Fine, A. 1998. The viewpoint of no-one in particular. *Proceedings and Addresses of the APA* 72 (2): 9–20.

Friedman, M. 1953. The methodology of positive economics. In *Essays in positive economics.* Chicago: University of Chicago Press.

Galilei, G. [1623] 1960. The Assayer. In *The Controversy on the Comets of 1618.* Trans. S. Drake and C. D. O'Malley. Philadelphia: University of Pennsylvania Press.

Gul, F., and W. Pesendorfer. 2008. The case for mindless economics. In *The foundations of positive and normative economics: A handbook*, ed. A. Caplin and A. Schotter, 3–39. New York: Oxford University Press.

Haller, M. 2004. Mixing economics and ethics: Carl Menger vs. Gustav von Schmoller. *Social Science Information* 43(1): 5–33.

Hausman, D. 1992. *The inexact and separate science of economics*. Cambridge: Cambridge University Press.

Hayek, F.A. 1956. The dilemma of specialization. In *The state of the social sciences*, ed. L. White. Chicago: University of Chicago Press.

Herndon, T., et al. 2013. *Does high public debt consistently stifle economic growth? A critique of Reinhart and Rogoff*. Working paper. University of Massachusetts Amherst, Political Economy Research Institute (PERI). 322.

Hoover, K. 2012. *Man and machine in macroeconomics*. CHOPE Working Paper. Center for History of Political Economy, Duke University. No. 2012-07.

Hutchison, T. 1994. *The uses and abuses of economics: Contentious essays on history and method*. London: Routledge.

Keynes, J.M. 1925. Alfred Marshall, 1842–1924. In *Memorials of Alfred Marshall*, ed. A.C. Pigou. London: Macmillan.

Koopmans, T. 1947. Measurement without theory. *Review of Economic Statistics* 29(3): 161–171.

Krugman, P. 2009. How did economists get it so wrong? *New York Times*, September 2.

Mankiw, N.G. 2010. Spreading the wealth around: Reflections inspired by Joe the Plumber. *Eastern Economic Journal* 36: 285–298.

McCloskey, D. 2003. *How to be human (Though an Economist)*. Ann Arbor: University of Michigan Press.

Menger, C. [1871] 1950. *Principles of economics*. Glencoe: Free Press.

Menger, C. [1887] 1963. *Problems of economics and sociology*. Urbana: University of Illinois Press.

Mill, J.S. [1843] 1874. *A system of logic, ratiocinative and inductive*. New York: Harper.

Mill, J.S. 1844. On the Definition of Political Economy; and on the Method of Investigation proper to it. *Essays On Some Unsettled Questions of Political Economy*, pp. 120–164. London: Parker.

Nau, H.H. 2000. Gustav Schmoller's historico–ethical political economy: Ethics, politics and economics in the younger German Historical School, 1860–1917. *European Journal of the History of Economic Thought* 7(4): 507–531.

Naylor, R. 1990. Galileo's method of analysis and synthesis. *Isis* 81(309): 695–707.

Raphael, D.D. 2007. *The impartial spectator*. Oxford: Oxford University Press.

Reinhart, C. and K. Rogoff. 2010. *Growth in a time of debt*. Working paper. Cambridge, MA: National Bureau of Economic Research. 15639.

Reinhart, C. and K. Rogoff. 2013. *Reinhart and Rogoff: Responding to our critics*. New York Times, April 25.

Reiss, J. 2000. Mathematics in economics: Schmoller, Menger and Jevons. *Journal of Economic Studies* 27(4–5): 477–491.

Reiss, J. 2008. *Error in economics: Towards a more evidence-based methodology*. London: Routledge.

Reiss, J. 2011. A plea for (good) simulations: Nudging economics toward an experimental science. *Simulation & Gaming* 42(2): 243–264.

Reiss, J. 2013. *Philosophy of economics: A contemporary introduction*. New York: Routledge.

Reiss, J., and D. Teira. 2013. Causality, impartiality and evidence-based policy. In *Towards the methodological turn in the philosophy of science: Mechanism and causality in biology and economics*, ed. H.-K. Chao, S.-T. Chen, and R. Millstein. New York: Springer.

Ricardo, D. 1817. *On the principles of political economy and taxation*. London: John Murray.

Robbins, L. 1932. *Essay on the nature and significance of economic science*. Toronto: Macmillan.

Rogoff, K. 2012. Austerity and debt realism. *Project syndicate: A world of ideas* http://www.project-syndicate.org/commentary/austerity-and-debt-realism.

Schmoller, G. 1883. Zur Methodologie der Staats- und Sozial-Wissenschaften. *Schmoller's Jahrbuch* 7(3): 975–994.

Schmoller, G. 1900. *Grundriss der Allgemeinen Volkswirtschaftslehre*, Band 1. Leipzig: Duncker & Humblot.

Scriven, M. 2008. A summative evaluation of RCT methodology & An alternative approach to causal research. *Journal of Multi-Disciplinary Evaluation* 5(9): 11–24.

Sen, A. 1970. *Collective choice and social welfare*. Amsterdam: Elsevier.

Smith, A. [1776] 2008. *An inquiry into the nature and causes of the wealth of nations: A Selected Edition*. Oxford: Oxford University Press.

Snyder, L. 2011. *The philosophical breakfast club*. New York: Broadway Books.

Stiglitz, J. 2009. The anatomy of a murder: Who killed America's economy? *Critical Review* 21 (2–3): 329–340.

Teira, D. 2010. Frequentist versus Bayesian clinical trials. In *Philosophy of medicine*, ed. F. Gifford, 255–297. Amsterdam: Elsevier.

The Economist. 2009. What went wrong with economics. *The Economist*, July 16.

Trichet, J.-C. 2010. Reflections on the nature of monetary policy non-standard measures and finance theory. Opening address at the ECB Central Banking Conference. Frankfurt.

Weber, M. [1904] 1949. Objectivity in social science and social policy. In *The methodology of the social sciences*, ed. M. Weber, E. Shils, and H. Finch, 50–112. Glencoe: Free Press.

Yonay, Y. 1998. *The struggle over the soul of economics: Institutionalist and neoclassical economists in America between the wars*. Princeton: Princeton University Press.

Part III
Attributing Standards of Expertise

Chapter 8
Epistemology as a Social Science: Applying the Neyman-Rubin Model to Explain Expert Beliefs

Aviezer Tucker

Abstract I present a social scientific approach to epistemic questions about expertise such as: Which properties make people into likely experts? What is the epistemic significance of agreements among experts? Is there a special kind of expert agreement that is indicative of knowledge? Why do the beliefs experts accept seem to enjoy a higher likelihood of being knowledge than the opinions of non-experts?

There are three types of causes of correlations between people and the beliefs they accept: Expertise, in the sense of special knowledge and impartiality; bias; and coincidence. The Neyman-Rubin model is useful for finding which is most likely.

The Neyman-Rubin model infers types of causes of correlated types of effects in two stages: First, it proves or disproves that the correlations between the types of effects are likelier given the hypothetical common cause type than given alternative (unspecified) numerous types of causes. The tested common cause type hypothesis specifies the properties of the type of common cause; but the properties of the alternative numerous types of causes are not specified. If both experimental and control populations are affected by the same types of (unknown or unspecified) variables, but only the experimental group is affected by a particular cause type (the treatment), significant differences between the two populations are likely to result from that cause type. At the second stage, the Neyman-Rubin model attempts to find the exact causal relations or nets, which may be complex, requiring the construction of multicollinear, interactive, and so on models.

A. Tucker (✉)
University of Texas, Austin, USA
e-mail: avitucker@yahoo.com; http://www.amazon.com/author/aviezertucker

© Springer International Publishing Switzerland 2014   155
C. Martini, M. Boumans (eds.), *Experts and Consensus in Social Science*,
Ethical Economy 50, DOI 10.1007/978-3-319-08551-7_8

8.1 Introduction

I propose to naturalize parts of epistemology as social science. It is observable that some people have certain beliefs or at least accept those beliefs as the best available (Cohen 1992; Miller 2013, pp. 1296–7). Standard surveys can establish correlations between groups of people and clusters of beliefs that they accept. Hypotheses that explain the correlations can be epistemically significant and interesting. Such hypotheses may be tested and corroborated using social science statistical methodologies that are more reliable than the methods of armchair epistemology like thought experiments.

I present here a social science approach to epistemic questions about expertise such as: Which properties make people into likely experts? What is the epistemic significance of agreements among experts? Is there a special kind of expert agreement that is indicative of knowledge? Why do the beliefs experts accept seem to enjoy a higher likelihood of being knowledge than the opinions of non-experts?

The answers social science epistemology can offer to such questions are "external" in the sense that they do not trace the processes that generate knowledge, beliefs or their acceptance in the minds of individual epistemic agents. Nor can social science epistemology examine the logical process of inference from evidence. Social science epistemology is useful in cases when it is impossible or inconvenient to open and look into the mental or methodological-inferential "black boxes" that connect cognitive inputs with outputs, or when we want to look into those boxes but do not know where they are. Non-experts may be unable to follow critically the process of belief formation of experts or may not have the time and or other resources to do so. They may have to reach epistemic conclusions on the basis of social science analysis of the group of experts. This resembles Goldman's formulation of what he called "the novice-experts problem": "some sorts of limiting factors-whether they be time, cost, ability, or what have you-will keep our novices from becoming experts, at least prior to the time by which they need to make their judgment. So the question is: Can novices, while remaining novices, make justified judgments about the relative credibility of rival experts? When and how is this possible?"[1] (Goldman 2001, p. 89).

Epistemologists interested in examining a type of inference of knowledge may not know where to start, where the expertise that should generate knowledge is exactly, especially when expertise is contentious. In the case of, say, quantum physics, it is obvious that if there is any expertise in the field, it is held by contemporary quantum physicists who publish papers in the field in prestigious peer reviewed journals. However, in other areas like economics, business, medicine, climatology, and environmental studies, the social location of expertise is not as obvious and may be contentious. Before epistemologists can study the cognitive processes that generate epistemically significant outputs, they need to know where

---

[1] I do not think that social science epistemology can distinguish between rival claims of experts. It can however distinguish likely from unlikely experts with rival claims.

to look, where expertise lies and who the experts whose practices they should study are likely to be. For example, in attempting to explicate the epistemology of our knowledge of the past, it is useful to know first which group of experts is likely to possess such knowledge, who are the historians who are likely to possess knowledge of the past (Tucker 2004).

The Neyman-Rubin model of causal inference is used by scientists, in particular social scientists, to infer types of causes from types of correlations (Morgan and Winship 2007; Sekhon 2010; Tucker 2012). Epistemology as a social science begins with epistemic hypotheses that connect types of epistemic causes (such as knowledge, expertise, or types of bias) with correlations between types of epistemic effects such as between types of people and types of beliefs. The transition from tokens to types of causal relations is achieved by the averaging of causal effects.[2] For example, there is significant correlation between scientists and belief in Darwinian evolution, in comparison with the populations in which the scientists live. This does not mean that each token scientist believes in a token of the theory of evolution; only that on average, there is a higher correlation between scientists and belief in evolution than the correlation between comparable populations of non-scientists and their belief in evolution. Another correlation may be between scientists and the belief that the more public funds are allocated by the government for scientists, the higher will economic growth and job creation be. Again, not every token scientist must hold this type of belief. On average scientists should have a greater tendency to accept it than comparable ordinary people. However, the cause of this correlation may be professional interest rather than expertise. The Neyman-Rubin method may help epistemologists to distinguish between such causes of correlation between scientists and beliefs, between expertise and bias.

Generally, from an epistemic perspective, there are three types of causes of correlations between people and the beliefs they accept: Expertise (which as I argue next means special knowledge and impartiality), bias, and coincidence. The Neyman-Rubin model is useful for finding out which of the three possible types of causes is most likely to have been effective in causing the correlation.

The Neyman-Rubin method infers types of causes of correlated types of effects in two stages: In the first stage, it proves or disproves that the correlations between the types of effects are likelier given the hypothetical common cause type than given alternative (unspecified) numerous types of causes. The tested common cause type hypothesis specifies the properties of the type of common cause; but the

---

[2] It is possible to characterize a type as having a certain property even if not all its tokens have the property. Though many tokens (for example of letters and words) resemble each other and share properties, not all do: "The analogy to zoology is helpful. Not every so-called black bear is black; not every grizzly is four-legged, brown or has a hump ... It may be permissible to characterize the species in terms of such properties anyway. In many cases, one extrapolates from properties of the tokens, individually or collectively, to properties of the type. However, ... even if the overwhelming majority of the tokens have a property it does not entail that the type has it" (Wetzel 2009, pp. 119–20). Some properties of a type are not shared by any of its tokens; for example, "the grizzly bear is endangered" (Wetzel 2009, p. 120).

properties of the alternative numerous types of causes are not specified.[3] For example, medical researchers are interested in finding out whether the correlation between an experimental group and healing is the result of the type of treatment (medicine) all its members received or the result of myriad other unspecified factors that affect healing. If both experimental and control populations are affected by the same types of (unknown or unspecified) variables, but only the experimental group is affected by a particular cause type (the treatment), significant differences between the two populations are likely to result from that cause type, e.g. the medicine increased the correlation between the experimental group and healing. If there is no significant difference in the correlations of the treatment and control groups with healing, the medicine probably was not causally effective.

Epistemologists, as social scientists using the Neyman-Rubin model of causal inference, may obtain a random sample of a population and divide it into two randomly assigned groups, whose only difference is the presence or absence of an epistemically interesting type of cause like a cognitive input or a biasing factor that the experimental group is introduced to but the control group is not. It is possible then to measure the average effect of the input or bias on the cognitive outputs (knowledge, beliefs, acceptance of beliefs) of the experimental group by measuring if there is a significant epistemic output difference between the beliefs of the two groups. Such experiments are common in behavioral economics and have produced most interesting results.

At the second stage, assuming that the correlation between types of effects is more likely given the specified type of cause type than given numerous unspecified different types of causes, the Neyman-Rubin method attempts to find the exact causal relations or nets, which may be complex, requiring the construction of multicollinear, interactive, and so on models. In the process, the method needs to eliminate possible confounders, common cause types of both the hypothesized type of cause and the correlation between its apparent effects. For example, personalized medical attention may cause both the administration of medicine and healing. Types of stress may cause both smoking and cancer. If statistically significant number of members of the experimental group are cured *except* a sub-group that is homogeneous in say, sharing the stage of development of the disease or in having a particular genetic makeup, it is still warranted to assign the cure to the new drug because the best explanation of the exceptional, dissenting, group is its homogeneous makeup.

In the experimental sciences, experimental designs control types of variables to isolate their effects. When such experiments are impossible, scientists resort to *statistical observational data analysis*. Using a variety of statistical control techniques to hold different variables constant while measuring others, social scientists

---

[3] I emphasize that the inference is of a common cause *type* rather than common cause *token*. Confusions between the inferences of common cause types and tokens have been rife and destructive in philosophy since Reichenbach. I have argued that the distinction between the inference of common cause types and tokens distinguished the theoretical from the historical sciences (Tucker 2007, 2012).

conduct multivariate regression analyses that generate causal maps that measure levels of causal influence that each variable exerts on the others.

"Natural," undesigned, experiments, can be just as effective in confirming hypothesis as laboratory experiments when nature cooperates. The experimental group should be as identical in type to the control group as possible. For example, in studying the causes of a type of cancer, random assignment is impossible. Instead, scientists select a random sample of people with cancer and a random sample of the population that contains the cancer sufferers and compare them to see if some causes seem to be more significantly correlated with the first than with the second group, e.g. smoking.

8.2   Expertise as the Explanation of Belief

In the following discussion I consider *expertise* to mean *impartiality* and *special knowledge*. Goldman (2001) discussed the meaning of expertise at some length. I agree with him in broad terms about the link between knowledge and expertise, but I add impartiality as a necessary condition. Knowledge could not generate experts unless they are also impartial; otherwise, their accepted beliefs would reflect their biases rather than their knowledge.

"Anthropological" reliance on professional organizations or academic institutions, affiliations and certifications to identify experts is a tempting alternative pragmatic approach that we use in everyday life to navigate society. At their best, professional and academic institutions should promote, promulgate, regulate and enforce expertise that makes agreements among their members epistemically significant and likely. However, historically, this appeal to authority has failed too often. Academic and professional institutions have been too susceptible to political pressure and coercion from without, economic interests and graft from within, internal power and seniority hierarchies, or the shared biases of a class of people who share professional interest and sometimes social background. The alternative approach I endorse does not have to rely on institutional authority.

The question is whether expertise in the sense of impartiality and special knowledge is a better explanation of correlations between groups of people and clusters of accepted beliefs than coincidence or bias. The Neyman-Rubin method can test the expertise hypotheses first against the coincidence hypothesis and if it passes that test, against the bias hypothesis.

People may adopt beliefs or even reach consensus on them (perfect correlation) coincidentally, just like an experimental group in medicine can be cured irrespective of the medicine because of the various different properties of the patients; or a group of people with lung cancer may have become sick irrespective of their smoking because they were exposed to myriad other risk factors. A complex alternative theory to the hypothesis that expertise accounts for a significant correlation between a group and its accepted beliefs, may combine conjunctions and disjunctions of different factors to explain the correlation. Miriam Solomon (2001) advocated such explanation of scientific consensus. Solomon suggested that scientific consensus on beliefs results from many different "decision vectors" that somehow have the same effect. Better scientific theories are affected by a greater variety and distribution of decision vectors than theories that follow a more narrow range of them, *e pluribus unum*. Solomon did not regard "decision vectors" such as ideology or pride, deference to authority or agreement with scriptures, as impediments to the achievement of scientific knowledge, but as inevitable necessary prerequisites for scientific progress. If Solomon is right, experts such as scientists do not agree because they share expertise, *despite* their different genders, cultures, interests and so on, but exactly because they are men and women of different cultures and of various interests and so on. Solomon collapsed the distinction between evidence ("empirical vectors"), cognitive values ("theoretical vectors"), and biases ("social vectors"). Altogether, Solomon (2001, pp. 62–3) estimated there are 50–100 decision vectors of all kinds that affect theory choice by themselves or in interaction with each other.[4]

Miller (2013, pp. 1307–8) introduced the historical example of broad acceptance by most medical scientists that excess acidity in the stomach caused peptic ulcers. In Miller's opinion, this consensus resulted from several decision vectors: Academic hierarchical status and power disparity between powerful supporters and weak deniers of the acidity hypothesis; prevailing physiological theory that held that the stomach was too acidic for bacteria to survive in; and the economic interests of pharmaceutical companies in a chronic illness that required a lifelong supply of anti-acids rather than a single round of antibiotics. Miller acknowledged that there were competing internal explanations of this episode in the history of science that did not resort to social biases. It does not matter for the current discussion if Miller's historical example is correct or not. Miller is right that "on occasion" coincidences can and do happen and various interests, biases, and so on coalesce in high correlation with the same set of beliefs. The same can happen in medicine, despite proper experimental design, significant statistical gap between treated and control groups can follow different causes rather than the treatment. Still, *ceteris paribus* in most cases the treatment is more likely to be the cause of the difference than many different causes. This conclusion is probable and not certain and hence fallible. The Neyman-Rubin method acknowledges that outcomes such as beliefs can be affected by the coincidence of large number of known and unknown factors (or vectors). But

---

[4] Solomon suggested that diversity of decision vectors is the best explanation of consensuses on beliefs among scientists. Still, *ceteris paribus*, even without using the Neyman-Rubin method, the likelihood of consensus is higher given a single common cause type such as expertise or an overwhelming bias for all the opinions of the experts than given many diverse decision vectors because of the low probability that all different biases will cause identical types of beliefs. In Bayesian terms, it would require multiplying the independent likelihoods of the beliefs given each independent type of bias by each other. Even if each likelihood is high to begin with, the result of multiplying many such factors by each other would reduce the total likelihood to close to zero. Miller (2013) noted correctly that this criticism is valid only when the vectors should explain a consensus in the sense of absolute agreement among all. A weaker but still significant correlation may be likely given different causes that generate the correlation with high likelihood.

if a control group (general non-expert population) is very likely to share those vectors with the experimental group (of experts), they probably cancel each other and expertise remains last standing as the best explanation of the doxastic outcomes.

8.3   The Limits of the Neyman-Rubin Method
in Epistemology

The Neyman-Rubin method can generate interesting epistemic results. But it can function only within bounds: Statistical samples of the tested "expert" group must be large enough to cancel out the various vectors of the larger control, non-expert, group. Smaller samples would not necessarily reproduce the various "decision vectors" or biases of the control group and may have a higher concentration of some decision vectors and so may generate results (beliefs) that do not result from the expertise "treatment." For example, a consensus on an esoteric topic by a handful of professionals may follow peculiar social dynamics in comparison with society, for example the domination of a single or few authoritative figures, "a guru" or "a cabal" (Goldman 2001, p. 98) that determine who is and is not hired in a small academic social milieu, and consequently who teaches and publishes. Such correlation or even consensus cannot function as an indicator of expertise according to the Neyman-Rubin method because the sample is too small, it does not replicate the distribution of properties in the population at large, and it has a higher concentration of authoritarian control by a small cabal than in society at large where many different concentrations of power can countervail each other.[5] This can happen only in isolated academic oligopolistic hierarchical structures where a small cabal can leverage its control over other institutions lower down on the hierarchy to impose its opinions. Once expertise goes global and outside the academy, it spins out of control and no oligopoly can usually achieve control any more than any financial cartel can control global markets and prices for a substantial period of time in today's global economy. For this reason, the correlation between scientists and Evolutionary and Relativity theories or historians and much of what they agree on about the past (which conspiracy theorists dispute) cannot be reduced to a small sample with a rigid social hierarchy, as in some parts of the academic humanities.

---

[5] Goldman's (2001) analyses the position of a layperson deciding between experts in terms borrowed from the epistemology of testimony. Only independent testimonies matter and they should be evaluated according to their reliabilities. Experts have higher reliabilities than lay people about esoteric subjects they specialize in. Despite the Bayesian framework, Goldman left out the prior estimation of the probability of what the experts testify for. As Bovens and Hartmann (2003) demonstrated, when that prior is low enough, two even unreliable but independent testimonies are sufficient for inferring knowledge. This Bayesian epistemology of testimony approach cannot discriminate between competing expert opinions if the experts who testify are independent and have similar credibility and their testimonies-opinions are similarly surprising.

The Neyman-Rubin method is also useless for identifying expertise if there are multiple groups with inconsistent beliefs that nevertheless seem to have the same expertise and the same social composition in comparison with the same control group of non-experts. The Neyman-Rubin method is useless for choosing which group is most impartial and knowledgeable. The *uniqueness* of the social correlation between the group of people affected by expertise and beliefs is essential for utilizing the Neyman-Rubin method in epistemology. If more than one group possesses the same expertise but forms different conclusions, an external social science method cannot identify which one is more likely to be in possession of impartial knowledge.

Multiple sub-groups with strong correlations with inconsistent beliefs are not a problem for the Neyman-Rubin method if all the groups of people who have inconsistent beliefs to those of the "expert" group are homogenous and their beliefs can be explained by that homogeneity. In such a case it can be argued that the otherwise heterogeneous expert group is the only impartial group. For example, the claim for impartial expertise of the scientists who believe in Darwinian Evolution is supported by the fact that all those who deny evolution, belong to fairly homogenous religious groups, while believers in evolution include members of virtually all religions. Similarly, there are historiographic accounts that are accepted by all or almost all historians except homogenous partisan groups. For example, the Holocaust, the deliberate genocide of about six million Jews during the Second World War, is believed by all the experts on the Second World War irrespective of their national, religious or ideological background. All Holocaust deniers are Neo-Nazis of various shades.

8.4 Confounding the Confounders

When it is seems likely that a correlation between a group and its beliefs is the result of expertise and not numerous other unknown factors, epistemic social scientists must be wary of confounding factors, either alternative single causes to expertise that also distinguish the expert from the control group, or common causes that affect both the expertise and the correlation between the group of experts and its accepted beliefs. If not the result of coincidence, the significant correlation between a group and its accepted beliefs may result from bias.

An alternative common cause type to expertise can be coercion. Coercion is no foundation for real consensus, but for "unwilling acquiescence" (Caws 1991, p. 379). Coercion may take many forms, violence, intimidation, threats, manipulation by economic dependence, or plain browbeating. Even oppressive coercion is rarely sufficient for coercing a full consensus of expressed opinions. Some people are not easily intimidated, others have a strong character and do not react to threats, and others take their own beliefs sufficiently seriously to express them regardless of the effect it may have on their personal fortunes. Historical experience demonstrated that the establishment of even a local coerced consensus on public expressions of belief in a state-sanctioned dogma required the extensive and extreme use of violence. Both the Inquisition and the Soviet NKVD secret police could not coerce without killing dissenters. Still, coercion can affect the correlation between groups of people and the opinions they express, whether or not they believe in them. Coercion may lead to the establishment of a discursive hegemony. Coercive bodies, most notably the state, may be interested only in the publicly accepted opinions of experts known for their special knowledge and expertise. This interest rather than expertise may create the apparent significant doxastic gap between the expert and control, non-expert, groups; the state may not care for the public opinions of the uneducated masses.

Confounders that affect both the expertise and the correlation between the group of experts and their beliefs may include social factors that select the experts and then affect their judgment. For example, if all medical doctors were male and they considered the male body the standard *human* body, there is a strong case for claiming that their beliefs about human anatomy as well as the social criteria that selected them to become experts reflected male biases rather than expertise. Masculinity confounded expertise.

If social science epistemologists eliminate known confounders, there is a *fallible* case for expertise. For example, scientists who endorse Darwinian evolution are an incredibly heterogeneous group. It is difficult to imagine one or more confounding biasing factors that would turn the apparently heterogeneous scientific community into a homogeneously biased group in a way that would confound the hypothesis that expertise causes the significant correlation between scientists and belief in Darwinian evolution. Yet, this conclusion is fallible. It is always possible that social science epistemologists overlooked a doxastic biasing factor, and an apparently heterogeneous sample was actually homogenous in a doxastic relevant way. A new hypothesis that discovers a confounding bias in a group may undermine its claim for expertise. For example, feminist philosophers of science developed hypotheses that discovered correlations between male biases in scientific communities in medicine and biology and their scientific beliefs (cf. Longino 1990, pp. 103–214; Okruhlik 1994). Before the introduction of feminist philosophy of science, historians and philosophers of science surely noticed that all doctors were males, but did not consider the gender composition of scientific groups significant for the explanation of their beliefs.

Conversely, a hypothesized confounding bias may be rejected by using the Neyman-Rubin method. For example, Communist ideologues claimed that Mendelian genetics and Darwinian evolution were biased by capitalist free market competition ideology. The Nazis claimed that the concentration of scientists of Jewish descent in branches of sciences like relativity theory biased them as "Jewish science." But the social background of geneticists and the religious practices of the ancestors of physicists were irrelevant for the acceptance of their knowledge as impartial and for recognizing them as experts. From a social science epistemic perspective, all expertise must emerge somewhere, sometime, among some people. The question, when applying the Neyman-Rubin method to epistemology, is whether *over time* the beliefs that emerged and developed among a specific, even homogenous, group of experts become accepted by very different kinds of people who then serve to refute social bias confounding hypotheses and support an expertise hypothesis that explains better the high correlation between people of very different backgrounds and accepted beliefs, in Mendelian genetics and relativity theory for example.

In natural experiments, especially because of the absence of random assignment, it is possible to guard only against conceivable confounding biases that are connected with alternative hypotheses to the expertise hypothesis. It is always possible that a relevant confounding bias has been overlooked and the expertise hypothesis is false despite the apparent heterogeneity of the consensus group. Confidence in the expertise hypothesis is directly related to the variety and diversity of alternative confounding hypotheses. The more varied alternative confounding hypotheses there are, the easier it is to guard against bias.

8.5   Cognitive Values

One particular possible confounder may undermine the whole idea of implementing in epistemology the Neyman-Rubin method for discovering expertise: shared cognitive values. Arguably, expertise is just an intermediate variable between shared cognitive values and correlations with beliefs. If so, expert agreement is not a reflection of knowledge and impartiality, but of shared cognitive values.

Cognitive values determine which statements are worthy of being considered knowledge, absolutely or in comparison with competing statements. Arguably, cognitive values may confound expertise. Kuhn (1996, pp. 184–6) suggested that the scientific community is constituted by cognitive values: accuracy, consistency, scope, simplicity and fruitfulness. Cognitive values changed more slowly than theories in the history of science. If shared cognitive values are necessary for forming beliefs, the expertise hypothesis may have to be at the very least qualified as relative to particular sets of cognitive values as biases that are shared by the putative expert group.

It is possible to reapply the Neyman-Rubin method to epistemology to examine cognitive values. The *conduciveness hypothesis* explains the high correlation between experts and types of cognitive values in comparison with a comparable control group of non-experts by their greater conduciveness to knowledge, in comparison with other cognitive values. For example, the birth of science was accompanied by a shift from cognitive values that considered knowledge to be the result of faith, revelation, ancient wisdom and tradition, to empiricist values that are arguably more conducive to knowledge. The conduciveness hypothesis can then be supported by the Neyman-Rubin method just like the expertise hypothesis, and be fallibly corroborated. Experts who possess impartial special knowledge unsurprisingly correlated more strongly with cognitive values that are conducive to the attainment of knowledge than comparable groups that are not in the business of obtaining special knowledge, or fail to achieve it. Competing hypotheses that claim to explain a significant correlation of experts with cognitive values by any other (particularly external social or cultural) variables would find it quite difficult to explain the appeal of these values to very different experts and their lower appeal to very similar groups of non-experts. The size of the group (not a sample) that upholds scientific cognitive values is much larger than that of any group of experts with special knowledge; it is the set of all the sets of experts. Accordingly, a comparable control group of non-expert will have to be just as universal. The heterogeneity and sizes of these groups should prove any bias in the achievement of expert correlation with scientific cognitive values highly unlikely.

8.6   Comparison with Consensus Accounts of Expertise

The Neyman-Rubin method's fallible inference of expertise from significant correlations between sufficiently large, uniquely heterogeneous, and unconfounded groups and accepted beliefs, in comparison with control groups is preferable to alternative epistemic attempts to use consensus or consensus inducing procedures as markers of knowledge, rationality, and expertise. The application of the Neyman-Rubin method to social science epistemology should make epistemology clearer, more parsimonious, pragmatically applicable to everyday contexts rather than to ideal situations, better reasoned, and politically unproblematic.

A literally universal consensus about any belief in any group is very rare, a utopian ideal with few instantiations in the real world (cf. Miller 2013, p. 1297). Epistemologists who resorted to a concept of consensus had to specify a particular meaning of this concept that could make it useful or resort to vagueness: "Consensus is typically not all encompassing ... since usually some dissent remains. The decision whether or not to call a state of affairs 'consensus' or 'dissent' is to *some extent arbitrary*" (Solomon 2001, p. 118, my italics).

One popular approach substitutes a process or a procedure that should generate a consensus for the consensus itself. For example, in Rescher's (1993) interpretation, Habermas limited his philosophic discussion of consensus to an ideal rational type, according to an *ideal process*. But an account of epistemic consensus that reduces it to a *process* that should generate the proper, significant, type of consensus begs the question. If a consensus is epistemically significant only if it follows a particular process, then the process is epistemically important, not the ensuing consensus. Similarly, the use of consensus to elucidate rationality must presuppose an account of rationality to discover which consensus is rational. Nicholas Rescher (1993, p. 13) criticized what he took to be Habermas's concept of consensus as begging the question of rationality. Rescher noted that if "consensus" is used in the sense of an *ideal* consensus under ideal circumstances that allow for a process of unconstrained rational consideration, consensus is reduced to the outcome of unbridled rationality. Unbridled rationality does not require a consensus or even a process. If a single individual or a machine possesses all the relevant evidence, background knowledge and pure rationality, a rational result will be inferred inevitably and a consensus would be superfluous.

An epistemic focus on an ideal consensus excuses ignoring the absence of actual literal consensuses where all experts agree on all their expert beliefs as well as actual cases of consensus that were irrational or founded on false beliefs, as deviations from the ideal. Habermas followed Peirce in attempting to understand truth by analyzing an ideal consensus that should follow a reflexive process of argumentation, mutual criticism, and airing of cultural values.[6] Since for Habermas only the results of an ideal speech situation were rational, less than ideal speech situations, practically all real situations of agreement and disagreement in society, were to varying degrees, less than rational. It would stand to reason then for experts to proceed on what an ideal speech situation *would have* resulted in, rather than bother with necessarily imperfect actualizations of the ideal of consensus (Habermas 1990, p. 67).

Since for Habermas only the results of an ideal speech situation are rational, less than ideal speech situations are less than rational. It is rational for a Habermasian to proceed on what an ideal speech situation *would have* resulted in, rather than bother with a necessarily imperfect actualization in something like anarchic democratic process. An intellectual minority can then conveniently define and represent the hypothetical rational consensus that *would have* resulted from an ideal procedure. Historically, this was the Jacobin interpretation of Rousseau's general will, a *hypothetical* general will that could not be ascertained empirically.

The Jacobins legitimized their dictatorship by claiming that the opinions of the people do not count, are not the general will, as long as they are hungry, dominated and misled by the rich who hire venal journalists to manipulate them (Talmon 1970, p. 106). Jacobin "democracy" is not about listening to the people or counting their votes, but about the creation of conditions for the true expression of the general will. Till then, the intellectual revolutionary vanguard may follow the common will, not the democratic majority vote (ibid., pp. 105–7). "The majority in the real sense is where the true general will resides, even if that will happens to be expressed by a numerical minority" (ibid., p. 99) of Jacobin activists. The idea that popular majority vote does not count as democratic until certain egalitarian prerequisites are satisfied runs from the Jacobins through to Habermas. Habermas's utopian vision, like that of the Jacobins, was the homogenization of society, an end to power distinctions and power biased "knowledge." Accordingly, the second task of

---

[6] Charles Peirce (1877, pp. 132–3) believed that the scientific process will ultimately generate consensus on objective truth. His faith in an unspecified scientific process of investigation was combined with an eschatological rhetoric about consensus as the "destiny", "destined center", "foreshadowed Goal", and "predestined opinion" of the history of science. Consensus for Peirce was not concrete, but a chiliastic ideal to be realized at the end of time, a form of epistemic messianism. Before the promised consensus comes about at the end of the scientific process, it is impossible to know which beliefs are true and which will be forsaken during the future history of science, just as it is impossible to distinguish the righteous from the sinners, the city of god from the city of man, before judgment day.

the rational intellectual or expert who knows which consensus should emerge from a rational process of deliberation is to obtain the kind of political power that would allow them to destroy all competing power centers to create the homogenous society that can then finally reach a rational consensus, the Jacobins' reign of terror.

> Only in an egalitarian public of citizens that has emerged from the confines of class and thrown off the millennia-old shackles of social stratification and exploitation can the potential of an unleashed cultural pluralism fully develop – a potential that no doubt abounds just as much in conflicts as in meaning-generating forms of life. But in a secularized society that has learned to deal with its complexity consciously and deliberately, the communicative mastery of *these* conflicts constitutes the sole source of solidarity among strangers. (Habermas 1996, p. 308)

Rescher (1993, pp. 156–7) traced back Habermas's utopian consensus to Hegel's march of reason in history and Marx's dream of a homogenous society without special interests. The totalitarian power required for such radical egalitarian transformation of society, to allow the emergence of "authentic complete democracy," has never been used for that purpose. Once any group achieved totalitarian power, it used it in its own interests. The Jacobins first excluded from discussion the special interests, the upper classes and the clerics; when that proved insufficient, they decapitated them, when that proved still insufficient they proceeded to decapitate other classes and special interests, culminating with themselves.

Other theories within the Habermasian orbit proposed different and sometimes less radical lists of necessary conditions for the emergence of epistemically significant consensus. Helen Longino (1994) argued that the consensus that counts must result from critical dialogues among individuals and groups from different points of view, an "interactive dialogic community" (1994, pp. 142–3). Longino stipulated further the properties of the community that can transmute subjective points of view into scientific objectivity: there must be public *fora* for criticism; the community must be responsive to criticism; there must be revisable public standards, cognitive values, to which participants in the discourse can appeal to reach agreement; and the community should be intellectually egalitarian, where decisions about beliefs are not taken by appeal to authority. Critical discourse should explain how different biases and points of view are transformed into consensus on beliefs. Still, like Habermas, Longino could not be interested in consensus *per se*, but in an ideal process for generating knowledge. The conditions she stipulated have been satisfied very rarely. These conditions are also too narrow because there can be a consensus or broad agreement among experts without deliberation, when a conclusion is obvious, given cognitive input, and discussion is superfluous, for example, when a surprising piece of evidence is discovered or the results of a crucial experiment become known.

The use of the Neyman-Rubin method releases epistemology from having to rely on vaguely defined or ideal consensus or from being forced to allow ideal presuppositions and procedures to substitute for the elusive consensus. From the perspective of the Neyman-Rubin model, a consensus is just an extreme and historically rare case of statistically significant correlation between a group and beliefs. Statistically significant correlation in comparison with a control group does not stipulate any particular epistemic process, nor does it demand the satisfaction of utopian preconditions whose self-defeating satisfaction requires political dictatorship. Epistemologists who are interested in the procedures that produce the significant correlation with beliefs can then pursue a different, intrinsic, research project inquiring *how* the group of experts reached its beliefs.

Boaz Miller (2013) proposed that knowledge is likely to be the best explanation of epistemic consensus the more three conditions are met: Apparent consilience of evidence, shared evidential standards in a consensus community, and diversity of social backgrounds. Miller's three conditions are intrinsic (the relation between types of evidence and knowledge), pragmatic (evidential standards and use of language that describes the evidence), and social (diversity of backgrounds). However, if the first criterion is well satisfied, the other two are redundant. If epistemologists can trace and judge the relation between evidence and beliefs, measure the consilience of the evidence and how it supports the posterior probability of hypotheses, the other criteria do not matter for the epistemic evaluation of whether the support of the evidence to the hypothesis is sufficient for considering it knowledge. For example, suppose the epistemologist concludes from studying the relation of evidence to hypothesis that it is well corroborated, though all the scientists who accept the hypothesis are white male zombies. Would the possible zombie bias matter here?! Arguably, not, because the epistemologist can trace intrinsically the process of inference from evidence irrespective of the identity of the experts. The "zombie hypothesis" that shared beliefs may reflect zombie culture and biases is relevant only if we cannot, or do not have the resources, to check the evidential justification of the hypothesis ourselves. Miller defended his social diversity requirement against this sort of argument, claiming that without sufficient social diversity the evidence cannot be sufficiently consilient. Social diversity should control against two kinds of biasing influences, expected and unexpected. Known hypotheses connect expected biases such as the financial interests of researchers with the results of the research. "[D]iversity is also required for controlling for unexpected influences. There may be influences of which we are unaware, and the more diversified the consensus, the less likely they will affect it. This is similar to the rationale behind the design of randomized clinical trials, which are required to control for both known confounders (sex, age, etc.) and unknown confounders" (Miller 2013, p. 1312). Miller implies that the Neyman-Rubin method can guard against both expected and unexpected biases and he is right; this is what I have been arguing for in this chapter.

Diversity is *not the only* way to guard against biases. It should be possible for qualified observers with sufficient resources to detect faulty research design or inference from evidence irrespective of expected or unexpected biases. Diversity or the Neyman-Rubin method is useful when it is *impossible* or *too expensive* in terms of time and other resources to examine the relation between evidence and accepted beliefs, or when we want to trace this process but are not sure where to look for it. In this second case, the Neyman-Rubin method may be social scaffolding that holds an epistemic edifice while it is being built.

8.7 Down with the Scaffoldings!

Epistemology as a social science has the advantage of attempting to build an edifice of expertise "from the ground up," from the observable social effects of epistemic processes, rather than "top down," from ideal definitions of knowledge and rationality. Epistemology can use the results of the search for expertise to locate a social and historical space of expertise.

Sufficiently large and uniquely heterogeneous groups that are strongly correlated with sets of beliefs, more than comparable control groups, enjoy a fallible presumption of expertise in the absence of confounders. Members of such groups are likely to be experts. This presumption of expertise precedes any knowledge and analysis of their epistemic practices. Epistemologists can use then the Neyman-Rubin method to know where to look for expert special knowledge. Epistemologists who are interested in an *internal* epistemic account of the generation of knowledge by experts, can investigate further which methodologies generate expert knowledge within each putative group of experts. I applied this method in the philosophy of historiography (Tucker 2004). Before attempting to answer questions about the epistemology of our knowledge of the past, I asked first where, when and among which group of expert historians such knowledge has emerged, spread, and become accepted. The answer to this question provided a natural basis for an epistemology of the knowledge of the past. This external, social scientific conclusion allowed me to build an epistemology of historiography from the ground up, by studying the theories and methodologies that enabled the emergence of this uniquely heterogeneous group that reached such a broad agreement about so much of what it believed about the past.

Similar epistemic applications of the Neyman-Rubin method can benefit other epistemic sub-fields that attempt to understand knowledge derived from expertise, like the philosophies of the special sciences. Epistemic inquiry can then investigate what kind of special knowledge expert groups possess that allow them to reach significant correlations with beliefs. This corresponds with standard scientific search for mechanisms, after establishing correlations between the treatment and the correlated results, for example, if the medicine correlates with healing in comparison with a control group, or if smoking correlates with higher rates of cancer among smokers in comparison with a non-smoking comparable group, scientists ask for the physiological and chemical mechanisms that cause the healing or the cancer. Similarly, epistemologists can find out how particular groups of experts obtain their knowledge, after they establish the likelihood of their expertise, and drop the scaffolding of social science epistemology.

References

Bovens, Luc, and Stephan Hartmann. 2003. *Bayesian epistemology*. Oxford: Oxford University Press.

Caws, Peter. 1991. Committees and consensus: How many heads are better than one. *Journal of Medicine and Philosophy* 16(375): 91.

Cohen, L. Jonathan. 1992. *An essay on belief and acceptance*. Oxford: Oxford University Press.

Goldman, Alvin. 2001. Experts: Which ones should you trust? *Philosophy and Phenomenological Research* 63: 85–110.

Habermas, Jürgen. 1990. *Moral Consciousness and Communicative Action*. Trans. Christian Lenhardt and Shierry Weber Nicholson. Cambridge, MA: MIT Press.

Habermas, J. 1996. *Between Facts and Norms: Contributions to a Discourse Theory of Law and Democracy*. Trans. William Rehg. Cambridge, MA: MIT Press.

Kuhn, Thomas S. 1996. *The structure of scientific revolutions*, 3rd ed. Chicago: Chicago University Press.

Longino, Helen E. 1990. *Science as social knowledge: Values and objectivity in scientific inquiry*. Princeton: Princeton University Press.

Longino, H.E. 1994. The fate of knowledge in social theories of science. In *Socializing epistemology: The social dimensions of knowledge*, ed. Frederick F. Schmitt, 135–157. Lanham: Rowman and Littlefield.

Miller, Boaz. 2013. When is consensus knowledge based? Distinguishing shared knowledge from mere agreement. *Synthese* 190: 1293–1316.

Morgan, Stephen L., and Christopher Winship. 2007. *Counterfactuals and causal inference: Methods and principles for social research*. Cambridge: Cambridge University Press.

Okruhlik, Kathleen. 1994. Biology and society. *Canadian Journal of Philosophy* 20(Supplementary): 21–42.

Peirce, Charles S. [1877] 1958. How to make our ideas clear. In *Selected writings*, ed. Philip P. Weiner, 113–136. New York: Dover.

Rescher, Nicholas. 1993. *Pluralism: Against the demand for consensus*. Oxford: The Clarendon Press.

Sekhon, Jasjeet S. 2010. The Neyman-Rubin model of causal inference and estimation via matching methods. In *The oxford handbook of political methodology*, ed. Janet M. Box-Steffensmeier, Henry E. Brady, and David Collier, 271–299. Oxford: Oxford University Press.

Solomon, Miriam. 2001. *Social empiricism*. Cambridge, MA: MIT Press.

Talmon, Jacob L. 1970. *The origins of totalitarian democracy*. New York: Norton.

Tucker, Aviezer. 2004. *Our knowledge of the past: A philosophy of historiography*. Cambridge: Cambridge University Press.

Tucker, A. 2007. The inference of common cause naturalized. In *Causality and probability in the sciences*, ed. Jon Williamson and Federica Russo, 439–466. London: College Press.

Tucker, A. 2012. Sciences of tokens and types: The difference between history and the social sciences. In *The oxford handbook of philosophy of the social sciences*, ed. Harold Kincaid, 274–297. Oxford: Oxford University Press.

Wetzel, Linda. 2009. *Types and tokens: On abstract objects*. Cambridge, MA: MIT Press.

Chapter 9
The Expert Economist in Times of Uncertainty

Maria Jimenez-Buedo

Abstract In view of the upsurge in the interest in the role of the economist as expert, the chapter analyses critically the conceptual strategies of several recent important contributions. The article identifies the main conceptual dilemma associated with the social scientific study of experts, stemming from the emphasis in either the objective or the relational dimension of the phenomenon of expertise. In this article the attributional or relational aspect of expertise, normally downplayed either explicitly or implicitly by a majority of recent contributions to the literature, is instead vindicated in the study of the expert status and its role in policy-making processes. The claim is sustained by reviewing some well-known theses in ideational and related approaches in Comparative Political Economy.

9.1 Introduction

The idea that expertise and democracy are often in tension has long been a concern in several strands of social scientific and philosophical literature, but since the 1990s several research programs in the field Science and Technology Studies have claimed an increase in this tension, driven by citizens' rising demands for a greater accountability of the scientists. With important parallels in their aims and scope, a number of related approaches have helped disseminate the idea of a profound transformation of science in the direction of a greater permeability to societal demands and preferences. This transformation has been referred to as "Mode 2 of scientific production", or "post-normal science", in contrast to a classic period of science dominated by the interests and preferences of scientists themselves (Gibbons et al. 1994; Funtowicz and Ravetz 1993; Nowotny et al. 2001, 2003). Though the main original aim of these contributions was descriptive, these approaches often share a strong normative leaning towards greater participation of the citizen in the science and technology policymaking processes. Moreover, these and related theoretical developments have managed to gradually reach the policy-making

M. Jimenez-Buedo (✉)
Department of Logic, History and Philosophy of Science, UNED, Madrid, Spain
e-mail: mjbuedo@fsof.uned.es

© Springer International Publishing Switzerland 2014   171
C. Martini, M. Boumans (eds.), *Experts and Consensus in Social Science*,
Ethical Economy 50, DOI 10.1007/978-3-319-08551-7_9

sphere and currently permeate the parlance of policy makers and official documents in science policy bodies (Jasanoff 2003).

Against this background, the increasing attention paid to the role of the economist as expert can thus be interpreted as one manifestation of a broader phenomenon. Yet the discussion of the public role of economists has a few distinct elements that perhaps make the debate more pressing. To consider just two examples: First, and with regard to the more open and public aspects of economic expertise, we find that the professional discussion around which policies could potentially end the Great Recession are the subject of an intense, high-profile, and unusually (very) public debate, especially considering that the discussion deals with relatively technical matters (see the example of the Krugman-Bernanke controversy over the adequacy of current inflation targets). This public debate has led to increased questioning of the legitimacy of the expert status of the economist profession. Second, and with respect to the less public aspects of economic expertise, certain sectors of the citizenry are increasingly wary of the type of economic expert knowledge that can be exploited, for example, to bet against the market and make a profit in the midst of a financial crash.

In this charged environment, we can expect that the public interest in the role of the economist as expert will only grow, and it is foreseeable that much of this public interest could be tainted by an anti-elitist sentiment against the role of economists in the present crisis. In turn, this could further boost academic interest in the role of the economist. In this context, one of the issues to discuss is conceptual: what notion of "expert" do we have in mind when we think of the expert economist? What is distinctive of the economist as expert from other scientific experts? Can any economist be an expert economist? The main purpose of this chapter is to clarify a few conceptual aspects regarding the general phenomenon of expertise and the specific phenomenon of the economist as expert. In particular, the chapter deals with the problematic relation between two aspects of expertise that can be also seen as two ways of conceptualizing the source of the expert status, i.e., a relational, attributional dimension, and an objective, realist dimension of expertise.

The chapter first provides a brief overview of some recent philosophical and social scientific works that have dealt with the question of the economist as expert and reviews the concept of expertise implicit in those works. The chapter then introduces Collins and Evans's definition of expertise as found in their *Studies of Expertise and Experience* and examines their main contentions. After reviewing Collins and Evans's account of expertise, which explicitly embraces an objective, realist account of expertise, the next section of the chapter argues that this approach is limited as a general account of expertise, and cannot properly be used to analyze some of the relevant aspects of the problem of the economist as an expert. In order to illustrate these limitations, we review some well-known results of ideational and related approaches in the field of comparative political economy, and we argue that the *attributional* aspect of expertise is crucial for an integral understanding of the role of the expert economist.

9.2   The Economist as Expert

In recent years, the nature of expert judgment and the role of the expert in the policy making process has become an issue of growing importance for several strands of literature that reflect upon the nature of social science knowledge and collective decision making processes (Collins and Evans 2007; Selinger and Crease 2006; Tetlock 2005; Kurz-Milcke and Gigerenzer 2004).

With respect to the question of expertise in economics, several interesting and influential works have recently discussed an important criterion for assessing the expert status of the economist, that of predictive success. These works offer a rather dismal view of economists' capacity as predictors. Among these, Philip Tetlock's (2005) work on expert political judgment is the most encompassing attempt to date to document the predictive capacities of professional specialists in the social sciences, in particular in the fields of international politics and political economy.

Tetlock is a political psychologist previously interested in the role of cognitive biases in political thinking, and his well-known 2005 book is built around a database collected from the end of the 1980s to the mid-1990s, recording the predictions of a stable group of experts. These experts were asked to make predictions on the potential developments of standard political variables like the relative success of certain political parties, or economic variables such as government spending and interest rates. In addition, he also asked this expert panel to make predictions on variables related to significant historical events such as potential developments regarding the outbreak of wars, or the evolution of the European Union.

Tetlock measures the predictive performance of experts on two dimensions that are often conjectured to trade off. *Calibration* refers to the degree to which a forecaster's assignment of probabilities to an event actually matches the actual frequency with which the event takes place (so that an expert shows a high calibration score if outcomes assigned a 50 % likelihood happen more or less 50 % of the time). *Discrimination* refers to the ability of forecasters to do better than the strategy that would simply predict the base rate probability of an event (so an expert gets a high discrimination score when she assigns probabilities close to one to events that do end up happening and probabilities close to zero to events that do not take place).

According to Tetlock's analysis, political and economic experts tend to do better on both of these dimensions than undergraduate students, but they do not outperform what the author classifies as "dilettantes", that is, people who regularly consult the mildly specialized media, reading sources such as the *New York Times* or the *Economist*. On the discrimination score, both experts and dilettantes outperform the random-guessing strategy, but both of these groups do a poorer predictive job in their calibration of probabilities than mere random assignment. Consistent with previous accounts of predictive success in the social and medical sciences, simple statistical models seem to do better than experts on all accounts (Camerer and Johnson 1991).

Angner's study on the causes and consequences of overconfidence that characterize experts in economics are congruent with the results of Tetlock's. Angner (2006) offers an in-depth case study based on the experience of Anders Aslund, a reputed Swedish economist who offered advice to the Russian government in the years between 1991 and 1994. Aslund, who also stood out in the media as a prominent public figure, was a firm defender of the use of "shock therapy" for countries in the geographical area of influence of the former USSR, advocating for the rapid deregulation of the existing economic and productive institutions in order to transform the country into a market-based economy. In his work, Erik Angner reports the results of the extensive literature documenting the general phenomenon of overconfidence in prediction. As mentioned, a calibrated judgment is one in which the probability assigned to an event coincides with the observed frequency of that event. Overconfidence is defined as occurring if the measure of confidence in one's predictions is higher than their success rate. An extensive psychological and decision-making literature reports the results of laboratory experiments displaying persistent overconfidence in judgment, whether subjects are students, laypeople, doctors, market analysts or experts in a wide range of topics. These laboratory studies also show an interesting list of related phenomena. For example, overconfidence seems to increase with the difficulty of the judgment task, with the motivation or incentives attached to getting an accurate judgment, or with the confidence of the subjects (the higher the confidence of a subject in his or her judgment, the higher the probability this confidence is unwarranted).

Julian Reiss's analysis of expertise (2007) also reviews the problems associated with the predictive role of experts, but he deals with the more general question of expert judgment as a type of evidence in the absence of more standardized, impersonal, or objective sources of data. His focus is on cases in which collectively binding expert judgment is called upon precisely because of a lack of standardized procedures or protocols for atomized, personal judgment. This characterizes Reiss's case study, the Boskin commission: an expert panel in charge of revising the official calculation of the US inflation rate during the 1990s. In Reiss's depiction, one of the problems with using expertise as a source of evidence is often the lack of objective standards against which expert judgment can be assessed. This is the case in the Boskin commission example: inflation must be defined in terms of the measurement procedure that a given group of experts may agree upon and cannot be contrasted with the "real" number out there. In order to assess whether expertise is optimally deployed, Reiss contrasts the functioning of the Boskin commission against a series of normative principles that should guide the relationship between the laypeople seeking expert advice and the potential specialists that could provide it. These principles are:

1. The subsidiarity principle: experts should be invoked only when there is reason to believe that they perform better than mechanical rules or when mechanical rules cannot be applied.
2. The supporting evidence principle: in so far as possible, experts should underpin their judgment with supporting evidence.

3. The relevant expertise principle: laypeople should seek advice only from an expert who is a specialist in the relevant area, avoiding the common problem of putative experts that are called specialists in one domain because their skills in other (possibly insufficiently related) areas are already well-known.
4. The democratic principle: expert advice should be made on the basis of the goals and values of the advice seeker, not the advisor.
5. The impartiality principle: as a rule, the expert should not have a stake in the matter considered.

Though Reiss's analysis is explicitly normative in setting the series of principles, he admits that the conditions under which real expertise is sought after and deployed often fall short of complying with these desiderata. According to Reiss's critical analysis of the procedure and performance of the Boskin commission, many of these principles were not sufficiently met. Nevertheless, Reiss himself acknowledges that very often, and in particular in the case of the social sciences, many of these principles cannot ever be met, i.e. economists and social sciences deal often with issues for which no impartial, perfectly relevant committee of experts can be formed that will provide advice that is unaffected by the goals and values of the advisor. And yet, even if no such ideal individual expert or committee thereof exists, there are situations in which an expert report is needed, for lack of a better source of evidence, and situations in which experts are indispensable in a given decision making process, for lack of a better decision rule.

Although Angner and Tetlock's analyses are mainly descriptive, both engage in a series of normative recommendations, prompted by their rather dismal picture of the performance of the expert economist as predictor. Both Agner and Tetlock engage in a normatively driven plea for the increase in accountability of both media experts and those working for private and public organizations, including the need to collectively sanction those experts giving ambiguous or vague predictions (since those can be ex post facto accommodated with almost any kind of evidence), or to dismiss those experts whose predictions are consistently wrong.

Prediction is indeed a sound place from which to start assessing experts' performance, especially if we are looking for an objective measurement of the quality of expertise. However, and despite their emphasis on the predictive performance of specialists, a close reading of Angner and Tetlock's analyses suggest that prediction is only arguably so crucial an aspect of social scientific expertise. Angner rightly points out the vagueness with which experts like Aslund formulated their predictions, yet we can be sure that a more precise forecast could neither save nor condemn these economists as advisors, for their function as experts was not to issue predictions, but to provide general guidance in an unprecedented process with mostly unknown outcomes. Despite their normative pleas for an improved relationship between experts and the public that appoints them, Tetlock and Angner's analyses actually provide a number of reasons why we should expect the relationship between experts and citizens, regarding public matters, to be intrinsically problematic.

First, as Angner points out, there is evidence that overconfident subjects tend to self-select themselves into advisory posts more often than well calibrated subjects, precisely because they to overestimate their predictive capacities.

Second, and as Tetlock's results attest, it is often the case that the better known and sought after an expert is, the worse his or her predictions tend to be. It is Tetlock himself who rescues the role of the expert from the radical skeptic view whereby experts are not useful at all: some experts are sought after for their cognitive style, which allows them to derive innovative prognoses that depart from common knowledge. This would be the case of the *hedgehog* type of expert, in Tetlock's typology, defined as those intellectuals who view the world through the lens of one big theory. This cognitive style, in turn, does nevertheless cause the hedgehogs to be outperformed, in their predictive abilities, by the *foxes*, i.e., those experts defined by the eclectic sources of their beliefs and models, whose way of thinking departs less often from common knowledge.

What seems to transpire in the works reviewed here is a certain tension between, on the one hand, the normative pleas for an improved relation between the expert economist and the public (motivated, in turn, by a rather negative view of their performance), and on the other hand, the implications of their research, that suggest that there are structural reasons that explain why expert economists underperform relative to our expectations. It thus seems somewhat contradictory to expect that the relationship between the expert and the public be exemplary, after detailing the reasons that explain why the incentives faced by experts can account for some of their bad performance. This chapter contends that behind this lack of congruence lies the tension between two different dimensions of the phenomenon of expertise: an objective sense in which expertise is seen as a real, deployable capacity of individuals (like that of issuing accurate predictions) and a relational sense in which expertise is linked to the reputation of certain individuals, or the authority that others concede, to the expert, that may or may not be justified by his or her superior knowledge over a particular matter. This tension, which is the subject of the next section, is driven by the two concepts of expertise: objective and relational.

9.3   Two Understandings of Expertise

In recent years Robert Evans and Harry Collins, an essential contributor to the Sociology of Scientific Knowledge and father of the "empirical programme of relativism", have tried to revive the debate around the sociology of expertise. Their efforts have given rise to a new research program that they have called Studies of Expertise and Experience (SEE) (Collins and Evans 2007). Their starting point comes from their perception that there is the need to set off a third wave of Science Studies that could serve as a corrective for the relativist excesses of its recent past. A first wave, tainted by positivism, in which the privileged social and epistemological status of science made the question of the determinants of expertise redundant, was followed by a second one, in which under the influence of an unrestrained social constructivism, Science Studies made both implicit and explicit calls for the reform of science and scientific institutions that would be participatory and inclusive of the whole of the citizenry. This, according to Collins and Evans, has led to a watering down of the role of the expert, and of the notion itself, via for example, the coining of terms like the "lay expert" and other such theoretical attempts normatively inspired by the need to democratize science.

Collins and Evans see these developments, stemming from a general call towards the democratization of expertise, as suffering from two problems, one epistemological, and one of a pragmatic, technical, nature. The first of these problems comes from viewing expertise, as a merely relational and attributional phenomenon, whereby the determination of who is an expert is entirely defined socially. For Collins and Evans, the difficulty of this approach is that it leaves little or no room to assess normatively, and ex-ante, what exactly constitutes optimal expertise (i.e., there is no way to discriminate among better or worse types of expertise). The second, technical problem comes directly from this one: collective decision-making in which there is a universal inclusion of all those concerned is infeasible, unless citizen participation is to be retained at a very shallow or superfluous level.

For these reasons Collins and Evans want to contain the constructivist view of expertise and underline that though the status of expertise is attributed and rela-tional, expertise is, more importantly, a *real* capacity. For the authors, expertise is acquired through experience and comes as a result of successful socialization within a relevant community linked to a particular domain of knowledge, be this scientific or technical. Thus, according to Collins and Evans, only by embracing a realist conception of expertise, can one differentiate between successful and failed instances of expertise attribution. A relational, attributional conception of expertise dilutes its content: anyone can be an expert.

Within their realist conception of the phenomenon, one of the main concerns for the authors and contributors to the SSE literature is that of distinguishing and classifying among different types of expertise. Since their motivation behind the launching of the SEE research program is mainly to contribute to the problem of extension (i.e. the extent to which participation in the science policy making must be amplified), they find that classifying types of expertise is central to the building of a conceptual framework that can help set guidelines about who and on which basis is able to contribute as an expert, based on their specific experiences and knowledge.

Though Collins and Evans's classificatory attempts have evolved from their first works to the more recent ones, partly as a result of the theoretical and empirical contributions to the approach, the core of their classification has remained the same. This basic tenet is the distinction between interactional expertise and contributory expertise. In this way, and following from some of the authors' previous projects, Collins and Evans emphasize that having the skills and aptitudes to communicate scientific knowledge and interact with scientists does not imply having the capacity to generate this very knowledge, while they insist that both sets of aptitudes are crucial. The other, less central types of expertise coined by Collins and Evans (ubiquitous and referred or *meta-expertise*) complete the picture. This classification is briefly reviewed next.

According to Collins and Evans's classification, *ubiquitous expertise* is embodied in those skills shared by all members of a community, such as a normal mastering of a natural language. Arguably, the authors defend that though counter-intuitive, this type of knowledge needs to be included in their "periodic table" because it is the kind of ability that serves as a prerequisite for all the others types of expertise. This is so because it allows the socialization of an individual in the relevant community in which expertise is either acquired or displayed.

More central to their classification is the distinction between interactional and contributory expertise. *Interactional expertise* is the kind of ability displayed by an agent that can engage in active conversation with a specialist in a given field without displaying the kind of formal knowledge that would allow him or her to contribute substantively to the field. An example of this would be that of a sociologist that immerses in a laboratory long enough to understand the practices and the object of the scientists that she studies (and is capable of discussing intricate and technical questions on the matter), but is nevertheless unable to contribute with her knowledge to the laboratory activity. In contrast, *contributory expertise* would be the kind of experience that allows a person to contribute to a given body of knowledge.

Finally, *referred expertise* is the kind of expertise that is created in one field and then referred to, or transferred into another one, and it is typical of the managers of large scientific projects, where typically one manager moves from one project to the next applying knowledge acquired in yet another field. Referred expertise is one type, if the most important one, among the ones that Collins and Evans classify as *meta-expertise*: the capacity to judge the expertise of others without possessing that expertise.

SEE has received much attention and its approach towards expertise has been widely cited, giving rise to various collective works (Collins and Evans 2007, Studies in the History and Philosophy of Science 2007). Collins and Evans's classification of types of expertise has now been applied to a wide array of phenomena and, through a series of collective amendments, has been enlarged to include several subcategories. Much of the emphasis has been put into the category of interactional expertise. In particular, this type of expertise has been the focus of some experimental work (Collins et al. 2006). Also, the interplay between interactional, contributory, and meta-expertise has been studied in the case of the development and application of econometric models, in the collaboration between businessmen and modelers (Evans 2007).

Regardless of their other empirical and theoretical merits, Collins and Evans's deserve much credit for their introduction and clear account of the two main terminological possibilities in the conceptualization of the phenomenon of expertise. Collins and Evans address in this way an issue that is often overlooked by recent contributions to the social scientific study of the role of the expert, i.e., the bi-dimensional character of the phenomenon of expertise. As we have seen, Collins and Evans clearly distinguish a realist, objectivist dimension, based on the experience and knowledge of the specialist in a particular subject or activity, and a relational, social dimension based on the existence of a constituency that attributes epistemic authority to the expert with regard to a particular domain. This distinction between the relational and objective dimensions of the phenomenon is reflected in the nuances that differentiate the folk meanings of expertise, as they are collected, for example, by Selinger and Crease's recount of folk dictionary meanings of the term, where some of the definitions refer to the idea of being "trained by experience and practice", or to the "gain[ing] skill from experience", and others refer also to the reputational aspect, as in the idea of a type of knowledge or skill that causes a person "to be regarded as an authority" (Selinger and Crease 2006, p. 1).

We can see how the two aspects or dimensions of expertise (realist versus relational) overlap, in turn, with two possible approaches in studying the phenomenon. Collins and Evans are explicit about this in their account: because they consider that a relational approach is incapable of being useful in solving the problem of extension, they choose a realist approach to the phenomenon. In their view, adopting a relational approach to expertise can only exacerbate the confusion around who should be an expert, since, according to a relational approach; anybody can be an expert as long as there is a constituency that thinks so. We take issue with this idea in the light of Collins and Evans's conceptual proposal in the remaining sections of the chapter.

9.4 A Conceptual Dilemma

Collins and Evans's reception to their SEE project has generally been rather enthusiastic, though some aspects of their approach have been critiqued. Jasanoff (2003), for example, has been critical of Collins and Evans's depiction of the STS field, more than of their substantive theses, since she thinks the authors do not give enough credit to those research programs that had previously tried to limit the sense in which science and science policy should be inclusive. Wynne (2003) in turn, has criticized the SSE program for having leaned too heavily on a realist notion of expertise: in Wynne's view this leads Collins and Evans to accept too readily the credit of expertise that powerful institutions extend to their members, disregarding to some extent the potential for redefining more radically current boundaries between the scientists and the public. In this way, Wynne engages fully with the assumptions behind Collins and Evans's opting for a realist approach to the study of expertise. In other words, Wynne, too, believes that embracing a relational conception of the expert assumes that one wants to extend or blur the frontiers between the specialist and the layperson. Or, we could say that he implicitly accepts, too, the counterpart to this idea: that defending a realist account of expertise means that one wants to preserve the role of the specialist, unthreatened by contamination of the public.

In the rest of this section assesses Collins and Evans's conceptualization of expertise, and we argue that, though their approach offers many interest insights on the phenomenon, their conceptual strategy has limits as a tenet for a wide-ranging social scientific agenda on expertise. However, our argument against their realist approach to expertise differs from Wynne's: our assessment and critique of Collins and Evans's conceptualization of expertise is not based on its normative implications, but on the fact that it does not pay sufficient attention to certain aspects of the phenomenon that matter to a social scientific understanding of the expert role.

Both Wynne and Collins and Evans adhere to the assumption that the conceptual choice one makes regarding the notion of the expert carries with it a series of normative commitments, related to the problem of extension (to recall, the problem of the extent to which expert status should be extended to agents that in virtue of having stakes in a given domain, may also have some form of relevant knowledge). Wynne rejects an objectivist concept of the expert on the basis that he considers it to limit our capacity to extend expertise to relevant stakeholders. Inversely, as mentioned, Collins and Evans think that accepting a relational notion of expertise implies an overextension of the status of the expert.

There is reason to argue that the conceptual choices one makes regarding expertise are perhaps not so clearly or straightforwardly connected to particular normative stances. In fact, Wynne's charge against Collins and Evans strategy is actually partially disproven by some of their categories in their Periodic Table of expertise: the notion of *ubiquitous expertise*, for example, reflects that the SEE program is able to conceive of inclusive ways of viewing expertise, to the extent of being able to extend it to all the members in a given community; the limits of Collins and Evans's conceptual strategy thus seem to lay elsewhere. The problem with a realist strategy of the kind deployed by Collins and Evans is not that it can only conceive of expert knowledge in an elitist or technocratic (i.e., restrictive) form, but rather, as we will claim, that expertise and knowledge become indistinguishable.

If examined closely, the categories in Collins and Evans's periodic table amount to an exhaustive and illuminating classification of the different types of embodied knowledge: the authors' emphasis in the realist dimension of expertise (i.e., in the skills or knowledge gained by experience, rather than in the reputational or authoritative aspects of the phenomenon) ends up committing them to a classification of expertise that is indistinguishable from a classification of the types of knowledge that an agent can embody. Since the SEE program conceives of expertise as fully expressed by the skills or knowledge that an agent *can* gain by experience, expertise then automatically and necessarily amounts to the knowledge that can be embodied by an agent. Thus conceived, a strictly realist conception of expertise renders the phenomenon indistinguishable from knowledge. This conceptual strategy, we argue, carries with it a series of limitations, in that it cannot account for a number of properties of the phenomenon of expertise that are of interest to social scientist or the philosopher of social science. Before we go over these, though, it is important to see how a realist conceptual strategy conforms to one of the two horns of a dilemma associated to the study of the phenomenon of expertise.

On the one hand, and according to Collins and Evans, an exclusively relational concept of expertise necessarily leads to the stretching of the expert status and the blurring of the distinction between the expert and the lay person. On the other hand, and as we have just seen, an exclusively realist conception, renders expertise indistinguishable from knowledge. We are thus faced with a conceptual dilemma: if we are relationalists about expertise, we are bound to face problems if we want to issue normative recommendations regarding who is better suited to be an expert, since an expert is whoever claims to be one (and is successful in finding a suitable constituency that thinks he or she is an expert). And yet, if we are realists about expertise, in the sense of considering that the study of experts should be restricted to those that objectively possess the best available knowledge in a given domain, we can end up not having a distinct object of study: we might as well turn to do the epistemologist or the psychologist's old job and study the determinants of embodied knowledge (since it is indistinguishable from expertise).

In view of this conceptual dilemma, we argue that an approach to expertise that explicitly integrates both aspects of the phenomenon should be advocated. That is, the social scientist must embrace an alternative conceptualization of expertise that avoids both horns of the dilemma by integrating the relational and the realist dimensions of the phenomenon. In fact, and implicitly, this is what a good number of empirical works interested in the phenomenon of expertise attempt to do, for it is often the case that the expertise-related case studies that social scientists tend to favor are precisely those in which the relationship between the objective and relational dimensions of the phenomenon are problematic, or disputable: instances, for example, in which we find that there is a problematic match between whom is considered, relationally, an expert, and his or her objective performance.

The focus on this type of "problematic" cases, in our view, can explain, at least partially, why we now find a growing interest among social scientists and philosophers in the idea of the expert economist, or the perennial, if perhaps also cyclical, interest in the expert in the social sciences- an interest that we do not find as often in the case of, say, the expert engineer. Whereas in the engineering case there seems to be a rather smooth match, in a majority of cases, between the objective knowledge and skills of the specialist and the expectations of the layperson that demands his or her expertise, there often is, in the case of the expert economist, a significant gap between the public expectations regarding his knowledge and his performance. In contrast, the question of how an engineer acquires his or her skills or to what extent these skills are due to certain innate capacities is a question of obvious appeal to the psychologist, yet these kinds of questions are probably not central to a social scientific research program, and only very unlikely to a philosophical one: the social scientists or the philosopher are more likely interested in those cases in which what is at stake is precisely, a problematic relation between the objective and the relational aspects of the phenomenon.

9.5   The Limits of a Realist Conceptualization of Expertise

Our contention is that a realist conceptual strategy, with its emphasis on the objective dimension of expertise, is not optimally suited to deal with instances in which the attribution of expertise is contested, or problematic, nor is it adequate to deal with some aspects of expertise that are necessarily relational. To see why, we reference Steve Fuller's account (2006), in which he defends the idea of expertise as a *constitutively social* phenomenon. Fuller has identified four ways in which this social character manifests itself (in order of intuitiveness):

1. Skills are the product of specialized training that is acquired purposefully, rather than being picked up casually or as the byproduct of some other form of learning.
2. No expertise carries universal applicability: any given type of expertise is relevant only on certain occasions.
3. The organization of expertise is dependent on the collegial practices of experts: extended internal disputes over fundamentals will typically erode expertise.
4. The significance of a given expertise is affected by the availability of expert training and of expert judgment, relative to the need for expertise. Too many experts relative to demand will typically depreciate the expertise in question.

Of these four factors, the first two can be incorporated by a realist account of expertise without problems. In fact, we can see that the first factor is a crucial part of the SEE program, a significant share of which is devoted to the study of the acquisition of expert knowledge. Something similar can be said about the second factor: a realist account of expertise should find no problem in the study of how different types of expertise are rendered useful in different contexts.

In the case of Fuller's fourth claim, regarding the value of expertise as related to its scarcity, the issue is murkier: as we saw, in Collins and Evans's taxonomy, even those types of knowledge that are virtually universally shared by a given community are considered expert knowledge. Yet, we can think that the social scientist interested in the general question of expertise is normally uninterested in this type of ubiquitous knowledge, but rather in those other cases in which the attribution of expertise to a particular agent or body of agents by a given constituency is not automatic, manifesting itself in an asymmetric relationship between the expert and the layperson. The SEE's realist approach to expertise, by equating expertise with knowledge, ends up being committed to include as pertinent objects the types of knowledge that are universally shared by a given community, even if the attributional aspect of expertise is irrelevant in such cases. And, more importantly, such an approach is not meant to take into account the dynamics by which a given type of expertise becomes more valuable through scarcity, since those are elements that lie outside of the domain of phenomenon of expertise, whenever the latter is defined objectively.

Perhaps the limitations of a realist account of expertise appear even more clearly when confronted with Fuller's third claim, which deals with how disputes among experts can erode the value that the public attribute to expertise. Regarding this third factor in Fuller's list, it seems that a realist account of expertise must choose between two options. The first option would be to remain silent about this fact, and in fact, this is probably why the SEE program initially claimed to shy away from types of expertise where knowledge is contentious: Collins and Evans's approach was initially explicitly devoted to areas in which political or normative statements were not intermingled with scientific ones, thus excluding, regrettably, an important share of scientific domains, and a majority of the social sciences. This option, however, appears as an undesirable one, since as philosophers or as social scientists we are clearly drawn to cases in which expertise is problematic, or *eroded*, by dissent. As a matter of fact, and despite the initial programmatic claims, Evans has, fortunately, contributed both in the past and recently, with very interesting works to the study the role of the expert economist as a forecaster (2007, this volume).

The second option that is left for the realist account in the face of controversial claims to expertise presents also its own problems: a realist about the concept of expertise must be committed to the idea that among the contending experts one is right where others are wrong, or alternatively, he or she must be committed to the idea that the controversy is based on the fact that all putative experts are wrong, i.e., none of them are genuine experts. Both of these options appear as unappealing, though, to the social scientist interested in expert dissent: a sociologist of expertise can think that contending forms of expertise regarding one particular problem represent alternative, and yet legitimate claims to knowledge about an issue, as we will see in some of our examples in the next section. Or, as is often the case within expert panels or expert boards, the social scientist might be interested in finding out the ways in which expert consensus is carefully negotiated and manufactured in order to be presented to the public, by again, genuine experts that are acutely aware of the fact that their disputes can erode their credibility in the eyes of outside critics.[1]

In sum, while Collins and Evans's program is a novel and valuable approach regarding the classification and deployment of types of knowledge as it is embodied by different agents, a realist research program regarding the concept of expertise is not optimally suited to understand how certain types of knowledge become valued and regarded authoritatively and others fall into disregard, nor how the value of some forms of knowledge depends on the number of individuals possessing that knowledge. Additionally, it is also not optimally equipped to analyze the role of experts in fields like economics, where the role of the expert is often debated, and where politics and science often intertwined.

Our contention here is thus that the social scientific study of expertise needs a concept that takes into account, and grants equal importance to, both the objective and the relational aspects of the phenomenon of expertise. To recap the conceptual dilemma associated with expertise: if we follow an only relational conception of

---

[1] For a study expertise as "performance" in a dramaturgical model illustrated by the debates in the US National Academy of Sciences Nutrition Board, over the period from 1977 to 1989, concerning estimates of human nutritional requirements, see Hilgartner (2000).

expertise, then we dilute the status of the expert. Yet, if we follow an exclusively objective conception of expertise, we equate expertise and knowledge, and render the two concepts indistinguishable. In order to avoid the dilemma, an inclusive perspective integrating the relational and the objective dimension of the phenomenon of expertise should be advocated. Such an integrative strategy can allow us to look into the objective features and skills of the putative experts that cause them to have a constituency of laypeople regarding them as experts, but also, can allow us to look into the contingent sociological or historical factors that can assist the public in their choice among contending experts that have objectively equally good (or equally suspect) knowledge credentials, or even, to understand those cases in which an expert is favored over his contenders in spite of a his having a less solid claim over whatever we consider to be his objective knowledge.

After all, and as the examples in the next section illustrate, social scientists tend to find more of an interest in those processes in which the expert status of a given specialist is debated, or only recognized by a particular constituency and disputed by relevant segments of the public. The analyst committed to a concept of expertise that is not exclusively objectivist nor exclusively relational can analyze these cases without feeling compelled to determine who is the better expert (which may not always be feasible) or without feeling compelled to appeal to the irrationality of the public in those instances in which they end up favoring a given expert over others even in the absence of compelling reasons based on the experts' qualifications or other objective measures.

In the next section, we analyze a series of works that have dealt with the issue of the expert economist without assuming an objectivist perspective of expertise, and thus do without the need to presume that the public's choice regarding expert's selection needs to be judged as optimal, or correct. These are works that, from a comparative perspective (integrating the disciplines of political economy and intellectual history) have tackled the issue of which economists' get to be regarded as the relevant authority at critical political junctures, and have investigated the ways in which different countries train and recruit the economists that are then destined to become elite experts.

Reviewed very briefly, the purpose of including these works' main conclusions here is to illustrate the usefulness of approaches that can help illuminate, by means of empirically informed case analyses, the nature of the relation between the objective and the relational dimensions of expertise. Through their results, these works make apparent that although experts' educational background and professional record are absolutely crucial in their selection as relevant advisors, there is more than the qualifications of experts that determine their public influence. The analysis of these economic experts' influence also illuminates the importance of historical or sociologically contingent factors, and the comparative approach sheds doubts on the always tempting functional tendencies that can lead us to think that influential experts are always chosen optimally given the public's needs, and exclusively on the basis of the best available experience and training.

9.6   The Political Economy of Economic Expertise

Marion Fourcade's "Economists and Societies" (2009) is devoted to understanding the forging of economists into experts, i.e., how economics became professionalized, and how it obtained a monopolistic claim to a particular knowledge jurisdiction within the state administration during the twentieth century. As Fourcade acknowledges, economics provides a particularly interesting case, since it is a privileged discipline within the social sciences, both for its impact in policymaking, and for its (currently perhaps more contested) prestige among the general public. Even if the latter were permanently eroded, economics as a discipline has reached higher levels of internationalization and professionalization than all other social scientific disciplines.

Fourcade's work deals with the different ways in which economists came to be recognized as experts in a particular knowledge domain, and how these processes differed in France, the United Kingdom, and the United States. Fourcade shows how these different paths towards the professionalization of the discipline depended on the different national intellectual and educational traditions, which were defined, in turn, by their distinct relationship with an elite class of politicians. In the case of France, the legitimation of economics as an autonomous discipline came relatively later, due, in part by the conflict between academics, on the one hand, and state officials on the other. This division was reflected in divisions between mathematicians and engineers (represented, institutionally, the ENSAE and the ENA) competing in gaining influence within the policymaking elite with regard to economic matters.

In the case of Great Britain, Fourcade characterizes the case by the relatively blurred line between the expert and the layperson in regard to economic matters: according to her, a tightly knit elite network linked to top institutions such as Cambridge, Oxford, and LSE composed of a group of intellectuals who influenced public economic discourse even if they were not professional economists. In contrast, the United States came to be defined by its heavy reliance on formal markers of competence and their highly technical approach to economics, precisely, to compensate for the lack of a pre-existing elite of public technocrats. Fourcade thus attributes the US emphasis on technical skills and a quantitative approach in economics to the need of a newly established select group of professors from top universities to deliver reports and assessments that would look as objective and free of bias as possible.

The American model would eventually spread to other countries, as the result of the growing prestige of top US universities and international organizations, and in parallel, due to the growing technological applications of quantitative economics to fields such as finance. Fourcade's analysis thus questions the "naturalness" of the way in which expertise in economics has currently developed around the notions of market efficiency and quantitative and technical skills by showing how, for years, different traditions and different ways of being an expert economist coincided in different political contexts.

A second relevant stream of literature that can be useful to those interested in stressing the relation between the objective and the relational aspects of expertise is to be found among ideational approaches in comparative political economy. Ideational analyses study the question of which economic ideas, embodied in experts, end up influencing the policy making process. The work of Peter Hall (1993, 1989) on the impact of Keynesian ideas in post-world war II Western economies is a particularly relevant example of the ideational approach, in which experts play the role of carriers of policy advice and policy innovation. Hall's pioneering work, together with Peter Haas (1992; Adler and Haas 1992), were based on the idea that structural interests alone (like class or resource-based interest) could not explain alone the content of particular policy choices. In Hall's terms, politics, and in particular economic policy, was not only about power, but also about puzzles that politicians needed to solve with the help of experts and the theories and ideas they embodied. Ideational approaches were built, in part, to try to understand the conditions under which experts were most able to exert the most influence. More recently, Mark Blyth (2002) and Lindvall (2006, 2009) have taken up the ideational project, and have tried to clarify, both conceptually and empirically, the impact of experts and their ideas on policy outcomes, through the analysis of the determinants of institutional change during economic crises.

Summarizing grossly the results of the ideational approach, all authors underline the crucial role of uncertainty in explaining the influence of experts into policy making. In their view, expert ideas tend to become particularly influential at times in which the main economic actors face uncertainty about the courses of action that are more likely to fulfill their interests. According to Blyth's theory, in times of economic uncertainty, expert ideas can help provide substance to these interests, and thus determine the form and content of institutional change. This approach has come up with a series of findings regarding the role of expert ideas in long-term institutional change: in periods of economic crisis, expert ideas reduce uncertainty (1); following uncertainty reduction, these expert ideas can help make collective action and coalition-building possible (2); in the struggle over existing institutions, expert ideas act as weapons and thus empower agents (3); following the de-legitimation of existing institutions, new expert ideas act as blueprints in the construction of new institutions (4); and following institutional construction, expert ideas coordinate agents' expectations and thus reproduce institutional stability (5).

Thus, and while in ordinary times, we can expect the content of policies to be determined, more or less mechanically, by the interests of the main political and social actors involved, during uncertain or extraordinary times, experts can play a crucial role in determining (via their theories and ideas) which course of action better suits the interests of those main actors, which is almost equivalent to say that experts can play a crucial role in determining what those interests are. A paradox (which has been long pointed out by proponents of ideational approaches, and that Evans, in his contribution to this volume also admits) immediately arises: experts are normally most needed in times in which it is harder to assess their performance, or where their criteria by which to judge on objective grounds who is the better expert is at its weakest.

9.7   What Concept of Expertise?

The approaches overviewed in the previous section offer us a complex picture regarding how economists are appointed as experts and get to shape the content of policies by making collectively binding decisions, based on their expertise. This expertise, however, is not only explained by their objective skills, nor solely, either, by their connections, or by the interests of the laypeople that appoint them, but by an intricate relation between both – a relation which the social scientist interested in expertise must disentangle. We have brought attention to these works and the research avenues they suggest because we find that their focus and conclusions substantiate the idea that a social scientific approach to expertise necessitates a concept that looks both at the relational and the objective aspects of the phenomenon, as well as to the interaction between them.

   We have argued that a realist conceptual strategy, with its emphasis on the objective dimension of expertise, may not be optimally suited to deal with instances in which the attribution of expertise is contested, or problematic, nor is it optimal to deal with some aspects of expertise that are necessarily relational. In recent years, some of the works that have dealt with the expert economist or the expert social scientists seem to have toyed with an objectivist notion of expertise, often only ambiguously. In this context, Collins and Evans's conceptual stand does have the merit of explicitness and consistency, in that their approach relies on a clear notion of expertise. These are crucial merits of a given concept of expertise in that they can allow the reader to assess whether the particular conceptualization we embrace has any normative implications.

   In this sense, it is problematic (and representative of some of the recent literature on the economist as an expert reviewed earlier here), to evaluate the performance of experts understood in the relational sense (i.e. an expert is whomever happens to be regarded as one), to then issue a set of desiderata regarding how the expert-layperson relation that seems to be grounded on an ideal, objective sense of expertise (i.e., without taking into consideration the real constraints under which actual experts might be selected or appointed) . Evans's work (2007, this volume) on the expert economist as a forecaster does not fall into this trap, and in this sense departs from other recent contributions to the debate, since it tries to find rationality in the actions of a public composed of laypeople demanding the forecasts of experts, even though they know these forecasts too often fail. In Evans's depiction, the expertise deployed by the professional economist contributes to, and benefits from, the narrative and knowledge that stem from the interaction between the forecasters and their clients.

   We still dissent, though, with Collins and Evans in a crucial aspect regarding the connection between conceptual choices and their normative implications: against their approach, we do not endorse the idea that stressing the relational aspects of expertise equates to giving up entirely the possibility of issuing any normative recommendations regarding who should be an expert. Underlining the constitutively social character of expertise does imply admitting that, de facto, just about anyone can potentially be considered an expert, yet, this does not amount to saying that anyone should be one: by trying to integrate as much as possible the realist and relational components of expertise we are best suited to learn about the conditions in which citizens are prone to demand the services of a specialist to whom they grant expert status, both when they are right and when they are wrong in doing so. By learning about these conditions, we think, we are better suited to discuss a series of normative questions about the rationality and the pitfalls of such expert attributions. Whenever we encounter situations, as it is often the case, where these attributions are not in the best interest of the laypeople making them, we are still able, by embracing the relational aspect of expertise, to be critical of their choices, rather than merely puzzled by them.

References

Adler, E., and P.M. Haas. 1992. Conclusion: Epistemic communities, world order, and the creation of a reflective research program. *International Organization* 46(1): 367–390.

Angner, E. 2006. Economists as experts: Overconfidence in theory and practice. *Journal of Economic Methodology* 13(1): 1–24.

Blyth, M. 2002. *Great transformations: Economic ideas and institutional change in the twentieth century*. Cambridge: Cambridge University Press.

Camerer, C.F., and E.J. Johnson. 1991. The process-performance paradox in expert judgment: How can experts know so much and predict so badly? In *Towards a general theory of expertise: Prospects and limits*, ed. K.A. Ericsson and J. Smith, 195–217. New York: Cambridge University Press.

Collins, H., and R. Evans. 2007. *Rethinking expertise*. Chicago: Chicago University Press.

Collins, H., R. Evans, R. Ribeiro, and M. Hall. 2006. Experiments with interactional expertise. *Studies in History and Philosophy of Science* 37: 656–674.

Evans, R. 2007. Social networks and private spaces in economic forecasting. *Studies in History and Philosophy of Science Part A* 38(4): 686–697.

Fourcade, M. 2009. *Economists and societies. Discipline and Profession in the United States, Britain, and France, 1890s to 1990s*. Princeton: Princeton University Press.

Fuller, S. 2006. The constitutively social character of expertise. In *The philosophy of expertise*, ed. E. Selinger and R. Crease. New York: Columbia University Press.

Funtowicz, S., and J. Ravetz. 1993. Science for the post-normal age. *Futures* 25(7): 739–755.

Gibbons, Michael, Camille Limoges, Helga Nowotny, Simon Schwartzman, Peter Scott, and Martin Trow. 1994. *The new production of knowledge: The dynamics of science and research in contemporary societies*. London: Sage.

Haas, Peter M. 1992. Introduction: Epistemic communities and international policy coordination. *International Organization* 46(1), Special Issue on Knowledge, Power, and International Policy Coordination, 1–35.

Hall, P. 1989. *Keynesianism across nations. The political power of economic ideas*. Princeton: Princeton University Press.

Hall, P. 1993. Policy paradigms social learning and the state. *Comparative Politics* 25(3): 275–296.

Hilgartner, S. 2000. *Science on stage: Expert advice as public drama*. Stanford: Stanford University Press.

Jasanoff, S. 2003. Breaking the waves in science studies: Comment on H. M. Collins and R. Evans, "The third wave of science studies". *Social Studies of Science* 33(3): 389–400.

Kurz-Milcke, E., and G. Gigerenzer. 2004. *Experts in science and society*. New York: Kluwer.
Lindvall, Johannes. 2006. The politics of purpose: Swedish economic policy after the golden Age. *Comparative Politics* 38(3): 253–272.
Lindvall, J. 2009. The real but limited influence of expert ideas. *World Politics* 61(4): 703–730.
Nowotny, Helga, Peter Scott, and Michael Gibbons. 2001. *Re-thinking science. Knowledge and the public in an age of uncertainty*. Cambridge: Reino Unido, Polity Press.
Nowotny, H., P. Scott, and M. Gibbons. 2003. Introduction. "Mode 2" revisited: The new production of knowledge. *Minerva* 41: 179–194.
Reiss, J. 2007. *Error in economics. Towards a more evidence-based methodology*. London: Routledge.
Selinger, E., and R. Crease. 2006. *The philosophy of expertise*. New York: Columbia University Press.
Tetlock, P. 2005. *Expert judgment. How good is it? How can we know?* Princeton: Princeton University Press.
Wynne, B. 2003. Seasick on the third wave? Subverting the hegemony of propositionalism: Response to Collins & Evans (2002). *Social Studies of Science* 401–417.

Chapter 10
Validating Expert Judgment with the Classical Model

Roger M. Cooke

Abstract The classical model derives performance based weights for combining expert judgments based on calibration or seed variables from the experts' field. Since publication of the TU Delft expert judgment database in 2008, various authors have attempted to use this data base for cross validation, splitting the seed variables into training sets and test sets. These attempts are reviewed. Many pitfalls and biases in cross validation efforts are identified and explained. A proposal for performing cross validation, based largely on the work of Eggstaff et al. (Reliab Eng Syst Saf 121:72–82, 2014) is formulated and illustrated with data from recent expert judgment studies.

10.1 Introduction

In 2008, Cooke and Goossens (2008) published the TU Delft data base (compiled up to 2006) comprised of 45 studies in which experts assessed calibration, or "seed" variables; variables for which true values are known post hoc. The Classical Model[1] (Cooke 1991) was used to derive Performance Weight (PW) and Equal Weight (EW) combinations (Decision Makers, DM). For an explanation of performance weighting and performance measures see (Cooke 1991, 2008a; Flandoli et al. 2011 or Eggstaff et al. 2014). Suffice to say that calibration or statistical accuracy is measured as the p-value of the "null hypothesis" that an expert's probability statements are statistically accurate (we want not to reject the null hypothesis) and informativeness is measured as Shannon relative information with respect to a uniform or loguniform background measure. An expert's combined score is the product of his/her p-value and informativeness, and satisfies an asymptotic scoring rule constraint. This entails that an expert is weighted only if his/her p-value is

---

[1] So called because of an analogy with classical hypothesis testing.

R.M. Cooke (✉)
Resources for the Future, Washington, DC, USA

Department of Mathematics, TU Delft, Delft, The Netherlands
e-mail: cooke@rff.org

© Springer International Publishing Switzerland 2014
C. Martini, M. Boumans (eds.), *Experts and Consensus in Social Science*,
Ethical Economy 50, DOI 10.1007/978-3-319-08551-7_10

above a threshold, which is chosen so as to optimize the combined score of the DM. In global weighting the informativeness score is averaged over all calibration variables, and the same weights are applied to all variables; with item specific weighting the informativeness for each item is used and the weights differ from item to item. All results reported here, except those in Cooke (2008b) use only global weights.

The TU Database is unique in providing expert assessments of variables in their fields whose true values are known post hoc. Researchers have used this data base to explore new models and to study whether performance on the calibration variables predicts performance on the variables of interest. In a few studies, variables of interest were later observed, enabling out-of-sample validation. In most cases the variables of interest are not observable on timescales relevant for the decision problem. Therefore, various forms of cross validation have been suggested. Clemen (2008) proposed a Remove-One-At-a-Time (ROAT) method according to which the calibration variables were removed one at a time and predicted by the model initialized on the remaining calibration variables. The predictions, though originating from different decision makers, were pooled and compared with the equal weight decision maker. On the 14 studies selected for this exercise, Clemen found that PW outperformed EW on 9, which was not statistically significant. Cooke (2008b, 2012) noted that this procedure is biased against PW since each calibration variable is predicted by a decision maker in which experts who assessed that particular item badly are up-weighted. It is commonly observed that removing one calibration variable can influence an individual expert's statistical likelihood by a factor 3 or more, a feature explained by the fact that statistical accuracy is a very fast function.

Variations on the ROAT approach have been performed by other researchers. Lin and Cheng (2008) examined 28 of the 45 studies and found PW significantly out performing EW, although PW's out-of-sample performance was degraded. Lin and Cheng (2009) used ROAT on 40 studies finding no significant difference between PW and EW.[2] Lin and Huang (2012) used ROAT with the Brier score in a regression based study of the effects of aggregation method, dependence, number of experts and seed variables and overconfidence on the Brier score (defined as 1 minus the quadratic scoring rule).

Other researchers have undertaken cross validation without ROAT. Cooke (2008b) looked at half-half splits in 13 studies with at least 16 calibration variables. Flandoli et al. (2011) examined five datasets, choosing 30 % of the number of calibration variables as the size of the test set, provided this number was at least 8, otherwise the test set was 8. They recoded the classical model in R, but did not implement item weights or the log uniform background measure. They randomly drew 500 partitions into training and test sets of the fixed sizes. The most extensive study of this kind is Eggstaff et al. (2014), which initializes the global weights

---

[2] There large differences between the in-sample values in these two papers, and those found in the original studies.

model on *all* non empty subsets of seed variables and in each case predicts the complementary subset, again using only global weights. Studies with large numbers of seed variables were split into separate studies to prevent combinatoric explosion. In total 62 expert judgment studies were analysed.

Studies differ in expert subject matter, in numbers and training of experts, in the methods of recruitment and methods of elicitation. For this reason, a numerical representation of out-of-sample validity at the study level would be desirable. For each study, Eggstaff et al. (2014) average the combined scores of PW and EW for each number K of variables in the training set, for $K = 1$ to $N - 1$, where N is the number of seed variables. The same experts, the same calibration variables, and the same information background measures apply for all training set choices within one study. However the statistical power of the test set goes down as the training set size increases, there are many more comparisons for values of K near N/2, and these comparisons have overlapping training sets. With this in mind the PW and EW combined scores are averaged for each size K, for $K = 1 \ldots N - 1$. To aggregate these up the study level we may either average the score differences (PW – EW) or take the geometric mean (geomean) of the ratios PW/EW.

Whereas the difference of scores inherits the scores' dimension (meters minus meters is meters), the ratio of scores is dimensionless (meters divided by meters is an absolute number). In aggregating ratios of positive numbers we must take the geometric mean, or geomean.[3] The ratio of PW and EW can be compared across training set sizes and across studies. The geomean of the ratios of combined scores of all comparisons per study are plotted in Fig. 10.1. In 45 of the 62 studies (73 %) the geomean of combined score ratios PW / EW was greater than unity. When PW's combined score exceeded that of EW, it tended to exceed by a greater amount than when EW's combined score exceeded that of PW. The best eyeball assessment is to compare the mass of lines above and below the baseline of 1. The geomean of the geomeans for each study was 2.46. Summarizing, PW outperforms EW in out of sample cross validation on more than two thirds of the studies, and the combined score of PW is more than twice that of EW.

The accuracy of a DM in terms of proximity of the median to the true value is not directly related to the scoring variables of statistical accuracy and informativeness. Eggstaff et al. (2014) report an accuracy advantage of PW over EW comparable to the differences in combined scores; however that feature is not pursued in this chapter.

This chapter addresses cross validation. First, the issue of scoring rules for individual variables is dealt with, followed by a demonstration of the bias in

---

[3] To see this suppose on two comparisons the scores were (PW $= 4$, EW $= 1$) and (PW $= 1$, EW $= 4$) The performance is identical, but the average of ratios is $1/2(4 + 1/4) = 2.125$. The Geomean is $(4 \times 1/4)^{1/2} = 1$. Eggstaff et al. (2014) report only the average scores for each size of the training sets, so we consider the ratios of averages. Since the average is always greater or equal to the geomean, the numerator and denominator in these comparisons would both be smaller if we took the geomeans of combined scores of each separate K-tuple of training variables. It's impossible to say if there is an overall effect of this choice.

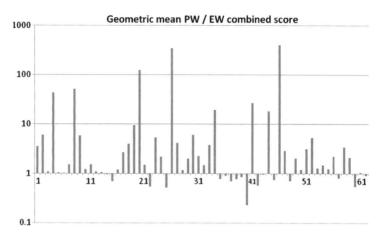

Fig. 10.1 62 studies, per study: geomeans of comparisons of PW/EW combined score ratios

Remove-One-at-a-Time (ROAT) cross validation. Realistic expectations for cross validation are developed in Sect. 10.3. Comparisons based on 5 or fewer seed variables would require a large number of independent and statistically identical studies to detect significant differences; 10 seed variables provide a more powerful basis for comparison. Section 10.4 analyses 4 studies reported since 2012 which involved at least 10 seed variables. Based on a suggestion of Eggstaff et al. (2014) initializing the model on all subsets of one or two seed variables, and evaluating on all seed variables attests to the superiority of Performance Weighting (PW) over Equal Weighting (EW), or when that is not attested, enables understanding in terms of the number of experts and their individual performance.

The cross validation exercises reported here were performed with the software system EXCALIBUR, which has been extensively tested in over 20 years of use. It is freely available at http://www.lighttwist.net/wp/. For cross validation of the Asian Carp data, the MATLAB code used in Eggstaff et al. (2014) was graciously provided by the authors.

10.2 Scoring Rules for Individual Variables

Scoring rules were originally introduced as a tool for elicitation. An expert gives a mass or density function for an uncertain quantity which is later observed, and a scoring rule assigns a number to the assessment-plus-realization. Strictly proper scoring rules are such that an expert achieves his maximal expected score by and only by giving the assessment which correspond to his/her true belief. The classical model uses asymptotically strictly proper scoring rules based on sets of assessments and sets of realizations. Many authors have suggested using strictly proper scoring rules for individual variables, and summing the scores over a set of variables, an idea strongly discouraged in Cooke (1991). A simple example tees up the issue. Suppose an expert assess the probability of Heads with a coin of unknown composition as 1/2. On each toss with the coin, the score is the same for Heads and Tails. If these individual scores are added, then the sum score after 100 tosses is also independent of the actual sequence of outcomes; 50 Heads and 50 Tails gets the same score as 100 Heads. Table 10.1 compares the quadratic score (positively sensed, on $[-1,1]$) averaged over 1,000 predictions of rain of two experts. Both experts are equally informative in the sense that they both attribute 5 % probability to 100 next days, etc. Expert 1 is statistically perfectly accurate, expert 2 is massively inaccurate, yet expert 2 scores higher than expert 1. The reason is that such rules decompose as the sum of a "calibration" and "resolution" terms (De Groot and Fienberg 1986). Resolution measures the expert's ability to separate the variables into statistically distinct subsets, regardless whether the distributions assigned to the subsets correspond to the expert's assessments. High resolution overwhelms bad statistical accuracy in the above example.

10.3 ROAT Bias

To understand the ROAT bias, suppose two experts state the probability of heads. Let $P_1(\text{Heads}) = 0.8$ and $P_2(\text{Heads}) = 0.2$ be the probability of heads for experts 1 and 2. Suppose that the decision maker's probability is a weighted combination of the experts' probabilities, $P_{dm} = wP_1 + (1 - w)P_2$, where the weight of each expert, given observed data, is proportional to the likelihood of each expert's distribution, given the data.[4] After observing n Heads and m Tails, the experts' likelihood ratio is

$$\frac{0.8^n \times 0.2^m}{0.2^n \times 0.8^m} = 0.8^{n-m} \times 0.2^{m-n} \qquad (10.1)$$

If $m = n$, then the weight ratio is 1, and $w = 1/2$. If $m = n - 1$ then the weight ratio is 4 and $w = 4/5$ Thus if we remove *one* Tail, re-initialize our model and predict the Tail which was removed, we find that the predicted probability of Heads is $P_{dm}(\text{Heads}) = (4/5) \times 0.8 + (1/5) \times 0.2. = 0.68$. Removing one Tail, strongly tilts the model toward expert 1, and our prediction probability for heads is 0.68. At the same time we evaluate this model on the Tail which we removed, hence the likelihood for this model on this observation is 0.32. The same holds, mutatis mutandis, when we remove a Head. Suppose we observe $n = m$; then the PW model would use $w = \frac{1}{2}$. If we truly validated out of sample with $n = m$ fresh observations, the PW likelihood would be 0.5^{2n}, but the ROAT value would be 0.32^{2n}. ROAT punishes PW relative to EW by a factor $(0.32/0.5)^{2n}$. The classical

---

[4] Such likelihood weights are not proper scoring rules, and do not account for informativeness, nonetheless there is a strong analogy with the classical model, as the driving term in that model is the likelihood of the hypothesis that an expert is well-calibrated.

Table 10.1 Two experts assessing next day probability of rain on 1,000 days

Probability of Rain next day:		5 %	15 %	25 %	35 %	45 %	55 %	65 %	75 %	85 %	95 %	Totals
Expert 1	**Assessed**	100	100	100	100	100	100	100	100	100	100	1,000
	Realized	5	15	25	35	45	55	65	75	85	95	500
Expert 2	**Assessed**	100	100	100	100	100	100	100	100	100	100	1,000
	Realized	0	0	0	0	0	100	100	100	100	100	500

Quadratic score expert 1 = 0.665; Quadratic score expert 2 = 0.835

Table 10.2 Weights for ROAT in Eudisp

Removed variable	Expert							
	1	2	3	4	5	6	7	8
None	0	0	0	0.7683	0.2317	0	0	0
1	0	0	0	0.8086	0.1914	0	0	0
2	0	0	0	0.7928	0.2072	0	0	0
3	0	0	0	0.8071	0.1929	0	0	0
4	0	0	0	0.7303	0	0.2697		
5	0	0	0	0.4094	0.5906	0	0	0
6	0	0	0	0.7022	0.2978	0	0	0
7	0	0	0	0.6777	0.3223	0	0	0
8	0	0	0	0.7928	0.2072	0	0	0
9	0	0	0	0.806	0.194	0	0	0
10	0	0	0	0.8645	0.1355	0	0	0
11	0	0	0	0.7003	0.1638	0	0	0.1359
12	0	0	0	0.7042	0.1632	0	0	0.1325
13	0	0	0	0.7659	0.2341	0	0	0
14	0	0	0	0.6996	0.1654	0	0	0.135
15	0	0	0	0.6287	0.1637	0	0.07593	0.1317
16	0	0	0	0.704	0.296	0	0	0
17	0	0	0	0.6996	0.1655	0	0	0.1349
18	0	0	0	0.6286	0.1638	0	0.07588	0.1317
19	0	0	0	0.704	0.296	0	0	0
20	0	0	0	0.6499	0.1537	0	0.07101	0.1254
21	0	0	0	0.5016	0.1307	0	0	0.3677
22	0	0	0	1	0	0	0	0
23	0	0	0	0.4094	0.5906	0	0	0

model is more complex than this simple probabilistic model, but the same behavior can be observed in simple artificial examples.[5]

ROAT sampling is NOT out-of sample validation. Each seed variable is removed one at a time, the model is re-initialized on the remaining seed variables and used to predict the removed variable. Each prediction is made by a *different* model. To appreciate how much these models may differ, Table 10.2 gives the 23 different performance weights for the eight experts that arise as the 23 seed variables in the Eudisp case are removed one at a time. Evidently, the differences between ROAT and true out-of-sample validation can be substantial. The weight for expert 4 varies from 1 to 0.4; that of expert 5 from 0 to 0.59. This is a

---

[5] Take expert 1 (2) with 5, 50 and 95 percentiles equal to 0, 4, 8 (2, 6, 10). Take 3 realizations equal to 0.5, 3 realizations equal to 9.5, 2 realizations equal to 4 and 2 realizations equal to 6. PW and EW coincide and hence should be identical on out of sample validation; however, the score of PW under ROAT is a factor 105 lower than that of EW.

consequence of the well know volatility of the calibration score, which is observed on every robustness analysis of every study. The recalculation of weights when item j is removed tends to give more weight to experts who assessed item j badly, and hence this volatility is put to work *against* the PW model.

10.4   Cross Validation Without ROAT: What to Expect

Absent observation of variables of interest, one option for some form of cross validation splits the calibration variables into a training set used to initialize the model and a test set used to assess performance. Cooke (2008a) applied this method to 13 studies having at least 16 seed variables. In 20 of the 26 cases the PW outperformed Equal Weights (EW). The probability of seeing 20 or more "successes" on 26 trials (77 %), if the probability of success were 0.5, is 0.001247. In this exercise both global and item weights were used, according to which performed best on the training set. Cross validation with item weights is possible with EXCALIBUR, but it is extremely time consuming. A large exercise enabling the choice between global and item weights would require recoding the model.

Intuitively, if we select experts who are 'statistically more accurate than average' in-sample, it is implausible that they should consistently be statistically less accurate out of sample. At worst they might be no better than randomly chosen experts out of sample (reversion to the mean). Further it is plausible that averaging a large set of experts will be less informative than averaging a small subset. How many similar studies we need to detect these effects depends on the size of the effects, the number of seed variables in each study and the number of studies. This section performs some indicative calculations.

We consider $p = (0.05, 0.45, 0.45, 0.05)$ as the interquantile interval probabilities, and let $s(N) = (s_1(N), s_2(N), s_3(N), s_4(N))$ be the sample distribution based on N independent samples from p. The likelihood ratio test statistic

$$2N\,I\big(s(N)\big|p\big)\ =\ 2N\Sigma_{i=1\ldots4}s_i(N)\,\ln\big(s_i(N)/p_i\big) \qquad (10.2)$$

is asymptotically chi square distributed with 3 degrees of freedom if s consists of independent samples from p. If F_3 is the cdf of the chi square distribution with 3 df, then $1 - F_3(2N\,I(s(N)\,|\,p))$ is the p-value of s(N), and it is asymptotically uniformly distributed on the interval [0, 1]. For small N the distribution is not uniform. Figure 10.2 shows the p-value distributions for s(5), s(10), and s(20) based on independent samples from p. Note that s(5) is concentrated in the middle of the [0, 1] interval, its 17th percentile is 0.394 and not 0.17 (the value for a uniform variable).

If the distribution s is not sampled from p then the mass functions of the three cases in Fig. 10.2 shift toward zero, however the shift is much slower for smaller N. Suppose the samples were actually sampled from the distribution $p^{**} = (0.2, 0.3, 0.3, 0.2)$. This would be the sampling distribution of an expert who has only a

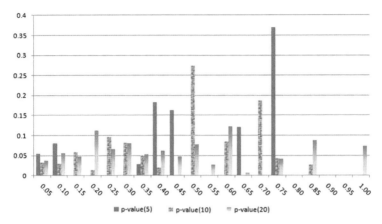

Fig. 10.2 P-values for s(5) (solid), s(10) (hatched) and s(20) (graduated) sampled independently from p

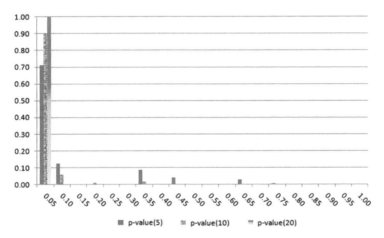

Fig. 10.3 P-values for p**(5) (solid), p**(10) (hatched) and p**(20) (graduated) sampled independently from p**

60 % chance of catching the realizations in his 90 % central confidence band, corresponding to severe overconfidence. Figure 10.3 shows the mass function of p-values for p**(5), p**(10) and p**(20).

The p-value of p**(5) has a 36 % chance of falling below the standard rejection threshold 0.05; for p**(10) that chance is 54 %. If two experts generate sample distributions from p and p**, then on 5 seed variables there is a 24 % chance that the p-value of p** will be *greater* than that of p; on 10 seed variables that chance drops to 14 %.

Suppose we have three types of assessors, the first type's interquantile hits are sampled independently from p. The second type's hits are sampled independently from p**; the third are sampled independently from p* = (0.1, 0.4, 0.4, 0.1).

Table 10.3 Mean and
standard deviation of p-values
on 5 seed variables for three
types of DM

5 seed vbls	Mean	σ
p	0.50	0.23
p*	0.41	0.25
p**	0.23	0.23

Fig. 10.4 Mean p-values of
p, p* and p** as function of
number of seed variables

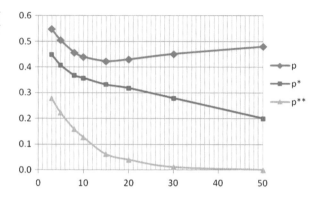

Type p* shows overconfidence, though not as severe as p**. The first type is perfectly calibrated, and his p-value is asymptotically uniform as the number of seed variables goes to infinity. The second type (p**) has p-values distributed as in Fig. 10.3, for 5, 10 and 20 seed variables. When an assessor of each type states a 5 percentile, for example, the probability that the realization falls beneath that 5 percentile is 30 % for p** and 15 % for p*. The mean and standard deviations of the p-values on 5 seed variables of these three types are shown in Table 10.3, as computed by simulation.

Figure 10.4 plots the mean of p-values for p, p* and p** as a function of the number of seed variables.

Note that the mean for p starts above the asymptotic value of 0.5, then dips down to 0.42 after 15 seed variables before climbing back to 0.5. The expected value of the severely overconfident assessor doesn't drop below 0.05 until 17 seed variables. On 5 seed variables the distribution with severe overconfidence and a location bias, p*** = (0.5, 0.3, 0.1, 0.1), will have and expected p-value of 0.06.

We may think of p and p* as representing high scoring assessors, while p** and p*** are representative of low scoring assessors. The following thumb rules apply: assuming that the information scores are equal, we cannot statistically distinguish between high scoring experts (p and p*) on 50 seed variables (the highest number on any study was 55). High scoring assessors can be statistically distinguished from severe overconfidence (p**) on 20 seed variables,[6] while severe overconfidence

---

[6] This is a thumb rule, the 5 % lower confidence bound for p is 0.05, for p* this bound depends on the number of seed variables, since the expected p-value of p* goes to zero as the number of seed variables goes to infinity. For 5, 10 and 20 seed variables the 5 % lower bounds are 0.02, 0.01 and 0.005 respectively.

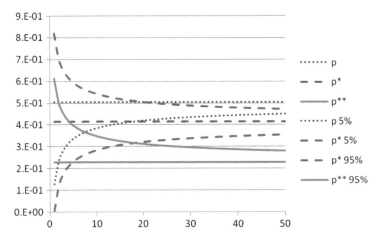

Fig. 10.5 Number of studies with 5 seed variables for distinguishing DMs

plus location bias can be statistically distinguished from high scoring assessors on 10 variables.

We now consider T independent studies with 5 seed variables, where on ALL studies the DM is p, p* or p**. How many studies would we need to decide which type of DM we have? An approximate answer is derived by noting that the mean of averaging p-values over T independent studies is the mean value in Table 10.3, and the standard deviation is approximated by $\sigma/\sqrt{T}$. Figure 10.5 shows the 5 percentile of p's sample average (dotted), the mean, 5 and 95 percentiles of p*'s sample average (dashed) and the mean and 95 percentile of p**'s sample average (solid); each is a function of the number of studies T. The 5 and 95 percentiles of p and p** cross at $T = 8$. That means that if we average p-values over 8 studies, each based on 5 seed variables, we can be 95 % certain that the average of p**'s p-values will be in the critical region for p; and conversely if we average p's p-values, we can be 95 % certain of being in the critical region for p**. Put a bit loosely, if two DM's had interquantile probabilities corresponding to calibration scores 0.5 and 0.23 on 5 seed variables, we could distinguish them statistically on 8 identical and independent studies.

Note that slopes of the percentiles go to zero, making the point of intersection unstable to small perturbations. Table 10.4 gives the number of studies need to distinguish these DMs.

Whereas perfect calibration can be distinguished from severe overconfidence based on 8 studies with 5 seeds, distinguishing perfect calibration (p) from mere overconfidence (p*) on 5 seeds requires 75 studies.

Table 10.5 combines the information of Tables 10.3 and 10.4, but for studies involving 10 seed variables. Overconfidence and severe overconfidence can now be distinguished on 11 studies, instead of 19. Curiously, the mean of the p-values for p has dropped (one can see this in Fig. 10.4) with 10 seeds the distribution is still far

Table 10.4 Number of studies to distinguish DMs with 5 seed variables

Number of studies to distinguish pairs of DMs		
p vs p*	Perfect vs overconf (p vs p*)	75
p vs p**	Perf. vs severe overconf (p vs p**)	8
p* vs p**	Overconf vs severe overconf (p* vs p**)	19

Table 10.5 p-values of DMs based on 10 seeds, and number of studies to distinguish DMs

10 seed vbls	Mean	Std	Number of studies to distinguish pairs of DMs		
p	0.44	0.21	p vs p*	Perfect vs overconf	90
p*	0.36	0.25	p vs p**	Perfect vs severe overconf	5
p**	0.13	0.20	p* vs p**	Overconf vs severe overconf	11

from uniform. As a result, distinguishing perfect calibration (p) and overconfidence (p*) actually requires more studies (90 instead of 75).

These results circumscribe what we can realistically expect from cross validation with appropriate caveats:

- The DM's of individual studies are not all the same,
- Calibration dominates the weighing, but information is also important
- The number and value of the experts in a study is also important. If there are several high scoring experts in a study, then fluctuating scores of experts will tend to cancel, keeping PW's performance high, but with one or no high scorers, extra instability can be expected, causing PW to perform poorly.

Most studies use 10 seed variables; if we split the seed variables into training at test sets of 5, then we may need in the order of 20 studies to distinguish the type of differences between p* and p**, but we need many more to distinguish p and p*, which is the range within which PW and EW calibration scores typically lie.

In contemplating cross validation, the first question is, what questions do we want to answer? On could formulate the following:

- Do the DM's calibration and information scores in-sample predict those out-of-sample?
- Is PW better than EW out of sample?

When a cross validation study initializes the performance based DM on K of the N calibration variables, the following issues arise: (1) If K is close to N, then the number of out-of-sample predictions, N-K, is small, statistically unpowerful, and predictions are subject to the ROAT bias. (2) If K is small, then the power of the calibration score is lowered, thereby reducing the ability to distinguish high and low statistical accuracy of experts. (3) A straddling bias may arise when training and testing sets are complementary halves of the seed variables. The intuition behind this is as follows: two independent random numbers X and Y become negatively correlated if we conditionalize on their sum. When the sum is fixed, one variable can get larger only at the expense of the smaller.

10.4.1 Straddling Bias

The straddling effect can be observed theoretically as follows: repeatedly draw independently 10 realizations from the distribution p*, divide them into disjoint sets of five, and denote by V_1, V_2 the distribution of p-values in the first and second sets. Since V_1, V_2 are independent, their correlation ρ_{12} is zero. The partial correlation given the p-value of the whole set S is defined as

$$\rho_{12}\big|s = \frac{\rho_{12} - \rho_{1s}\rho_{2s}}{((1 - \rho_{1s}^2)(1 - \rho_{2s}^2))^{1/2}} = \frac{-\rho_{1s}^2}{1 - \rho_{1s}^2}.$$

since $\rho_{1s} = \rho_{2s}$; $\rho_{12} = 0$. If S represents the "reduced power p-value" of all 10 variables,[7] and if this negative partial correlation is strong, then the p values of the first and second sets of 5 will tend to straddle the p-value of the whole set. This combined with the fact that the performance weight scores have higher variance than equal weight scores will tend to cause performance weights to outperform on only one of the two subsets, giving an overall 50 % chance that PW exceeds EW, assuming the informativeness scores are roughly equal. Note that if the size of disjoint sets decreases, then ρ_{1s} decreases as well; if the size is greater than one half, then ρ_{12} will be positive. In either case the partial correlation will move towards zero. The effect of a straddling bias in real datasets has not yet been studied, but it is a potential problem.

Table 10.6 shows the partial correlations for p, p* and p** for seed variable sets of size 3, 5, 10, 20 and 50. Notice that the partial correlations are rather weak for the perfectly calibrated assessor whose interquantile probabilities are p. However, for p* and p** the effect is sizeable, even for disjoint subsets of size 3 in a set of 10 seed variables.

Using the data of Eggstaff et al. (2014), Table 10.7 breaks the out-of-sample geomean of mean-score ratios PW/EW and arithmean of mean-score differences PW-EW into the number of variables in the training set and in the test set. For each training set size K (dot-shaded), we collect all comparisons with K in the training set, and consider the geomean of their out-of-sample score ratios and the arithmean of their out-of-sample score differences. This procedure aggregates over test sets of different sizes since the 62 studies differ in total number of seed variables. Similarly we aggregate over all test sets of size K (plane-shaded), thus aggregating over

---

[7] This would hold after the power p-values on samples of size 10 has been reduced to the power of sample size 5. We find that for assessor p (perfect calibration) V_1 and V_2 straddle the reduce power 10 sample p-value with probability 0.24. For assessors p* and p** straddling occurs with probability 0.32 and 0.54 respectively. Note that for p all p-values have approximately the same expectation (namely $\frac{1}{2}$). For p* and p* the expected p-value is decreasing in sample size, which is why we have to equalize power to see the straddle effect.

Table 10.6 Partial correlations

Partial correlations of p-values given whole set

p		Whole set		
		10	20	50
Subset size	3	−0.18	−0.01	0.00
	5	−0.17	−0.01	0.00
	10		−0.17	−0.02
	20			−0.13
p*		**Whole set**		
		10	20	50
Subset size	3	−0.33	−0.09	−0.03
	5	−0.32	−0.09	−0.03
	10		−0.30	−0.06
	20			−0.18
p**		**Whole set**		
		10	20	50
Subset size	3	−0.37	−0.09	0.00
	5	−0.39	−0.09	0.00
	10		−0.24	−0.01
	20			−0.05

Table 10.7 Geomean and Arithmean as function of training size and test size, using data of Eggstaff et al. (2014)

# Train	Geomean	# Test	Geomean	# Studies	# Train	Arithmean	# Test	Arithmean
1	3.14	1	1.20	62	1	0.031	1	0.216
2	5.96	2	1.35	62	2	0.059	2	0.211
3	4.66	3	1.59	62	3	0.087	3	0.180
4	3.52	4	1.88	62	4	0.114	4	0.139
5	2.83	5	2.20	61	5	0.133	5	0.121
6	2.24	6	2.66	59	6	0.142	6	0.101
7	1.88	7	3.06	59	7	0.174	7	0.067
8	1.60	8	3.84	55	8	0.220	8	0.043
9	1.41	9	2.84	53	9	0.197	9	0.022
10	1.23	10	3.02	35	10	0.031	10	0.017
11	1.13	11	3.32	32	11	0.017	11	0.014
12	1.06	12	4.45	25	12	0.005	12	0.018
13	1.08	13	4.03	20	13	0.029	13	0.011
14	0.96	14	1.65	15	14	0.002	14	0.044
15	1.05	15	2.25	10	15	0.033	15	0.042
16	1.09	16	1.79	7	16	0.040	16	0.030
17	0.98	17	1.22	6	17	0.001	17	0.016
18	0.81	18	1.28	2	18	-0.102	18	-0.001
19	0.96	19	0.95	1	19	-0.015	19	-0.013
20	0.85	20	0.93	1	20	-0.015	20	-0.019
21	1.04	21	0.93	1	21	0.012	21	-0.018

The number of studies with training set size 16 and greater are too small to draw conclusions

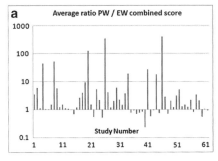
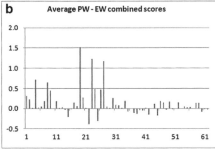

Fig. 10.6 Geomean and arithmetic mean of PW and EW: geomean (*left*) of PW and EW score ratios and arithmetic mean (*right*) of PW and EW score differences, for each of 62 studies analysed in Eggstaff et al. (2014). If a study had N seed variables, the PW and EW scores were averaged over training sets of size K, K = 1 . . . N − 1 and aggregated with either geo- or arithmetic means to determine an out-of-sample performance indicator per study

different sizes of training sets. There are 62 studies in total, and 62 with training sets of size one, and also 62 with test sets of size 1. The 35 studies with at least 11 seed variables have a training set of size 10, and these same 35 studies also have a test set of size 10. Displaying the data in this way, we see that the geomean "likes" small training sets and large test sets. The arithmean "likes" larger training sets up to size 9. Large test sets have greater statistical power, which tends to drive down both the PW and EW scores, and also drives down their difference. This explains arithmean's decreasing behaviour in test size.

Figure 10.6 compares the results of aggregating up to the study level by taking the geomean of the mean-score ratios (left panel) and the arithmetic mean of the mean-score differences (right panel), where "mean-scores" refers to combined scores averaged over training sets of the same size, per study. The left panel of Fig. 10.6 was already presented in Fig. 10.1. Since the studies are indexed from small to large numbers of seed variables, we readily note that a larger number of seed variables lowers the PW and EW scores and also the score differences. A similar effect was noted in Table 10.7. Figure 10.6 highlights the differences between geometric versus arithmetic aggregation, but the superiority of PW over EW is evident from either perspective.

The "small training set" cross validation has the advantages of avoiding the ROAT and the straddle bias. Eggstaff et al. (2014) noted that with small training set the actual scores did not predict the scores on the larger set of calibration variables, but the superiority of performance weighting against equal weighting was attested. If this finding is corroborated, then a smaller number of calibration variables would be defensible, if a smaller number achieved adequate coverage of the problem domain. Based on the results of Sect. 10.3, the current recommendation is that the test set should comprise at least 8, preferably 9 variables.

10.5 Cross Validation of Recent Data

The four studies discussed here are recent and have not yet been published. Figures 10.7, 10.8, 10.9, and 10.10 show the results of initializing the PW model on all subsets of size $K = 1$ and $K = 2$, and using these to predict all calibration variables. Using all seeds instead of the out of sample seeds is done to enable uniform comparison with all-sample results. The difference between all-sample and out of sample is modest for small K values. The curve is the contour of calibration × information that corresponds to the all-sample EW. The all-sample EW and PW are indicated by solid and outlined stars respectively. Geomeans are given in the caption to each figure for the ratio of the PW combined score based on one and two seed variable initializations and all-sample EW. The geomean of all geomeans in the cases analysed here is 2.57

In the Fistula case there is no discernible pattern for PW to outperform EW out of sample, for the others there is. In addition to numbers of experts and seed variables, out of sample performance depends on the experts themselves. In the Fistula case, there were eight experts, all of whom scored poorly. However, on one or two seed variables, one expert may have achieved a high score and gathered dominant weight, only to degrade on the entire set of seed variables.

The Asian carp study with 15 seed variables allows us to illustrate aggregation while keeping at least 9 variables in the test set. Table 10.8 shows results for each size of the training set from 1 to 6. "Arithmean" means that the experts' combined score results were averaged over all tests with the same size of training set;

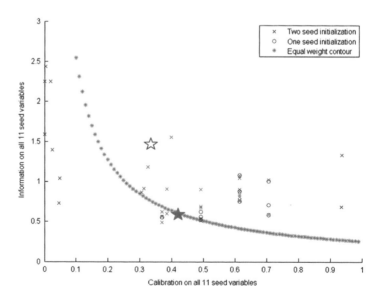

Fig. 10.7 Ice sheet, 11 seed variables: geomean PW/EW one seed = 1.48, two seeds = 0.59. PW > EW on 9 of 11 one seed initializations, and on 34 of 55 two seed initializations, overall on 43/66 = 65 % of these initializations

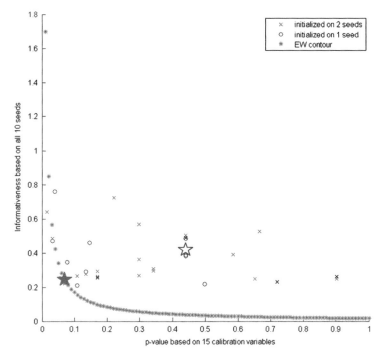

Fig. 10.8 Obesity, 10 seed variables: geomean PW/EW one seed = 3.46, two seeds = 6.19. PW > EW on 9 of 10 one seed initializations, and on 39 of 45 two seed initializations, overall on 48/55 = 87 % of these initializations

similarly "geomean" indicates that the geometric mean was taken. Column 9 considers the ratio of arithmeans, column 10 takes the ratio of geomeans, and column 11 considers the difference of arithmeans.

Note that all of the PW and EW scores increase in the training set size, reflecting the diminishing power of the test set. Note that the difference between the PW arithmean and geomean is greater than this difference with EW. The geomean is always less than or equal to the arithmean, and the difference becomes greater as the (positive) numbers are more variable. Indeed, if one of the aggregated non-negative numbers is zero the geomean is zero, no matter how large the other numbers are. This tendency of the geomean to be driven by the smallest of highly variable non-negative numbers cautions against uncritical use of the geomean. The geomean of a normal variable with mean 1 and standard deviation 0.8, truncated at 0.001 is 0.42, while its mean is 1.04. With this in mind, the ratio of geomeans (column 10) would punish PW for its greater variability. The difference of arithmeans (column 11) is affected by the decrease in statistical power. The ratio of arithmeans (column 9) avoids both these issues and is the current favorite. The geomean of column 9 is 2.62, which is the geomean of column 4 divided by the geomean of column 7. Figure 10.11 compares

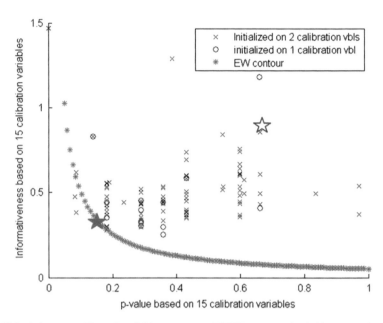

Fig. 10.9 Asian carp, 15 seed variables: geomean PW/EW one seed = 2.64, two seeds = 3.22. PW > EW on 15 of 15 one seed initializations, and on 101 of 105 two seed initializations, overall on 116/126 = 92 % of these initializations

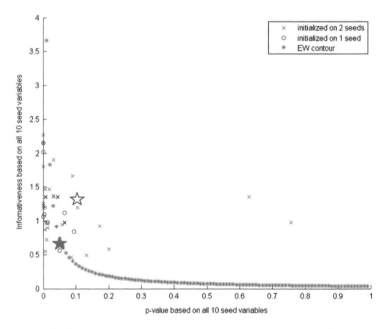

Fig. 10.10 Fistula, 10 seed variables; geomean PW/EW for one seed = 34.8, for two seeds 0.34. PW > EW on 2 of 10 one seed initializations, and on 19 of 45 two seed initializations, overall on 21 / 55 = 38 % of these initializations

Table 10.8 Asian Carp cross validation

1. Nr in Training set	2. Nr of training sets	3. PW median	4. PW Arithmean	5. PW geomean	6. EW median	7. EW Arithmean	8. EW geomean	9. Arith(PW)/ Arith(EW)	10. Geo(PW)/ Geo(EW)	11. Arith(PW) – Arith(EW)
1	15	0.1134	0.1260	0.1173	0.0688	0.0582	0.0554	2.1648	2.1158	0.0678
2	105	0.1470	0.1953	0.1491	0.0561	0.0670	0.0613	2.9170	2.4311	0.1284
3	455	0.1679	0.2019	0.1636	0.0755	0.0764	0.0678	2.6438	2.4136	0.1255
4	1,365	0.2001	0.2406	0.1695	0.0957	0.0864	0.0747	2.7852	2.2676	0.1542
5	3,003	0.2285	0.2626	0.1962	0.0864	0.0971	0.0822	2.7059	2.3858	0.1656
6	5,005	0.2382	0.2808	0.1970	0.1114	0.1084	0.0902	2.5918	2.1834	0.1725

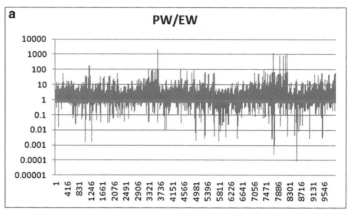

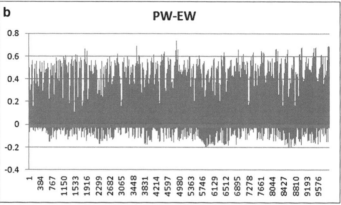

Fig. 10.11 Ratios and differences of PW, EW scores for Asian Carps, based on 1–6 training variables out of 15 calibration variables

the PW and EW scores ratios and differences, for each of the 9,949 training sets of size 1.6.

10.6 Conclusion

Cross validation is more complex that appears at first sight. It is easy to see that single variable scores like the Brier or quadratic score are inappropriate, although they are still misused for this purpose. Less evident but still readily demonstrable is the bias in the ROAT method. Cross validation without ROAT is more challenging. Considering the straddle bias and the power loss relative to the expected size of the PW – EW differences, and the number of studies, the training set should be less than half of the total number of seed variables, and should leave at least 8, preferably 9, seed variables in the test set.

To derive a single out-of-sample validation number for each study, the following procedure reflects the best current insight:

I. Average the PW and EW combined scores (calibration $\times$ information) scores over training sets of size K which leave at least 9 variables in the test set. Call these averages PW(K), EW(K).

II. For each K, compute the ratio PW(K) / EW(K) and the difference PW(K) – EW (K).

III. Take the geomean over K of these ratios: $\prod_{K=1..K^*} [PW(K)/EW(K)]^{1/K^*}$ (preferred) and the arithmean of the differences: $(1/K^*) \sum_{K=1...K^*} PW(K) - EW(K)$ (for comparison); where $N - K^* = 9$, and N is the number of seed variables. If $N = 10$, use $K^* = 2$.

The geomean is preferred in (III) as the ratio PW(K)/EW(K) is dimensionless, and PW(K) – EW(K) is affected by the statistical power of the test set. Throughout all these comparisons, the experts, and seed variables are the same, and the information scores can be meaningfully compared. Taking the geomean over all comparisons with the same training set size is not recommend, as (a) the number of comparisons can be very large, (b) the geomean is strongly influenced by the minimum value, and (c) the PW has greater variability than EW.

Future work could be profitably directed to performing cross validation with item weights and performing cross validation on all studies in the TU Delft base including recent studies. Of course, the studies are designed to pick up the large differences in expert performance, and are fit for that purpose. However we parse the Eggstaff data, PW seems to outperform EW convincingly. Since these are out of sample results, it is not surprising that the difference in performance is less than in sample. Further, these studies were not designed to optimally enable cross validation. As we better understand how cross validation should be done, we may modify the study designs.

References

Clemen, R.T. 2008. Comment on Cooke's classical method. *Reliability Engineering and System Safety* 93(5): 760–765.

Cooke, R.M. 1991. *Experts in uncertainty*. Oxford: Oxford University Press.

Cooke, R.M. 2008a. Special issue on expert judgment, Editor's introduction. *Reliability Engineering and System Safety* 93(5): 655–656, Available online 12 March 2007.

Cooke, R.M. 2008b. Response to comments, Special issue on expert judgment. *Reliability Engineering and System Safety* 93(5): 775–777, Available online 12 March 2007.

Cooke, R.M. 2012. Pitfalls of ROAT cross validation comment on effects of overconfidence and dependence on aggregated probability judgments. *Journal of Modelling in Management* 7(1): 20–22. ISSN 1746–5664.

Cooke, R., and Luis L.H.J. Goossens. 2008. TU Delft expert judgment data base. *Reliability Engineering & System Safety* 93(5): 657–674.

De Groot, M., and S.A. Fienberg. 1986. Comparing probability forecasters: Basic binary concepts and multivariate extensions. In *Bayesian inference and decision techniques*, ed. P. Goel and A. Zellner. New York: Elsevier.

Eggstaff, J.W., T.A. Mazzuchi, and S. Sarkani. 2014. The effect of the number of seed variables on the performance of Cooke's classical model. *Reliability Engineering and System Safety* 121 (2014): 72–82. doi:10.1016/j.ress.2013.07.015.

Flandoli, F., E. Giorgi, W.P. Aspinall, and A. Neri. 2011. Comparison of a new expert elicitation model with the classical model, equal weights and single experts, using a cross-validation technique. *Reliability Engineering and System Safety* 96: 1292–1310. doi:10.1016/j.ress.2011.05.012.

Lin, Shi-Woei and Chih-Hsing Cheng. 2008. *Can Cooke's model sift out better experts and produce well-calibrated aggregated probabilities?* Department of Business Administration, Yuan Ze University, Chung-Li, Taiwan Proceedings of the 2008 I.E. IEEM.

Lin, Shi-Woei, and Chih-Hsing Cheng. 2009. The reliability of aggregated probability judgments obtained through Cooke's classical model. *Journal of Modelling in Management* 4(2): 149–161.

Lin, Shi-Woei, and Ssu-Wei Huang. 2012. Effects of overconfidence and dependence on aggregated probability judgments. *Journal of Modelling in Management* 7(1): 6–22.

Chapter 11
The Truth About Accuracy

Filip Buekens and Fred Truyen

> *The goal of inquiry is substantial, significant, illuminating truth.*
>
> (Haack 1994, p. 203)

Abstract When we evaluate the outcomes of investigative actions as justified or unjustified, good or bad, rational or irrational, we make, in a broad sense of the term, evaluative judgments about them. We look at operational accuracy as a desirable and evaluable quality of the outcomes and explore how the concepts of accuracy and precision, on the basis of insights borrowed from pragmatics and measurement theory, can be seen to do useful work in epistemology. Operational accuracy (but not metaphysical accuracy!) focuses on how a statement fits an explicit or implicit standard set by participants involved in a shared project. While truth can remain a thin semantic property of propositions, operational accuracy, as a quality of an outcome of inquiry and typically attached to a statement, a model, a diagram or a representation is an evaluation based on the non-epistemic goals set by the goal of inquiry (which every inquiry has), and a substantial evaluative notion. The goals, often made explicit by relevant questions in a context of inquiry, act as a filter, with truths a reliable epistemic method has access to functioning as input, and *accurate representations* as its output. Responsible inquiry seeks pragmatic equilibrium between what reliable knowledge on the one hand and degrees of accuracy required by the goal of inquiry.

F. Buekens (✉)
Department of Philosophy, University of Leuven, K. Mercierplein 2, 3000 Leuven, Belgium

TILPS, Tilburg University, Tilburg, The Netherlands
e-mail: filip.buekens@hiw.kuleuven.be

F. Truyen
Faculty of Arts, University of Leuven, Blijde Inkomststraat 22, 3000 Leuven, Belgium
e-mail: fred.truyen@arts.kuleuven.be

© Springer International Publishing Switzerland 2014
C. Martini, M. Boumans (eds.), *Experts and Consensus in Social Science*,
Ethical Economy 50, DOI 10.1007/978-3-319-08551-7_11

11.1 Introduction

When we evaluate the outcomes of investigative actions as justified or unjustified, good or bad, rational or irrational, we make, in a broad sense of the term, evaluative judgments about them.[1] We look at operational accuracy as a desirable quality of outcomes of investigative actions, typically put forward as contributions to purposive exchanges between informants engaged in shared projects. Following those who seek to distinguish good from bad knowledge (Stephen Hetherington), what one ought to and what shouldn't be known (Miranda Fricker) or what counts as valuable knowledge (Stephen Grimm), we ask what it takes to acquire and provide *accurate* information, as well as how accuracy and the reliability of investigative methods interact. Inaccurate truths are easy to obtain, and we could not easily be mistaken about them – our knowledge of them is "safe". So, while the truth exerts a powerful attraction, serious inquiry – inquiry with a purpose (and sheer curiosity can make any subject matter interesting) should deliver *accurate* truths. What counts as an accurate truth (or set of truths) ultimately depends on the non-epistemic goals of the exchange. Unimpeded by extra-epistemic constraints on what one ought to know, aiming at truth is reduced to a pointless game. Standards of accuracy – what will count as accurate information – will ultimately be dependent on what we ought to know given the project that motivates the investigative effort that engages us.[2]

The sake for which we seek knowledge about a subject matter cannot itself be defined in epistemic terms; any reason why X wants to know *p* derives from a non-epistemic project, perhaps ultimately driven by pure curiosity (as Hume pointed out in the *Treatise*, and Jane Heal forcefully argued). We want "truth as such, but not for its own sake" (Heal 1988; Sosa 2003). But accuracy, like *relevance* and *salience*, is an elusive notion (Schelling 1960). Our aim in this chapter is to *precisify* a useful concept in epistemology and philosophy of science by locating it within a network of epistemic and practical principles. Accuracy is too useful to be identified with truth.

Begin with a *prima facie* objection: isn't accuracy just a synonym for truth? Ernest Sosa begins a recent presentation of his acclaimed virtue approach to knowledge with the thesis that "[b]elief is a kind of performance, which attains one level of success if it is true (or accurate)" (Sosa 2011, p. 3).[3] The principle that "an epistemic agent ought to approximate the truth", is called *Accuracy* by Leitgeb

---

[1] We would like to thank Marcel Boumans, Carlo Martini, Chris Kelp and participants at the Bayreuth Conference for valuable suggestions.

[2] The *as such/not for its own sake-* qualification precludes the reduction of truth to some other value (the value we attach to the sake itself).

[3] Ernest Sosa holds that belief aims at truth and that we want correct answers (Sosa 2011, p. 56).

and Pettigrew (2010). In a paper that explores what makes truth good, Linda Zagzebski holds that "[b]elief aims at accurately representing some part of reality propositionally. When a belief is true it is accurate" (Zagzebski 2004, pp. 135–6, note omitted). Bernard Williams (2002) defines what the virtue of *Accuracy* (which is itself, according to him, the counterpart of another veritistic virtue, *Sincerity*) in terms of truth:

> If someone seriously wants to find out the truth on an issue, we can say that this is equivalent to his wanting to get into the following condition: If *p*, to believe that *p*, and if not *p*, to believe that not *p*. (Williams 2002, p. 133)

Williams characterizes *Accuracy* (as *he* uses the term) as "the desire for truth 'for its own sake' – the passion for getting it right" (Williams 2002, p. 126), but we have already indicated that the desire for truth "for its own sake" is questionable. Williams is of course aware of that: the conversational implicature suggested by the definite article in "finding out *the* truth", intimates that the concern is to find the accurate and/or relevant truths in view of one's non-epistemic aims and goals.[4] In "accurate truths" the adjective's role is not pleonastic. "True, but wholly inaccurate" suggests a severe criticism.

While accuracy is arguably a thick evaluative concept, truth-minimalists reject that truth itself is an evaluative concept (Horwich 1998). Although the concept often appears in norms like "one should assert what is true", minimalism holds that such norms are mere generalizations of particular norms as "One should asserts that grass is green only if grass is green". Moreover, the normativity of a concept does not follow from its appearance in a norm, for that would entail that any concept is normative ("being over 18" can appear in a hypothetical norm, but it is clearly not an intrinsically normative concept). Donald Davidson and Allan Gibbard have questioned whether truth can count as the aim of inquiry (Davidson 2005; Gibbard 2007), suggesting that truth is a goal in name only and that what matters are the justifications one provides. Jane Heal (1988/89), in a neglected paper defending minimalism about truth, holds that we never seek truth for its own sake. When someone's actions can be described as trying to find out the truth, a further more specific description under which her investigative action was intentional is always possible, and the description articulates a goal the agent holds because it is derived from the overall project in which her investigative action has a proper place.

---

[4] If, as Grimm (2008) points out, "we think that pursuing the truth is intrinsically valuable, then why are we unapologetically indifferent to so many truths? If you propose an evening memorizing the phone book for Topeka, Kansas and I decline, have I really missed an opportunity to enrich myself, from an epistemic point of view? If the truth is always intrinsically worth pursuing, then it seems that I have. And yet that conclusion seems ridiculous" (Grimm 2008, pp. 725–26). Talk of pursuing the truth is highly misleading, as Hookway (2007) points out: "We seek answers to our questions which are relevant, illuminating and useful, so truth is, at most, one among a set of standards that we use in evaluating inquiries" (Hookway 2007, p. 2).

Goldman (1999) concurs. Heal also points out that this strategy need not assume a non-relational conception of truth. Even if we seek "correspondence" between us and the world, correspondence as such is not the goal of inquiry. Inquiry aims at finding out whether p, not whether a certain relation between the inquirer and the world holds. It is the fact that p that matters for one's projects, not the relation between the inquirer and that fact.

Our first proposal is therefore to distinguish the *thick* concept of accuracy from the thin notion of truth.[5] What counts as accurate or inaccurate information clearly varies with the purpose of the model or representation it is supposed to qualify. As Van Fraassen puts it, "[t]he evaluation as accurate or inaccurate is highly context-dependent. A subway map, for example, is typically not to scale, but only shows topological structure. Relative to its typical use and our typical needs, it is accurate; with a change in use or need, it would at once have to be classified as inaccurate" (van Fraassen 2008, p. 15).[6] Note that Van Fraassen does not speak of the truth of a subway map (can maps be true?) and that few would accept that truth or falsity would be highly context-dependent.

According to Teller (2004, 2009), scientific representations should not be thought of as true or false. While it makes perfect sense to talk of one theory being more accurate than another and therefore "closer to the truth", none of our theories are flat-footedly true. Teller's suggestion, however, confuses the useful idea of approximating standards of accuracy with the more contentious idea of metaphysical truth approximation.[7] Moreover, it would involve an implausible *error theory* about accuracy because, if Teller were right about ineliminable discrepancies between a representation and its target, no representation could ever be completely accurate.[8] Secondly, the claim that every model misrepresents its object and that all representations are therefore inaccurate confuses what is *absent from a representation* with what a representation *misrepresents as being the case*. Thirdly, inaccurate knowledge is – on the account presented here – not an oxymoron, for known truths can be inaccurate, and inaccurate statements often

---

[5] Minimalists can hold that the descriptive element in the concept of accuracy is simply truth; a theory of what counts as accurate explores the evaluative aspect of accuracy. The extension of a thick concept cannot be determined without sharing or imaginatively entering the insider's evaluative point of view. The insider's point of view in the case of accuracy is recognition of the project one needs accurate information for.

[6] According to G.L. Hallett, "[i]t is in general desirable for tables, maps, statistics and descriptions to be accurate, as it is for statements to be true. Accuracy is usually a virtue, as truth is, and to say that something is accurate is generally to praise it" (Hallett 1988, p. 83).

[7] Tal (2011) suggests that the correlate concept of metaphysical measurement accuracy is truth. The counterpart of operational measurement accuracy is standardization. More on the relevance of standards in Sects. 11.2 and 11.3.

[8] An error theory about *flatness* was famously developed in Unger (1975).

convey falsehoods and/or reveal inappropriate choices of standards.[9,10] It seems then that cashing out accuracy as "approximating the truth" doesn't really capture what is useful about the concept. Teller's measurement-analogy suggests that it might useful to turn to the science of measurement for further refinement of the concept and we will pursue that analogy later in this chapter. Tal (2011) discusses, in the context of measurement theory, no less than five different notions of measurement accuracy. *Metaphysical measurement accuracy* is the closeness of agreement between a measured value of a quantity and its true value which suggests, under a traditional understanding of truth as correspondence with a mind-independent reality, a form of realism about quantities. Epistemic accuracy refers to the closeness of agreement among values reasonably attributed to a quantity based on its measurement. The correlate concept is (un)certainty. Comparative accuracy refers to the closeness of agreement among values of a quantity obtained by using different measuring systems. Its correlate concept is reproducibility. Finally there is the pragmatic measurement notion of being accurate for, where the measurement meets the requirements of a specific application (Tal 2011). Operational measurement accuracy – closeness of agreement between a measured value of a quality and a value of that quantity obtained by reference to a measurement standard – serves best the concept under scrutiny. Metaphysical measurement accuracy, on the other hand, is the closeness of agreement between a measurement value and its "true value", but it is usually assumed in physics that, in this sense, the true value of a physical magnitude is simply unknowable. The analogy would make truth (and therefore accuracy) by definition unattainable. The focus must therefore be on the relation between a statement and some standard in view of which it will be evaluated as (in)accurate.[11] This suggests a further objection to Teller's approach: the operational accuracy of a measurement result assumes that the standards are set in such a way that they are attainable and that attainment can be recognized by us. If truth were the fixed standard of accuracy that holds in all contexts of inquiry,

---

[9] Teller (2009) connects precision, accuracy and truth as follows: "The way we talk, and even more strikingly, the way we think about our subject matters, all seems to operate in terms of determinate truths, unqualified in any way by either imprecision or inaccuracy. How can this be if, as I claim, inexactness is ubiquitous?" (Teller 2009, p. 15). See http://maleficent.ucdavis.edu:8080/paul/manuscripts-and-talks/T-F%20In%20Science (consulted July 2013). In the same paper, Teller holds that "A representation is inaccurate insofar as there are discrepancies between the representation's target and the way the representation represents the target as being. If the true value of a quantity is 6, characterizing that value as 5.9 is precise, but inaccurate" (Teller 2009, p. 2). If (public) representations are seen as models, it should be obvious (hence not a disqualifying feature) that they will be imprecise, incomplete, not without assumptions, etc. Is the well-known model of London's subway map accurate? Yes – for the purposes of the visitor.

[10] Braun and Sider (2007) defend an error theory about truth: "Truth is an impossible standard that we never achieve. [...] (I)t would be pointlessly fussy to enforce this standard to the letter, requiring the (exact) truth, ... nor would it be desirable to try, for the difference between the legitimate disambiguations of our sentences are rarely significant to us" (Braun and Sider 2006, p. 135).

[11] Tal's definitions are inspired by the *International Vocabulary of Metrology* (VIM).

recognizing the accuracy of a statement would be problematic since, as Frege pointed out in *Der Gedanke*, truth is an unrecognizable property.

In Sect. 11.2 we explore and defend the distinction between truth and accuracy and show that they qualify different objects. In Sect. 11.3 we look at accuracy as a distinctive quality of contributions to conversational exchanges: how is accuracy created, how are investigative actions with accurate outcomes obtained, and who is in charge of saying what is and what isn't going to count as accurate information? We start with some Gricean examples, but the key analogy will be drawn from measurement theory and the interaction between accuracy and precision in measurement (Sect. 11.4). In the final section (Sect. 11.5) we reject Alvin Goldman's *veritistic* characterization of experts as those who "know more about a subject matter" (Goldman 1999). A key element in distinguishing laymen from experts is the degree of accuracy (and not just truth) of the latter's contributions, relative to their domain of expertise, combined with the capacity to set the appropriate standards of accuracy required by the goal of the investigative action in which they are engaged or are being asked to contribute.[12]

11.2 Accuracy Entails Truth

What speaks against identifying of truth with accuracy is that while truth is a thin concept, accuracy is arguably *thick*. Qualifying a model, representation, diagnosis, assessment or contribution as accurate (or not accurate, or not very accurate, or as more accurate than was required) is an appraisal, not only of the contribution itself but also of the agent who made it, who was responsible for the accurate model or result. Accuracy, unlike truth, easily transfers from statements to agents, and one can be accurate at one epistemic task but not at others. Unlike truth, accuracy unproblematically admits of degrees.

Against identifying the concepts of truth and accuracy (or speaking the truth and speaking accurately) also speak broadly Gricean considerations, which suggest that an accurate statement can be false. "Everyone in the room speaks French" may be accurate, but not (strictly) true. A model or simulation may be said to be accurate enough for some purpose but not for another, even if the model itself is strictly speaking false which explains why models and simulations are sometimes thought of as "useful fictions." "France is hexagonal" is literally false, but seems accurate if "Italy is booth-shaped" is also accepted as accurate. We discard this family of objections, first on the grounds, already mentioned, that truth and accuracy are often used interchangeably, which suggests that a statement's being accurate (for some purpose) but strictly speaking false depends on how we single out the proposition

---

[12] Another argument against a purely veritistic characterization of experts is that, paradoxically, laymen run a lesser risk of having false beliefs because they have fewer beliefs about a domain or subject matter.

expressed by the statement to be qualified. By invoking the principle that propositions expressed by assertions can contain unarticulated constituents and that one such unarticulated constituent is (in the relevant cases) the "roughly" or "more or less"-operator: if *France is hexagonal* is roughly true, then it is and objective, unqualified truth that France is roughly hexagonal. Similarly, if it is more or less true that the room is full of speakers who speak French, it is true (simpliciter) that the room is more or less full with speakers who speak French (Horwich 1998, p. 63). Statements that are "more or less", "roughly" or "approximately" or "sort of" true are equivalent with *unqualified* truths when the unarticulated constituent – in this case an operator – is integrated in the proposition qualified as true or false. What is *strictly speaking* false may, with the help of unarticulated "more or less" or "sort of"-operator, be transformed into an asserted plain truth. Interpretative charity (of the Gricean or Davidsonian kind) suggests that some such operation is ubiquitous in micro-interpretation. The fact that the compositionally determined minimal semantic content of a sentence – its *literal meaning* – is almost never literally true on occasions of use doesn't entail that we cannot successfully use such a sentence to make true or accurate assertions (Borg 2005; Cappelen and Lepore 2004). What we literally say is often under-articulated, underspecified and/or imprecise because a more precise articulation would take too much time and/or cognitive effort. What can be plausibly inferred by the intended audience need not be explicitly articulated by the speaker (Levinson 2000). Semantic and pragmatic considerations thus speak *for* and not *against* the claim that accuracy entails truth. Finally, it should be noted that while every accurate statement is also true, not every useful statement (or belief, for that matter) need to be true. There are patently false beliefs that are useful – just think of placebo effects, for example, and how they constitutively depend on having false beliefs about certain pills. No amount of tinkering with semantic contents can make such useful-but-false beliefs true.

11.3 Accuracy Is More than Truth

Further arguments give credence to the claim that accurate truths involving a domain *D* are a strict subset of the possible informative truths about *D*. Consider Grice's well-known example: A is planning with B an itinerary for a holiday in France. Both know that A wants to see his friend C, if doing so would not involve too great a prolongation of the journey.

A: Where does C live?
B: Somewhere in the South of France.

B's answer is, as he very well knows, less informative than is required to meet A's needs. This infringement of the *Maxim of Quantity* ("Make your contribution as informative as is required for the current purposes of the conversation") can be explained only on the supposition that B is aware that being more informative would require saying something that infringed on the *Maxim of Quality*, ("Don't say what you lack adequate evidence for"). Consequently, B implies that he does not know in which town C lives (Grice 1967/1989, p. 34). Grice's abductive explanation assumes that it is common knowledge among the participants what would count as an accurate answer. Although what B says is true, a more informative answer would infringe on the maxim of *Quality*. This would explain why B's contribution implicates that he does not know where C lives, *given* the informal standard of what would count as accurate in the conversation (and made explicit in Grice's gloss that accompanies his example; the gloss is supposed to make explicit what the participants, on the basis of the Cooperative Principle, agree is the purpose or general direction of the conversation).

The example illustrates how the *practical purpose* of the informative transaction fixes what will count as an *accurate* (and not just *true*) answer.[13] If A and B were to discuss C's secret whereabouts on a need-to-know standard, B's original answer would have been accurate enough. The operative standards of accuracy in an epistemic exchange are therefore a function of the project one is engaged (where to go, how to build a plane that carries 520 passengers over at least 8,000 miles, etc.,).[14] Merely telling and acquiring truths (or justified truths) independently of a mutually recognized project would be a parody of a purposive conversation. Note that I can provide accurate information, given that I know what you need to know in order to realize your non-epistemic purposes. But I do not thereby have to adopt your goals, which determine why you want to know what you just asked me.

An assertion's accuracy cannot be transferred to what the proposition that specifies the asserted content logically entails. If there were 520 passengers on the plane, there were also more than 200 on the plane, but the latter truth is inaccurate if we want to know how many passengers died in the crash. Although one can *say* that it is "not inaccurate" to assert that there were more than 200 passengers on the plane (and especially so if one doesn't know better), such a remark would in this context surely be dismissed as inappropriate or even misleading.

Epistemologists often object to the unqualified principle *that we should believe the truth*, under the bidirectional reading that (i) we ought to believe what is true, and that (ii) our beliefs ought to be true (Goldman 1999; Sosa 2003; Piller 2008). Why invest costly epistemic efforts in irrelevant subjects just because the epistemic actions yield true beliefs (Grimm 2008, p. 731)? Acquiring true beliefs is, as such, not a good way to measure how we benefit from investigative actions (Heal 1988) Ernest Sosa demurs concerning the claim that truth itself ("as such") is valuable:

> At the beach on a lazy summer afternoon, we might scoop a handful of sand and carefully count the grains. This would give us an otherwise unremarked truth, something that on the view before us [truth as such is valuable] is at least a positive good, other things equal. This view I hardly understand ... it is hard to see any sort of *value* in one's having that truth. (Sosa 2003; pp. 44–5)

---

[13] Pragmatists would define the *true* answer with the one that satisfies our non-epistemic purposes. This cannot be correct, for false beliefs also help us realize extra-epistemic goals. There are useful falsehoods and useless truths.

[14] See Hempel 1965, p. 333 for a defense of a purely intellectual interest in truth.

Lots of truths can be found in any domain, but a genuine interest in a domain or subject matter will necessarily be motivated by projects which determine what will be accurate information about that subject matter, the kind of things you *need to know* in order to successfully move forward. Even if one's investigative efforts into a domain are motivated by Humean curiosity, any sensible inquirer will set for himself standards of accuracy, and only when attainable by the inquirer, will they count as reasonable standards (an observation already made by David Hume in the Treatise, but going back to remarks of Cicero in *De Officiis*). Indicators of the veritistic quality of an assertion or belief, like coherence or simplicity, do not suffice to turn truths into accurate truths (an inaccurate truth can be perfectly well justified). Neither is accuracy a direct function of the evidence one possesses. It is *the sake for which we seek truths* – the project in which inquiry is necessarily embedded – from which standards of accuracy must derived. The value of the goal of truth is fully swamped by the further goal of acquiring and exchanging accurate knowledge (recall that accuracy entails truth). The question "Why do you want to know that?" points at what will provide the source of the standard of accuracy required to give a useful answer.

Thirdly, we already pointed out that unlike accuracy, truth doesn't admit of *degrees* (Crane 2014). If two statements *S* and *S'* both express true propositions, one cannot be *more* true than the other, but in the same context of inquiry *S* can be more accurate than *S'* (but see Elgin 2004, Braun and Sider 2006 for dissent).[15] William James held that truth itself is created ("Truth is made, just as health, wealth and strength are made, in the course of experience" (James 1907, p. 218)). What James mistakenly attributes to truth *is* in fact true of accurate statements. Standards of accuracy are created and not found, and they must be designed so that they can be recognizably attained in the course of inquiry by the inquirer. What is going to count as an accurate result, answer or statement depends on an implicitly or explicitly set standard, set by agents in view of their projects and the subject matter they investigate. Experts can decide what is going to count as accurate enough in a certain context, given a well-designed project or purpose.

Fourth, the accuracy of a statement is a relational and recognizable property, while truth is, not only on the minimalist account of the concept, neither relational nor recognizable. Where Frege held in *The Thought* that the property of being true, unlike the property of being yellow, is *not* recognizable, Dummett's analogy between truth and winning a game assumes that truth is a recognizable property:

> It is part of the concept of winning a game that a player plays to win, and this part of the concept is not conveyed by a classification of the end positions into winning ones and losing ones. Likewise, it is part of the concept of truth that we aim at making true statements. We cannot in general suppose that we give a proper account of a concept by describing those circumstances in which we do, and those in which we do not make use of the relevant word, by describing the usage of the word; we must also give an account of the point of the concept, explain what we use the word for. (Dummett 1959, pp. 142, 149)

---

[15] J.L. Austin famously held that "true" and "false" indicate "a general dimension of being a right or proper thing to say, as opposed to a wrong thing, in these circumstances" (Austin 1962, p. 145).

One can recognize a winning position on a chessboard, but the truth of a belief or statement does, as Donald Davidson put it, "not come with a 'mark' like the date in the corner of some photographs, which distinguishes them from falsehoods. The best we can do is test, experiment, keep an open mind . . . Since it is neither a visible target, nor recognizable when achieved, there is no point in calling truth a goal" (Davidson 2005, p. 6). Since Accuracy relates a statement with a standard, the operative standards of accuracy should be recognizable by us.[16,17] The assessment of a statement as accurate (in a context) involves a comparison of a statement or obtained result with a (public) operational standard. (It may well be that identifying truth with accuracy explains the tendency to seek recognizable standards for truth.) The setting of operative standards for what is going to count as accurate and their attainability is informed by what ultimately motivates inquiry. Not that setting the standard is always a difficult matter. The operative standard may sometimes simply be set by the relevant Yes/No-question ("What happened? Did a bomb explode, or was there a gas leak?"), where the conversational context indicates what counts as an accurate (and not just true) answer. "Something happened" is a true but inaccurate answer.

11.4 Accuracy and Reliability: Interactions

We now leave behind the Gricean analogy and explore a further analogy with accuracy as used in measurement theory. In measurement theory, the degree of *accuracy* indicates the degree of closeness of a measured or calculated quantity to its reference value, sometimes misleadingly referred to as the "true value", for no measurement is absolutely (i.e. metaphysically) accurate.[18] Its complementary concept is *precision*, which indicates the degree to which a *series* of measurements or calculations have similar outcomes. Precision reflects the reliability of the method that yields measurement results. This gives us four qualifications of the outcomes of such an inquiry:

Accurate and precise (d)
Inaccurate, but precise (a)
Accurate but imprecise (b)
Inaccurate and imprecise (c)

---

[16] Frege held that "[t]ruth is not a quality that corresponds with a particular kind of sense-impression. . . . That the sun has risen is seen to be true on the basis of sense-impressions. But being true is not a material, perceptible property" (Frege 1918/1999, p. 88).

[17] "In principle", because we may not yet have designed or developed the instruments or measurement tools that yield results accurate enough for our purposes, and it may be impossible to design tools that will work sufficiently accurately to realize our non-epistemic goals. Thanks to Chris Kelp for help here.

[18] It is impossible to make a perfectly precise measurement (see footnote 3).

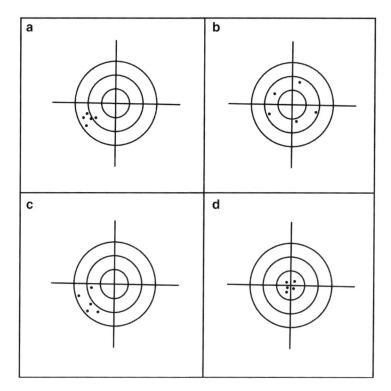

Fig. 11.1 Accuracy and precision

In measurement theory *precision* refers to the similarity of a series of measurement results, while *accuracy* is obtained if a token is close enough to an independently fixed value (the *standard*). Only when *accuracy* (a property of a token result) and *precision* (a property of a pattern of tokens, or a type) are as required by the standards is a measurement result deemed *valid*. The relevant correlative concept of the measurement-theoretic notion of precision in epistemology is that of a *reliable process*. Note, first, that even extremely reliable methods need not yield accurate truths. Very precise measurements can be "off the mark" (see Fig. 11.1, upper left corner). Just as the overall precision (reliability) of a series of measurement results depends on its repeatability, a reliable epistemic process must be robust, *i.e.* hold in the actual world and in nearby possible worlds.[19] In his version of a reliabilist account of knowledge, Robert Nozick's *modus operandi* are tracking connections which correspond with the fact believed (see Nozick 1981): (i) if p were not true, the agent wouldn't believe that p, and (ii) if p were true (under circumstances slightly differing from those actually obtaining), he would (still) believe that p obtains. Once it is assumed that knowledge is, among other things, true belief

---

[19] Repeatability and reproducibility can be given an intra-world reading or an inter-world reading.

acquired via reliable methods – a quite uncontroversial assumption – the question arises what the method is supposed to be reliable for: producing a true belief in exactly those circumstances in which it is actually deployed, producing a true belief in circumstances much like those actually obtaining, producing a true belief in all the circumstances likely enough to be worth considering, or producing a true belief in all possible circumstances (Craig 1999, p. 54)? The answer must refer to the project in which the investigative efforts are embedded, and it can reflect what the epistemic risks one is prepared to take: can we afford to come to know a very accurate truth with a method which, in very nearby possible worlds, would yield blatant falsehoods? A variant of Nozick's account is the safety approach (Williamson 2000): S knows that p only if, in many nearby worlds where S believes that p, p is true. One knows that p only if the belief could not have easily been false. What if the standard of accuracy requires that in many nearby worlds one's methods no longer yield reliable results?

Reliability is, like its counterpart *precision* in measurement theory, characterized by a *consistent pattern* in the outcomes (as in cases (a) and (d) in Fig. 11.1) and a type-token distinction: a token is reliably produced if it falls under a type of process that produces "true" tokens in similar circumstances and/or under similar conditions. But however reliable the outcomes, true beliefs produced by a reliable process R may be wholly *inaccurate* (see case (a) in Fig. 11.1). To return to Grice's example: suppose that B is a very reliable informant with respect to C's country-wise whereabouts: in the actual world and in many nearby worlds, B has true beliefs about C's location – France or England. Yet it doesn't follow that B can give the information required by those who seek C's *exact* location in France or England. His expertise (expertise here defined in terms of reliability) doesn't yield accurate information. Alternatively, B may have come to know C's exact location in France, but only accidentally so (he may have incidentally overheard a conversation in which C's whereabouts were pointed out in quite some detail). Under such conditions he provides accurate information based on an unreliable process. Since accuracy, unlike precision, is a property of individual tokens, the unreliability of the method undercuts the epistemic status (true belief, but not knowledge), but not its accuracy. What he said was accurate relative to the purposes at hand. Note that if A does not knows that C is in France, then B's assertion is informative, yet inaccurate while if he does know that C is in France, the statement is both uninformative and inaccurate.

There is a further difference between reliability and accuracy. The kind of accuracy required for an investigative action to be successful is fixed by goals and projects of the inquirer and features of the domain of investigation. Fixing one's goals usually falls under intentional control: we deliberate about them, they are often subject to negotiation, and they may be morally and practically evaluated. These goals determine what we should or need to know, and fix standards for what will count as accurate information. The reliability of belief-forming processes, on the other hand, is typically *not* directly accessible to agents (think of perception, for example). One can be very reliable at a cognitive task, with little or no understanding of what makes one reliable. Our grasp of belief-forming mechanisms may be largely tacit. This is one further reason why reliable believers cannot be praised as such: only when the appropriate reliable processes are mobilized to further the acquisition of accurate beliefs – things they need to know – can their epistemic actions be evaluated. In order for reliability to become a feature agents can bring under intentional control, it is therefore useful to make a distinction between the *reliable methods* on the one hand and *reliable processes* agents don't have access to. The choice of a method is, like the standard of accuracy set for oneself, determined by one's extra-epistemic goals and an epistemic agent is responsible for the choice of method.

11.5 How Accuracy and Reliability Interact

Truth doesn't compete with accuracy. Both fit together in the sense that the focus of our epistemic aim is set by non-epistemic goals that direct investigative actions towards finding out the accurate truths, the ones we need to know in order to realize our projects (again, the project may simply be to come to understand the issue, or to satisfy our curiosity). The degree of accuracy required by a project in a context c will interact with the epistemic methods available to the agent in c: the standards must be such that the method to be followed can attain them. Obtaining accurate information can be costly. On the other hand, it doesn't make sense to seek very accurate information if that would require costly epistemic efforts unmotivated by goals that motivated the inquiry. Progress in science and technology is often indicated by setting more ambitious standards of accuracy, driven by the attainability of new goals by improved technology.[20]

Second observation: Agents need not *share* non-epistemic goals to agree about what will count as accurate data, given one of the participant's non-epistemic goals and the epistemic actions required to achieve that goal.[21] Setting standards unrealistically high, given the available methods in the agent's context of inquiry, puts one at fault for being too ambitious. Setting standards too low makes accurate truths easily attainable but almost certainly useless for the purposes they are supposed to serve. Responsible inquirers manage to strike a balance between the choice of epistemic methods weighted against the level of accuracy required by their goals; the required level of reliability sometimes requires that one lowers the standards of accuracy: too accurate truths may be difficult to obtain. The promise of acquiring very accurate truths can justify costly epistemic efforts, the cost mainly due to maintaining sufficient reliability of the methods deployed. In general, it cannot be

---

[20] Goldman (1986, p. 98) holds that "truth acquisition is often desired for its own sake, not for ulterior ends". But we are not interested in every truth: it is a *subject matter* that elicits curiosity but even then only *accurate* truths will interest us.

[21] When stakes are high or become more complex, negotiating the relevant standards will take on a more formal character. *Standardization* has become a thriving industry.

the purpose of epistemic interactions that contributors feed each other with inaccurate truths collected via extremely reliable methods, or extremely accurate truths acquired via very unreliable methods. When asked for information that cannot be obtained via reliable methods or that will be highly inaccurate, epistemically responsible informants should *signal* a disequilibrium between standards and the epistemic method deployed.[22]

The account of accuracy proposed here suggests that it is questionable whether it is even *prima facie* good to believe or seek trivial truths, as Lynch (2004, p. 55) seems to hold. What *is* open-ended and by definition true is that any subject matter may be of interest to us, but it does not follow that it is the truth *as such* that we want (Grimm 2008, p. 730). Aristotle's dictum that all humans desire knowledge is therefore only half true (as one might say). We desire *accurate* knowledge because epistemic efforts are by their very nature embedded in non-epistemic projects (Heal 1988). Even pure curiosity requires a sense of what accurate truths about a subject matter would consist in (trivial, easily obtainable truths about a subject matter do not satisfy one's curiosity). The familiar dictum that "the truth is hard to find" must mean that *accurate* information about a designated subject matter may be hard to find. As Craig (1999, p. 223) points out, it is implausible that one can responsibly recommend an informant (qua expert) without knowledge of the purposes of the inquiry, which is to say that an informant's *expected* accuracy, *given* standards of accuracy, will be a determining factor for selecting him/her as an expert. These considerations plead against a purely veritistic account of expertise. Goldman (2001) holds that cognitive expertise should be defined in "veritistic" (*i.e.* truth-linked) terms:

> Experts in a given domain ... have more beliefs (or higher degrees of belief) in true propositions and/or fewer beliefs in false propositions within that domain than most other people (or better: than the vast majority of people) do ... To qualify as a cognitive expert a person must possess a substantial body of truths in the target domain. (Goldman 2001, p. 91).

> An expert ... in domain *D* is someone who possesses an extensive fund of knowledge (true belief) and a set of skills or methods for apt and successful deployment of this knowledge to new questions in the domain. (idem., p. 92)

However, one can, on this account, be a very reliable agent with respect to domain *D,* while not being in a position to deliver operationally accurate information about *D*. Nobody counts as an expert just because she is blindly amassing truths on the basis of reliable methods or processes. He/she should know which standards are operative in the context of inquiry, whether they can be realistically attained given the epistemic actions afforded by the environment, how refined the method should be by which they can be attained, and why the operative standards should be accepted by the intended audience that takes him/her to be the expert on the subject

---

[22] Reliability looks at the informant's competence to provide true information in a range of possible worlds, one of which is the actual one.

matter. Craig speaks of "indicator properties" as what an inquirer seeks to identify in an informant as a guide to her *truth-telling* ability (Craig 1999, p. 135). Our account of operational accuracy suggests an indicator property for experts: their ability to set appropriate standards of accuracy and to deliver on those standards.[23]

11.6 Conclusion

Ernest Sosa's famous analogy of the archer and her target is particularly helpful to illustrate our main claims: accuracy is to hit the point, and as she practices, she hits closer to the target and her accuracy improves (Sosa 2011). When her shots are more tightly clustered they are precise, and the archer has become more reliable. Hitting the intended target involves compensating for whatever is causing her precision to veer from the target – she is trying to map actual precision to the public standard of accuracy (hitting the point). Similarly, in inquiry, we want to be reliable agents who can provide exactly those truths that satisfy the operative standards of accuracy relevant in the context of inquiry. What counts as accurate information cannot be defined in terms of the truths an expert can detect just in virtue of being a reliable detector of truths. That would be like drawing a circle around clustered arrows on a board and then claiming that the target was hit. But it would turn *any* reliable method into one that yields accurate results. Practical goals, standards for accuracy, the reliability of one's epistemic methods in view of these goals and the operative standards set in view of these goals are interacting in practical epistemic rationality.[24]

References

Austin, J.L. 1962. *How to do things with words*. Oxford: Oxford University Press.
Borg, Emma. 2005. *Minimalism in semantics*. Oxford: Oxford University Press.
Braun, D., and T. Sider. 2006. Vague, so untrue. *Noûs* 41(2006): 133–156.
Braun, D., and T. Sider. 2007. Vague, so untrue. *Noûs* 41: 133–156.
Cappelen, H., and E. lePore. 2004. *Insensitive semantics*. Oxford: Blackwell.
Craig, William. 1999. *Knowledge and the state of nature*. Oxford: Clarendon.
Crane, Tim. 2014. *Aspects of psychologism*. Cambridge, MA: Harvard University Press.

---

[23] A good informant is not just someone who is sufficiently likely to be right about the issue (as Craig suggests) but also sufficiently accurate. Indicator properties of good informants need to indicate not just reliability but also their accuracy.

[24] Goldman (2009) seems to identify both values when he describes Sosa's view: "Like an archer's shot at a target, a belief can be accurate, it can manifest epistemic virtue or competent (roughly, reliability)." See http://plato.stanford.edu/entries/reliabilism/ (last consulted March 1, 2011).

Davidson, Donald. 2005. Truth rehabilitated. In *Truth, language and history*, ed. D. Davidson. Oxford: Oxford University Press.

Dummett, Michael. 1959/1978. *Truth and other enigmas*. London: Duckworth.

Elgin, Catherine Z. 2004. True enough. *Philosophical Issues* 14(1): 113–131.

Frege, G. 1918/1999. The thought: A logical inquiry. In *Truth*, ed. S. Blackburn and K. Simmons. Oxford: Oxford University Press.

Gibbard, Allan. 2007. Rational credence and the value of truth. In *Oxford studies in epistemology*, vol. 2, ed. Tamar Szabo Gendler and John Hawthorne, 143–165. Oxford: Oxford University Press.

Goldman, Alvin. 1986. *Epistemology and cognition*. Cambridge, MA: Harvard University Press.

Goldman, A. 1999. *Knowledge in a social world*. New York: Oxford University Press.

Goldman, A. 2001. Experts: Which ones should you trust? *Philosophy and Phenomenological Research* 63: 85–110. Reprinted in E. Selinger, and R. Crease (ed.). 2006. *The philosophy of expertise*. New York: Columbia University Press.

Goldman, A. 2009. Social epistemology: Theory and applications. *Epistemology. Royal Institute of Philosophy Supplement* 64: 1–18.

Grice, P. 1989. Logic and conversation. In *Studies in the way of words*, ed. H.P. Grice. Harvard: Harvard University Press.

Grimm, Stephen. 2008. Epistemic goals and epistemic values. *Philosophy and Phenomenological Research* 77(3): 725–744.

Haack, Susan. 1994. *Evidence and inquiry: Towards reconstruction in epistemology*. Oxford: Wiley-Blackwell.

Hallett, G.L. 1988. *Language and truth*. New Haven: Yale University Press.

Heal, Jane. 1988/89. The disinterested search for truth. *Proceedings of the Aristotelian Society New Series* 88: 97–108.

Hempel, Carl. 1965. *Aspects of scientific explanation and other essays in the philosophy of science*. New York: Free Press.

Hookway, C. 2007. Fallibilism and the aim of inquiry. *Proceedings of the Aristotelian Society Supplement* 81: 1–22.

Horwich, Paul. 1998. *Truth*, 2nd ed. Oxford: Oxford University Press.

James, William. 1907. *Pragmatism*. New York: Longman Green & Co.

Leitgeb, H., and Richard Pettigrew. 2010. An objective justification of bayesianism I: Measuring inaccuracy. *Philosophy of Science* 77(2): 201–235.

Levinson, Stephen. 2000. *Presumptive meanings*. Cambridge, MA: MIT Press.

Lynch, Michael. 2004. *True to life. Why truth matters*. Cambridge, MA: MIT Press.

Nozick, Robert. 1981. *Philosophical explanations*. Cambridge, MA: Harvard University Press.

Piller, Christian. 2008. Desiring the truth and nothing but the truth. *Noûs* 43: 193–213.

Schelling, T. 1960. *The strategy of conflict*. Cambridge: Harvard University Press.

Sosa, Ernest. 2003. The place of truth in epistemology. In *Intellectual virtue: Perspectives from ethics and epistemology*, ed. M. DePaul and L. Zagzebski, 155–180. Oxford: Oxford University Press.

Sosa, Ernest. 2011. *Reflective knowledge*. Oxford: Oxford University Press.

Tal, E. 2011. How accurate is the standard second? *Philosophy of Science* 78(5): 1082–1096.

Teller, Paul. 2004. How we dapple the world. *Philosophy of Science* 71: 425–447.

Teller, P. 2009. *Modelling the conception of truth* (draft, last downloaded March 7, 2009). http://philosophy.ucdavis.edu/paul/manuscripts-and-talks/Idealized%20and%20practical%20truth%208.pdf

Unger, Peter. 1975. *Ignorance: The case for skepticism*. Oxford: UP.

Van Fraassen, Bas. 2008. *Scientific representation*. Oxford: Oxford University Press.

Williams, B. 2002. *Truth and truthfulness*. Princeton: Princeton University Press.
Williamson, T. 2000. *Knowledge and its limits*. Oxford: Oxford University Press.
Zagzebski, Linda. 2004. Intellectual motivation and the good of truth. In *Intellectual virtue. Perspectives from ethics and epistemology*, ed. M. DePaul and Linda Zagzebski, 135–154. Oxford: Oxford University Press.

Part IV
The Democratic Dimension

Chapter 12
Expert Advisers: Why Economic Forecasters Can Be Useful Even When They Are Wrong

Robert Evans

Abstract The dilemma posed by expert consensus can be summarized as follows. On the one hand, it seems perfectly reasonable to give special weight to an agreement reached by those who have studied a topic in great detail. On the other hand, does the very same specialization that confers expert status also mean that the group is unable to consider all alternatives equally? In other words, do the shared analytic models and other practices that expert groups rely on provide an enhanced understanding or mean that they focus only on those aspects of the problem that fit neatly into their pre-conceived way of thinking?

The problem for policy-makers and those who would rely on experts is thus to identify which experts they need to consult. If the boundary is drawn too tightly, reaching consensus may be easy but its practical applicability may be highly restricted. If the boundary is too porous, then consensus may never be reached and the epistemic quality of deliberations may suffer as a result of irrelevant or unfounded concerns. If we accept that non-coercive decision-making is appropriate, then the problems of expert consensus are twofold: first, the members of the expert group must be identified and, second, the relationship between these experts and the wider society must be clarified.

12.1 Introduction

This volume is about expertise and consensus. In this chapter I focus on the nature of expertise and how it can be used to inform decision-making in the public domain. The aim is twofold. First, I consider a particular case of specialist expertise – economic forecasting – and use this to examine the relationship between experts as policy-advisers and policy-makers as users of expert advice. The emphasis is on the role of judgment in giving expert advice and the importance of knowing whose judgment to trust. Secondly, I consider what this need for judgment means for

R. Evans (✉)
Centre for Study of Knowledge Expertise and Science, School of Social Sciences, Cardiff University, Glamorgan Building, King Edward VII Avenue, Cardiff CF10 3WT, UK
e-mail: evansrj1@cardiff.ac.uk

© Springer International Publishing Switzerland 2014   233
C. Martini, M. Boumans (eds.), *Experts and Consensus in Social Science*,
Ethical Economy 50, DOI 10.1007/978-3-319-08551-7_12

policy-making institutions. My conclusion is that, despite the popularity of arguments for democratizing expertise, there remains an important need to keep the
expert and political aspects of policy-making as distinct and separate forms-of-life.

The chapter begins by examining economic forecasts made around the start of
the financial crash of August 2007. Here we have a group of highly specialized
experts who largely agreed about what the economic future would hold but who
turned out to be quite wrong. Despite the terrible social consequences of the
collapse in bank lending that followed this forecasting failure, the same kinds of
experts continue to play the same important role in UK monetary policy. What is
more, or so I will argue, this is a reasonable way of making monetary policy
decisions, so long as we understand what such technical expertise can and cannot
provide.

The case of the economic forecasters can be contrasted with two other cases of
expert consensus – the use of AZT to prevent mother-to-child-transmission of HIV
and the use of the MMR vaccine – where the outcomes were rather different. In the
case of AZT we have a strong expert consensus being over-ruled by a policy-maker,
the South African President Thabo Mbeki. In the case of MMR, we have another
strong expert consensus being rejected by lay people. Comparing the three cases,
shows how the successful use of expert advice requires careful judgments about
who the relevant experts are. It also shows that specialist technical expertise needs
to be nurtured and valued even if, on occasion, it appears to be worse than useless.

12.2   Limits of Expertise: Forecasting the Financial Crisis

August 2007 is often seen as the start of the financial crisis that has dominated the
recent past.[1] It is also one of the months in which the UK central bank, the Bank of
England, publishes its Quarterly Inflation Report.[2] These reports set out the economic analysis that informs the interest rate decisions of the Bank's Monetary
Policy Committee, which meets each month to set the key "base" interest rate
through which the Bank aims to fulfill its responsibilities for controlling inflation and
supporting government policies for growth and employment. The Inflation Reports
draw on a wide range of economic data and indicators and include, amongst other
things, 1 and 2 year forecasts for GDP growth and prices. Because of their role in
determining UK monetary policy these forecasts have a profound impact on the daily
lives of the UK population. These include relatively direct effects, such as changes to

[1] For example, 2 August 2007 is the date on which BNP Paribas became the first major bank to
react to the crisis in the US sub-prime lending market by closing several hedge funds that traded in
this debt.

[2] Bank of England Quarterly Inflation Reports are available from: http://www.bankofengland.co.
uk/publications/pages/inflationreport/default.aspx

mortgage and savings rates, as well as more indirect effects from aggregate outcomes like inflation, GDP growth and employment.

12.2.1   *Economic Forecasting at the Bank of England*

Before discussing the Bank's forecasts I must emphasize that I have not picked the Bank of England's forecasts because they are especially bad. In fact, the reason is the exact opposite. I have picked the Bank of England forecasts because their forecasting method, their account of how judgment enters into this forecasting procedure, and the way these judgments are reflected in their published output are all exemplary. There is also no suggestion that the forecasters working for the Bank are less accomplished than those working elsewhere: the research produced by the Bank's economists is published as official working papers and in peer-reviewed academic journals.[3] Focusing on the Bank of England forecasts means that questions about competence, bias and other avoidable failures of forecast performance can be excluded.

Turning now to the forecasts themselves, we see that, unlike most other forecasting organizations, the Bank of England does not present its forecasts for GDP and inflation as single numbers. Instead, the Bank publishes these forecasts as "fan charts" that indicate the range of possible futures that might develop (see Fig. 12.1). Within the fan, the darkest, central band represents the central 10 % of the forecast distribution, with the other shaded bands each representing a further 5 %. In all, the shaded area includes 90 % of the forecast distribution, meaning that the white space outside the shaded fan represents the remaining possible outcomes.[4]

For August 2007, the GDP forecast fan chart showed that the Bank's central estimate was that GDP growth would be just over 2.5 % in 2007 and slightly lower in 2008. Thanks to the fan chart, we can also see that the probability of these outcomes is only about 10 %. The "90 %" range of outcomes is given by the upper and lower limits of the fan. For GDP growth in 2007, this range runs from about 1.5 % up to about 4 %. For 2008, the range of possibly outcomes is slightly wider, going from about 0.75 % to just over 4 %.

---

[3] For more information on the Bank of England's economic research see: http://www. bankofengland.co.uk/research/Pages/default.aspx

[4] More details on the Bank of England's fan chart are available at: http://www.bankofengland.co. uk/publications/pages/inflationreport/irprobab.aspx

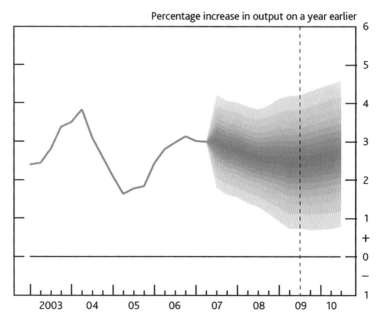

Percentage increase in output on a year earlier

Fig. 12.1 Bank of England GDP forecast, August 2007 (Source: Bank of England Quarterly Inflation Report, August 2007. available on-line at: http://www.bankofengland.co.uk/publications/ Pages/inflationreport/default.aspx)

12.2.2   Failure to Forecast the Financial Crash

As is now well known, what actually happened in 2007 and 2008 was nothing like this at all. Instead, 2007 saw the start of a major economic contraction that left the UK economy in a deep recession. As shown in Fig. 12.2, GDP growth fell throughout 2007 and this decline continued throughout 2008. Most seriously of all, the character of the economic situation was completely different to that implied in the August 2007 fan diagram. Rather than 18 months of more or less trend growth what actually happened was the start of an almost catastrophic recession. For policy-makers, this meant that plans based on any of the futures predicted by the fan diagram were of little or no use as the situation had changed and, from their perspective, had changed with very little warning.

Given the difference between what was forecast and what happened, the obvious question to ask is whether the Bank of England got it wrong and other forecasters got it right. There is no evidence that this is the case, however. The Bank of England's forecasts were very similar to those produced by other forecasting organizations at the same time. The HM Treasury monthly round up of economic forecasts published in August 2007 shows that the average of all GDP growth

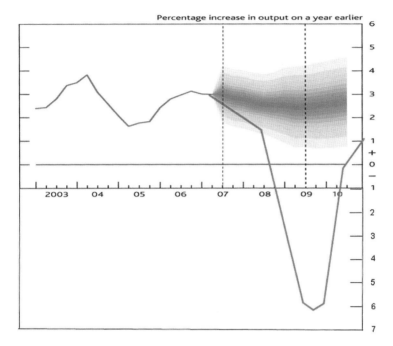

Fig. 12.2 UK GDP growth forecast and outcome (Source: as for Fig. 12.1 but adapted by author to show outcome data)

forecasts for 2007 was 2.8 %, with a range of 2.4–3.1 %.[5] In terms of the fan chart, virtually all the other forecasts lie within the central 50 % band and none of the mainstream forecasting organizations was predicting the downturn that happened. Asking a different forecaster would not, therefore, have given a significantly different answer.

Turing to the forecasts for 2008 leads we see a similar picture. Once again the Bank's forecasts are well in line with those produced by almost every other forecasting organization in the Treasury's list. The mean forecast for 2008 is for GDP growth of 2.2 %, compared with the Bank's forecast of just under 2.5 %, and every forecast except one falls between 1.5 and 2.8 % (see Fig. 12.3).

With the benefit of hindsight, the one outlying forecast, which comes from the economic consultancy firm Economic Perspectives, obviously takes on a particular interest.[6] We know now that the Economic Perspectives team, led by Peter Warburton, were correct in predicting some kind of recession. The key question, however, is whether or not this forecast implies that policy-makers should have acted differently at the time. It is significant, therefore, that in his contribution to the

---

[5] Source: http://webarchive.nationalarchives.gov.uk/20100407010852/http://www.hm-treasury. gov.uk/d/forecast_150807.pdf

[6] See: http://www.economicperspectives.co.uk/

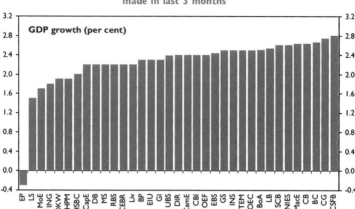

Fig. 12.3 HM Treasury summary of forecasts for 2008 (Source: http://webarchive. nationalarchives.gov.uk/20100407010852/http://www.hm-treasury.gov.uk/d/forecast_150807.pdf)

Shadow Monetary Policy Committee – a group of independent economists that monitors the work of the official Bank of England Monetary Policy Committee – Warburton voted for monetary policy to remain unchanged in August 2007.[7] This was also the decision taken by the Bank of England's Monetary Policy Committee.

12.3   Expert Consensus: Robust Knowledge or Partial Perspective?

The discussion so far has focused on economic forecasts. We have seen that the forecasts produced by different forecasting teams were often fairly similar. We have also seen that they were also mostly wrong, with what actually happened lying well outside what was expected by the vast majority of forecasters. Whilst it is tempting to see this as a problem for economics I want to argue that the issues raised are best seen as more general problems of expert advice.

---

[7] Minutes of Shadow Monetary Policy Committee, August 2007. Available online at: http://www. iea.org.uk/smpc

12.3.1 Specialization and Expert Consensus

Economic forecasters, like all other experts, are experts in *something*. They have become experts by following some program of training and they bring this specialist knowledge to problems in ways that become increasingly taken-for-granted and, to the expert, unremarkable (Ericsson et al. 1993; Dreyfus and Dreyfus 1980; Collins and Evans 2007). In the case of economic forecasting, economists typically work within a shared economic paradigm that includes standard economic theories and their problems, familiarity with econometric techniques and their use to model economic behavior, and a shared professional culture of conferences and meetings. There are differences between economists over the correct way to interpret economic data but the basic approach is largely shared and most disagreements result from differences in the weight given to different variables rather disputes about which factors need to be considered in the first place.

Although the economic crisis made the consequences of this conformity particularly apparent for economic forecasters, the opportunity cost of specialization is not unique to economists. The same risk is faced by all experts who, by definition, bring with them deep, specialist knowledge that has been built up over years of experience.[8] The price of this sustained immersion in the traditions and practices of their own domain of practice is that they have learned to see the world in a particular way (Kuhn 1996; Collins 1992; Winch 1958/1988). This, in turn, means that experts with a similar professional background are pre-disposed to agree about how to diagnose a problem because they all start from a similar position and make similar judgements about what is and is not salient. As a result, it is not surprising if they also end up reaching similar conclusions about the kinds of actions that should be taken next.

Recognizing this problem lies behind many of the calls for more inter- or multi-disciplinary teams as well philosophical arguments around ideas such as active or reasonable pluralism (see Chap. 14 by Lefevere and Schliesser, this volume). To the extent that different disciplinary traditions emphasize different variables and different causal pathways, then it is possible that using different experts will provide a more wide-ranging analysis of a policy problem. By tasking these groups with reaching some form of consensus, the idea is that the advice policy-makers receive will be epistemically more robust as it will have been subject to test from a wider variety of perspectives.

12.3.2 Accountability and the Democratization of Expertise

Within the STS literature, however, the argument typically goes one step further and links the idea of more heterogeneous expert groups to the political legitimacy of

---

[8] Taleb (2007) makes a similar argument though does so from a different starting point.

the advice and not just its epistemic quality. The idea is that by including a wider range of experts, and hence including a wider range of perspectives, the advice will more accurately reflect the interests of the wider society and not just the elite groups of establishment experts. In this analysis, arguing for more participatory decision-making is about giving a voice to excluded groups.[9] Public debate about the legitimacy and applicability of expert authority, which may include both technical concerns and more general issues, is therefore contrasted with the universalizing tendencies of technocracy in which uncertainties are suppressed and local knowledge ignored. As Sheila Jasanoff (2003) has written:

> the presumption in democratic societies is that all decisions should be as far as possible public
> ... Without such critical supervision, experts have often found themselves offering irrelevant
> advice on wrong or misguided questions ... and powerful institutions can perpetuate unjust
> and unfounded ways of looking at the world unless they are continually put before the gaze of
> lay persons who will declare when the emperor has no clothes. (Jasanoff 2003, pp. 397–8).

On this account experts – but particularly scientists – are like the Emperor's courtiers: they have a vested interest in maintaining the status quo and their privileged position within it. Such experts do not to ask the "difficult" questions that an outsider would pose as their specialization, coupled with a lack of reflexivity, means that they take the key assumptions and framings for granted (Wynne 1992; Harding 2006; Longino 1990). In contrast, lay people are like the child in the story. Because they are outside the institutions of power, they do not suffer from this pressure to conform and do not have the blinkers of specialization to limit their perception (see e.g. Wynne 1992; Irwin 1995; Epstein 1996). Indeed, some writers go further and argue that lay people can be more reflexive and/or sensitive to a wider range of factors than the more officially recognized experts (Peterson 1984). Seen this way, expert consensus becomes a potentially risky thing that needs to be managed by close and critical scrutiny of the ways in which problems are defined and expert status awarded. As this scrutiny is invariably couched in democratic terms, the problem of expert scrutiny becomes linked to, and putatively solved by, increased opportunities for citizen participation.[10]

---

[9] See e.g. Evans and Plows (2007); CST (2005); Epstein (1996); Fischer (2011); Funtowicz and Ravetz (1993); Grin et al. (1997); House of Lords (2000); Irwin (1995); Office of Science and Technology (2002); POST (2001); Rip et al. (1995); Wynne (1992).

[10] Examples include : Post Normal Science and the extended peer community (Functowicz and Ravetz 1993), Rethinking Science and the agora (Nowotny et al. 2001), Wynne's claim that legitimate participants in debate about framing are every democratic citizen (Wynne 2003), Jasanoff's (2003) argument that the 'worldwide movement' is towards greater public involvement and that STS should not seek to critique this, Frank Fischer's emphasis on the continued need to challenge technocratic forms of decision-making (2011).

12.4   Third Wave of Science Studies: Studies of Expertise and Experience

The idea that expert-claims should be properly scrutinized before being used to inform policy decisions is hard to dispute. The devil, however, is in the detail: who is best placed to perform such technical scrutiny and how should they be selected? If, as many in STS appear to do, you see science as essentially political, then extending the norms of democratic theory to the scrutiny of science, and by extension to the scrutiny of expertise in general, makes perfect sense. If, however, you see science as being something different – a culture or form-of-life in its own right – then imposing the norms of a different culture risks destroying science by undermining the values and norms that made it distinctive in the first place.[11]

It is this latter approach that characterizes the Third Wave of Science Studies (Collins and Evans 2002, 2007). Rather than try to subsume one into the other, Collins and Evans argue that it is better to ensure that each sticks to the tasks for which it is best suited. In other words, rather than extend democratic norms into expert debate, it would be better if the distinction between expert and political forms-of-life was re-affirmed and even celebrated:

> Democracy cannot dominate every domain – that would destroy expertise – and expertise cannot dominate every domain – that would destroy democracy. (Collins and Evans 2007, p. 8)

The normative point that follows from this – and the claim that lies at the heart of the debate about the Third Wave of Science Studies – is that more lay participation is not always justified and the testing the limits of expert consensus is a matter for experts and experts alone.

12.4.1   Problems of Legitimacy and Extension

The argument for a more inclusive expert debate stems from the problems of legitimacy faced by technocratic decision-making in which expert advice dominates even as it rides roughshod over the concerns and knowledge of local groups. Including these groups in the policy process produces epistemic gains in that the expert claims are now better tested. There are also some political gains as citizens can see that a wider range of views, including the ones that resonate with their own lives, are now being taken into account. The problem of extension arises when the

---

[11] A sporting analogy might help. In the US baseball and basketball are both games that share some characteristics (e.g. they are competitive, players are expected to train and try hard, cheating is not permitted and so on). On the other hand, they are also different in important respects (you cannot bring a large stick onto a basketball court, for example) and imposing the rules of one sport on the other makes no sense.

epistemic benefits of more diverse scrutiny start to diminish as the new participants lack the expertise to ask appropriate questions or make informed judgments.

Using expertise as the criteria for participation has no effect where decision is a political one. This is because all citizens are assumed to be capable of carrying out their civic duties and so the problem of extension cannot arise in a democratic process. Where the decision is a technical one, however, and the criteria for entry is the meritocratic one of relevant expertise, the same assumption – that all people are equally capable – cannot be justified and the problem of extension can arise.

The difference between the democratic norms of political decisions and the meritocratic process of expert scrutiny can be illustrated with some examples. Starting first with the case for more heterogeneous expert debate, many of the classic case studies in STS show how the failure of meritocratic norms (i.e. the failure to recognize legitimate expertise) has undermined confidence in technological decision-making. In these cases, expert consensus had formed too easily as official and/or elite experts met with other like-minded experts and confirmed the validity of their own world views. Although concerns were raised, these were often dismissed as being anecdotal or uninformed, with the result that potentially important evidence and insights were overlooked. Including this expertise by extending participation might have made consensus more difficult to reach but it would, nevertheless, have been the right thing to do.

To see why there might be a limit to expert participation requires paying attention to a rhetorical move that has become increasingly common in the social sciences. In many of the studies that inform the call for more inclusion, the non-scientist experts are often called lay experts (Prior 2003). This formulation puts the stress on their ordinariness rather than their expertise and it is a relatively short step from here to argue for more lay (without the expert) participation. The flaw in the argument is that the lay experts were generally valuable because of their "expert-ness" rather than their "lay-ness". As the following two examples show, when genuinely lay (i.e. non-expert) people become embroiled in those parts of technological decisions that require specialist, technical expertise the outcome can be far worse than if it had been left to experts alone.

12.4.2 AZT for Preventing Mother-to-Child-Transmission of HIV

When Thabo Mbeki was the President of South Africa he took the decision to block the use of AZT to prevent mother-to-child-transmission of HIV in pregnant women (Weinel 2010). Speaking in October 1999 to the National Council of Provinces, the upper house of the South African parliament, he explained his decision as follows:

> There also exists a large volume of scientific literature alleging that, among other things, the toxicity of this drug [AZT] is such that it is in fact a danger to health. These are matters of great concern to the Government as it would be irresponsible for us not to head the dire warnings which medical researchers have been making . . . To understand this matter better,

I would urge the Honourable Members of the National Council to access the huge volume
of literature on this matter available on the Internet, so that all of us can approach this issue
from the same base of information.[12]

The reference to the internet is important as it appears that this conclusion is
based entirely on Mbeki's own reading of the scientific literature and not as the
result of any specialist technical advice. The outcome is that he gives much too
much weight to views that have long since been discredited by the mainstream
research community.

The consequences of this non-expert reading of the technical debate were
disastrous: the introduction of the treatment was delayed for several years as
Mbeki's decision was challenged and eventually over-turned but, while this was
happening, several thousand babies were born with HIV that could have been
prevented if the evaluation of medical research had been left to those with the
expertise needed to undertake the task properly. If this had been done then the most
likely outcome was a clear expert consensus that AZT was safe to use and could
prevent at least some babies being born with HIV. Note, however, that this expert
consensus would not, by itself, have compelled Mbeki to approve the policy. He
could still have decided not to make the drug available. The only difference would
be that he would have had to justify this decision on other grounds and not by
invoking a long-dead scientific controversy (Weinel 2008).

12.4.3   MMR Vaccine Controversy

The controversy about the MMR vaccine began in 1998 with a paper published in
the peer-reviewed literature and involves a man – Andrew Wakefield – who was a
qualified doctor.[13] The main facts of the controversy are that Wakefield
et al. published a paper in the Lancet in February 1998. The paper, which was
based on study of 12 autistic children, explored the relationship between a measles
virus and autism. Although the paper itself does not make an explicit causal link
between the MMR vaccine and autism, Wakefield did suggest that the MMR
vaccine could be a risk factor when presenting the research at a press conference.
This claim was taken up by a number of patient groups and some newspapers and a
vociferous campaign for a change in UK vaccination schedules was launched.

In response, the UK government insisted that the MMR vaccine was safe and
that there was no reason to change policy (e.g. by allowing parents to opt for single
vaccinations rather than the combined one). In making this claim they were

---

[12] http://www.dfa.gov.za/docs/speeches/1999/mbek1028.htm

[13] For more information see Boyce (2007).

supported by the overwhelming majority of medical experts and could point to epidemiological data from many countries and covering several decades.

Sadly, however, the loss of faith in experts caused by previous failures of inappropriately technocratic policy-making meant that this expert consensus lacked credibility. The anti-MMR campaign continued to attract public support and parents continued to give credibility to Wakefield's claims. Vaccination rates fell and herd immunity was gradually lost. The result is that, at the time of writing, measles epidemics have re-emerged in the UK and emergency vaccination campaigns have been launched in several areas.[14]

12.5   Technical and Political Phases

As the examples discussed in this chapter show, technological decision-making in the public domain invariably includes an element of specialist or technical expertise but it cannot be reduced to this alone. Wrapped around and related to these technical issues are broader public concerns that are the legitimate responsibility of all citizens. Working out how these expert and democratic institutions should be related can only be done by distinguishing between the technical and political phases of a technological decision.

The political phase refers those aspects of technological decisions that are the responsibility of democratic institutions and processes. Its guiding principles are those of democratic theory: participation is open to all so every citizen is able to contribute freely and equally to the debate. In contrast, the technical phase refers to those aspects of technological decisions that are legitimately delegated to specialist expert communities. The guiding principles here are meritocratic and draw on the values and norms of science. Participation is necessarily limited to those with the appropriate expertise but, as noted above, the definition of expertise used here includes non-scientists with relevant experience (see Chap. 2 by den Butter and ten Wolde, this volume). The relationship between the two phases is summarized in Fig. 12.4.

Applying these ideas to the canonical examples from the STS literature, the normative conclusion that follows is that experience-based experts should be recognized as legitimate contributors to the formation of expert consensus in the technical phase. This is broadly consistent with the standard interpretation of the classic STS case studies although the emphasis is on the expert status of new participants rather than their lay qualities. Where the political phase is involved then the argument would be that all citizens should be involved, either directly through political activities (e.g. standing for office, campaigning, lobbying, taking part in elections) or through their actions as a consumer (e.g. the classic options of

---

[14] See for example: http://www.bbc.co.uk/news/uk-wales-politics-23244628

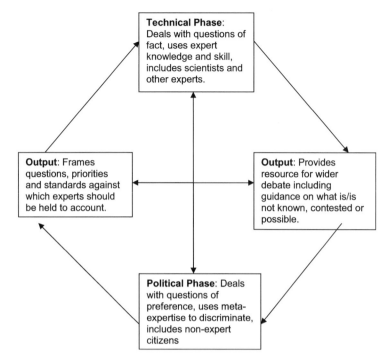

Fig. 12.4 Technical and political phases (Source: Diagram is from Evans and Plows (2007))

exit, voice, and loyalty). The other three examples require a slightly more detailed explanation.

12.5.1 Economic Forecasting and the MPC

Despite not predicting the economic events of 2008 with any great accuracy, the Monetary Policy Committee of the Bank of England provides a good example of how technical expertise can fit into a wider political process. The Committee has a clearly defined role that has been given to it by Parliament, namely to meet each month in order to determine the level of interest rates consistent with price stability and other government objectives.

In order to do this, a group of economic experts meets and considers a range of economic data and evidence. The decision, the analysis that informs it, and the minutes of their discussion are all made available for inspection by others, though the work itself is always and only carried out by the experts and their forecasting team. Most importantly of all, the economic analysis produced goes to unusual lengths to convey the rationale for the decision and the risks that accompany it. As

Mervyn King, the then Governor of the Bank of England explained to journalists, the MPC is not engaged in the Sisyphean task of developing ever more accurate models in order to control the economy. Instead, the true value of the Committee is found in the consensus that emerges about what the risks to economic growth are and how those risks will be monitored.

Speaking in wonderfully colorful language, King tells a journalist who has just asked a question about the differences of opinion between Committee members:

> if you're really interested in the question of what will happen to interest rates ... then forget getting out a ruler, throw your rulers away, be liberated ... and start to think. That's what we're trying to help you to do, to think for yourself, by our identifying what to us are the main risks. And what will happen to interests rates will not depend on whether people can get their rulers sufficiently accurate ... What will happen to interest rates will depend on whether or not the risks that we discuss in this report crystallise.[15]

From the perspective of a Third Wave analysis, this is exactly what technical advice should do. Experts need to advise in order that others can take note of their analysis and decide how best to proceed.

It is, of course, always possible to argue that the limited number of external appointments – 4 out of a total of 9, the other 5 being employees of the Bank – mean the MPC is unlikely to represent the full spectrum of economic analysis. If this happens, then the outcome would be analysis that considers only a sub-set of legitimate concerns and gives too little weight to some risks. Changing the balance between Bank and external appointees or deliberately appointing more heterodox economists might provoke a more wide-ranging discussion and could be considered. For example, in addition to having experts from the main theoretical schools in economics, it might be useful to have experts with experience of working in different sectors of the economy. To some extent this does happen and how much current practice would need to change in order to make an appreciable different is hard to say without actually trying it.

Finally, it should be noted that the fact that the official Bank of England MPC is responsible for acting on its recommendations makes no difference. If, for some reason, the remit was changed so that the outcome of each meeting was a recommendation for the government to either accept or reject very little of what has been said would change. The reason is that, within the Third Wave approach, the starting point is that the political phase always has primacy over the technical phase. In other words, technical advice is only ever advice; decision-making authority resides with the political process even if, as in this case, they choose to delegate it.

---

[15] Source: transcript of press conference. Available from http://www.bankofengland.co.uk/publi cations/Pages/inflationreport/ir0703.aspx

12.5.2 AZT for Preventing Mother-to-Child-Transmission of HIV

In the case of Thabo Mbeki, the normative recommendation is more straightforward. All the evidence suggests that, by 1999, there was a strong expert consensus that AZT was safe to use. As such, policy making should start from that position. The recommendation does not go any further than this, however. Recognizing the existence of the consensus does not mean that Mbeki would then have been compelled to introduce the AZT policy. Rather the point is that, if he were to decide against the use of AZT, he should not justify this choice by reference to an expert disagreement that does not, for all practical purposes, exist.

Had the technical consensus about AZT been much weaker and the controversy Mbeki referred to real, then the situation might have been different. If there was still significant uncertainty about the efficacy of the treatment, then Mbeki could have been justified in waiting for further trials or deciding that other interventions offered a better chance of success. Two things need to be stated about this hypothetical scenario, however. The first is that assessing the strength of the technical consensus remains an expert task and is not something that lay people can do. Secondly, whatever the outcome of the technical phase turns out to be, the political phase has to represent it fairly and accurately. In other words, just as Mbeki was wrong in 1999 to say there was a controversy, he would also be wrong in this hypothetical scenario to claim that there was no expert disagreement and no uncertainty about what lay ahead. In other words, the expert consensus, whatever its strength or content, should always inform policy-makers but it should not be distorted by them.

12.5.3 MMR Vaccine Controversy

The MMR case appears trickier because the source of the controversy is a doctor and this appears to suggest there is a legitimate expert disagreement that needs to be acknowledged. In fact, as other experts were able to point out, although the paper was published in a peer reviewed journal, the results were based on a small study and did not provide anything like the evidence needed to justify the change in policy that Wakefield and his supporters wanted. Indeed, the peer-reviewed paper does not actually make a causal link between MMR and autism; this was done in a press conference about the paper. Given this, there seems no compelling technical reason to recommend a change in vaccination policy as there is no expert controversy that policy makers should be responding too.

In political phase, parents and others obviously have the right to campaign for changes to any policy. Given that, prior to the publication of Wakefield's paper there was no evidence that MMR was harmful and it was already well-known that measles is a highly contagious and potentially dangerous disease, the government's decision to continue with the policy of MMR vaccinations can be seen as reasonable. As with AZT in South Africa, there is a strong expert consensus that the current policy is the best one and, for the government to respond to Wakefield's claims, would be to make the same mistake as Mbeki did when he endorsed the maverick science of the AIDS skeptics.

Seen this way, the public health problem of MMR is really public relations problem caused by earlier scandals of expert advice. Put simply the government and its expert advisers were not trusted and there was a strategic decision to take about whether or not an alternative policy, such as making single vaccines available for children whose parents refused to consent to the MMR vaccine, could be justified on the purely pragmatic grounds that the current policy had lost legitimacy, albeit for completely spurious reasons.[16] In fact, the one thing that probably would have made the difference in this crisis of trust was the Prime Minister, Tony Blair, saying that his son had received the vaccination. His refusal to comment on what decision he and his wife had made about their own child inevitably led to speculation that he had refused to consent to the vaccination and this could only reinforce the doubts of those who were already skeptical. A more principled response would have been for him to declare that, as the leader of the country, he was following the advice of his own experts.

12.6   The Value of Expert Advice

The preceding analysis of expertise has been based around three main points:

- Expertise is limited to specific fields and domains (e.g. economics, medicine, public health)
- Heterogeneous expert institutions are needed to ensure full and robust testing expert claims
- Not everyone can be an expert so these expert institutions should not be open to non-expert lay citizens

What is missing, however, is a general argument that would justify the continued use of specialist technical expertise within policy making. The problem here is that the most obvious normative arguments for experts are epistemic arguments. As such, they only really work when the experts are right or are at least known to have a very high probability of being right. Thus, for example, we can see why expert advice was relevant in the two medical examples given above: it was known with a high probability that AZT would reduce the risk of Mother-to-Child-Transmission and that MMR does not cause autism. In contrast, the case of the economic fore-casters is much less clear cut as here the epistemic argument does not appear to

---

[16] There was some debate about this but the research evidence suggest that single injections are less effective than the combined injection as children are less likely to have all the injections needed.

work: not only were they wrong in 2007, we also know that the probability of them being right in the future is low, especially when compared to sciences like medicine and physics.

In practice, however, this problem is not limited to economists and might even be the more standard case of expert advice. If we ask when is expert advice most likely to be needed, then the answer seems to be when there is doubt or debate about the best course of action to take. In other words, the problem of expertise is most acute at the very times when expert advice is most needed and who counts as an expert is itself a matter of dispute. In these circumstances, the epistemic justification for expertise is of little use and other arguments are needed if we are to avoid a purely political resolution in which expert status is granted to those best able to mobilize resources in their support.

In fact there are three main reasons for continuing to defend the idea of expertise and for promoting institutions in which the expertise needed to provide specialist, technical advice to policymakers can be developed. These are:

- *The Expert Community as Boot Camp*: Being an expert typically involves providing advice that goes beyond the routine application of pre-determined rules. Instead, nuanced judgment and the ability to respond to novel situations are essential. As this requires going beyond simple rule-following behavior, some form of tacit knowledge is needed in order to know how to apply disciplinary knowledge in new settings. Maintaining the expert community enables these tacit skills to be honed by providing a context in which novices can be trained and experience shared. Of course, this does not guarantee that the expertise developed in this way will be useful or even relevant but, without some social community to hold the knowledge, then the only outcome is that whatever expertise currently exists will be lost.

- *The Expert Community as Aspiration*: The philosopher Nelson Goodman has argued that it is important to retain the notion of art forgery even if it is impossible to distinguish between real and counterfeit works of art. The argument is that, even it is currently impossible to tell the real from the fake, there may be a time in the future when new technologies do make it possible. If, however, the need for the distinction is not defended now, and the difference between real and fake loses its significance, then the opportunity to tell them apart may be lost forever. The same argument can be extended to expertise in general: even if an expert community is not particularly good at predicting now, allowing them to continue to develop their skills and methods keeps alive the possibility that they may improve over time. If the community is disbanded then the possibility of future success is also abandoned.

- *The Expert Community as Part of Modern Society*: This argument follows most directly from the Third Wave of Science Studies paper (Collins and Evans, 2002). Here the claim is that the scientific community is characterized by a distinctive set of values that are good in themselves. In other words, the argument for science, and by extension expertise, is not an epistemic one but one based on values. Retaining an expert community modeled on the scientific community means retaining a form-of-life within which scientific values provide the formative aspirations. Under this argument, choosing not to value expertise means allowing a core part of contemporary democratic societies to wither.

Of course, none of these arguments are arguments for or against expert consensus. Instead, they are simply arguments for turning to experts when the problems of technological decision-making require some specialist, technical input. Having made the choice to seek advice, the normative argument is not that policy-makers should defer to scientists but that the technical advice is provided by experts whose actions conform to scientific values. What happens after this depends, in part, on what the expert advice turns out to be, though it would be quite wrong to say that the fact of expert agreement is enough to close the policy debate. To say this is to argue for technocracy.

Instead, the requirement is that the technical advice – be it consensual or contested – should be accurately portrayed within public debate. Where expert consensus is strong, this should be acknowledged and policies that reject this advice should say why this has been done. In other words, a strong technical consensus does not restrict the policy choices available; what it restricts are the reasons that can be given in order to justify them. In the opposite case, where expert advice is contested, then policy-makers have exactly the same freedom to determine policy but the justifications remain equally restricted as they can no longer claim that a strong expert consensus exists to legitimate their policy.

12.7 Conclusions

Expert advice is an essential part of technological decision-making in the public domain. To attempt to defend it on epistemic grounds is not helpful, however, as experts can be wrong and, when this happens, may lose their legitimacy. Defending the role of experts requires a different approach to understanding what technical experts can do and how this contributes to the broader process of technological decision-making in the public domain.

Drawing on the example of economic forecasters in particular I have argued that maintaining the distinction between the technical and the political is crucial. Distinguishing between the two is best done on the basis of the formative intentions that characterize the two cultures and this is also the reason why expert institutions need to be preserved and valued in their own terms. Without this defense of scientific values, then the institutions of expertise risk being politicized, with the result that the scientific form-of-life becomes corrupted and, ultimately, lost.

In practice, the problem is inevitably how to strike the right balance between the technical and political. The argument set out here is that the political always trumps the technical but that it cannot distort or miss-represent it. Where advice is based on a clear and strong agreement then policy makers should not claim that experts disagree. Conversely, where experts do disagree, then policy-makers should not legitimate policy choices by citing some experts and ignoring others in order to create the impression of agreement.

Finally, there is the problem of how to choose experts. Here the principles are clear, even if how to put them into practice is not. Expert advice needs to be sufficiently diverse that it does not simply allow elite institutions to impose their own priorities and unjustly further their interests at the expense of others. On the other hand, political decision makers and lay citizens must resist the temptation to accept any skeptical claim as valid and so end up undermining the idea of expertise itself. Technological decision-making in the public domain thus requires both decision-makers and citizens to understand what expertise is and to have the courage to put limits on where it resides.

Acknowledgements I am grateful to Carlo Martini and Marcel Boumans for the invitation to workshop and for encouraging me to write up my presentation so it could be included in this volume. It is also a pleasure to thank the other participants in the workshop for two great days of thought-provoking presentations and discussion. In writing this chapter, I have drawn on two previous papers: Evans (2007) and Collins et al. (2010); an early version of the opening section was presented at the "Expert Knowledge, Prediction, Forecasting: A Social Sciences Perspective" held in Bucharest in November 2010. Finally, I am grateful to both the Bank of England and HM Treasury for their permission to re-produce the inflation forecast charts that are used in this chapter.

References

Boyce, Tammy. 2007. *Health, risk and news: The MMR vaccine and the media.* New York: Peter Lang.

Collins, Harry. 1992. *Changing order: Replication and induction in scientific practice,* 2nd ed. Chicago/London: University of Chicago Press.

Collins, Harry, and Robert Evans. 2002. The third wave of science studies: Studies of expertise and experience. *Social Studies of Sciences* 32(2): 235–296.

Collins, Harry and Robert Evans. 2007. *Rethinking expertise.* Chicago: University of Chicago Press.

Collins, Harry, Martin Weinel, and Robert Evans. 2010. The politics and policy of the third wave: New technologies and society. *Critical Policy Studies* 4(2): 185–201.

Council for Science and Technology (CST). 2005. *Policy through dialogue.* London: CST.

Dreyfus, S.E., and H.L. Dreyfus. 1980. *A five-stage model of the mental activities involved in directed skill acquisition* (No. ORC-80-2). Berkeley: California University Berkeley Operations Research Center.

Epstein, Steven. 1996. *Impure science: AIDS, activism, and the politics of knowledge.* Berkeley: University of California Press.

Ericsson, K.A., R.T. Krampe, and C. Tesch-Romer. 1993. The role of deliberate practice in the acquisition of expert performance. *Psychological Review* 100: 363–406.

Evans, Robert. 2007. Social networks and private spaces in economic forecasting. *Studies in History and Philosophy of Science* 38(4): 686–697.

Evans, Robert, and Alexandra Plows. 2007. Listening without prejudice? Re-discovering the value of the disinterested citizen. *Social Studies of Science* 37(6): 827–854.

Fischer, Frank. 2011. The 'policy turn' in the Third Wave: Return to the fact–value dichotomy? *Critical Policy Studies* 5(3): 311–316.

Funtowicz, Silvio O., and Jerome R. Ravetz. 1993. Science in the post-normal age. *Futures* 25(7): 739–755.

Grin, J., H. van de Graaf, and R. Hoppe. 1997. *Technology assessment through interaction: A guide*. The Hague: Rathenau Institute.

Harding, Sandra. 2006. *Science and social inequality: Feminist and postcolonial issues*. Urbana/ Chicago: University of Illinois Press.

House of Lords. 2000. *Science and society: Science and Technology Select Committee, third report*. London: HMSO.

Irwin, Alan. 1995. *Citizen science: A study of people, expertise and sustainable development*. London/New York: Routledge.

Jasanoff, Sheila. 2003. Breaking the waves in science studies; Comment on H.M. Collins and Robert Evans, 'The third wave of science studies'. *Social Studies of Science* 33(3): 389–400.

Kuhn, Thomas S. 1996. *The structure of scientific revolutions*, 3rd ed. Chicago/London: University of Chicago Press.

Longino, Helen. 1990. *Science as social knowledge*. Princeton: Princeton University Press.

Nowotny, Helga, Peter Scott, and Michael Gibbons. 2001. *Re-thinking science: Knowledge and the public in an age of uncertainty*. Cambridge: Policy.

Office of Science and Technology. 2002. *The government's approach to public dialogue on science and technology*. London: OST.

Parliamentary Office of Science and Technology (POST). 2001. *Open channels: Public dialogue in science and technology*. Parliamentary Office of Science and Technology, Report No. 153. London.

Peterson, James C. 1984. Citizen participation in science policy. In *Citizen participation in science policy*, ed. James C. Peterson, 1–17. Amherst: University of Massachusetts Press.

Prior, Lindsay. 2003. Belief, knowledge and expertise: The emergence of the lay expert in medical sociology. *Sociology of Health and Illness* 25(3): 41–57.

Rip, Arie, Thomas J. Misa, and John Schot (eds.). 1995. *Managing technology in society: The approach of constructive technology assessment*. London/New York: Pinter Publishers.

Taleb, Nassim Nicholas. 2007. *The black swan: The impact of the highly improbable*. New York: Random House.

Weinel, Martin. 2008. *Counterfeit scientific controversies in science policy contexts*. Cardiff School of Social Sciences Working paper, 120. http://www.cardiff.ac.uk/socsi/research/publi cations/workingpapers/paper-120.html.

Weinel, M. 2010. *Technological decision-making under scientific uncertainty: Preventing mother-to-child transmission of HIV in South Africa*. PhD thesis, Cardiff University.

Winch, P. 1958/1988. *The idea of a social science and its relationship to philosophy*. London/New York: Routledge.

Wynne, Brian. 1992. Misunderstood misunderstanding: Social identities and public uptake of science. *Public Understanding of Science* 1(3): 281–304.

Wynne, B. 2003. Seasick on the Third Wave? Subverting the hegemony of propositionalism. *Social Studies of Science* 33(3): 401–418.

Chapter 13
The Role of Experts in the Condominium Model as Republican (Re-) Solution of Social, Economic, and Political Problems

Rafał Paweł Wierzchosławski

Abstract Problems about expertise have been discussed quite intensively in philosophy and in the social and political sciences in recent years. My contribution aims to examine how the analysis of experts question provided by Stephen P. Turner in *Liberal Democracy 3.0.* (2003) and *The Politics of Expertise* (2014) apply to political theory, and, in particular, to the neo-republican theory proposed by Philip N. Pettit in *Republicanism* (1997) *A Political philosophy in public life* (2010), with José Luis Martí, and *On the People's Terms* (2012). The republican state promotes freedom as non-domination in relations between the state and the citizen as individual (imperium) and the citizens as collectivity (dominium). Republican democracy consists of the mixed government, rule of law, and contestatory citizenry. Its functioning may be presented in the condominium model. One of the proposed conditions of achieving non-domination is referral of certain decisions to independent bodies, auditors, solicitors and impartial experts. However, problems arise when one takes into account the variety of expert types, and especially the fact that not all of them fulfill the impartiality condition. This may pose some challenges to the condominium model. In this chapter I present and address those challenges.

13.1 Introduction

In recent years the role experts and their advising activity have called the attention of scholars from different domains of the social sciences (sociology of knowledge, STS). In most cases, the experts' problem is considered in the framework of social conditions and set-ups, pointing up privileged epistemic position of experts against that of laics, and their specific place in social stratification of knowledge, to refer to phenomenological sociological traditions (Schütz 1964; Sprondel 1979).

R.P. Wierzchosławski (✉)
Faculty of Philosophy, The John Paul II Catholic University of Lublin, Lublin, Poland
e-mail: rafalw@kul.pl

© Springer International Publishing Switzerland 2014
C. Martini, M. Boumans (eds.), *Experts and Consensus in Social Science*,
Ethical Economy 50, DOI 10.1007/978-3-319-08551-7_13

In the social contexts experts' considerations may deal with such topics like the role of science in democratic societies, knowledge based societies in particular (Beck 1992; Stehr 1994) and contributions of experts in social and political decision making which should make them more effective and efficient. The multitude of experts' activities and variety of domains in which they are engaged make it possible to provide more general typologies of experts and expertise, which aim to cover the complicated subject matter of expertizing in various domains of social and political life of modern societies in particular. The expert questions may deal with such divergent questions as ecology and climate change as well as with structural/dynamic interpretation of different social and political systems, both totalitarian and democratic ones (Callon et al. 2009; Collins and Evans 2007; Turner 2001, 2003, 2006, 2010, 2014; Brown 2009; Fischer 2009; Hilton et al. 2013; Selinger and Crease 2006).

The aim of my contribution is to examine how analyses of expertizing (typologies) provided by Stephen Turner (2003) may apply to the problems of politics and by consequence how they may help to resolve social and economic problems. The "experimental field" is going to be the modern neo-republican approach proposed by Philip Pettit (1997, 2013; Martí and Pettit 2010). The 15-M Movement in Madrid might be considered as a case study of the republican contestatory democracy ideal in time of economic crisis in Spain.

The republican idea of freedom and government has a venerable tradition, and it has enjoyed a significant revival in recent years, competing with other genres in reflection on politics, such as liberal and communitarian ones. The republican idea of freedom claims that we are free when we are not dominated i.e. we are not under mastery and possibility of capricious intervention in the domain of our actions, by a possible master – we are not *in potestate domini*, but we live *in sui juris* (Martí and Pettit 2010, p. 37). The domination in question can happen in two areas: imperium and dominium: the first one deals with relation state-individual (institutional and public) and the other one deals with relations between individuals in the social realm (i.e. family), as well as in the economy domain (i.e. work conditions and regulations). We can avoid domination when we can point it out and when we are able to protect our freedom applying various mechanisms, which can eliminate, or at least diminish the possibility of domination.

In the first context of non-domination the main aim is to ensure that institutions are limited and controlled by non-dominating law (*contestatory* principle) and constitutional devices of mixt-constitution, which ensures individual liberty. In the other context, the aim of civic republicanism is to formulate social-democratic ideas of progressive intervention in favor of the most dominated groups of society – a postulate, which has got a full voice in the recent stage of development of the republican interpretation of dominium (Martí and Pettit 2010).

> The state should intervene so as to guard against the private domination and should organize itself so as to guard against public domination. The civic republican project is to translate those principles into specific designs for the civic control of public power and into specific policies for the establishment of a social order in which even the poorest citizens can command the respect of their fellows, conscious of not being exposed to private power in the basic domains of human choice. (Martí and Pettit 2010, pp. 52–53)

In my chapter I would like to provide an analysis of the condominium model as an alleged method to resolve decision-making problems of diverse opinion presented by its participants, which has been proposed by Philip Pettit in his recent publications (Martí and Pettit 2010; Pettit 2008a, b, 2010a, b, 2011, 2012).

Martí and Pettit (2010) refer to independent bodies, auditors, solicitors as experts and prescribe them essential roles to play in the condominium model as well as constraints:

- *Regulatory constraints* that subject the committee to monitoring by **independent officials** and bodies, appointed from among owners or from outside, such as **auditors** and **solicitors**
- *Outsourcing constraints* that require committees to outsource decisions to an **independent arbitrator** or **advisor** in arenas where rival, individual interests are engaged
- *Tie-breaking constraints* that ensure that decisions between equally acceptable policies are not indefinitely delayed and are made by procedures that themselves fit with common concerns: depending on the case, these might authorize a committee vote, or a referendum, or referral to **an expert** or **impartial body**. (Martí and Pettit 2010, p. 64)

The main presumption of Pettit deal with experts' impartiality and independence as far as resolution of conflicting situations, which may happen in the condominium. However it seems that he takes the experts or independent arbiters impartiality for granted, if not by definition. One may claim that he omits in his considerations the problem that experts' opinions might be dependent on the type and domain of expertizing she/he belongs to. In my opinion this presumption should be examined in the light of expert studies, and I will do it applying Stephen Turner's experts taxonomy and his analysis of various cases of experts' activities in solving political, economic, and social questions (Turner 2001, 2003, 2006, 2008a, b, 2010, 2012 – most of them now collected in 2014).

I will focus my attention in particular on (1) Pettit's understanding of common concerns versus sectarian interests as far as public goods are concerned; (2) the condominium model which should "have to conduct its life on the pattern of the mixed constitution and the contestatory citizenry [. . .] give an important role to civic deliberation [. . .] in public decision-making" (Martí and Pettit 2010, p. 68); (3) Turner's taxonomy of experts to the requirements the condominium model and (4) consideration of profits and limits of experts' referral demand for the condominium model in the context of republican theory and model of democracy (Pettit 2012).

The structure of my chapter is the following:

1. The idea of freedom as non-domination;
2. Pettit's understanding of the republican state;
3. The common concerns vs. sectarian interests as far as public goods are concerned and its applicability in different realms;
4. various forms of democratic control of effective vs. ineffective and representative vs. non-representative types of governments;
5. the condominium model which should "have to conduct its life on the pattern of the mixed constitution and the contestatory citizenry [. . .] give an important role to civic deliberation [. . .] in public decision-making" (Martí and Pettit 2010, p. 68).

6. Stephen Turner typology experts and its application as an evaluation and feasibility test of Pettit's condominium model;
7. Some republican reflections on system/government contestation in practice in a context of *15-M Movement* in Madrid 2010.

13.2   The Revival of Republican Tradition

Republican idea of freedom and government has a venerable tradition originating with Athenian democracy and the Roman republic. It has been an important point of reference for late medieval and renaissance authors (civic humanism), and it has been treated as a framework of political system in England (1640–1650), the Dutch republic, as well as the Polish and Lithuanian Commonwealth of seventeenth to eighteenth century (Grześkowiak-Krwawicz 2011). Republican ideas have been seminal for the American Revolution and as well as for the French Revolution and constitution of new states, which have originated from those events (Pettit 2012; Skinner and Van Gelderen 2002). Not only can one point out the historical significance of republicanism, but also its proponents claim that republicanism might be a real alternative to a variety of liberal and communitarian approaches to political freedom and its institutional implementation. In recent years one can observe a significant revival of republican tradition both as historical research and more systematic project applicable to conditions of modern politics.

There are two different types of neo-republican restorations, i.e. the Athenian and Roman ones (Pettit 1998b), or in recent formulation: Franco-Prussian (Rousseauvian-Kantian) and Mediterranean-Atlantic (Martí and Pettit 2010; Pettit 2012, 2013). The differences between the two are going to be pointed out later on.[1]

Since the neo-roman idea of republican freedom and government has got a vivid resonance in various domains of social and political thought, I will consider the second interpretation of republican heritage, which got its modern formulation in the writings of Quentin Skinner and Philip Pettit and their followers (Skinner 1998, 2002; Pettit 1996, 1997, 2012).

In recent literature we can find certain applications of the republican idea of freedom as proposed by Pettit's into the domain of social and political sciences, such as: Cecile Laborde (2008), David Miller (2008), Robert Bellamy (2007), John Maynor (2003), Cecile Laborde and John Maynor (2008), Iseulet Honohan (2002), Honohan and Jennings (2006), James Bohman (2007), Daniel Weinstock and

---

[1] "I regret that usage now, since as a matter of history – if not in later representations, which were deeply influenced by Polybius – Athens had many of the characteristics of a mixed constitution; it was not a city ruled by an assembly with Rousseauvian powers" (Pettit 2012, p. 12). The distinction between various Republican traditions have been recently clarified by Pettit in his contribution *Two Republican Traditions* (2013) and further extended in his key-note lecture *Rousseau Bequest to Kant* during the conference *Kant and Republicanism* held at the University of Hamburg 8–10. 04. 2014. (https://lecture2go.uni-hamburg.de/veranstaltungen/-/v/16151).

Christian Nadeau (2004), Samantha Besson and Jose Martí (2006, 2009), Samantha Besson and John Tasioulas (2010), Andreas Niederberger and Philipp Schink (2013).

Among the problems that are discussed from the republican point of view, there is for example a discussion concerning European *versus* national citizenship, critical republicanism as a solution to the hot question of French school politics of the manifestation of ethnic and religious traditions (hijabs) in the public sphere (i.e. public schools), and non-dominating international relations, in relation to legal and political systems. From this very short overview of republican discussions we can learn that the topics, which are touched by the discussants cover a wide range of current problems.

I have mentioned that one of the aims of my chapter is to consider the feasibility of the republican project as applied to modern societies, its limitations, as well as applicatory problems, which it can face in various contexts and circumstances. The idea is to go beyond the ivory tower of philosophical deliberations and to profit from the very fact that Pettit's republican idea of freedom and government has been recognized as a "philosophic" program of Zapatero's government in Spain and some of his crucial ideas have been incorporated in the political agenda of Spanish government. What makes the project interesting is: (1) Pettit's theoretical project has been in certain measure tested by its actual application in Zapatero's Spain, and by that token it can be considered whether the accountability test has been passed or failed. In that context we may consider Pettit's position *vis-à-vis* both the Zapatero's government and adopted politics, as an expert. What should be noticed is that Pettit has stipulated a rather limited understanding of his expertizing activity, restricting it to purely philosophical point of view, i.e. fidelity of policy with the principles.[2] (2) Pettit has made a self-assessment (auto-evaluation) of his "platonic

---

[2] However, it should be mentioned that the very problem of "philosophical couching" is going beyond the scope of our considerations. Pettit himself has pointed out the limited influence of his couching activity upon the actual decisions of Zapatero's government: "I should make clear that I am not a personal friend or advisor of Zapatero. I have met with him on two occasions. [...] My detachment is emphasized by the fact that I have had to prepare the review on the basis of my own research, in which I have mainly relied on independent, outside commentators" (Martí and Pettit 2010, p. 69). Another question is a "philosophical audit" of political action, i.e., if, and if yes, to what measures the results of political program, are consistent with the declared program, or whether the governmental agenda has been effectively implemented into social and political actions (institutional design). "My focus is on how far the government's program has been true to republican principles. They are the product of two forces, one philosophical, the other practical. [...] I shall be looking at how far the policies have been reflected a concern for republican principles. But I shall not be making a judgment on whether the policies adopted were, from a practical point of view, the best means for advancing those principles" (Martí and Pettit 2010, pp. 69–70).

One should distinguish the inspiration of political action by a philosophical theory (quite a vague relation), which is claimed by the politician, from its "application" or being translated as a political program. Pettit himself has done such an audit twice. Once for the social democratic government of Australia *Governance of The Australian Capital Territory* (1998c), and for the second time for the Spanish government *Examen a Zapatero* (2008b) and with José Luis Martí *Philosophy in the Public Life* (2010, pp. 69–94, 95–108), which incorporates the first book in Spanish (2008b).

couching" for the social-democratic "tyrant from Madrid", when facing the financial crisis of 2008 which has cost Zapatero's government loss of power in the elections of 2011. In this context, Pettit's *Republican Reflections on the 15-M Movement* may be read as a "case study" not only of a self-reflecting expert reconsidering his expertizing in an above defined sense and limits, i.e. restricted to results of philosophical coaching only, but also, as a case of limits of expertizing as such (problem of expertizing predictability). Following that second case, we should take into account not only narrow the understanding of the philosopher-in-expertizing, but also to embrace some sociological or economic contexts, which in spite of going beyond his scope, should not be lost from sight of the experts' analysis, and which might provide a some evidence of effectivity measures of expertizing in question. The problem, however, deserves more attention in further considerations (Pettit 2011).

13.3 Definition of Domination

Before I start my presentation of the condominium model I will briefly introduce the republican idea of freedom, which claims that we are free when we are not dominated i.e. we are not under mastery of others and by no means there is a possibility of capricious intervening in the domain of our actions, even by a benevolent master. Simply speaking, we are not *in potestate domini*, but we live *in sui juris* (Martí and Pettit 2010, p. 37).

The domination in question can happen in two areas:

1. *imperium* and it deals with relations between state-individual (institutional and public) and;
2. *dominium*: the other one deals with relations between individuals in social realm (i.e. family, social and work relations).
3. Both dimensions of domination can be considered on local, national and international levels (between states and international organizations: UN, EU, IMF) (Bellamy 2007, 2008; Bohman 2007, 2008; Miller 2008; Pettit 2010a, b).

We have already mentioned that domination consist of intervening in the scope of one's actions, however it should be noticed, that: "one agent dominates another if and only if they have a certain power over that other, in particular a power of interference on an arbitrary basis" (Pettit 1997, p. 52). It means that the domination in question deals not only with actual interference, but also with a possible one – with a possible danger of interference.

Domination is a two part relation: the dominating party might be an individual or collective agent and the dominated party always is to be – at least ultimately – a single individual. In reverse, non-domination involves a sort of immunity or security against any possible interference on arbitrary basis, not the mere actual absence of such interference (a liberal position). In other words, one can say that the advantage of the republican idea of freedom over its liberal competitor consist of, that it is a secure concept of freedom, since it stresses the possible danger of loss of freedom when we are exposed on the arbitrary will of alien subjects and it looks after possible remedies against such a possibility.

It has been noticed that freedom as non-domination has both subjective and inter-subjective significance for such understanding of liberty. The subjective deals with the psychological status of the single individual – as non-dominated *she can look in the eye* of others, she is self-confident, and does not live on the mercy of others. The inter-subjective aspect of liberty as non-domination has three dimensions: (1) *internal*: it is not an accidental relation, but a constitutive one, when we have a social order and civic virtues, so the liberty (franchise) appears; (2) *social*: that its realization presupposes the existence of a number of people who display intentional attitudes and perhaps intentional activities (idea of social holism see: Pettit 1993, ch. 3, 1998a); (3) *common* (interactive): to the extent that it cannot be increased for one without being increased for all (Pettit 1997, p. 121). The importance of both dimensions will be shown later on.

As far as remedies are concerned it is said, that we can avoid or decrease the level of domination when: (1) we can point it out – i.e. when we have knowledge of domination in question, and (2) when we are able to protect our freedom applying various *institutional* mechanisms to eliminate domination, or at least to diminish possibility of domination.

We have already noticed that republicans used to distinguish two areas in which political freedom matter: *imperium* and *dominium*.

As far as the first domain is concerned non-domination in the context of *imperium* means that the main aim is to ensure individual liberty against the activity of the state. It means that state institutions should be limited and controlled by a non-dominating law (*contestatory principle*) and by constitutional devices like the mixt-constitution, which enables checks and balances mechanism. The republican state should be a self-limited state, responsive to possible grievances of its citizens and being prepared to channel them and to give a proper hearing. Pettit defines the republican state as a trustee, a corporate agent, which can be trusted as a body handling communal interests.

As far as the second domain is concerned, non-domination in the context of *dominium* spells out that the aim of civic republicanism is to formulate social-democratic idea of progressive intervention in favor of the most dominated groups of society – a postulate, which has got a full voice in the recent stage of development of the republican interpretation of dominium (Martí and Pettit 2010; Pettit 2012). A good exemplification might be the case of modern Spain under the government of Zapatero, which may be treated as the playground for neo-republican freedom for all. There is an important criterion of non-domination, *the eyeball test* – "everyone can look the others in the eye" without fear or deference, and with a shared consciousness of equal status – (see. subjective aspect of non-domination).

> This is, in the end, what to be undominated means. A free citizen is able to require respect from others and to feel equal to them, to enjoy the same dignity and status, independent of economic, cultural, or personal differences. (Pettit 1997, p. 166; Martí and Pettit 2010, p. 18)

In order to pass the "eyeball test" the state: "should intervene so as to guard against the private domination and should organize itself so as to guard against public domination." That is why the civic republican project has to translate its principles into specific designs for the civic control of public power and to find some applications by introducing "specific policies for the establishment of a social order in which even the poorest citizens can command the respect of their fellows, conscious of not being exposed to private power in the basic domains of human choice" (Martí and Pettit 2010, pp. 52–53).

As far as the dominium sector of non-dominating republican polity/policy, which promotes equality of all citizens is concerned, it applies a social-democratic agenda focusing its attention on citizens' rights much more than neither on economic equality, which used to be a traditional socialist ideal, nor on economic effectivity, which used to be stressed by supporters of the Third Way approach of Tony Blair and Gerhard Schröder or their sociological patrons like Anthony Giddens (1994, 1998), Urlich Beck (1992, 1997) or Beck et al. (1994). The civic republicanism is going to differ significantly from the Third Way ideas as an intellectual platform promoting Spanish modernization (Martí and Pettit 2010, pp. 8–9).[3]

However, among some other questions of the non-dominating state agenda in the Spanish case have been focused on solutions to some (serious) social problems of the most vulnerable groups in society, like improvement of women's position (especially in traditional societies), rights of workers in the job market, migrants' status, right of sexual minorities, support of reproductive rights, and same-sex marriages (Martí and Pettit 2010, pp. 18–21, 78–85). There have been debates on the position of religious groups in society and state subventions for the Roman Catholic Church in Spain. The Zapatero reforms have met some social contestation and there has been a wide social debate in media (Martí and Pettit 2010, pp. 26–30). As far as the definition of governmental agenda, and *dominium* in particular, is strongly connected with the expert question since it is the state, as a trustee, which places itself in a position of an agent, who "knows" what should be done in order to introduce the non-domination in a given area of social problems, and by which means it might be implemented. There is a significant difference in comparison with the idea of freedom as non-interference, since in most social and cultural questions there is no state activity expected, or under libertarian reading, even prohibited. The question, which might arise in that context, especially when the policy introduced by a non-dominating state is going to meet no-acceptance of wide

---

[3] The civic republicanism's aim was to renovate the social democratic scene in Spain. "The first reason for discontent was that the Third Way did not sufficiently differentiate them [PSOE] from González [. . .] The Third Way in Spain was already done by González. And then we find the new way, the modernizing impulse, or whatever expression you prefer; Zapatero's 21st-century socialism. The second reason for discontent with the Third Way was that Zapatero and Nueva Vía were looking for a more refined and principled approach to social democracy – a solid ground for their political institutions – and an approach that would connect with first socialist in Spain, from whom they had drawn inspiration. The Third Way's pragmatism and ambiguity over neoliberalism made it unsatisfactory for these purposes." (Martí and Pettit 2010, p. 10)

social groups i.e. more traditional oriented part of society (sectarian approach). In my opinion, the problem is more complicated. When we take into account Pettit's declaration, that:

> neorepublicanism, as we have repeatedly emphasized, is a research program, not a comprehensive blueprint or ideology [...] The challenge in political philosophy is to hone and elaborate these guiding ideas, connecting them with congenial developments such as deliberative democracy or the capabilities approach as well as with historical antecedents. The challenge in political science and cognate disciplines – law, economics, sociology – is to explore models and practices of institutional design with a view to determining the best form in which republican ideals can be realized. The challenge in political practice is to seek support and influence for a way of thinking about government that, in our opinion, has a uniquely commanding claim on our attention and allegiance. (Lovett and Pettit 2009, p. 16).

The complication I have in mind deals with the "empirical" sense of freedom as non-domination of those, who are (still) unable to accept its inclusive character and state intervention into the social and cultural domain of *dominium*. The problem has been nicely pointed out by Stephen Turner in his paper *Was "Real Existing Socialism" Merely a Premature Form of Rule by Experts?* (2006). He argues that the system of real existing state socialism a kind of experiment in the construction of a model of relating expertise, the bureaucratic state, and the political forces arising from "civil society". Was this system of rule by a party of experts with control of a real administrative structure a fulfillment of the Saint-Simonian dream, in which the enlightened actually ruled (2006)?[4] The problem, Turner has mentioned, in spite of all structural and contextual differences, might be treated as a *caveat* of possible troubles for a neo-republican regime, in process of imposing

---

[4] An excellent exposition of expert's position in the democracy may be found in Stephen Turner's paper *Public Sociology and Democratic Theory* (2007). He points out a structural conflict between public opinion and as far as the position of public sociology is concerned in the structures of the democratic state. "There is a conflict in the abstract, and recognized explicitly in Comte and others, between liberal democracy and a 'social science' that makes 'political' pronouncements, whether it does so by asserting intellectual authority over topics that public discussion takes as its domain or by participating as a state-sponsored source of opinion within public discussion. This conflict takes other forms as well, such as the issue of classroom indoctrination. [...] As we have seen, sociology occupies an uncomfortable and anomalous position. **Sociology purports to have expert knowledge about matters which are in the domain of public discussion in liberal democracy** (bold mine) It's value lies in the ability of sociology to do something that public discourse ordinarily cannot or does not. The claim that sociology makes for public support and recognition depends on this purported ability. But once recognized and supported, what status do sociological claims have? Ordinarily the state in liberal democracies does not fund political viewpoints. If sociological claims are part of public reason, they would run afoul of this practice. But if sociology were a more limited activity, it would undercut the *raison* d'être for sociology, for it would limit its contribution to public discussion. The issue can be put differently. **Is sociology, as a publicly funded activity, an anomaly for liberal democracy, fundamentally in conflict with it because it is an attempt to usurp the functions of public discussion by expertizing it?** (bold mine) Or is it a means by which liberal democracy is supported and improved, and a legitimate object of state support?" (Turner 2007, p. 791). I suggest that the issue observed by Turner might also be a problem for republican theory: how to define and where to place the republican expertizing in the domain of pubic opinion?

"non-dominating regulations" which should protect the most vulnerable (top-down relation). Both their content and the measures of applicability, depend on the "experts'" recognition of republican principles from which they are derived and properly applied. The expertizing in question deals with the defining of aims of state policy, both as far as *imperium* and *dominium* are concerned, which are going to pass the "eye-ball test". The definition in question may be the result of bottom-up channeling of particular grievances, which might be recognized as common avowable interests. However, there is also a top-down aspect of such a definition, which sometimes goes against traditional views and customs. In this sense, we may have a case of republican system colonization of local *life-worlds*, to use Habermasian terms. And such "systemic" colonization refers to experts' opinions, by means of which they are going to "modernize" and to "transform" social reality (republicanism as a progressive political philosophy). If that intuition is sound, we may face the question of resolution of the clash un-colonized *life-world* approach with the expertizing view of the republican "system". However we may ask whether the experts' system is a homogeneous one. Should we expect the same solutions for the same cases in all worlds in question?[5]

To recall the observation Cecile Laborde has made in *Critical Republicanism* (2008), the application of republican ideals may differ from country to country, according to local cultures, social traditions and may vary as far as application is concerned. That means, that application of republican principles is (at least partly) context dependent and demands certain socio-cultural flexibility. The ban on hijabs in French public schools might be treated as a suitable solution, while their wearing at German or English ones might be accepted. The solutions in questions are the results of local expertizing, both of the state and of civil society representatives. At the moment, this is only my working hypothesis, which I want to be noticed, but which deserves much more detailed considerations.

Two aims of the republican policy presented above, should be considered in the wider framework of Pettit's considerations concerning his concept of democratic state and types of democracy. He introduces a two-dimensional conception of democracy: electoral and contestatory *cum* non-electoral democratic institutions (Pettit 1998b, 2004, 2008a, 2009).

I am going just to mention his remarks on the problem. The distinction is important since if republican freedom means not living in subjection to arbitrary power, private or public (Pettit 1997, 1999), we can ask about the aims of the government and according to Pettit that premise "gives a satisfactory interpretation to the idea that government should be guided by all and only the common perceived

---

[5] It is worthwhile to keep in mind some insights of phenomenological perspective to the experts-layman problem, which might be found by Alfred Schütz in his *The Well Informed Citizen: An Essay on Social Distribution of Knowledge* (1946/1964) and some developments of his ideas in sociology of knowledge by Walter Sprondel *'Experte' und 'Laie': Zur Entwicklung von Typenbegriffen in der Wissenssoziologie* (1979). The distinction between different levels of socially distributed knowledge might be of importance as far as the social context of expertizing in politics, and of the republican democratic project in particular, is concerned.

interests of the people", and he stresses that "the relevant interests of the governed are not their special or sectional interests, but rather, their shared or common interests." (Martí and Pettit 2010; Pettit 2009, 2012)

But how to define such common interests which would be accepted by all citizens? And he answers that a certain good will be counted as representing a common interest of a population, just so far as cooperatively avowable considerations might support its collective acceptance.

In context of the common good which the state and its institutions are going to support, states might be described with reference to two relevant dimensions: (1) the first one which is related to the measure in which they operate effectively: effective vs. ineffective states; (2) the second one which is related to the measure in which they represent their people properly: representative vs. - non-representative states. In his formulation, effective states have the capacity to provide basic services to their populations and ineffective states that lack this capacity. Signs that a state is ineffective in the intended sense will be civil war, unchecked famine, continuing genocide, a class of warlords, and general lawlessness. On the other hand he claims that effective states are those that are fit to speak for their people as a whole and ineffective states are those that are not. We can spell out what it means: "A state will be fit to speak for its people to the extent that it gives them the institutional resources – say, of election, contestation and accountability – that will enable them to exercise control over the government and its policies" (Martí and Pettit 2010; Pettit 2008a, b, 2009, 2012). However, it can be claimed that there are many possible types of governmental control and the question is which of those types might be the best one from the republican point of view?

13.4 Popular Institutional Control as an Ideal of Democracy: The Condominium Model

In order to answer the question Pettit considers whether there is any other sort of goal that we might identify as a suitable target for the popular control that democracy is meant to establish.

From his point of view a useful analogy is provided by the sort of association exemplified by the condominium, in which the owners of apartments in the same building combine to run their affairs after what will intuitively count as an acceptable manner. So, the condominium is designed as a "functional" model prescribing various *modi operandi* of state institutions, state as a body as well, and certain procedures by which the institutions in question and the state itself should be bound. It also provides certain elements of a "structural" model since it enumerates various bodies, institutions, levels on which those are located, and their mutual relations.

In the republican design the condominium will not usually operate as an assembly but will elect a committee on a periodic basis to discharge its business.[6] The main target of the projected model is that of forcing the committee to act according to terms of reference endorsed by the members as a whole (Pettit 2004, pp. 58–62; List and Pettit 2011).

We may find three formulations of the condominium model presented by Pettit in his subsequent writings *Three Conceptions of Democratic Control* (Pettit 2008a), *Philosophy of Public Life* (Martí and Pettit 2010) and *On the Peoples Terms* (Pettit 2012). They reflect the development of the concept and they differ as far as certain formulations are concerned. That is why I will present three of them in order to pick up (notice) references to experts, auditors and other independent bodies, which are of my interest.

We have mentioned that the committee will be charged with: (1) promoting certain goals that are important from all points of view (like: maintenance of the quality of the building and surroundings, fostering civility in the relations between residents in the building), (2) pursuing no goals other than these, unless they happen to be related as means to the realization of the primary goals; (3) treating all members more or less equally, both in giving them a hearing and in selecting policies that deal fairly with those in different categories of membership (Pettit 2007, p. 52).

The committee will need to find a certain terms of reference – such as public or civic reasons – which are going to constrain and channel what the committee does in the condominium's name, since the members of the committee are going to discuss the issues, and since they may weigh them in a different way, they will disagree on various questions. How might they overcome the disagreement and obtain the public good? The sort of procedure used by the committee might involve (1) a vote on the committee itself, (2) a vote among the members as a whole, (3) reference to an *outside consultant* or *expert*, (4) or even resort to an impartial lottery of some kind (Pettit 2007, pp. 52–53). Pettit asks the question of how the members of a condominium may ensure that its committee acts so as to satisfy such terms of reference, acting in all and only those ways that are supported by the reasons that will be accepted in the group. Taking into account the fact of abuses that elected officials may practice, he claims that the members of the condominium may also be expected to implement other institutional devices for ensuring that the committee operates according to the terms of reference under which it is appointed. The devices we might expect to be established fall into five categories:

1. The members of the condominium have certain rights, for example in respect of how they furnish their apartments, that the committee may not breach.
2. The requirement that any committee rulings have a rule-of-law form, applying equally to all, and only from the time of their introduction, not retrospectively.

---

[6] This condition may be read as a significant difference between the neo-roman and the Franco-Prussian versions of republicanism, where the idea of popular assembly is praised (*la volonté géné ral* of Jean Jacques Rousseau) (Pettit 2013).

3. Provisions that force the committee to record its proposals, give members a right to object, and time to object, thus enabling members to invigilate its doings.
4. Provisions that force the committee to declare conflicts of interest and submit its performance to *independent audit*, thereby reducing the danger of abuse.
5. Arrangements for adjudicating and disciplining the committee in the event that there is evidence of any breach of such rights or rules or provisions.

Pettit is convinced that the condominium model suggests a parallel for how the people in a democracy, even a large-scale democracy, might – and in some measure do – exercise popular control over government. Specifically, it suggests an image under which the democracy will give the people control of a sort that forces government to satisfy a demanding set of constraints (Pettit 2007, pp. 53–54).

The condominium model obtains its formulation in his book written in collaboration with J-L. Martí, however the chapter in question, *The Philosophy of Public Life*, has been written by Pettit himself (Martí and Pettit 2010, pp. 63–64).

1. *Rule-of-law constraints* on committee decisions, ensuring that the committee can act only on the basis of established principles that apply to all and do not discriminate against any individual or group.
2. *Private-right constraints* that block the committee from taking actions that would intrude on the affairs of individual owners, say by requiring them to furnish the interiors of their apartments in a certain pattern.
3. *Invigilation constraints* that require the committee to publicize its decisions or plans, and its reasons for supporting them, inviting public discussion and challenge and establishing means for having objections heard and adjudicated (p. 63.).
4. *Separation-of-power constraints* that subject committee proceedings to the checking of other bodies, say, an oversight "senate," and that require bodies that adjudicate objections to be independent of the committee.
5. *Regulatory constraints* that subject the committee to monitoring by independent officials or bodies, appointed from among owners or from outside, such as auditors or solicitors.
6. *Outsourcing constraints* that require the committee to outsource decisions to an *independent arbitrator* or *advisor* in areas where rival, individual interests are engaged.
7. *Tie-breaking constraints* that ensure that decisions between equally acceptable policies are not indefinitely delayed and are made by procedures that themselves fit with common concerns: depending on the case, these might authorize a committee vote, or a referendum, or *referral to an expert* or *impartial body*.
8. *Amendment constraints* that make it possible to alter electoral arrangements or any of the constraints on this list – including the amendment constraints themselves – but only in a certain manner, say, by a supermajoritarian support in a committee-of-the-whole.

And the final formulation from the most recent book of Pettit *On the People's Term*:

As owners talk, try out proposals and then vote on remaining candidates, they will inevitably establish norms that rule their communal life together. These will determine:

1. The reasons why they should collectively organize the servicing of elevators, the tending of common areas, the maintenance of a sinking fund, and such endeavours.
2. The features of collective decision-making that are acknowledged on all sides as desirable: openness, consultation, deliberation, efficiency, and the like.
3. The duties of individuals in relation to the group in the matter of body corporate fees, committee participation, general civility, etc.
4. The equality of individuals in collective decision-making, despite the variations in the fees paid by the owners of different apartments.
5. The rights of individuals to furnish and decorate their apartments internally to their own taste.
6. The benefits that individuals can expect to be able to claim from the group corporate in dealing with particular problems like ground-floor flooding.
7. The penalties that ought to be meted out to apartment owners who breach commonly established procedures.
8. The value of giving authority to an elected committee, while allowing for challenges by other members to its resolutions.
9. The utility of outsourcing certain decisions to **independent advisers** and **auditors**, given **possible conflicts of interest**. (Pettit 2012, p. 258)

Pettit stresses that the fact that a group operates under an acceptability regime in which certain norms of argument dictate the terms of argument and association does not mean that members will always behave in a saintly, or even a salutary, manner. However, they have to be prepared to make their local community work, and work in a manner that gives each a role in community governance. He stresses that by their very participation in deciding on common policies, or in revising the processes under which policies are decided, they show that they are ready to accommodate themselves to others in various ways, making whatever compromises and concessions are required. That means that the participants are ready to overcome possible disagreements, conflicting and sectarian interests. And that they are able to do it since they are willing to think from the point of view of the group as a whole, rather than living in isolation and resentment or seeking after a community that is more congenial to their tastes. This commitment to the group amounts to a local counterpart of what would count as patriotism at the national level (List and Pettit 2011; Pettit 2012, pp. 258–259).

In this short presentation of the condominium model, which provides an institutional solution of conflicting interests and fractional positions, which might be found between its members – among other structural and functional elements of the condominium – the solution in question depends on independent auditors, advisers and experts who are invited from outside by the committee, to serve the condominium with their procedural knowledge, or maybe of some subject matter knowledge important for taking up decisions important for the group. It seems to me that Pettit is akin to taking the advisors, auditors, experts etc. as *impartial* by definition, and by the same token the services provided by them, can be accepted by all the parties of the condominium, since they have been offered a solution, which is above and beyond their individual perspectives.

The main point I would like to make is that in the recent experts literature the picture is not so unproblematic, as we might infer from his presentation. The experts and other authority bearers mentioned by Pettit in the context of solving by their authority conflicting disagreement are not always as independent, as impartial as he has used to claim. Such an image of expert activity as proposed by Pettit is – in my opinion – due to stressing the purely procedural aspect of their activity. When we have reasons of group agency and the formal procedures of deliberations of those reasons, then we can expect that an auditor from outside of the group, who is bound by the procedures in question (meta-procedures, or rules) might provide a solution, that will be accepted by all the parties. But when his or her activity goes beyond procedural regulations, which are suggested in most of the examples, then his impartiality and her independence, in spite of her being form outside the group, are not so obvious and evident. The problem is, that in some cases of experts activity we cannot expect such a clarity as far as the content of their expertizing is concerned, that would lead the audience of their services to their acceptance without its questioning, or using another expression, that they are taken for granted.

To illustrate the problem I would like make a reference to one of the experts studies, where the experts problem has been presented in more complicated manner, I do mean Stephen Turner's experts typology form his *Liberal Democracy 3.0. Civil Society in an Age of Experts* (2003). My aim is neither to dismiss Pettit's interpretation of possible independent experts position, nor to claim that his stipulation is unsound, but to consider how the more complicated picture of experts landscape may enrich his project of the condominium model.

The reason I refer in this context to analysis of Stephen Turner is that he has provided an extensive presentation of various types of experts in the context of politics, and in the framework of liberal democracy in particular. He states an interesting observation that the system of representative democracies based on liberal principles and electoral control is evolving in the direction of discretionary power of experts, certain types of experts. Turner defines all experts by relating their cognitive authority to the domain of expertizing (filed) and their respective audience, which recognizes them as experts in the field. According to above mentioned definition he has distinguished five types of experts:

1. Scientist (i.e. physicist, scientist)
2. Theologian
3. Hobby-horse or cook-book Expert
4. The Expert with a Cause – acting on public stage
5. The Expert with a Cause – acting from behind the public stage.

(1) Scientists possess their cognitive authority when they speak as representatives of science. The cognitive authority of scientists is a corporate one since it is the scientific community, which confirms or disconfirms an authority of i.e. physicist. Therefore these social control mechanisms are crucial to the cognitive authority of science, as they are to professions (see. R.K. Merton). However, even in the domain of the science we may observe some problems of the social acceptance of

some experts in due to status of the scientist-expert in the social sciences, like economists or sociologist. The degree of disagreement between economists is much greater than between physicists – varieties of schools and orientations (Turner 2003, p. 25).

(2) Another type of expert described by Turner is theologian who is a "restricted audience" expert, whose cognitive authority extends only to the specific audience of the sect, i.e. is accepted only within the (conceptual and practice) framework of his/her religious community. Relation between theologian (theological authorities) and audiences of believers – how can mysterious assertions of special knowledge come to be regarded as authoritative? In which way is highly esoteric knowledge granted the same, or similar deference (credibility) as scientific knowledge? Thinking of the audiences of the expert – the audiences for whom the expert is legitimate and whose acceptance legitimates her claims to expertise – illuminates a puzzle in the discourse of the problem of expertise and democracy.

(3) The third type of expert usually appears in the area of various services, i.e. the massage therapist is paid for his knowledge or for his skills, but payment depends on the judgments of beneficiaries of that knowledge to the effect that the therapy worked, and they can claim to be experts for a wider audience. But some people don't benefit from the massage therapy, and don't find the promise to be fulfilled. So, the experts of this type have a created audience, a set of followers for whom they are an expert because they have proven themselves to this audience by their actions.

Experts of three first types whose cognitive authority is: (1) generally (universally) accepted by the scientific community, (2) accepted by a religious group of believers, (3) accepted by some group of self-selected followers who profit from the experts knowledge, according to Turner, each of them have a place in the scheme of liberal democracy (Turner 2003, p. 27).

(4) The fourth type selected by Turner may be called the expert with a cause. Consider the "expert" who is subsidized to speak and claim expertise in the hope that the views he advances will convince a wider public and thus compel them into some sort of political action or choice. This is a type of expert, that has come to prominence at the end of the nineteenth century in the USA, and has been established concurrently with the development of foundations (Rockefeller and founding of the University of Chicago, Russell Sage Foundation).

(5) The fifth type is a variant of the fourth one and it differs in its target audience. Where the audience of the fourth type is the general public, the audience of the fifth is professionals, typically bureaucrats who have discretionary power. It may be claimed that in some context the fifth type has been an historical development of the fourth. The fifth type of expert is distinguished by a crucial difference in this triad: the fact that the primary audience is not the public. The legitimacy of the cognitive authority exercised by these individuals is not a matter, ordinarily at least, of direct public discussion, because they deal with issues, such as administration, that are not discussed in newspapers until after they become institutional fact, and indeed are rarely understood by reporters, and may be subject of administrative secrecy of some time. A paradigm case of this fifth kind of expertise is public administration

which contains the three distinctive elements of the type: a distinctive audience of "professionals", experts whose legitimacy is a matter of acceptance of these professionals, but who are not accepted by the public, and experts whose "professional" audience is itself recognized as possessing, at most, only partial expertise by the public.[7]

Turner's claim is that it is with this step that the problem of democracy and experts become salient. The experts whose expertise is employed are so in the sense that they have an audience that recognizes their expertise by virtue of being trained by these experts (Turner 2003, p. 35). With respect to the audience, this expert more closely resembles the theologian whose expertise is recognized by the sect he successfully persuades of his theological expertise (see. J. Habermas and the "experts cultures").

Conflicts between democratic and expert opinion are – in Turner's opinion – inevitable, not so much because experts possess some secret information, but that it is a consequence of the fact that the processes by which knowledge is validated by audiences are separated. Eventually, the processes of validation of theological expertise by sects are distinct from those by which public validation is achieved (Turner 2001, 2003). What public audiences can do in each case is to legitimate, or to accept the claims to expertise. Legitimation is the "solution" to the conflict. But in the case of bureaucratic expertise the legitimation is very indirect (Turner 2003, p. 36).

What kind of experts are involved in Pettit's republican project? The problem of experts' impartiality and neutrality as far as their services are concerned may resemble the two last types of experts. In what terms should we think about relation: experts and the public (a state as trustee) who do we trust on?

I would like to notice that the conclusions which might be drawn from this short overview is that expertizing is going to be a much complicated and context dependent enterprise than it has been claimed in the condominium model. That the impartiality and independence of subjects who are involved in expertizing (audits or advisory consulting) depends not only on their "professional stance", as Pettit would suggested, but also on the domain, audiences, types of expert authority and its validation in question. And those "structural" factors – at least to some extent – predetermine the results of the experts activity. Think about the expert with the case who is employed by some lobby which is going to pay him for convincing the audience of some social reforms, the lobby may even found a research institute or university to "covert" the expertizing in question with the science-experts clothes, but the question is still open whether the policies she is opting for, let it be implementation of some projects as far as the *dominium* is concerned, might be recognized by the audience – both the committee and the members of condominium as "independent" and "impartial". The point, that such an expert is hired form outside from the condominium members is not sufficient; the claim that his or her

---

[7] In this context a very interesting analysis of the fifth type of experts activity in the process of policy making in the structures of European Union (Turner 2008b).

services are taking into account the avowed interest of all citizens and that they might pass the "eyeball test" may in this context be discussable, since to represent the avowed interest of all citizens may appeal to different experts who go from different premises.

My remarks are very preliminary ones and my main aim at this stage of development is to point out the possible problem for the republican idea of democratic control in the framework of the condominium model, which is intended to provide a platform of overcoming possible disagreements and excluding opinions. A possible solution of this question would demand much more detailed analysis of the case studies, it would also demand a more precise spelling out of the republican "conceptual scheme" as far as understanding of experts activity and their condition is concerned.

What I have in mind is an introductory and provisional analysis which is, in fact, an analysis of Pettit's expertizing to the Zapatero government which has been provided by Pettit himself in *Republican Reflections on the 15-M Movement* in September 2011. We can call his remarks the condominium in practice.

Pettit is very conscious that the civic republican policy which has been introduced by the Zapatero government is now in danger and that it has to face the protest of young people from the *Puerta del Sol*. "What do you say to thousands of young people who gather in frustration at a political system that has utterly failed them? Is there anything to say that can reach the depth of their wholly understandable outrage at the disappearance of jobs and the collapse of prospects?" he asks (Pettit 2011, p. 1). And he admits that in thinking about the future of Spain under the Zapatero government – indeed under any government – he made two serious mistakes. "I was naive about the reliability of the international financial system in providing the infrastructure that would enable the government in a country like Spain to provide for its people's economic welfare. I failed to realize how far the country's options for responding to a downturn of economic fortunes would be restricted by its membership in the Eurozone." (Pettit 2011, p. 1) The question we may ask: but where were the experts, both on the national and supra-national level, who were responsible for the allowance of the home construction bubble, for example?

However, admitting his fault he tries to balance the negative outcomes of the situation, pointing out the positive one: "I continue to commend the performance of the Zapatero government for its attempts to equalize the position of women in society, for its regularization of the status of many illegal immigrants, for the law of dependency that it established in protection of the vulnerable, and for the introduction of same-sex marriage" (Pettit 2011, p. 2).

From our point of view, it may be interesting what strategy he is going to propose in order to cope with the crisis situation. The strategy in question reflects his understanding of a role of the state *vis-a-vis* the domain of economics and market processes. The state should take into account that the crisis "showed us all that the reliance of governments on the international financial system amounts, in an old phrase, to riding the tiger" (p. 2). He points that all governments depend on the banking system and stock market, of course, for the capital that nurtures job-creating enterprises and this dependence makes for a serious vulnerability to how well the international financial system performs.

In his opinion there are two extreme responses that the financial crisis and its aftermath have provoked. The first approach may be exemplified in the stance of the Tea Party in the United States. It gives the government the task of law and order and calls for the abdication of the state in the sphere of production, commerce and employment. The first response puts its faith in the invisible hand of market-based adjustment. It would license a plutocratic regime in which markets allow enormous concentrations of personal and corporate wealth and the polity does nothing about restraining the power of those thereby enriched. The second approach would support a rejection of dependence on the sort of beast that the international financial system constitutes; it puts its faith in a more attractive object than the first, appealing to the sense of our collective power as a democratic people; it is populist in character rather than plutocratic; "Where the first approach would give the tiger free range, this would simply kill the animal" (Pettit 2011, p. 3).

If the two remedies, which have been registered in popular answers to the crisis are not to be accepted from the republican point of view, how then should we respond to the financial crisis and its aftermath? In his view one should certainly avoid the iconoclastic tendency to seek the demolition of either the governmental or the financial system. To follow his phrase "The tiger is not to be given free range and the tiger is not to be hunted down and killed" and the proposed response provides a third alternative that our metaphor suggests, that is to "rein in and regulate the tiger: to put it to work for democratic ends, under restrictions that make sure it serves those ends." (Pettit 2011, p. 7) This is a democratic and not just a technocratic challenge, and he claims it will certainly require a lot of technical expertise to identify means whereby a financial system that has novel instruments at its disposal can still be regulated and harnessed to the common good. In this remark we may read that expertizing is always provisional and temporal since the conditions are changing all the time, so the solutions, which are proposed are exposed to permanent adjustability to signals and information which the system obtains from its environment (N. Luhmann's *autopoiesis*). How should we place this remark in the Turnerian experts landscape?

And he asks two important questions: how to understand that "it is up to a responsible parliament and a contestatory citizenry to explore the strengths and weaknesses of different proposals and to maintain oversight of whatever proposal is eventually enacted? How can a contestatory citizenry function in a role of this kind?" (Pettit 2011, p. 7).

What is important in the answer he proposes is that the Italian-Atlantic tradition of republicanism suggests that if citizens are to exercise the contestatory control that democracy requires, then they must divide the civic labour of contestation between them, with different groups specializing in different areas of governmental activity. And there is a reference to expertizing, which he has introduced – in this case – expertizing from the bottom, we may call it bottom-up expertizing: "It is essential for the proper invigilation of those in power that different civic associations can monitor the decisions of the authorities in different areas of policymaking, can muster the best available expertise in assessing what the authorities decide, and can hold them to effective, public account." (Pettit 2011, p. 7). The reference to the bottom-up expertizing is introduced in order to avoid some populist tendencies which he ascribes to the 15-M movement, since however it has been important in giving expression to the insistence of the people at large that government should live up to their expectations on the economic and related fronts, it engages democracy on the international as well as the national front.

Since the nature of the crisis is international (begun in the USA), it does mean that if people are to address it seriously in the contestatory mode Pettit has envisaged, then they have to do so via civic associations that reach across boundaries. "Fully alerting governments to the urgency of popular demand may be better achieved by marches across Europe than by mass gatherings in national squares" (Pettit 2011, p. 8).

The answers and remedies Pettit has proposed to the Spanish, and more general to the European crisis, reveal republican strategy as far as the problem solving in such a situation might look like. We may treat them as a (provisional) illustration of how the condominium model might work in the situation of divergent opinions, in particular, when emotional stance of the condominium inhabitants has lost its balance. The proposals he provides are realistic, at list as far as technocratic questions are concerned, however it might be discussable whether the Spanish *Indignados* are going to accept his shifting application of contestatory principles onto a higher international and supra-national level, and to what extend they could not claim that at least partial responsibility for the crisis can be addressed to the national or local governments which have not been far-sighted and cautious enough in their policies.

I would like to end my considerations on the experts' activity in the republican framework with one remark. I am very conscious that the application of Turners experts taxonomy to the condominium model would need a much more detailed analysis then might be provided it this provisional and preliminary contribution, but I hope that the point which I have tried to make, that the experts position, as well as their activity in solving the conflicting situations, deserves much more attention and consideration than just stipulated proclamation of their impartiality and independence, which by definition will guard the expected outcome, i.e. the sooth cooperation of all parties in defining and finding the common good of the community in question.

References

Beck, Ulrich. 1992. *Risk society: Towards a new modernity*. London: Sage.
Beck, U. 1997. *The reinvention of politics: Rethinking modernity in the global social order*. Cambridge: Polity Press.
Beck, Urlich, Athony Giddens, and Lasch Stott. 1994. *Reflexive modernization: Politics, tradition and aesthetics in the modern social order*. Stanford: Stanford University Press.

Bellamy, Richard. 2007. *Political constitutionalism: A republican defense of the constitutionality of democracy*. Cambridge: Cambridge University Press.

Bellamy, R. 2008. Republicanism, democracy, and constitutionalism. In *Republicanism and political theory*, ed. C. Laborde and J. Maynor, 159–189. Malden: Blackwell.

Besson, Samantha, and José Luis Martí. 2006. *Deliberative democracy and its discontents*. Farnham: Ashgate Publishing.

Besson, S., and J.L. Martí. 2009. *Legal republicanism. National and international perspectives*. Oxford: Oxford University Press.

Besson, Samantha, and John Tasioulas (eds.). 2010. *The philosophy of international law*. Oxford: Oxford University Press.

Bohman, James. 2007. *Democracy across borders: From Demos to Demoi*. Cambridge, MA: MIT Press.

Bohman, J. 2008. Nondomination and transnational democracy. In *Republicanism and political theory*, ed. Cecile Laborde and John Maynor, 190–216. Malden: Blackwell.

Brown, Mark B. 2009. *Science in democracy: Expertise, institution and representation*. Cambridge, MA: MIT Press.

Callon, Michel, Pierre Lascoumes, and Yanick Barthe. 2009. *Acting in an uncertain world: An essay on technical democracy*. Cambridge, MA: MIT Press.

Collins, Harry, and Robert Evans. 2007. *Rethinking expertise*. Chicago: The University of Chicago Press.

Fischer, Frank. 2009. *Democracy and expertise: Reorienting policy inquiry*. Oxford: Oxford University Press.

Giddens, Anthony. 1994. *Beyond left and right. The future of radical politics*. Cambridge: Polity Press.

Giddens, A. 1998. *The third way. The renewal of social democracy*. Cambridge: Polity Press.

Grześkowiak-Krwawicz, Anna. 2011. Noble republicanism in the Polish-Lithuanian commonwealth (an attempt at description). *Acta Poloniae Historiae* 103: 31–65.

Hilton, Matthew, James McKay, Nicholas Crowson, and Jean-François Mouhot. 2013. *The politics of expertise: How NGOs shaped modern Britain*. Oxford: Oxford University Press.

Honohan, Iseult. 2002. *Civic republicanism*. London: Routledge.

Honohan, Ieult, and J. Jennings (eds.). 2006. *Republicanism in theory and practice*. London: Routledge.

Laborde, Cecile. 2008. *Critical republicanism: The Hijab controversy and political philosophy*. Oxford: Oxford University Press.

Laborde, Cecile, and John Maynor (eds.). 2008. *Republicanism and political theory*. Malden: Blackwell.

List, Christian, and Philip Pettit. 2011. *Group agency: The possibility, design and status of corporate agents*. Oxford: Oxford University Press.

Lovett, Frank, and Philip Pettit. 2009. Neorepublicanism: A normative and institutional research program. *Annual Review of Political Science* 12: 11–29.

Martí, José Luis, and Philip Pettit. 2010. *A political philosophy in public life. Civic republicanism in Zapatero's Spain*. Princeton/Oxford: Princeton University Press.

Maynor, John W. 2003. *Republicanism in the modern world*. Cambridge: Polity.

Miller, David. 2008. Republicanism, national identity, and Europe. In *Republicanism and political theory*, ed. Cecile Laborde and John Maynor, 133–158. Malden: Blackwell.

Niederberger, Andreas, and Philipp Schink (eds.). 2013. *Republican democracy: Liberty, law and politics*. Edinburgh: Edinburgh University Press.

Pettit, Philip. 1993/1996. *The common mind: An essay on psychology, society and politics*. New York: Oxford University Press.

Pettit, P. 1996. Freedom and antipower. *Ethics* 106: 576–604.

Pettit, P. 1997. *Republicanism: A theory of freedom and government*. Oxford: Oxford University Press.

Pettit, P. 1998a. Defining and defending social holism. *Philosophical Explorations: An International Journal for the Philosophy of Mind and Action* 1(3): 169–184.

Pettit, P. 1998b. Reworking Sandel's republicanism. *Journal of Philosophy* 95: 73–96.

Pettit, P. 1998c. *Review of Governance in the Australian Capital Territory Dept of Urban Services, ACT Government, April 1998*. Presented to the Chief Minister and the Federal Minister of Territories on behalf of the Working Party for the Review of Governance in the ACT. Canberra.

Pettit, P. 1999. Republican liberty, contestatory democracy. In *Democracy's value*, ed. C. Hacker-Cordon and I. Shapiro. Cambridge: Cambridge University Press

Pettit, P. 2004. Depoliticizing democracy. *Ratio Juris* 17: 52–65.

Pettit, P. 2008a. Three conceptions of democratic control. *Constellations* 15(1): 46–55.

Pettit, P. 2008b. *Examen a Zapatero*. Madrid: Temas de Hoy.

Pettit, P. 2009. Varieties of public representation. In *Representation and popular rule*, ed. Ian Shapiro, Susan Stokes, and E.J. Wood. Cambridge: Cambridge University Press.

Pettit, P. 2010a. A Republican law of people, 'Republicanism and international relations', special issue. *European Journal of Political Theory* 9(1): 70–94.

Pettit, P. 2010b. Legitimate international institutions: A Neo-republican perspective. In *The philosophy of international law*, ed. Samantha Besson and John Tasioulas, 139–160. Oxford: Oxford University Press.

Pettit, P. 2011. Republican reflections on the 15-M Movement. *booksandideas.net* – 20 September 2011.

Pettit, P. 2012. *On the people's terms: A republican theory and model of democracy*. Cambridge: Cambridge University Press.

Pettit, P. 2013. Two Republican traditions. In *Republican democracy: Liberty, law and politics*, ed. Andreas Niederberger and Philipp Schink, 164–204. Edinburgh: Edinburgh University Press.

Schütz, Alfred. 1946/1964. The well informed citizen: An essay on the social distribution of knowledge. *Social Research* 13: 463–478. Reprinted in Alfred Schütz. 1964. *Collected papers, Vol II, Studies in social theory*, ed. Arvid Brodersen, 120–134. The Hague: M. Nijhoff.

Selinger, Evan, and Robert P. Crease (eds.). 2006. *The philosophy of expertise*. New York: Columbia University Press.

Skinner, Quentin. 1998. *Liberty before liberalism*. Cambridge: Cambridge University Press.

Skinner, Q. 2002. *Visions of politics*. Cambridge: Cambridge University Press.

Sprondel, Walter M. 1979. «Experte» und «Laie»: Zur Entwicklung von Typenbegriffen in der Wissenssoziologie. In *Alfred Schütz und die Idee des Alltags in den Sozialwissenschaften*, ed. Walter M. Sprondel and Richard Grathoff, 140–154. Stuttgart: Ferdinand Enge Verlag.

Steher, Nico. 1994. *Knowledge societies*. London: Sage.

Turner, Stephen P. 2001. What is the problem with experts? *Social Studies of Science* 31(1): 123–149.

Turner, S.P. 2003. *Liberal democracy 3.0. Civil society in the age of experts*. London: Sage.

Turner, S.P. 2006. Was real existing socialism a premature form of rule by experts? In *Democracy and civil society east of the Elbe*, ed. Sven Eliaeson, 248–261. London: Routledge.

Turner, S.P. 2008a. Balancing expert power: Two models for the future of politics. In *Knowledge and democracy: Is liberty a daughter of knowledge*, ed. Nico Stehr, 119–141. New Brunswick: University of British Columbia Press.

Turner, S.P. 2008b. Expertise and the process of policy aking: The EU's new model of legitimacy. In *Building civil society and democracy in new Europe*, ed. Sven Eliason, 160–175. Cambridge: Cambridge Scholars Publishing.

Turner, S.P. 2010. Normal accidents of expertise. *Minerva* 48: 239–258. doi:10.1007/s11024-010-9153-z.

Turner, S.P. 2012. Double heuristics and collective knowledge: The case of expertise. *Studies in Emergent Order* 5: 64–85.

Turner, S.P. 2014. *The politics of expertise*. London: Routledge.

Van Gelderen, Martin, and Quentin Skinner. 2002. *Republicanism: A shared European heritage*. Cambridge: Cambridge University Press.

Weinstock, Daniel, and Christian Nadeau (eds.). 2004. *Republicanism: History, theory and practice*. London: Frank Cass.

Chapter 14
Private Epistemic Virtue, Public Vices: Moral Responsibility in the Policy Sciences

Merel Lefevere and Eric Schliesser

Abstract In this chapter we address what we call "The-Everybody-Did-It" (TEDI) Syndrome, a symptom for collective negligence. Our main thesis is that the character of scientific communities can be evaluated morally and be found wanting in terms of moral responsibility. Even an epistemically successful scientific community can be morally responsible for consequences that were unforeseen by it and its members and that follow from policy advice given by its individual members. We motivate our account by a critical discussion of a recent proposal by Heather Douglas. We offer three, related criticisms of Douglas's account. First, she assumes that scientific fields are communicative communities. Second, in a system where the scientific community autonomously sets standards, there is a danger of self-affirming reasoning. Third, she ignores that the character of a scientific community is subject to moral evaluation. We argue that these omissions in Douglas's theory leave it with no adequate response to TEDI Syndrome. Moreover, we deny that science ought to be characterized by unanimity of belief among its competent practitioners, this leads easily to the vices of close-mindedness and expert-overconfidence. If a scientific community wishes to avoid these vices it should create conditions for an active pluralism when it and its members aspire to the position of rational policy decision-making.

14.1 Introduction

In this chapter we provide a new approach to analyze the moral responsibility and duty of scientific communities and individual scientists in these, especially those engaged in policy science. We motivate our account by a critical discussion of a recent proposal by Heather Douglas. In particular, our approach addresses what we call "The-Everybody-Did-It" (TEDI) Syndrome. Our main thesis is that the character of scientific communities can be evaluated morally and be found wanting in

M. Lefevere (✉) • E. Schliesser
Department of Philosophy and Moral Science, Ghent University, Gent, Belgium
e-mail: merel.lefevere@ugent.be

© Springer International Publishing Switzerland 2014
C. Martini, M. Boumans (eds.), *Experts and Consensus in Social Science*,
Ethical Economy 50, DOI 10.1007/978-3-319-08551-7_14

terms of moral responsibility. In particular we argue that even an epistemically successful scientific community can be morally responsible for consequences that were unforeseen by it and its members and that follow from policy advice given by its individual members. We sketch what we call an active pluralism in order to give content to the duties that follow from the character failure of scientific communities.

In Sect. 14.2 we summarize Heather Douglas's proposal and elucidate its character. In Sect. 14.3.1 we offer three, related criticisms of Douglas' account. First, she assumes that scientific fields are communicative communities. Second, in a system where the scientific community autonomously sets standards, there is a danger of self-affirming reasoning. Third, she ignores that the character of a scientific community is subject to moral evaluation. We argue that these omissions in Douglas's theory leave it with no adequate response to TEDI Syndrome. In a fourth section we sketch an argument for the claim that if a scientific community wishes to avoid the vices of close-mindedness and overconfidence it should create conditions for an active pluralism when it and its members aspire to the position of rational policy decision-making.

Before we turn to our argument, we offer one methodological comment and a real-life (albeit stylized) example. We are primarily interested in recommendations from policy scientists to policy makers and the public. Most of our examples focus on economics, but our claims do not turn on these. However, the focus on economics is not only due to our scholarly interests; we argue that Douglas's conception of a scientific community has non-trivial similarities with an efficient market hypothesis in economics.

So, what do we have in mind when we talk about TEDI syndrome? Our example is grounded in a remarkable self-study of the Dutch Central Planning agency about the gross failures in considering the possibility of the macro-economic consequences (liquidity-trap, collapse in world-trade, etc.) of a Lehman style collapse in 2008. The self-study repeatedly points to this failure in "all other forecast agencies" (de Jong et al. 2010, p. 7, p. 27, p. 40, cf. p. 63). As the authors of the study admit, at the time, their whole modeling approach is unable to think systematically about such events.[1] We claim that the presence of TEDI syndrome is evidence that one may be dealing with an instance of *collective negligence*.

14.2   Science: Responsible Scientists

In her increasingly influential book (2009) *Science, Policy and the Value-Free Ideal*, Heather Douglas proposes that the longstanding idea of science as a value-free ideal is not only mistaken but also undesirable. Here we focus only on the

---

[1] They treat the fall of Lehman as a discretionary policy choice (61) that cannot be modeled. For more discussion of this case see Schliesser (2011).

fourth chapter of her book, where Douglas offers an account of the moral responsibilities of science. She argues that scientists need to consider the consequences of error in their work, without expecting them to be fortune-tellers. However, we do expect reasonable foresight and careful deliberation from scientists. This means that scientists are accountable for expected results and for certain side-effects of their actions. To elaborate on unforeseen consequences, Douglas returns to Joel Feinberg's well-known distinction between negligence and recklessness: "When one knowingly creates an unreasonable risk to self or others, one is reckless; when one unknowingly but faultily creates such a risk, one is negligent" (Feinberg 1970, p. 193). Thus, according to Douglas, a reckless scientist is fully aware of unjustified risks his choices entail, a negligent scientist is unaware of such risks, but he or she should have been (Douglas 2009, p. 71).

But how does one determine a scientist's negligence or recklessness? Difficulties arise in determining how much foresight and deliberation we ought to expect from scientists, without blaming them for every trivial use or misuse of their work. According to Douglas scientific communities provide the benchmarks of responsibility.[2] Reasonable foresight is to be evaluated in light of the judgments of the scientific community. While this still leaves a lot of details unanswered, Douglas offers a quite plausible suggestion; non-scientists generally lack the technical expertise to evaluate what would be foreseeable consequences of following policy advice. Her position can be strengthened intuitively: for a clear way to operationalize the very notion of expert-understanding of a scientific theory is to know how to reliably derive consequences from it.

Before we turn to our criticism of Douglas's approach, we provide some context for it. In particular, we argue that Douglas leans towards a juridical interpretation of scientific responsibility in terms of "what would a reasonable person do"?

14.2.1 The Reasonable Person

But how reasonable is that "reasonable person"? In current tort law and liability cases a person is considered responsible for his actions, or his negligence or imprudence. But the discussion about what is negligence and imprudence is still going on. Before we apply this to a more serious example, let's toy with this situation:

It's Monday morning, and as usual before work you pull over at your favorite magazine shop. You hop out of your car, leave the engine running, and quickly pop into the shop to pick up your journal. In the meantime a sinister figure approaches your car, sees that it is unlocked, jumps in and drives of. A few hundred meters further, the thief runs over a pedestrian.

---

[2] Douglas (2009), p. 83ff. Ian Hacking (1992) has developed a sophisticated treatment of the self-vindicating norms of various scientific communities.

Who's to blame for the death of the pedestrian? The thief you say? Not so fast. Are you not at least negligent or even reckless by not locking your car? Should you not have foreseen the possibility that an unlocked car attracts thieves? Sure, it's the thief that pushed the gas pedal, but if you had locked your car, he would not have stolen it and would not have hit the pedestrian. According to juridical standards, you may be co-responsible for the accident (especially if your insurance company has deep pockets), if a reasonable person would have acted in such a way that the accident would not have happened. So if a reasonable person would have locked his or her car, you may be, in part, to blame.

But who is that reasonable man (or woman) everyone should act like? The reasonable person is a legal fiction; it represents an objective standard to measure the actions of a real person against. While its philosophical roots may be traced back to impartial spectator theories of Hume and Adam Smith, it was first introduced into a legal context in 1837, in the case Vaughan versus Menlove. The defendant built a haystack on his land, close to the border of the plaintiff's land. The haystack had a "chimney" to prevent the hay from spontaneous inflammation. Unfortunately, the haystack caught fire anyway. However, the defendant had been warned several times in 5 weeks' time that the haystack was wrongly built, and thus dangerous, but he would not change it. The hay caught fire, spread to the plaintiff's land, and two of his cottages were destroyed in the fire. The jury was asked to judge whether the defendant's showed such reasonable caution as a prudent man would have acted with. This "reasonable person" test became a standard in the English and U.S. courts.

Steven P. Scalet argues that this "reasonable person" functions like an empty vessel, "allowing courts to use various norms and moral judgments to determine what seems reasonable in the circumstances" (Scalet 2003, p. 75). The standard of reasonableness is not very informative; it is the jury or the judges who interpret "reasonable" along the lines of community norms, legal principles, precedents, or moral judgments. This creates a serious tension. At one end, laws should be formulated in general terms, so that they can be applied to a variety of particular cases. At the other end, laws should provide the necessary information for citizens in order to guide their behavior. Reasonableness can indeed be applied to particular cases, but is no stable guide of conduct (ibid., p. 77). Scalet thinks of reasonable standards as "binoculars that focus our attention on some actual practices that have won our approval as an appropriate standard to guide our conduct" (ibid., p. 78). This changes the direction of interpretation: it is no longer the fiction of the reasonable man that instructs what is reasonable, but the behavior of actual people with certain relevant traits. The question remains which traits are relevant and which are not. There is a tendency in criminal law to individuate the characteristics of the reasonable man, and have a certain tolerance for traits such as hot-headedness or carelessness (ibid., p. 85). Others such as Honoré (1988), Holmes (1881) and Greenawalt (1992) argue for standards based on moral beliefs or other principles. Once the court has set the relevant traits, the conduct of the defendant has to be compared to the virtual or counterfactual conduct of the reasonable person. The case-law reflects these divergent tendencies (Scalet 2003, p. 85 etseq). In American jurisprudence guidelines are being formulated by the American Law Institute to give judges and lawyers information about general principles. For tort law there is the Restatement of Torts.[3] However in the legal literature those general principles have come under critical scrutiny. For example, Bernstein (2001) claims that the General Principles look at tort law from a gendered, mostly male, perspective. Hetchers argues that in the Third Restatement of tort law the interpretation of reasonableness is based on a normative characterization that transforms the reasonable person standard into a tool for promoting social welfare, and thereby ignores the moral heterogeneity of the community (Hetcher 2001).

For our purposes we need not take a stance on the debates over these general principles. All we claim is that without a lot of further contextual detail mere appeal to the legal framework of a "reasonable man" may not settle any interesting cases of scientific responsibility.[4] We now turn to a more critical engagement with Douglas's framework.

14.2.2 The Reasonable Scientist

In this subsection we show that Douglas uses something like a "reasonable person" framework to analyze responsibility in science. To argue for the responsibility of scientists, Douglas critically analyzes Bridgman's claim that "scientific freedom is essential and that the artificial limitations of tools or subject matter are unthinkable" (Bridgman 1947, p. 153). This means that scientists should have full autonomy and should not be bothered with social or moral responsibilities beyond ordinary responsibilities.

However, Douglas presents evidence that scientists do weigh epistemic goals against other non-epistemic considerations: the use of human subjects in research, animal rights, determining or cutting budgets for certain projects such as the supercollider in the 1990s, etc.[5] Douglas focuses on two particular cases in order to show that scientists even act against the weak interpretation of Bridgman; scientists frequently consider potential unintended outcomes of their research. For example, she provides historical evidence that before testing the explosive chain reaction of an atomic bomb, physicists worried that the energy that would come free with the explosion of such a bomb may generate an unwanted chain reaction in the earth's atmosphere itself. Similarly, before pursuing recombinant DNA techniques,

---

[3] Restatement Third of Torts: Liability for Physical and Emotional Harm (2010), Apportionment of Liability (2000), and Products Liability (1998).

[4] Neil Levy reminded us that in the United States courts use the so-called Daubert and Frye tests in evaluating admissibility of scientific facts and theories – both tests crucially make reference to widespread acceptance within a scientific community. From our vantage point this makes the question we are pursuing in the chapter only more urgent.

[5] Douglas 2009, p. 76. Of course, the requirements and incentives to take non-epistemic (e.g., legal, financial, ethical, etc.) factors into consideration may themselves be extra-scientific.

scientists discussed the possible risks for public health and changed lab practices in light of these. From these examples, Douglas infers that scientists themselves do not consider themselves free of social or moral responsibilities.[6] Of course, there are wide disciplinary divergences in such matters. For example, not all scientific professional societies have ethical codes or codes of conduct that govern their members. Economics does not.[7]

In Douglas's view *scientific* responsibility boils down to the duty to be neither reckless nor negligent as a scientist. (Of course, she allows that scientists may have all kinds of non-scientific responsibilities.) Even if we assume that scientists have good intentions, there can be (i) unintended foreseeable consequences and (ii) unintended unforeseeable consequences that may raise concern. But more central for Douglas are (iii) "the potential unintended consequences of making inaccurate or unreliable empirical claims" (Douglas 2009, p. 72). Externalizing the responsibility for situations like (iii) beyond the scientific community, is an unlikely option because "presumably only the scientist can fully appreciate the potential implications of the work" (ibid., p. 73). The only qualified people who can consider the potential errors and their consequences are often the scientists themselves.

Of course, we cannot expect scientists to be fortune-tellers. The responsibility they bear should be limited by the standards of reasonable foresight. While she discusses other cases, too, Douglas focuses on policy scientists (as will we). When giving advice, scientists should consider the consequences of error and avoid negligence or recklessness. "This means that when a scientist makes an empirical claim in the process of advising, they should consider the potential consequences if that claim is incorrect" (ibid., p. 81). A scientist should acknowledge uncertainties in empirical evidence, but the weighing and listing of potential consequences is at play in choosing to emphasize or minimize the importance of uncertainties.

As an aside: a note on our terminology: we deploy the old distinction between measurable risk (with, say, a probability distribution attached to it) and un-measurable uncertainty (Knight 1921; Keynes 1921). In practice, an event that is not possible within a model-world – like the fall of Lehman for the Dutch CPB in 2008 – is uncertain. Both (ii) and (iii) may be uncertain.

But which consequences should a scientist be able to foresee? Here the standard of reasonableness comes in. This standard should be provided by the scientific communities: "because scientists work in such communities, in near constant communication and competition with other scientists, what is foreseeable and what is not can be readily determined" (Douglas 2009, p. 83). Douglas claims that because a scientific community is essentially a communicative community,

---

[6] We leave aside to what degree this practice is itself a historic relic from a different scientific culture or organization.

[7] In private correspondence Heather Douglas pointed out that on her view "if there are scientific groups without ethical codes or indeed any sense of responsibility for the consequences of error … they are in moral error."

ideas of potential errors and their consequences will spread quickly and be discussed.

Douglas illustrates this by an example from nuclear physics. The discovery of the neutron by James Chadwick gave a boost to nuclear physics, but the discoveries that followed the neutron did not have important implication outside of the discipline. This changed when fission was discovered in 1938. In early 1939 scientists saw the possibilities of fission in bomb making or energy production, which started a political debate. But can we blame or praise Chadwick for the invention of the atomic bomb or nuclear power? According to Douglas the scientific community in early 1939 saw the potentially disturbing consequences of fission, and thus it is that community that provides the benchmark of what should have been foreseen. In Douglas's words, "what is reasonable is to expect scientists to meet basic standards of consideration and foresight that any person would share, with the reasonable expectations of foresight judged against the scientist's peer in the scientific community. [. . .] They are held to only what can be foreseen, and thus discussed and considered." (ibid., p. 84). Douglas's case nicely shows that once a view about a consequence reaches some threshold of wide currency within a scientific community in a field, it becomes reasonable to presuppose it in one's consideration of reasonable foreseeable consequence, and – if needed – change one's practices in light of them.[8] Of course, one might think that there is some further responsibility to conduct inquiry into whether there are relevant consequences. Below we argue that there is indeed such a duty for a class of scientific agents.

Before we turn to our three, interconnected criticisms of Douglas, we should note a qualification about our approach. According to adherents of the so-called "doctrine of double-effect," unintended consequences are never morally blameworthy. This doctrine states that "it is permissible to bring about as a merely foreseen side effect a harmful event that it would be impermissible to bring about intentionally."[9] The doctrine concerns circumscribing permissibility, but our views concern what, among those things that are impermissible, is blameworthy; we simply set it aside here.[10]

---

[8] This is a stricter standard than an appeal to what is to be found in textbooks, which are often trailing scientific findings at the so-called "research frontier." On the latter concept, see de Solla Price (1965).

[9] McIntyre (2011). Of course, as she remarks, "traditional formulations of double effect require that the value of promoting the good end outweigh the disvalue of the harmful side effect;" so it is not a blanket principle.

[10] We thank Neil Levy for this formulation.

14.3 Collective Negligence and the "Everybody Did It"-Syndrome

14.3.1 Three Criticisms of Douglas

In this section, we offer three, interconnected criticisms of Douglas: first, she assumes that scientific fields are communicative communities in a way that begs the question. Second, in a system where the scientific community autonomously sets standards, there is a danger of self-affirming reasoning. Third, she ignores that the character of a scientific community is subject to moral evaluation. We argue that these omissions in Douglas's theory leave it with no adequate response to TEDI Syndrome. Along the way, we introduce motivations to take our alternative approach, which we dub "active pluralism," seriously.

First, in practice it is not so obvious that scientific fields are always communicative communities of the sort required by Douglas. Recall that Douglas offers two characteristics of scientists who make up these: they are "[a] in near constant communication and [b] competition with other scientists." Douglas presupposes something like an efficient market in scientific ideas.[11] Even if there are no barriers to communication at all, any given scientist is exposed to a flood of information. So, the mere fact that an issue is discussed openly in a scientific community is not enough to ensure that any given scientist is aware of the discussion, let alone all the relevant details of it.[12]

Moreover, policy-sciences do not always instantiate constant communication and competition; there is plenty of classified (e.g., defense-related) or so-called sponsored research that often is bound by non-disclosure requirements. This is not an idle thought: financial trading houses try to keep their trading strategies and the consequences of their proprietary financial products a secret for competitive advantage – often these presuppose non-trivial technical and technological improvements that will not be available and, thus, not well understood by the larger community, including regulators and assessors of systemic risk. This issue generalizes more widely; in medical sciences and engineering it is quite common to keep new techniques secret by patenting first before publishing results. Some important results never get published when the financial stakes are high.

Further, policy scientists, in particular, are not always transparent about the explicit or subtler tacit financial incentives of their consulting work.[13] Also, fields

---

[11] For an influential statement of this idea within economics, see Stigler (1969). For recent critical engagement see Schliesser (2011), and Boettke et al. (2010).

[12] We thank Neil Levy for pressing this point.

[13] The locus classicus is Gordon Tullock: "Not all of the advocates of tariffs, of course, are hired by 'the interests.' But the existence of people whose living does depend on finding arguments for tariffs and the further existence of another group who think that maybe, sometime in the future, they might need the assistance of either someone who believes in tariffs or an economist who is in this racket makes it possible for them to continue to publish, even in quite respectable journals.

have very diverging practices when it comes to replicating results or sharing data (Feigenbaum and Levy 1993). There are well-known incentives and barriers against publishing replications or dis-conformations. So even if scientific fields are essentially communicative communities it is by no means obvious that scientific communities communicate the right contents. It is unreasonable to expect Douglas's approach to apply without some finessing.

Our two other criticisms also focus on Douglas's commitment to what can be reasonably foreseen is linked to what is discussed and considered within the scientific community. In both cases we highlight different problematic features of her implicit commitment to efficiency in ideas within scientific communities. So, our second criticism is that community standards are often the product of ongoing scientific practices. In general, these practices are tuned to facilitate *epistemic* practices not potentially *moral* implications of these practices or even the unintended *social* impacts of these practices. To rephrase this point slightly in economic terms: the incentives that govern the evolution of reasonably successful epistemic norms need not have taken into account possible social and moral externalities. For example, competent geneticists need not be well placed to foresee or calculate the potential social costs of their mistakes or successes.[14]

This is not to deny that various policy sciences can have evolved in certain directions in order to be attractive to policy-makers. For example, the mathematical econometric techniques and tools – and more generally inferential technologies that produce univocal and stable figures in calculating the implications of policy alternatives – were promoted since the 1940s within economics, in part, because they would make economists attractive as policy advisers (as opposed to say, sociologists, lawyers, anthropologists, and historians).[15] But it is not *prima facie* obvious that attractiveness to policy makers automatically translates into being socially responsible.

Be that as it may, in Douglas's system it is the scientific community itself that sets the benchmark for reasonable foreseeability. New findings are communicated through conferences, journals, books, and so forth to peer-scientists. During this contact (and the way it disseminates through graduate training and textbooks) a community develops something of a benchmark for what a reasonable scientist

---

Thus a dispute which intellectually was settled over a century ago still continues." The point generalizes. Tullock ([1966] 2005): Chapter VII: The Backwardness of the Social Sciences.

[14] In standard applied welfare economics distribution effects are ignored in calculating so-called "consumer surplus," but this means that some of the most controversial social consequences of policy-advice is systematically neglected. See Harberger (1971), for an important defense, and Khan (1992a) for criticism.

[15] This was also contested. See, for example the Koopmans-Vining debate; the papers are nicely available here: http://cowles.econ.yale.edu/P/cp/p00a/p0029.pdf, accessed on May 16, 2011. We thank Roger Backhouse for calling our attention to it. See also Harberger (1971). See also Düppe and Weintraub 2013.

should foresee and how he or she should deliberate. If enough scientists adopt this benchmark, it becomes the benchmark of the scientific community.[16]

The problem with this architecture is that there is a danger of self-affirming reasoning. It is the individual scientist, as a member of the scientific community, who determines the standard he or she will be judged by. Warnings of possible consequences that do not make it into journals or conference presentations, or that are not taken seriously by peer scientists, do not help shape the benchmark and are, even if they turn out to be prescient, after all, therefore not taken into consideration when blameworthiness (or praiseworthiness) of the scientific community is evaluated. There is no need for conspiracies or malicious intent here. After all, time is one of the scarcest commodities for active researchers; it is often not worth their effort to actively seek out all consequences of a theory. Such an individual cost-benefit analysis may well be replicated through a whole field. Moreover, if journal articles in a field do not reward publications of, say, lack of replication then there may well be incentives that prevent possible consequences from ever being noticed.[17] A socially significant question may never be asked in the pursuit of interesting science. Again, to put this in economic terminology: competition for scarce resources does not by itself guarantee that externalities are properly incentivized.[18]

In practice, self-affirming benchmarks may well be woven into a field's standard practice. It is well known that alternative models and even long-standing objections can get suppressed from a discipline's collective tool-kit and memory. In the philosophy of science literature, the suppression of long-standing objections or even reliable alternative approaches is known as a "Kuhn-loss."[19] In particular, insights of discarded theories that cannot be articulated or recognized by the new theory are instances of Kuhn-losses.[20] Here we use "suppression" in non-moral sense; we have in mind epistemically important practices that set aside, say, questions, anomalies, or results in pursuit of more epistemically promising alternatives. Kuhn is significant here for a related point. He helped popularize a view of paradigms that allowed social-scientific practitioners to claim that they need not

---

[16] This need not be explicit; criticisms of a new benchmark my come to an end. See Pickering (1992). In private correspondence Douglas insisted that on her view "it is not the case that what is foreseeable is only what is discussed and considered." The following goes beyond this point.

[17] Not all sciences have what we may label a *Popperian ethos* in which concepts, models, and theories are deliberately constantly stress-tested. Plenty of sciences have what we may call a *confirming ethos*; that is they seek to provide evidence for theories. For the sake of argument, we stipulate that such a confirming ethos may be the most efficient epistemic practice.

[18] See Mäki (2011), who points out that the attainable truths may not necessarily track the truths worth having. See also Schliesser (2005).

[19] According to I. Votsis (2011) the term "Kuhn-loss" seems to be coined by Heinz Post (1971).

[20] Hasok Chang (2004) offers ingenious arguments for the significance of Kuhn-losses, and he uses these to motivate the pursuit of non-standard science. For extensions of the argument, see Schliesser 2008, 2009.

answer all objections; a welcome result in some consensus-aiming policy sciences.[21]

So, the community standards themselves can be flawed for some (say) non-epistemic purposes, but still be accepted by the community. That is to say, the members of the community as well as their funders, grant agencies, and "consumers" (i.e., politicians and the public) may well unintentionally create the conditions by which a community instantiates the vice of close-mindedness and its related vice of overconfidence. In such cases there is *collective negligence*. Often the presence of TEDI syndrome is evidence that one is dealing with an instance of *collective negligence*.[22]

We propose that if the benchmark is created by the scientific community itself, there should at least be more to reasonableness than merely accepting the (vast) majority's opinion. In particular, if there is intolerance of alternative approaches and suppression of historical knowledge of the discipline's past (or the routine propagation of mythic history in textbooks) these may well be enabling conditions for collective negligence. Again, to put this in terms of Douglas's implied efficiency claim; there may well be institutional barriers to entry that prevent the kind of intellectual competition worth having within a scientific community from society's point of view.

Collective negligence is not the only flaw in Douglas's approach. Our third criticism is this: it is perfectly possible that every individual scientist has acted according to community standards, and therefore should be free of any moral responsibility, but that there is a problem with those community standards. One of those problems is that scientific communities seem to have difficulties to think outside their paradigm and have limited tolerance of heterodoxy. Moreover, expert over-confidence is a now well-established empirical fact (Angner 2006). To put this in modal terms: There is a tendency for experts to treat their own model as necessary.[23] This tendency can be reduced if we treat the model as just one *possible* world (or a member of a portfolio of theories).

The benchmark of foreseeability for any claim is often made within a "paradigm" itself. Sometimes this means that events that are or were foreseeable within an incommensurable paradigm become impossible to state within the ruling paradigm. For example, in the tool-kit of recent mainstream economics it became very difficult to talk about or even discern bubbles; the efficient market hypothesis (understood in terms of random walks and arbitrage-free environments) makes no conceptual space for it. When asked recently, "*Many people would argue that, in this case, the inefficiency was primarily in the credit markets, not the stock market –*

---

[21] Stigler 1975, pp. 3–4. We thank David Levy for calling our attention to it. Stigler was also an active promoter of Kuhnian views about science within economics. For the larger story, see Schliesser 2012.

[22] The desire to produce consensus may, in fact, sometimes be the distant cause of the negligence; in such cases philosophies of science that promote an image of science as a consensus activity may be thought complicit in the negligence.

[23] We thank David M. Levy for pressing this point.

that there was a credit bubble that inflated and ultimately burst," the economist that actively promoted so-called efficient market theory, Eugene Fama, replied: "I don't even know what that means. People who get credit have to get it from somewhere. Does a credit bubble mean that people save too much during that period? I don't know what a credit bubble means. *I don't even know what a bubble means.* These words have become popular. I don't think they have any meaning"[24] (emphasis added).

Fama's words here exhibit very nicely what we have in mind. His world-view is so caught up with his evidentially well-supported, particular paradigm that he finds concepts that do not fit it utterly unintelligible. To speak metaphorically: he sees and understands economic phenomena through his model. Anybody that adopted his toolkit – as was widely done among economists – could claim all scientists within the community are free from any blame, because "everybody did it". But, of course, if he had wanted to, Fama could have learned about serious, empirical studies of bubbles at the margins of the economics profession that seem to have no problem operationalizing the term successfully.[25]

This concludes our critical engagement with Douglas. We now turn to sketch a bit more fully our alternative approach that can promote a morally more sound character to scientific communities and the duties of individuals within them.

14.3.2   The Duty of Epistemic Pluralism

In this section we explore the duties and obligations that prevent collective negligence. The moral upshot of our analysis in the previous section can be articulated in Douglas's terms: the autonomy of a field with policy implications comes with increased responsibility if not an outright duty to be open-minded, that is, to be actively striving for a variety of pluralisms. For present purposes we adopt De Langhe's definition of pluralism, which is "an epistemic position which acknowledges the validity of different possible perspectives on reality in an active way, which means that they are not only tolerated but also taken into account when goals of knowledge (prediction, problem-solving, truth, curiosity, policy advice, funding decision, ...) are to be achieved" (De Langhe 2009, p. 87).

We now turn to exploring briefly what this entails. In order to obtain scientific pluralism it is not necessary that every individual scientist in a community is a pluralist, but the scientific community as a whole should be. We cannot stress this enough; we are tackling collective negligence at the level of the composition of the

---

[24] http://www.newyorker.com/online/blogs/johncassidy/2010/01/interview-with-eugene-fama.html#ixzz1f QoeflSE. See, for example, the canonical paper by Fama (1970), which has over 8,000 citations.

[25] Including work done by those awarded the Nobel prize in economics. See Smith et al. (1988).

community.[26] From individual scientists we expect no more than ordinary, scientific open-mindedness, this is why we focus on the *character* of the community. We also focus on the responsibilities and duties of a sub-set of policy scientists those involved in aggregating scientific knowledge.

At the community level we advocate the ongoing cultivation of competing, potentially incommensurable paradigms. So, we reject the once-widespread idea that a field's unanimity is trumping evidence for it to be considered scientific or a sign that a field is "mature" in Kuhn's sense.[27] We have in mind, of course, the reality that in the wake of Kuhn's *Structure* some fields of inquiry pursued near-unanimity *in order* to be considered scientific. For example, the Nobel-laureate, George Stigler defended this as a "fundamental tenet" of "those who believe in free discussion that matters of fact and logic can (eventually) be agreed upon by competent men of good will, that matters of taste cannot be."[28]

In fact, there may well be many reasons that a science naturally becomes pluralistic, if permitted.[29] Diversity in science, while no magic cure, can help ensure that a variety of research questions are asked and a corresponding variety of possible solutions, problems and applications are discussed. This is a long-standing concern of so-called standpoint theory that is very popular among feminists philosopher of science and critical race theorists.[30] To forestall misunderstanding: we are not arguing that some standpoints are *a priori* better because they are minority standpoints.

As an aside, while here we promote a pluralist approach at the level of the composition of approaches within a scientific community, it is worth noting that it is not the only possible way to avoid collective negligence. Given that even foreseeable consequences may also have unintended side-effects, creating (incentives for) a willingness to assertively articulate known or knowable uncertainty over possible consequences of policy may be a viable alternative approach.[31] Even if policy-

---

[26] Audiences to earlier drafts of this chapter worried that we demand a change of behavior in the epistemic practices of individual scientists.

[27] Some readers might wish to claim that our position has been decisively disproved in a famous article by Robert J. Aumann 1976, "Agreeing to Disagree,". But even if we grant the appropriateness of his Bayesian conceptual apparatus, Aumann does not provide an institutional framework that ensures that equilibrium in the information exchange will be reached such that rational disagreement becomes impossible. Our approach offers reasons for thinking that the preconditions that would make his proof actual for real scientific communities sometimes (often?) do not exist. We thank M. Ali Khan for urging us to consider Aumann.

[28] Stigler 1975, pp. 15–16. See Levy and Peart (2008). Stigler was an early, enthusiastic reader of Kuhn; within economics it is common to encounter Kuhnian concepts (see Schliesser 2011 for details).

[29] De Langhe 2009, p. 88. See also Kitcher 2001, pp. 55–62. Here we ignore the question of what causes a lack of pluralism. When we presented this material to an audience of economists at NYU, these proposed that government funding practices may be the source of monopoly power within many sciences.

[30] For an excellent introduction, see section "2. Feminist Standpoint Theory" in Anderson 2011.

[31] This is, in fact, the approach favored by one of the co-authors.

M. Lefevere and E. Schliesser

makers may not wish to hear about uncertainty this does not exculpate the policy-scientists who provide their "clients" with what they want to hear. Even independent of our approach, scientists have professional duties that regardless of their policy-makers' wishes may demand fuller disclosure or remaining silent.[32] This aside suggest that a community can be morally responsible for the unintended and unforeseen consequences of its research, namely if the community is not critical enough such that it does not pay enough attention to the potential consequences of the research. This means pluralism is not a necessary consequence of our criticism of Douglas.

We claim that in order to avoid collective negligence at the policy level, having different possible answers can help to make more responsible decisions. In the active pluralism view promoted here, what is reasonable for a scientist is not what is foreseeable according to the benchmark the majority has set, but it should be evaluated in light of all the different (empirically well supported) perspectives that are available in that discipline.[33]

Such evaluation is a requirement at the level where science and policy intersect. In what follows we call that level the "aggregate level;" policy scientists that work at an aggregate level do have special duties to seek out and be familiar with scientific approaches other than their own and, perhaps, different from the ruling paradigm(s). These duties follow from, in the first instance, from their ability to influence policy. In practice such policy scientists working at the aggregate level also gain special benefits from their status (e.g., recognition, access to lucrative consulting gigs, etc.). This means that if a policy scientist chooses to ignore more marginal voices within his or her discipline, this does not free him or her from responsibility to take potential warnings from that group seriously to weigh the consequences of possible error. There are known cases where, for example, in development economics economists with "local" backgrounds pointed out the biased assumptions of leading economists and were ignored.[34]

14.3.3 Some Distinctions[35]

Our chapter challenges a widely held truism: (I) one can never be blamed for things that were not foreseen (by you and your community). By contrast, our position is

---

[32] Such professional duties have long been recognized by economists, including Alfred Marshall and A.C. Harberger (1971).

[33] Boundary policing of a discipline makes it a bit tricky to say when such perspectives are still available. Moreover, different theories may, of course, be differently empirically supported. But even theories that are empirically less supported along many dimensions may do better in a sub-set of problems.

[34] See the criticism of Lawrence Summers by Khan 1992b, 1993 and the subsequent discussion by Ron Jones in the same issue, pp. 580–582.

[35] This section is greatly indebted to [names omitted].

that (II) a scientific community can be morally responsible/blameworthy for the consequences of its research even if they are unintended and unforeseen in the community. In particular, (III) a scientific community can be morally responsible or blameworthy for the consequences of its research even if these are unintended and unforeseen (by the community), namely if the broader community is not pluralistic (such that it does not pay enough attention to the potential consequences of research).

Of course, there is a closely related alternative to (I): (IV) One can never be blamed for things that were not foreseeable. This is more appealing than (I); if consequences of research are unforeseeable then one can never take them into account, no matter how much attention one pays to them. Nevertheless, (IV) is ambiguous between: (IV*) one is never to be blamed for things that were not foreseeable by a community at the time; (IV**) one is never to be blamed for things that were and are not foreseeable in principle, that is, genuine uncertainty. Let's grant (IV**) for the sake of argument (even if one can imagine cases where not preparing for, say, any unexpected emergencies may be inexcusable).

Now, let's operationalize the foreseeable in terms of the portfolio of models (and paradigm-preserving extensions of these) within the paradigmatic science. In particular, the foreseeable is the possible in the paradigmatic models (plus bridge principles, know-how of the expert, etc.). This suggests that (IV*) is too weak because due to Kuhn-loss phenomena, paradigmatic models never incorporate all the models available in discarded or non-paradigmatic models. So, a community may in some circumstances not be able to foresee consequences that would have been available if some of the non-paradigmatic models would be in use. So (V) a community can be blamable for things that were not foreseeable (in the sense of IV*) by a community at the time (because of overreliance on a ruling paradigm). In fact, (V) is our argument for pluralism.

14.4 Active Pluralism as a Condition for Rationality/ Reasonableness

Before we offer some modest, preliminary suggestions on how to meet such duties, we briefly characterize pluralism in epistemology in order to offer an account of benchmarking that can avoid the vices of collective close-mindedness and collective negligence.

14.4.1 Pluralism in Epistemology

Pluralism in science is part of an ongoing debate, especially in epistemology. There are philosophers who advocate pluralism in one specific issue of epistemology, such as explanation. Several *philosophers*[36] advocate an explanatory pluralism, by acknowledging that one can have different interests or types of questions, and thus requiring a different type of explanation. But there are also philosophers who have more expansive frameworks for articulating pluralism. For example, Mitchell and Dietrich show how "integrative pluralism" succeeds in biology[37]; Van Bouwel offers considerable motivation for pluralism in the social sciences and economics.[38] In both cases, pluralism seems to be positively received, but "if it is to be more than a liberal platitude, we need to delimitate more clearly"[39] what pluralism entails, where we want it and how we can achieve it. In the remainder of this subsection we'll dig deeper into the concept of pluralism.

Batens, Nickles, Nersessian and Schliesser[40] defend pluralism as a key concept in context-based epistemology.[41] On this view, a belief or decision is only justified if it is actively compared with available alternatives. This happens in a local process, a context, since not all of our knowledge is used, doubted or accepted at the same time. Accept this for the sake of argument. There are at least two important features of this context-based proposal that raise questions. The first question is what is considered an available alternative? This will be considered in Sect. 14.4.2. The second worry is whether we can demand from an individual, policy scientist to switch between views or hypotheses as if it were a change of clothes.

De Langhe (2009) addresses the second by making a useful distinction between pluralism at the level of the individual scientist and at the level of the scientific community. He argues that there are plenty of reasons to expect lack of consensus in science: its presence can be the consequence of the problem of underdetermination of theory by evidence (or data); the world's complexity; the limits to our cognition; the contingency thesis; experiential diversity and path dependence. If an individual scientist accepts all alternatives simultaneously, his decisions (such as research questions or methods) are empty. It could just as well have been another decision. If he considers the multiple alternatives as a reason not to make a decision at all, he would in a certain sense stop being a scientist.[42] How does one make choices as a pluralist, and how can those choices be warranted if there are multiple

---

[36] To ensure an anonymous referee process this sentence has been adapted. The original sentence can be found on the title page.

[37] Mitchell and Dietrich (2006). It turns on recognizing different levels that need not require general unification.

[38] Van Bouwel (in print) and Van Bouwel (2004, 2005).

[39] Keating and Della Porta 2010, p. S112.

[40] Batens (1974, 2004). There are other philosophers who advocate similar views, such as: Thomas Nickles (1980) Nancy Nersessian (2008) and Eric Schliesser (2005).

[41] For an interesting discussion about this form of contextualism, we refer to Demey (forthcoming).

[42] This is what happened to the Chicago economist Frank Knight, who indirectly created the foundations for an understanding of economics as an applied policy science as made famous by "Chicago-economics" (e.g., Milton Friedman, George Stigler, A.C. Harberger, and Gary Becker), but who himself was a deep pluralist about the way social science could influence policy and who

views rationally justifiable? De Langhe points out that this is a false dilemma, since it is not the individual scientist that needs to be a pluralist, it is the scientific community. "Warranted choice can go hand in hand with pluralism on the condition that pluralism is confined to the aggregate level. In other words, the cost of warranted choice is individual level pluralism" (De Langhe 2009, p. 92). The individual scientist qua scientist can continue doing research starting from his situation, his epistemic interest, his experience, and so forth. This makes his or her choices warranted at the individual level.

De Langhe infers that "advocates of pluralism should not bother trying to convince individual scientists of adopting pluralism in their own research nor blame them for not doing so" (p. 94). He advocates that it is far more important to concentrate efforts to structuring scientific community in such a way that it reflects the diversity at the community level. In particular, when scientific knowledge gets aggregated for policy-makers (and regulators) this diversity should be available. We have offered moral arguments for the same conclusion. We now return to discuss the problem of benchmarking in order to assess the moral responsibility of a scientific community and the duties of policy scientists within it.

14.4.2 Benchmarking in a Pluralist Epistemology

If a scientific community constitutes the benchmark by which the consequences of its policy recommendations are to be judged then we argue that this community should be pluralistic in a way that we characterize more exactly in this section. In doing so we build on Batens's proposal that reasonable decisions can only be made after comparing a certain proposed action (claim or hypotheses, etc.) with available alternatives (Batens 1974, 2004); we also agree with De Langhe's proposal that pluralism is only required at the aggregate level. By this aggregate level we mean not just the composition and methods of the scientific community as a whole, but also the manner in which these are deployed in policy advice. Here we focus on some suggestions that can assure a supply of alternatives for the aggregate level. We propose that an active pluralism can contribute to ensuring a morally responsible scientific community.

Douglas refuses to separate the roles of a scientist-as-researcher from a science-advisor (Douglas 2009, p. 82), but perhaps she would be inclined to accept De Langhe's distinction between the individual roles of a scientist (such as doing research, writing articles, giving lectures), and the aggregate roles such as editing a journal, organizing conferences, teaching, refereeing, policy-advisor, regulator, media spokesperson, etc.[43] On that aggregate or composite level, De Langhe writes,

---

embraced (epistemic) uncertainty as a fact of life in most policy decisions. For a very good discussion of Knight see Ross Emmett (2009), chapter 12.

[43] This distinction is in many respects a manner of degree, of course. A grant-making, lab-director straddles our distinction for example.

the effort should be focused on structuring scientific community in such a way that it reflects the diversity at the individual level. Unfortunately he stops, where the real problem begins.

We propose that scientists who work at the intersection with policy (understood in its widest sense, including consulting, editorializing, regulating, etc.) take that aggregate-responsibility seriously. Pluralism at the level of scientific content should then be a value of paramount importance.[44] Scientists who enter this level should be prepared to question the current structure of the scientific community. In particular, they have a *duty* to seek out alternative orientations within the scientific community to their own approach. To forestall misunderstanding: even within this pluralist framework we allow that many aggregating mechanisms (conferences, journals, etc.) will not be and need not be in themselves pluralist. All we claim is that when these mechanisms intersect directly or indirectly with policy that then policy scientists and those that fund and listen to them have a duty to consider more than one scientific perspective. Sometimes this can be as simple as letting, say, one group of social scientists (say, sociologists) evaluate the policy advice of, say, another group of social scientists (economists), or – recalling an earlier point – geneticists. We agree with Douglas that it should still be scientists who judge scientific claims.[45]

14.5   Conclusion

In the final paragraph of the section, our discussion has slid into practical suggestions. In our conclusion we will offer a few more in order to stimulate further reflection. For example, in grant-making or regulatory agencies one can try to create distinct panels that ensure aggregate diversity and pluralism. This may appear to make, say, the grant-process, or policy-advice generation less efficient and messier. But we assume, by contrast, that scientific monocultures, which may benefit from all kinds of economies of scale and internal efficiencies, can cause far worse kinds of social externalities.[46]

In practice this means that grants should be awarded to economists, physicists or psychologists of different positions, backgrounds, and so forth. We believe grant agencies and ought to incentivize the presence of such alternatives. For example,

---

[44] There are other potential benefits to our proposal: if one paradigm bluntly fails, there are alternatives available that can provide decent answers. Not to mention that scientific monocultures may be vulnerable to extinction. So our proposal may increase the robustness of science. We thank Dunja Seselja for pointing out this benefit.

[45] To forestall misunderstanding: an argument that all people affected by a policy decision should be included in policy discussion falls beyond the scope of our more limited concern here.

[46] This is not just arm-chair philosophizing. Consider the massive damage done to environments and indigenous people by large multinational lending institutions in the grip of one-sided economics paradigms.

10–25 % of a government research budget could be devoted to foundational and methodological criticisms of dominant research programs; to ensure proper replication of fundamental results; to promote transparency of data; to do effectiveness studies; to explore social consequences of policy; and to fund empirically or conceptually promising alternatives to the main approaches. None of these suggestions are radical and some would build on existing initiatives.[47] Of course, there would be plenty of resistance to such a proposal, too.

In public governance, and even in private companies, ombudspersons are appointed to mediate between an organization and the interested stakeholders of that organization. Plenty of institutions are capable of pursuing more than one (perhaps hierarchically organized) goal at once. Something similar could be set up within the policy sciences. Such an institution allows an individual scientist qua scientist to focus on his or her research, while improving the moral character of the scientific community. Moreover, such an institution can help the policy scientist who is active on the aggregate level to cope with responsibilities that come with his or her function.

Finally, our chapter challenges two deep-seated commitments in our thinking about science. First, we deny that science ought to be characterized by unanimity of belief among its competent practitioners. We have argued that this leads easily to the vices of close-mindedness and expert-overconfidence. Second, we deny that the current way in which research is organized is optimal if one wishes to prevent social externalities; rather it seems especially prone to what we call TEDI Syndrome. We advocate a reform of aggregate scientific institutions that promote active pluralism. We also believe that given the great privileges and powers accorded to policy scientists, it is their duty to seek this out.

Acknowledgments   We are grateful to M. Ali Khan, David Levy, Neil Levy, Roger Koppl, and Frank Zenker for very helpful suggestions. We are especially grateful for the generous feedback by Heather Douglas. We also thank audiences at Lund, New York University, George Mason University, and Bayreuth for very helpful comments. The usual caveats apply.

---

[47] Some grant agencies already do this on a modest scale: The NSF's "STS considers proposals for scientific research into the interface between science (including engineering) or technology, and society. STS researchers use diverse methods including social science, historical, and philosophical methods. Successful proposals will be transferrable (i.e., generate results that provide insights for other scientific contexts that are suitably similar). They will produce outcomes that address pertinent problems and issues at the interface of science, technology and society, such as those having to do with practices and assumptions, ethics, values, governance, and policy." http://www.nsf.gov/funding/pgm_summ.jsp?pims_id=5324

References

Anderson, Elizabeth. 2011. Feminist epistemology and philosophy of science. In *The Stanford encyclopedia of philosophy*, ed. Edward N. Zalta. http://plato.stanford.edu/archives/spr2011/entries/feminism-epistemology/.

Angner, E. 2006. Economists as experts: Overconfidence in theory and practice. *Journal of Economic Methodology* 13(1): 1–24.

Aumann, R.J. 1976. Agreeing to disagree. *Annals of Statistics* 4(6): 1236–1239.

Batens, D. 1974. Rationality and justification. *Philosophica* 14: 83–103.

Batens, D. 2004. *Menselijke Kennis: Pleidooi voor een Bruikbare Rationaliteit*, 2nd ed. - Antwerpen-Apeldoorn: Garant.

Bernstein, A. 2001. Restatement (third) of torts: General principles and the prescription of masculine order. *Vanderbilt Law Review* 54(3): 1367–1411.

Boettke, P.J., P.T. Leeson, and C.J. Coyne. 2010. Contra-Whig history of economic ideas and the problem of the endogenous past. *GMU Working Paper in Economics*, No. 10-31. Available at SSRN: http://ssrn.com/abstract=1686134.

Bridgman, P.W. 1947. Scientists and social responsibility. *Scientific Monthly* 65: 48–154.

Chang, H. 2004. *Inventing temperature: Measurement and scientific progress*. Oxford: Oxford University Press.

de Jong, Jasper, Mark Roscam Abbing, and Johan Verbruggen. 2010. Voorspellen in crisistijd: De CPB-ramingen tijdens de Grote Recessie. CPB Document No 207. http://www.cpb.nl/sites/default/files/publicaties/download/voorspellen-crisistijd-de-cpb-ramingen-tijdens-degrote-recessie.pdf. Accessed on 17 May 2011.

De Langhe, R. 2009. Why should I adopt pluralism. In *Economic pluralism*, ed. R. Garnett, E. Olsen, and M. Starr, 87–98. London: Routledge.

De Mey, T. Forthcoming. Human, all too human. In *Proceedings of logic reasoning and rationality*.

de Solla, D.J. 1965. Networks of scientific papers. *Science* 149(3683): 510–515.

Douglas, H. 2009. *Science, policy and the value-free ideal*. Pittsburgh: University of Pittsburgh Press.

Düppe, T., and E.R. Weintraub. 2013. *Finding equilibrium*. Princeton: Princeton University Press.

Emmett, R. 2009. *Frank Knight and the Chicago school in American economics*. London: Routledge.

Fama, E. 1970. Efficient capital markets: A review of theory and empirical work'. *The Journal of Finance* 25(2): 383–417.

Feigenbaum, S., and D.M. Levy. 1993. The market for (ir)reproducible econometrics. *Accountability in Research* 3(1): 25–43.

Feinberg, J. 1970. *Doing and deserving*. Princeton: Princeton University Press.

Greenawalt, K. 1992. *Law and objectivity*. New York: Oxford University Press.

Hacking, I. 1992. The self-vindication of laboratory sciences. In *Science as practice and culture*, ed. A. Pickering. Chicago: University of Chicago Press.

Harberger, A.C. 1971. Three basic postulates for applied welfare economics: An interpretive essay. *Journal of Economic Literature* 9(3): 785–797.

Hetcher, S. 2001. Non-utilitarian negligence norms and the reasonable person standard. *Vanderbilt Law Review* 54(3): 863–892.

Holmes, O.W. 1881. *The common law*. Boston: Little, Brown.

Honoré, T. 1988. Responsibility and luck. *The Law Quarterly Review* 104: 530–553.

Keating, M., and D. Della Porta. 2010. In defense of pluralism in the social sciences. *European Political Science* 9: S111–S120.

Keynes, John Maynard. 1921. *Treatise on probability*. London: Macmillan & Co.

Khan, M.A. 1992a. On measuring the social opportunity cost of labour in the presence of tariffs and an informal sector. *The Pakistan Development Review* 31(4 I): 535–564.

Khan, M.A. 1992b. Comments on Professor Summers. *The Pakistan Development Review* 31: 394–400.

Khan, M.A. 1993. On education as a commodity. *The Pakistan Development Review* 32: 541–579.

Kitcher, Philip. 2001. *Science, truth, and democracy*. Oxford: Oxford University Press.

Knight, Frank H. 1921. *Risk, uncertainty, and profit*. Boston: Hart, Schaffner and Marx/Houghton Mifflin Co.

Levy, David M., and Sandra J. Peart. 2008. Analytical egalitarianism. *American Journal of Economics and Sociology* 67(3): 473–479. Wiley Blackwell.

Mäki, U. 2011. Scientific realism as a challenge to economics (and vice versa). *Journal of Economic Methodology* 18(1): 1–12.

McIntyre, A. 2011. Doctrine of double effect. In *The Stanford encyclopedia of philosophy*, Fall 2011 ed, ed. Edward N. Zalta. URL = http://plato.stanford.edu/archives/fall2011/entries/double-effect/.

Mitchell, S., and M.R. Dietrich. 2006. Integration without unification: An argument for pluralism in the biological sciences. *The American Naturalist* 168: S73–S79.

Nersessian, N. 2008. *Creating scientific concepts*. Cambridge, MA: MIT Press.

Nickles, T. 1980. *Scientific discovery, logic, and rationality*. Boston: D. Reidel Pub. Co.

Pickering, A. 1992. *Science as practice and culture*. Chicago: University of Chicago Press.

Post, H. 1971. Correspondence, invariance and heuristics. *Studies in History and Philosophy of Science* 2: 213–255.

Scalet, S. 2003. Fitting the people they are meant to serve: Reasonable persons in the American legal system. *Law and Philosophy* 22: 75–110.

Schliesser, E. 2005. Galilean reflections on Milton Friedman's 'Methodology of Positive Economics', with thoughts on Vernon Smith's 'Economics in the Laboratory'. *Philosophy of the Social Sciences* 35(1): 50–74.

Schliesser, E. 2008. Philosophy and a scientific future of the history of economics. *Journal of the History of Economic Thought* 30: 105–116.

Schliesser, Eric. 2009. Prophecy, eclipses and whole-sale markets: A case study on why data driven economic history requires history of economics, a philosopher's reflection. *Jarhbuch für Wirtschaftsgeschichte* 50(1): 195–208.

Schliesser, E. 2011. Four species of reflexivity and history of economics in economic policy science. *Journal of the Philosophy of History* 5: 425–444.

Schliesser, E. 2012. Inventing paradigms, monopoly, methodology, and mythology at 'Chicago': Nutter, Stigler, and Milton Friedman. *Studies in History and Philosophy of Science* 43: 160–171.

Smith, Vernon L., Gerry L. Suchanek, and Arlington W. Williams. 1988. Bubbles, crashes, and endogenous expectations in experimental spot asset markets. *Econometrica* 56(5): 1119–1151.

Stigler, G.J. 1969. Does economics have a useful past? *History of Political Economy* 1(2): 217–230.

Stigler, G.J. 1975. *The citizen and the State: Essays on regulation*. Chicago: University of Chicago Press.

Tullock, G. 2005. *The selected works of Gordon Tullock*, The organization of inquiry, vol. 3. Indianapolis: Liberty Fund.

Van Bouwel, J. 2004. Explanatory pluralism in economics: Against the mainstream? *Philosophical Explorations* 7(3): 299–315.

Van Bouwel, J. 2005. Towards a framework for the pluralisms in economics. *Post-Autistic Economics Review* 30: art.3.

Van Bouwel, Jeroen. 2015. Towards democratic models of sciennce: Exploring the case of scientific pluralism. *Philosophy and Religion* (in press).

Votsis, I. 2011. Structural realism: Continuity and its limits. In *Scientific structuralism*, ed. P. Bokulich and A. Bokulich. Dordrecht: Springer.

Name Index

A

Angner, Erik, 174–176, 285

B

Beatty, John, 71, 84–87
Blair, Tony, 248, 260
Blanchard, Olivier, 5, 120, 121
Blyth, Mark, 186

C

Cartwright, Nancy, 127, 138, 140
Cassidy, John, 143–144
Chadwick, James, 281
Churchill, Winston, 89
Clemen, R.T., 11, 192
Colander, David, 121, 122, 127, 132, 146
Collins, Harry, 7, 12, 172, 173, 176–183, 187, 239, 241, 251, 254
Cooke, Roger M., 7, 9–11, 49, 51, 54–62, 65, 67, 68, 127, 191–211
Craig, William, 224, 226, 227

D

Dalkey, Norman, 3, 7
Dalton, John, 6
Davidson, Donald, 215, 222
De Langhe, Rogier, 286, 287, 290, 291
den Butter, Frank A.G., 7, 8, 17–47, 126, 244
Don, Henk, 67

Douglas, Heather, 12, 88, 275–277, 279–286, 288, 291, 292
Drees, Willem, 29

E

Edison, Thomas, 6
Ehrenfest, Paul, 66
Evans, Robert, 7, 11, 12, 125, 172, 173, 176–183, 186, 187, 233–251, 254

F

Fama, Eugene, 143–144, 286
Feinberg, Joel, 277
Feyerabend, Paul, 5, 6, 131, 144, 145
Fine, Arthur, 142, 146
Fourcade, Marion, 185
Franses, Philip Hans, 52, 61, 62, 65
Frege, Gottlob, 218, 221, 222
Fricker, Miranda, 214
Friedman, Milton, 141, 149, 290
Fuller, Steve, 182, 183

G

Galileo, Galilei, 135
Gibbard, Allan, 215
Gilbert, Margaret, 84, 85
Goldman, Alvin, 11, 156, 159, 161, 216, 218, 220, 225–227
Goodman, Nelson, 249

© Springer International Publishing Switzerland 2014
C. Martini, M. Boumans (eds.), *Experts and Consensus in Social Science*,
Ethical Economy 50, DOI 10.1007/978-3-319-08551-7

Subject Index

© Springer International Publishing Switzerland 2014
C. Martini, M. Boumans (eds.), *Experts and Consensus in Social Science*,
Ethical Economy 50, DOI 10.1007/978-3-319-08551-7

Printed by Printforce, the Netherlands